TITANFALL™

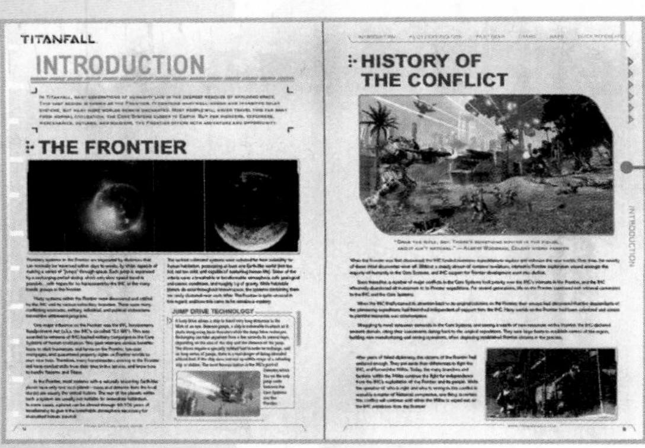

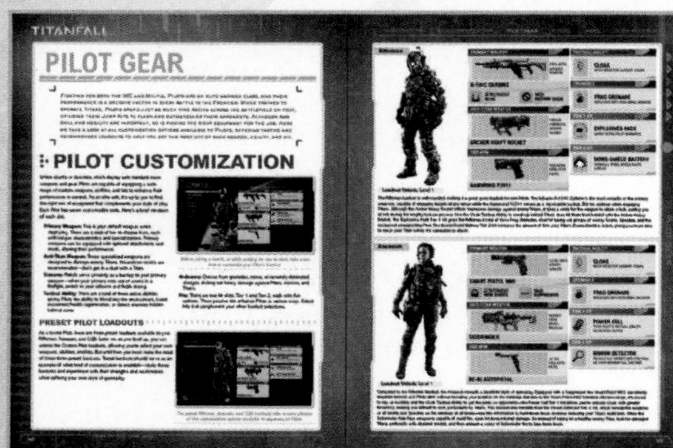
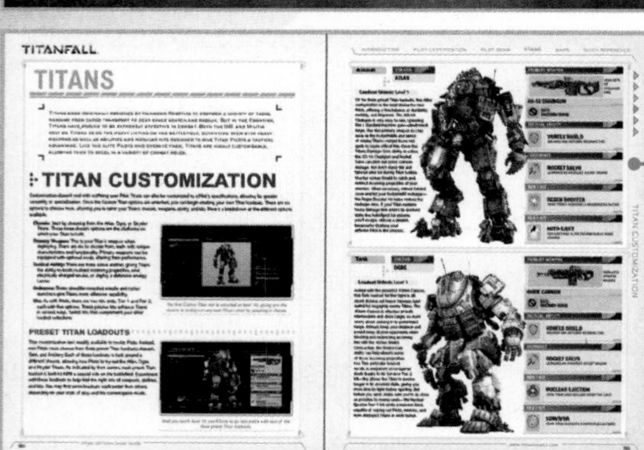
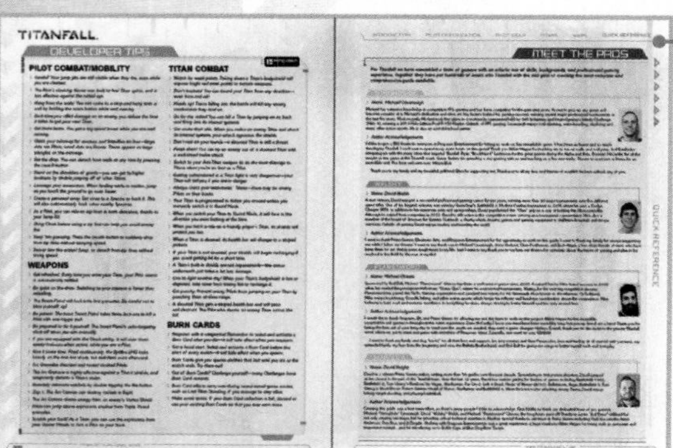

CONTENTS

Maps 124

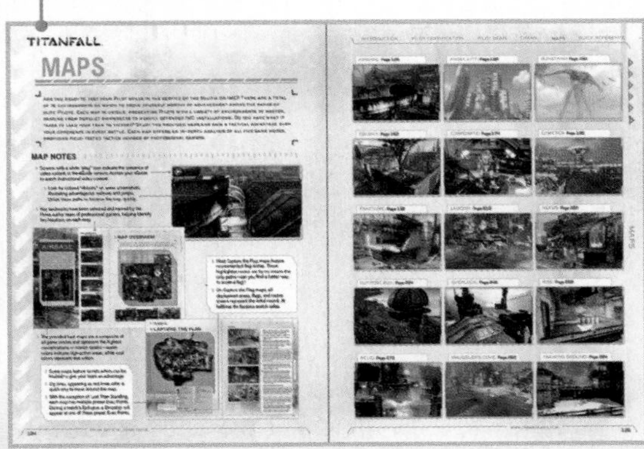

Quick Reference 306

INTRODUCTION

In *Titanfall*, many generations of humanity live in the deepest reaches of explored space. This vast region is known as the Frontier. It contains many well-known and inhabited solar systems, but many more worlds remain uncharted. Most people will never travel this far away from normal civilization, the Core Systems closer to Earth. But for pioneers, explorers, mercenaries, outlaws, and soldiers, the Frontier offers both adventure and opportunity.

THE FRONTIER

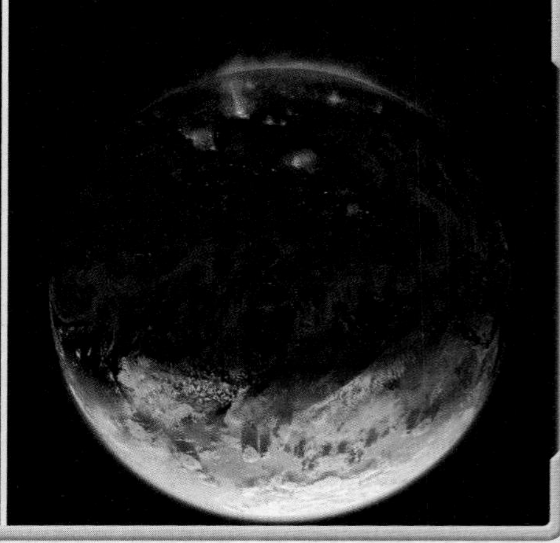

Planetary systems in the Frontier are separated by distances that can normally be traversed within days to weeks, by ships capable of making a series of "jumps" through space. Each jump is separated by a recharging period during which only slow speed travel is possible...with hopes for no harassment by the IMC or the many bandit groups in the Frontier.

Many systems within the Frontier were discovered and settled by the IMC and its various subsidiary branches. There were many conflicting economic, military, industrial, and political motivations behind the settlement programs.

One major influence on the Frontier was the IMC Servicemen's Readjustment Act (a.k.a. the IMC's so-called "G.I. Bill"). This was awarded to veterans of IMC-backed military campaigns in the Core Systems of human civilization. This gave veterans various benefits: loans to start businesses and farms on the Frontier, low-cost mortgages, and guaranteed property rights on Frontier worlds to start new lives. Therefore, many homesteaders arriving at the Frontier still have combat skills from their time in the service, and know how to handle firearms and Titans.

In the Frontier, most systems with a naturally occurring Earth-like planet have only one such planet—mass and distance from the local star(s) are usually the critical factors. The rest of the planets within such a system are usually not suitable for immediate habitation. In some cases, a planet can be altered through 60-100 years of terraforming to give it the breathable atmosphere necessary for unassisted human survival.

The earliest colonized systems were selected for their suitability for human habitation, possessing at least one Earth-like world (not too hot, not too cold, and capable of sustaining human life). Some of the criteria were: a breathable or terraformable atmosphere, safe geological and cosmic conditions, and roughly 1g of gravity. While habitable planets do exist throughout known space, the systems containing them are rarely clustered near each other. The Frontier is quite unusual in this regard, and how this came to be remains a mystery.

JUMP DRIVE TECHNOLOGY

A Jump Drive allows a ship to travel very long distances in the blink of an eye. Between jumps, a ship is vulnerable to attack as it plods along using basic thrusters while the Jump Drive recharges. Recharging can take anywhere from a few seconds to several days, depending on the size of the ship and the distance of the jump. The drives require a specially refined fuel in order to recharge, and on long series of jumps, there is a real danger of being stranded without fuel, if the ship does not end up within range of a refueling ship or station. The most famous station is the IMC's port of Demeter, which lies on the only jump route between the Core Systems and the Frontier.

HISTORY OF THE CONFLICT

"GRAB THE RIFLE, BOY. THERE'S SOMETHING MOVING IN THE FIELDS, AND IT AIN'T NATURAL." — ALBERT WOODMAN, COLONY HYDRO FARMER

When the Frontier was first discovered, the IMC funded numerous expeditions to explore and colonize the new worlds. Over time, the novelty of these initial discoveries wore off. Without a steady stream of constant revelations, interest in Frontier exploration waned amongst the majority of humanity in the Core Systems, and IMC support for Frontier development went into decline.

Soon thereafter, a number of major conflicts in the Core Systems took priority over the IMC's interests in the Frontier, and the IMC effectively abandoned all investment in its Frontier expeditions. For several generations, life on the Frontier continued with minimal connection to the IMC and the Core Systems.

When the IMC finally turned its attention back to its original colonies on the Frontier, their envoys had discovered that the descendants of the pioneering expeditions had flourished independent of support from the IMC. Many worlds on the Frontier had been colonized and access to plentiful resources was commonplace.

Struggling to meet consumer demands in the Core Systems, and seeing a wealth of new resources on the Frontier, the IMC declared eminent domain, citing their investments dating back to the original expeditions. They sent large fleets to establish control of the region, building new manufacturing and mining operations, often displacing established Frontier citizens in the process.

After years of failed diplomacy, the citizens of the Frontier had endured enough. They put aside their differences to fight the IMC, and formed the Militia. Today, the many branches and factions within the Militia continue the fight for independence from the IMC's exploitation of the Frontier and its people. While the question of who is right and who is wrong in this conflict is arguably a matter of historical perspective, one thing is certain: this conflict will continue until either the Militia is wiped out, or the IMC withdraws from the Frontier.

THE MILITIA

The Frontier Militia represents the military arm of the Frontier systems' territorial defense pact. The Militia is a loosely governed mishmash of homesteaders, bandits, mercenaries, and pirates, all rising up as "citizen soldiers" when the need arises. Many homesteaders have taken on a "if you can't beat 'em, join 'em" attitude regarding working alongside different criminal groups. Naturally the people in this melting pot don't always see eye to eye on how to deal with the IMC's exploitation of the Frontier, but they are unified in fighting against it.

The Militia is loosely divided into Brigades. Each Brigade is responsible for fighting in an assigned section of Frontier territory, which might span as far as several planetary systems. The Marauder Corps (M-COR) is a small part of a much larger Brigade tied to the Freeport System. Although some Brigades are little more than vast pirate organizations, the Militia has enough resources to be a real obstacle to the IMC's ambitions on the Frontier.

The Militia often claims that direct action against the IMC is in the best interests of the homesteaders whom they allegedly represent, but not everyone on the Frontier sees it that way.

KEY CHARACTERS

MacAllan

"THEY'LL CALL US TERRORISTS OR WORSE, BUT WE CAN'T WIN PLAYING BY THEIR RULES." — MACALLAN

A highly decorated veteran of the Titan Wars, MacAllan served as the executive officer of the *IMS Odyssey*, under the command of Vice Admiral Marcus Graves. The *Odyssey*'s mission was part of a peacekeeping operation on the Frontier for the IMC. Official IMC reports indicate that MacAllan led a mutiny aboard the *Odyssey* fifteen years ago, citing numerous grievances with the IMC's treatment of Frontier citizens. However, these reports have not been proven, in the absence of the ship's flight data recorder, which was lost when MacAllan and his people escaped with the *Odyssey* and disappeared into an uncharted sector of the Frontier.

Bish

"WE TRACED THE MODIFICATION. HAMMOND ROBOTICS HAS A WEAPONS DIVISION?" — BISH

The name Bish is short for Bishamon, the mythological god of warriors within the Japanese Seven Gods of Fortune. Bish is an IMC-trained electrical engineer, born and raised on Earth. After getting screwed over by the IMC on a Frontier job placement that cost him all his savings just to move out there, he ended up in the right place at the right time—the notorious "Bish bar brawl"—to take the Militia's timely offer of employment. Bish now serves as a Combat Intel Specialist, remote hacking into IMC systems during combat on behalf of ground forces, tracking mission progress, and giving tactical guidance to Pilots on the ground.

Sarah

"YOU SAW THOSE MACHINES FIGHT. WE NEED AN ANSWER AND WE NEED IT FAST." — SARAH

As a child, Sarah lost several close members of her family to incidents in which the IMC displaced Frontier citizens by force. As a result, she vowed to take revenge on the IMC at every possible opportunity, refusing to rest until they have been removed from the Frontier. For most of her career, she served in Covert Operations for the Militia, before moving into the command ranks of the Militia's Marauder Corps. Her long list of successful attacks on IMC installations landed her on the IMC's High Value Target List, where she remains listed as one of the 50 most dangerous Militia operatives still at large.

NOTE

Sarah is voiced by Respawn Entertainment's Community Manager, Abbie Heppe.

Barker

"WAIT! WE HAVE TO GO BACK. I LEFT MY SHOTTY AT THE BAR. I AIN'T LEAVING TOWN WITHOUT IT!" — BARKER

Barker served with MacAllan during the Titan Wars—a series of conflicts within the Core Systems many years ago. Their operations during the Titan Wars have been chronicled in many historical records, and have formed the basis of current IMC counterinsurgency doctrine. A tremendously gifted Pilot of both Titans and all things flying, Barker is rumored to have adjusted poorly to life outside of combat, sinking into a deep depression and becoming even more of an alcoholic than he was during active service.

THE IMC

The Interstellar Manufacturing Corporation, or IMC, started out small, in natural resource extraction industries, under the name Hammond Engineering. Fifteen years later, demand for Titan manufacturing materials, combined with Hammond's market-cornering planetary survey technology and map database rights, contributed to explosive growth for the company. Over the course of a century, a series of acquisitions, mergers, and re-brandings led to the transformation of Hammond Engineering into the sprawling commercial empire that is the IMC.

Despite their reputation for exploitative behavior on the Frontier, they receive little criticism from their shareholders and customers living in the Core Systems—the material conveniences and widely used products provided by the IMC generate considerable "consumer inertia", to the corporation's benefit.

With the Frontier's valuable shipping lanes and vast planetary resources ripe for exploitation, the IMC is dedicated to maximizing profits and shareholder wealth, using the legal application of force when necessary.

KEY CHARACTERS

Graves

"Sometimes rank has its privileges."
— Graves

In the IMC command structure, Vice Admiral Graves is formally known as the CINCFRONT, or Commander-in-Chief, Frontier Command. Despite the elaborate title, Frontier operations are notorious for their lack of adherence to traditional protocol, allowing Graves to personally command IMC forces in the field, and to operate far more informally than commanders in the Core Systems. Graves has a reputation as a maverick within the IMC. His calls for policy change have often been deemed too risky to IMC forces, and too lenient to Frontier citizens. During the inquiry into the *Odyssey* scandal, Graves maintained that the ship was forcibly commandeered by MacAllan and his band of mutineers.

Blisk

"I almost feel bad for them. Almost."
— Blisk

Blisk is a South African mercenary working under a new long-term contract with the IMC on the Frontier, providing Combat Intel and Counterinsurgency services. His first contract concluded with his outfit making enough money to retire to a tropical paradise, but after considering the excellent pay, and more importantly, the opportunity to lay waste to everything in sight with state-of-the-art hardware, Blisk decided that the IMC's offer of renewal was just too good to pass up.

Spyglass

"A Pilot survived the aftermath? Find out how and bring him and his Titan to me."
— Spyglass

Spyglass is a physical manifestation of the IMC's vast computational network identity, handling logistics, navigation, deployment, and communications between all IMC forces on the Frontier. Spyglass units are built on a modified Spectre chassis and are considered expendable in the field, often accompanying ground forces aboard dropships to provide up-to-date mission information and live surveillance.

TITANFALL TECH

PILOTS

Titan Pilots are rated by "certifications", most of which apply to civilian applications such as construction, shipping, and heavy salvage industries. The most prestigious of these is the Full Combat Certification—a widely published series of tests that grade a Titan Pilot's abilities. Because of the extreme physical and mental challenges of mastering both Titan combat and dismounted parkour movement, a fully combat-certified Titan Pilot is a rare find, and the combat skills of active Pilots in the field varies widely throughout the Frontier.

Some are formally trained by the IMC or Militia's dedicated programs, while the vast majority are trained by independent mercenary or pirate groups. A large black market surrounding the technology used by Pilots is rumored to have developed across the Frontier, covering areas such as weapons modifications, physical alterations and strengthening, stolen training simulation pods, and Titan-Pilot combat interface abilities.

JUMP KITS

Jump Kits are small jetpacks that are worn around the waist. They originated in the ship salvage industry—workers needed a way to quickly navigate through complex geometries with deadly drops and sheer vertical faces. Jump Kits provide a brief burst of thrust that is used to leap to higher locations. They also have a function that adjusts the deceleration on potentially fatal descents to safe levels, allowing Pilots to fall from great heights without injury. Combat Titan Pilots have informally adapted Jump Kits to their own purposes for many years. The Jump Kit enables sustained wall running, improving Pilot maneuverability in combat situations against regular infantry and other Titans.

TITANS

Titans are descendants of today's fledgling military exoskeletons. In addition to the obvious combat applications, unarmed forms of Titans are used in heavy industries like cargo transport and salvage. They are also used in special applications such as deep space search and rescue, and are very effective in inhospitable environments. The use of Titans is widespread throughout the Frontier in both combat and in civilian life.

DATA KNIFE

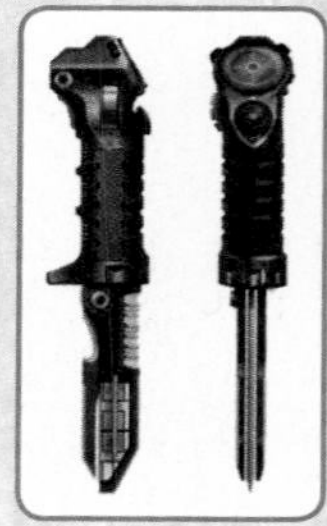

This is a special knife designed to infiltrate and reprogram enemy computer systems by plugging into a data port. A circular, backlit screen in the handle indicates progress. The "business end" of the device is a plug that works with many different types of hardware ports like a skeleton key. When used against Marvins and Spectres, the Data Knife will reprogram the robot to fight on the attacker's side. It also works as a knife.

GRUNTS

Standard infantry deployed by both the IMC and Militia are most commonly referred to as Grunts. Participating in battles dominated by Pilots and Titans, Grunts often serve in a supporting role, securing and defending objectives. Grunts are equipped with a variety of ballistic-based weapons ranging from carbines to shotguns. But some Grunts also carry shoulder-fired anti-armor weapons designed to damage Titans.

MARVINS

Subsidiaries of the IMC developed the MRVN (Mobile Robotic Versatile eNtity), commonly referred to as the Marvin. A Marvin is an anthropomorphic helper robot used in industrial and civilian applications. They are not designed for combat and they have a relatively primitive locomotion system compared to their Spectre counterparts. Marvins are used throughout the Core Systems and the Frontier, performing sanitation, construction, maintenance, and hazardous environment duties in both industrial and civilian markets.

HEAVY TURRETS

Heavy turrets are designed for killing everything—including Titans. When used out in the field, they are often braced into position in urban environments atop buildings, and have a considerable range of motion and excellent target tracking systems. Multiple Titans are usually required to disable a single heavy turret by focusing their fire on it. They operate autonomously and, in most cases, can be "flipped" (to fight for the other team) when a nearby console is compromised, often with a Data Knife.

SPECTRES

Defense contractor subsidiaries of the IMC developed the Spectre—a robotic anthropomorphic combat system derived from the MRVN project. The Spectre is officially classified in IMC manifests as a form of Automated Infantry. Their main use is urban pacification and occupation. Due to the corporate and military politics that plagued their development, Spectres inherited a data port vulnerability from their Marvin predecessors. When a Pilot reprograms a Spectre, the Spectre immediately begins to seek out and engage friendly combatants, both human and artificial, with extreme prejudice.

DROP PODS

Drop Pods are used to deploy automated and human infantry to the ground from orbit with high precision. Drop Pods can be pressurized for the deployment of human occupants. The pods may also be internally reconfigured in many ways to deliver a wide variety of payloads. Distortion Braking Technology allows Drop Pods to streak in but decelerate to a survivable speed prior to hitting the ground. The braking results in a visible donut-like distortion effect in the sky, and a bowel-shaking, low-frequency sound that is hard to miss.

DROPSHIPS

The Goblin dropship is the current generation of IMC troop and light cargo transport. It is manufactured in a variety of formats, each with different drive, shielding, and weapons systems. The Crow is an older generation of dropship based on the battle-forged and proven designs from the Titan Wars. Although it was superseded by the IMC's Goblin design several years ago, it is still seen everywhere throughout the Frontier. Many Crow-class dropships still remain in service with the Militia, either salvaged from the battlefield or stolen outright from the IMC.

The Dropship Combat Search and Rescue (D-CSAR) System is a collection of modifications that allows small dropships such as the Crow and Goblin to carry several Titan-grade bodyshield generators onboard. Dropships carrying the D-CSAR System are so heavily shielded that they are almost invulnerable to enemy fire, making them ideal for medical evacuation, even when under heavy fire from enemy Titans. However, the amount of power required to operate the system limits how often the ship can operate its jump drive (usually one jump for arrival and one jump for departure before requiring refueling) and disables all of the dropship's built-in weapons.

CAMPAIGN

Titanfall features a unique multiplayer campaign, further chronicling the conflict between the Militia and IMC. Players can choose to play on either side, resulting in different pre-match briefings and communications chatter during battle. To get the whole story, make an effort to play the campaign as both the Militia and IMC—there's achievements for completing the campaign as each faction. There are nine campaign matches, consisting of five Attrition matches and four Hardpoint Domination matches. Unlike traditional multiplayer matches, the campaign features a number of scripted events, helping enhance the story. So while engaging the enemy, pay close attention to your surroundings and the radio chatter—your team's performance on the battlefield impacts the outcome of the story.

THE REFUELING RAID

Map: Fracture
Game Mode: Hardpoint Domination

The 1st Militia Fleet, desperately low on fuel and on the run from the IMC, prepares to raid an IMC gas mining world. Years of aggressive fuel extraction have taken their toll on this former colony for the privileged. Now on the edge of defeat, the Militia forces must find a way to fight on, despite the loss of their commanding officer in an earlier battle. Meanwhile, unsure as to the exact time and place of the impending Militia refueling raid, IMC forces make defense preparations at several gas mining worlds in the Yuma System.

Team Tactics

Hardpoint Charlie can be neutralized and captured by Titans. Expect some intense Titan duels here.

In this Hardpoint Domination battle, both factions begin with one AI-operated Titan—consider rodeo attacking the enemy team's Titan to give your side an early advantage. Grunts of the IMC are likely to secure Hardpoint Alpha early during the round while the Militia's Grunts capture Hardpoint Charlie. This leaves Hardpoint Bravo up for grabs—assault this hardpoint with Arc Grenades and prepare for some close-quarter firefights, as Pilots tend to converge here early on. Hold on to at least two of the hardpoints for the majority of the match to secure a win for your team.

THE COLONY

Map: Colony
Game Mode: Attrition

Following the Militia's refueling raid and escape in the Yuma System, the IMC continue their search to eliminate the Militia fleet. The IMC deploys a small unit, led by Blisk, to an uncharted planet on the Frontier, where life signs have been detected. Blisk uses the opportunity to field test a platoon of Spectre automated infantry units on the local populace. The Militia, receiving a distress signal from this world, sends a strike force to investigate. During the battle, communications intercepts reveal that the colony was founded by the crew of the *IMS Odyssey*, led by James MacAllan. Now, forced out of hiding, MacAllan must once again confront Vice Admiral Graves, his former commanding officer from the *Odyssey* fifteen years ago.

Team Tactics

Take to the rooftops and ambush enemy Grunts, Spectres, and Titans—but watch for enemy Pilots doing the same thing.

Unlike Hardpoint Domination, Attrition is all about accumulating kills. Regardless of which faction you represent, make a push toward the center of the map and start eliminating Grunts and enemy Pilots as fast as you can—you get one Attrition Point for each Grunt and Spectre you kill, and four Attrition Points for enemy Pilots. Consider attaching a Suppressor to keep your Pilot off the minimap and utilize the various rooftops and second-story windows to maintain the high ground. The more damage you inflict on the enemy, the sooner you get your Titan. Coordinate Titan deployments with your teammates and then roam the map in groups of two or three Titans.

THE *ODYSSEY*

Map: Relic
Game Mode: Attrition

In exchange for the rescue of his fellow colonists from the forests surrounding the wreckage of the *IMS Odyssey*, the ex-IMC officer James MacAllan agrees to lead the Militia against the IMC. Despite Sarah's mistrust of MacAllan, Bish insists that getting the ex-IMC officer's help is their best chance of defeating the IMC. At the same time, Vice Admiral Graves tracks MacAllan's signal to its source, and deploys forces to secure the wreck of the *IMS Odyssey*. During the battle, MacAllan downloads the contents of the *Odyssey's* computer core, containing the schematics for Demeter, a critical refueling station linking the Core Systems to the Frontier—destroying Demeter would prevent the IMC from sending reinforcements to the Frontier for years to come.

Team Tactics

While fighting within the ship, use the Active Radar Pulse ability to detect enemy Grunts and Pilots.

This is another Attrition battle, this time set among the wreckage of the *IMS Odyssey*. Prepare for a mix of close and mid-range combat. Versatile weapons, like the R-101C Carbine, perform well here. While locating enemy minions is easy enough through the use the minimap, consider equipping the Active Radar Pulse Tactical Ability to locate enemy Pilots, including those using suppressed weapons. Eliminating Pilots nets your team more Attrition Points, plus you'll get your Titan faster. Titan combat on this map can get a bit claustrophobic, particularly inside the ship. Use the ship's bulkheads for cover, dashing in and out of cover to engage enemy Titans.

GET BARKER

Map: Angel City
Game Mode: Attrition

IMC informants in Angel City confirm Graves' suspicions as to MacAllan's next move. MacAllan is in the city, attempting to extract an ex-IMC pilot named Barker. IMC search parties are deployed, but they soon come under attack from Militia forces, who are attempting to delay the IMC so that MacAllan can get Barker out of the city. While getting Barker out via the city's sewer tunnels, MacAllan orders Militia fighters to attack an arriving IMC carrier called the *Sentinel*, despite Sarah's objections that it's a suicide mission for the fighter pilots.

Team Tactics

Early on, rodeo attack the opposing team's AI-controlled Titan to score some easy Attrition Points.

At the start of this battle, the Militia are in the process of sneaking Barker out of Angel City. Each team begins the battle with one AI-controlled Titan. Make it your objective to locate and eliminate the enemy team's Titan at the start of the battle. This is easily accomplished with a rodeo attack, netting your team five Attrition Points for its destruction. Once you gain access to your Titan, work with friendly Titans to isolate and engage the enemy team's Titans, picking them off one by one. The urban setting offers plenty of cover for Titans—hold at intersections and use the adjacent buildings for cover, dashing laterally around corners to engage.

ASSAULT ON THE *SENTINEL*

Map: Outpost 207
Game Mode: Attrition

Although Barker is successfully extracted from Angel City, he is reluctant to help MacAllan unless an IMC carrier, the *IMS Sentinel*, is destroyed. The *Sentinel*, according to Barker, is an impassable threat in this sector that must be eliminated before he can be of any help to MacAllan. MacAllan's gambit to send fighters against the *Sentinel* during the battle of Angel City now pays off. As part of their plan, the Militia first sends in a large decoy ship to draw fire from the orbital defense cannons, to allow their troop-carrying dropships to infiltrate IMC airspace.

Team Tactics

Hack the turret, then lure enemy Titans toward it—you get credit for any kills it scores.

In this Attrition battle, both teams begin with one AI-controlled Titan—hunt down the opposing team's Titan to score some quick Attrition Points. But the IMC team also benefits from a turret, positioned near their deployment area. If used wisely, this turret can be the deciding factor in close matches. Both teams should attempt to maintain control of this turret—this requires the Militia team to hack it. With the turret in your team's control, try to lure enemy Titans toward it—move toward the center of the map, then retreat toward the turret, drawing enemy Titans into its field of fire. Every enemy killed with this turret nets your team Attrition Points—and if you hacked the turret, you get XP for every kill it scores.

HERE BE DRAGONS

Map: Boneyard
Game Mode: Hardpoint Domination

Following the elimination of the *IMS Sentinel*, Barker flies a Militia strike force to an abandoned prototype of a tower designed to repel hostile wildlife. Using knowledge of Frontier war simulations he had developed with MacAllan in the past, Graves predicts MacAllan's move and sends a strike force to scuttle the tower. During the battle, both sides struggle for control of the generators that route energy to the old tower—the Militia try to operate the tower and analyze its workings, while the IMC attempt to overload and trigger it to self-destruct before the Militia learn too much about it.

Team Tactics

Bring your favorite Anti-Titan weapon to Hardpoint Charlie and prepare for some intense battles.

This is a Hardpoint Domination match, requiring your team to hold a majority of the hardpoints to win. The Militia are likely to take Hardpoint Bravo early on, while the IMC takes Hardpoint Alpha. Hardpoint Charlie can be accessed by enemy Titans, so expect heavy action here—once captured, consider placing Arc Mines at the entrances. While most of the action is focused on the hardpoints, don't miss the chance to hack the two turrets on this map—any damage dealt by a hacked turret reduces your Titan's build time. When moving around on foot, make use of the map's various zip lines to speedily move from one hardpoint to the next.

THE THREE TOWERS

Map: Airbase **Game Mode:** Attrition

IMC reinforcements are about to lift off and crush the Militia fleet approaching Demeter. To even the odds, Sarah leads a surgical attack on the airbase, armed with Bish's new tower-toppling invention, the "Icepick". As the battle comes to an end, MacAllan hails Vice Admiral Graves directly on comms, and questions his old friend's efforts to change the IMC from within, but the Vice Admiral dismisses MacAllan's remarks and terminates the connection.

Team Tactics

Doom the enemy's AI-controlled Titans in the hangar to secure an early lead.

At the start of this Attrition battle, each faction begins with two AI-controlled Titans. Chances are these four Titans will meet and battle in the large hangar. Assist your team's Titans in this early battle, lobbing Arc Grenades and firing your Anti-Titan weapon from a distance. You can even rodeo attack one of the Titans to secure the kill for your team—each Titan killed is worth five Attrition Points. Once the enemy's two AI-controlled Titans are down, make your way to the turret on the west side of the map and hack it. Once your team holds the turret, try to lure enemy Titans toward it to gain an upper hand in Titan battles. Holding this turret may be enough to tilt the odds in your team's favor.

THE BATTLE OF DEMETER

Map: Demeter
Game Mode: Hardpoint Domination

The Militia forces attack Demeter—the key refueling link that allows travel between the IMC's Core Systems and the Frontier. While his forces fight to start a devastating chain reaction that will wipe out the refueling facilities at Demeter, MacAllan plays out his endgame with Vice Admiral Graves. Again, MacAllan questions Graves' actions as a Vice Admiral in the IMC. He reminds Graves that fifteen years ago, Graves allowed him to desert with the *Odyssey*—not under the duress of a mutiny, but in an act of compassion to a friend burned out on war. In the end, MacAllan offers the Vice Admiral one last chance to redeem himself, and to change the fate of the Frontier, against all the bloodshed under his command.

Team Tactics

Once captured, consider posting two Titans at Hardpoint Bravo—this is the battle's most contentious hot spot.

In this Hardpoint Domination battle, the Militia deploys near Hardpoint Charlie while the IMC arrives near Hardpoint Alpha. Grunts and Spectres on both teams can usually capture these two hardpoints on their own, so Pilots should make an early round move toward Hardpoint Bravo. Accessible by both Titans and infantry, expect Hardpoint Bravo to be a major point of contention throughout the battle. Instead of taking heavy losses at Hardpoint Bravo, consider simply locking down Hardpoints Alpha and Charlie to hold out for a win. The turrets on the south side of the map cannot be hacked, so don't waste time trying to secure them. Instead, stay focused on the hardpoints. At the end of the battle, there is no Epilogue. Simply stay alive and rack up as many kills as possible.

MADE MEN

Map: Corporate
Game Mode: Hardpoint Domination

Graves defects to the Militia. Three months later, under his command, the Militia takes the fight to the IMC, striking at the first of many IMC robotics production facilities. Cut off from reinforcements following the destruction of Demeter, the IMC on the Frontier are increasingly dependent on automated infantry. Now, the hunters have become the hunted, and the IMC forces must fight to preserve their replication facilities on the Frontier. The fate of the Frontier remains uncertain, but for now, the Militia holds the upper hand.

Team Tactics

Most Titan battles occur at Hardpoint Bravo. Make sure you have backup.

At the start of this final battle, the IMC usually takes control of Hardpoint Alpha while the Militia makes a move for Hardpoints Bravo or Charlie. When hardpoints are captured on this map, Spectres emerge from the adjoining walls, serving as automated sentries for the capturing team. So when assaulting an enemy hardpoint, expect stiff resistance from enemy Spectres. Begin your attack by tossing an Arc Grenade toward the objective—one Arc Grenade is usually enough to wipe out most of the defending Spectres. Hardpoint Bravo is accessible by infantry and Titans, so expect plenty of activity here—Arc Grenades and Arc Mines work well when defending this location.

CAMPAIGN COMPLETION ACHIEVEMENTS

XBOX ONE	XBOX 360	NAME	CRITERIA	GAMERSCORE
		IMC Pilot	Complete the IMC Campaign	50
		Militia Pilot	Complete the Militia Campaign	50
		IMC Elite Pilot	Win every Campaign level as an IMC Pilot	25
		Militia Elite Pilot	Win every Campaign level as a Militia Pilot	25
		Frequent Flyer	Play 50 Campaign matches	50

PILOT CERTIFICATION

In *Titanfall*, you take on the role of an IMC or Militia Pilot. These elite combat specialists are respected (and feared) throughout the Frontier. Equipped with Jump Kits, Pilots are capable of performing some truly acrobatic maneuvers, aiding them in taking the high ground and dominating the battlefield. But Pilots are most known for operating Titans: mechanized war machines fitted with an array of devastating weapons.

To succeed in *Titanfall* you must master playing as both a Pilot and a Titan. This chapter is jam-packed with information on both topics, complete with insight from the game's developers at Respawn Entertainment. So whether you're new to the FPS genre or not, take the time to read up—*Titanfall* is easy to learn, but it takes skill and a broader knowledge of the gameplay mechanics to master the intricacies of Pilot and Titan combat.

CONTROLS

XBOX ONE

Aim Modifier
Tactical Ability
Move / Sprint
Scoreboard
[D-Pad]
Eject Sequence Initiation
Equip Anti-Titan Weapon
Titanfall / Titan AI Mode / Titan Core

Fire
Ordnance
Switch Weapons / Pick Up Weapon
Crouch
Jump / Dash
Use / Reload / Disembark Titan
Loadouts / Settings
Look / Melee

XBOX 360

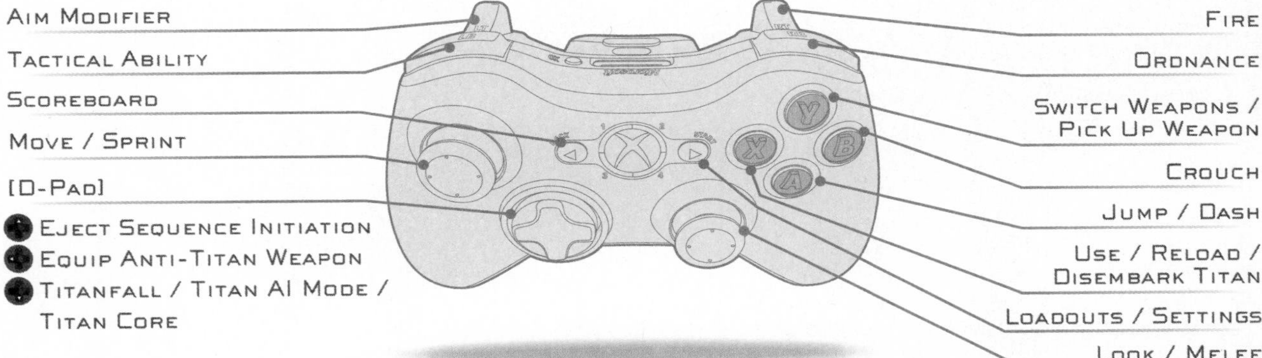

BUMPER JUMPER

The Bumper Jumper button/stick layout, accessible through the game's Options menu, is perfect for *Titanfall* since you're constantly jumping and wall running. If you are not familiar with this button/stick layout, it switches your Jump button (A) with your Tactical Ability button (LB). With this layout you can keep your right thumb on the right analog stick at all times, while jumping with LB. This allows you to maintain precise aim while jumping and moving around.

PC: DEFAULT KEY BINDINGS

ACTIONS	KEY
Fire	Mouse 1
Aim	Mouse 2
Melee	C
Ordnance	F
Tactical Ability	Q
Use/Disembark Titan	E
Reload	R
Eject	X
Titanfall/Titan AI Mode/Titan Core	V
WEAPONS	
Switch Weapons	Mouse Wheel
Equip Primary Weapon	1
Equip Sidearm	2
Equip Anti-Titan Weapon	4
Pick Up Weapon	G

ACTIONS	KEY
MOVEMENT	
Move Forward	W
Move Back	S
Move Left	A
Move Right	D
Sprint	Shift
Jump/Dash	Space
Crouch	Ctrl
MISCELLANEOUS/COMMUNICATION	
Scoreboard	Tab
Push To Talk	T
Chat Message	Y
Team Chat Message	U

INTERFACE

Pilot Interface

Titan Interface

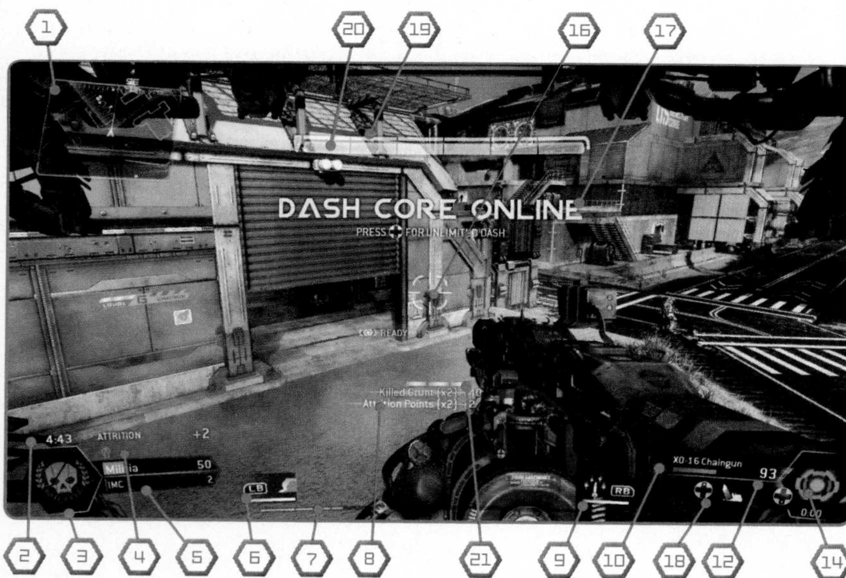

1. **Minimap:** This map provides a rudimentary top-down perspective of your current position on the map. Friendly units appear as blue icons while hostile units are represented by red icons.
2. **Match Timer:** This shows how much time is left in the current match.
3. **Faction:** This insignia shows which faction you're representing—Militia or IMC.
4. **Active Titans:** These icons show how many Titans are on the map. Colored icons show active Titans while gray icons represent Titans ready for Titanfall.
5. **Game Mode Info:** This display shows the current score for the selected game mode.
6. **Tactical Ability:** The selected Tactical Ability is shown here along with the input required to activate it.
7. **XP Bar:** This bar fills from left to right as XP is earned through various actions. When the bar is completely filled, the Pilot levels up.
8. **Scoring Update:** Every time a Pilot scores points or earns XP, a text notification appears beneath the reticle.
9. **Ordnance:** The selected ordnance is shown here along with the input required to deploy it.
10. **Equipped Weapon:** The name of the Pilot's equipped weapon.
11. **Anti-Titan Weapon:** A silhouette of the Pilot's Anti-Titan weapon appears here along with the input required to equip it.
12. **Ammo Count:** This number represents how much ammo is left in the selected weapon's magazine.
13. **Magazine Count:** This number shows how many magazines are remaining for the selected weapon.
14. **Build Timer:** This shows how much time is remaining before a Pilot's Titan or Titan's Core Ability is available for deployment.
15. **Kill Notification:** Recent Pilot kills/deaths are reported here.
16. **Reticle:** This is your weapon's aiming reticle. The reticle expands while moving, indicating an unstable firing stance. The reticle constricts while stationary or crouched, representing a stable firing stance.
17. **Status Update:** A variety of status updates appear here, reporting game mode information as well as leveling up, completion of challenges, and Titan/Core Ability availability.
18. **Core Ability*:** When your Titan's Core Ability is available, this icon appears along with the input required to activate it.
19. **Bodyshield Bar*:** This bar represents your Titan's bodyshield—once depleted it can be regenerated by taking cover.
20. **Health Bar*:** This bar represents your Titan's health—unlike the bodyshield, it can't be regenerated.
21. **Dash Bars*:** These bars represent how many dashes your Titan has. These bars slowly replenish after each dash.

* = Titan only

WELCOME TO THE FRONTIER: TRAINING

"EVERYONE OUT HERE'S EITHER RUNNING FROM THE PAST, OR CHASING THE FUTURE."
—MACALLAN

Begin your Pilot career by completing the training exercises in the Hammond Robotics Pilot Certification simulator.

Before jumping into the campaign or multiplayer matches, it's strongly advised to begin your Pilot career by completing the training tutorial. Here you learn the fundamentals of mobility and combat, both for Pilots and Titans. Training is broken up into fourteen separate modules, each focusing on a specific topic. While training doesn't cover every aspect of *Titanfall*, it serves as a good starting point, highlighting the basics. Here we take a look at each training module, offering a bit more insight and perspective on each topic.

NOTE

After performing the initial Look Calibration exercise, requiring you to look at two red lights, you're given the opportunity to reverse the vertical look input. If you prefer an invert setup, now's the time to do it. This can also be set later in the game's options.

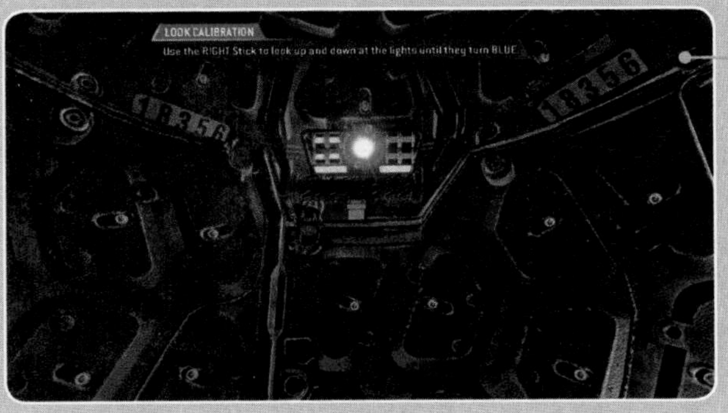

MODULE 01: MOVEMENT

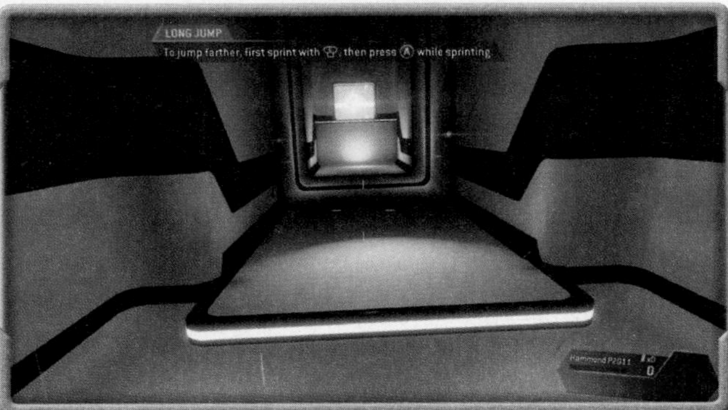

Sprinting prior to a jump allows your Pilot to jump greater distances.

In this exercise, familiarize yourself with walking, sprinting, jumping, and mantling. Move through the first tunnel, then sprint through the second tunnel before the sliding doors at the far end close. Upon exiting the second tunnel, jump over the low obstacle. Next, sprint and jump over the wide pit—if you fall, you can try again until you make it to the other side. Finally, approach the high ledge at the end of the corridor and jump toward it—your Pilot automatically grabs the ledge above. While holding on to the ledge, push forward to pull yourself up—this is called mantling. After mantling up to the ledge, walk into the blue glowing light in the adjoining chamber to complete this exercise.

MODULE 02: WALL RUNNING

Chaining together multiple wall runs is extremely effective, allowing you to cover great distance at an increased rate of speed.

Here you learn the significance of a Pilot's Jump Kit, which allows you to run on walls. Start by wall running across the first gap—sprint, then jump at an angle toward the wall on the right to start wall running. Continue sprinting upon making contact to run along the wall. Cross the next pit using the same technique, this time running along the wall on the left. The third pit is too long to cross with a single wall run. So start by running along the wall on the right, then jump toward the wall on the left to continue over the pit. Finally, wall run along the wall on the right to reach the ledge at the end of the corridor. After pulling yourself up to the ledge, continue into the blue light to complete this module.

PILOT CERTIFICATION

MODULE 03: FREEFORM WALL RUN

This exercise can be completed without touching the ground. Try linking wall runs to make it all the way to the exit.

Now it's time to put sprinting, jumping, and wall running to some practical use. There are several large pits in the corridor ahead, requiring the use of wall running to make it to the exit. After each wall run you can jump to a nearby platform before setting up the next wall run. However, it's entirely possible to make it through this corridor without touching any of the platforms—just keep linking wall runs, jumping back and forth between the wall on your right and the wall on your left. Complete the exercise by moving into the blue light at the end of the corridor.

MODULE 04: DOUBLE JUMP

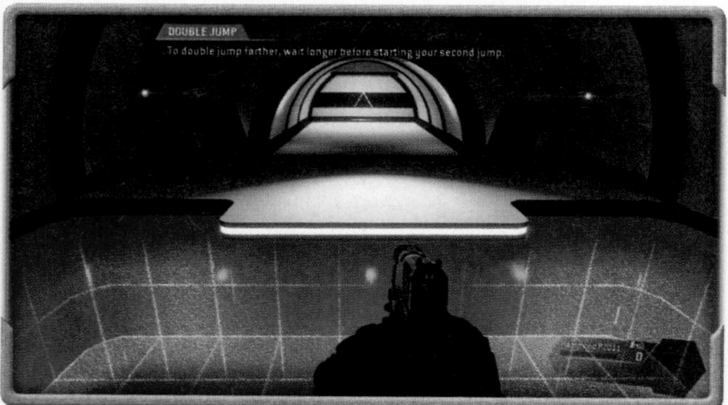

Perform these double jumps without sprinting to better gauge the distance you can travel with this technique.

A Pilot's Jump Kit extends their natural jumping ability, allowing them to jump once more after leaving the ground. This is called double jumping and it's useful to boost your Pilot to greater heights, perfect for reaching high ledges or hopping through second-story windows. Advance through this obstacle course using double jumps to leap over a couple of pits. When you reach the second pit, jump and then initiate the double jump just before your Pilot starts to descend. Delaying your double jump until you reach the apex of your jump allows your Pilot to travel greater distances, particularly when sprinting before initiating the first jump. At the end of the corridor, double jump vertically and mantle upward through a hatch in the ceiling to complete the exercise.

MODULE 05: FREEFORM DOUBLE JUMP

Don't worry about speed now. Instead, study your environment and identify multiple paths through each room.

Now combine double jumping with wall running to make your way to the exit. In this exercise, you must traverse two large hangar-like interiors filled with large crates and other objects. There are multiple paths through both rooms, so take the time to experiment—see if you can reach the catwalk on the upper-left side of the first room. When you enter the second room, simply perform a wall run along the vertical surface on the right side of the catwalk—at the end of the wall run, leap toward the exit. If you fall, use double jumps to make your way back to the catwalk above. Even once you reach the exit, consider returning to the first room and try again, this time racing through the obstacle course as quickly and as fluidly as possible.

MODULE 06: CLOAK

Cloaking makes you invisible to Grunts and Spectres—at least until you fire your weapon.

Cloaking, making yourself nearly invisible, is essential to Pilot survival. Using the Cloak Tactical Ability, sneak past the Grunts in the large room, passing directly beneath them without being detected. However, once cloaked, make haste. This ability is only active for a few seconds, as indicated by the Cloak meter in the bottom left of the HUD—once the meter is depleted, Cloak deactivates, making you visible. Cloak, and all other Tactical Abilities, must recharge after being deployed—the Tactical Ability icon and meter are grayed out during this recharge period, indicating the ability is unavailable. After sneaking past the Grunts, continue to the exit to complete this exercise.

MODULE 07: BASIC COMBAT

The Smart Pistol MK5 can lock on and engage multiple targets simultaneously with one pull of the trigger.

This module begins with a basic melee demonstration. Walk up behind the enemy Grunt and perform a melee attack, as indicated by the on-screen instructions. Melee attacking an enemy from behind results in a neck-snapping execution. Performing a frontal melee attack causes your Pilot to perform a lethal kick. Frontal melee attacks are faster, but also put your Pilot at risk. For the second part of the exercise, you're prompted to eliminate several enemies with the auto-targeting Smart Pistol MK5. Take note of the vertical brackets on the HUD—your targets must be between these two brackets for the weapon to achieve a lock. Once a lock is achieved, all you have to do is pull the trigger. Unlike weaker opponents, enemy Pilots require three separate locks to kill with one trigger pull. Eliminate all the targets using the Smart Pistol, then proceed to the exit.

MODULE 08: FIRING RANGE

Make a habit of aiming down your weapon's sights to improve accuracy.

Unlike the Smart Pistol MK5, the R-101C Carbine is a more traditional firearm. Start this exercise by aiming down the weapon's sights. As your Pilot shoulders the weapon, the iron sights are visible—this offers a more precise means to aim the weapon. While aiming down sights, engage the Marvins beyond the partition. For best results, place the iron sights over a Marvin's head and squeeze the trigger, firing off a few rounds. Scoring headshots always inflicts the most damage and aiming down your weapon's sights is the best way to ensure such precision. Eliminate all six Marvins, preferably without reloading. As you score hits, make note of the white X icon appearing within the weapon's sights. This hit indicator provides you with instant feedback, letting you know your weapon is scoring hits. If you don't see a hit indicator when firing, adjust your aim before reengaging. Once all six Marvins are destroyed, the exercise is complete.

MODULE 09: GRENADE RANGE

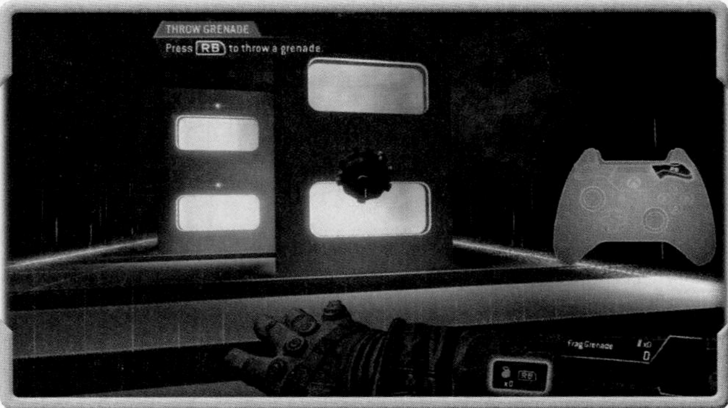

Aim directly for the center of the windows before tossing a grenade.

In this exercise you must throw a grenade through four different windows. Before throwing a grenade, place your aiming reticle directly over one of the windows. At this range you don't need to compensate for range by aiming high. Instead, place the reticle over the center of a window and throw. As you can see, grenades have a relatively flat trajectory, making them fairly easy to deploy with precision. Try to go four out of four in this exercise, tossing no more than four grenades—the simulator will be impressed.

MODULE 10: PILOT COMBAT SCENARIO

The Smart Pistol MK5 makes quick work of enemy Grunts. Lock on to multiple targets before firing.

Now it's time to put all you've learned about combat to the test. You're free to move about this training facility while engaging a large number of enemy Grunts with the Smart Pistol MK5, Frag Grenades, and melee attacks. To locate enemies, study the minimap in the top-left corner of the HUD. The red dots on this map represent enemies at your same elevation—the orange dots represent enemies either above or below your current elevation. Use the minimap to hunt down all the enemy Grunts. The Smart Pistol MK5 makes it easy to eliminate multiple Grunts at a time. If enemies are too far away for the weapon to achieve a lock, aim down the Smart Pistol MK5's iron sights to drop distant targets.

NOTE

You can pick up weapons dropped by enemies. Swap out your Smart Pistol MK5 with a dropped R-101C Carbine and engage the hostiles with automatic fire. It's more effective when engaging targets at intermediate and long range. Titans can also pick up dropped Titan weapons—this is a good way to try out weapons you haven't unlocked yet.

When firing the Sidewinder, aim for the red glowing parts of the Titan's hull to score critical hits.

For the second phase of the exercise you're tasked with engaging an enemy Titan while using the Sidewinder Anti-Titan weapon. The Sidewinder fires a rapid barrage of micro-missiles designed to inflict damage against armored threats. However, don't attempt to go toe-to-toe with a Titan. Instead, use cover, mobility, and your Cloak Tactical Ability to avoid taking damage—if your screen tints red, you are close to death. Your health automatically regenerates over time when you're behind cover and no longer taking damage. The Titan you're engaging is stationary, so try to sneak up on it and score a few hits before it can retaliate—if necessary, activate the Cloak Tactical Ability to make your escape. Hit-and-run attacks are essential to survival when engaging enemy Titans on foot. For best results, aim for the glowing red section on the Titan's hull—hitting this spot results in a critical hit, inflicting heavy damage. Continue playing cat and mouse with the Titan until it's down for the count.

These Grunts don't stand a chance against your Titan. Shoot, trample, or melee all the enemies.

Pilots earn credit towards their next Titan drop by engaging in combat. Once your Titan is built, you can drop your Titan onto the battlefield. To begin the next phase of the exercise, initiate Titanfall—aim at the desired location you want your Titan to drop, and press the button/key indicated on screen. Within seconds your Titan drops from the sky and lands at the desired point—rush to your Titan and mount up. Soon after entering your Titan, more enemy Grunts arrive in drop pods. Hunt them down with your Titan, firing the Quad Rocket primary weapon—you can also eliminate Grunts by punching or running them down.

MODULE 11: TITAN DASH

The green lights at the end of the hall indicate when rockets are about to be fired—dash laterally to prevent getting hit.

Titans can dash laterally to perform fast directional changes. Start the exercise by dashing in the directions indicated by the simulator. Make note of the dash meter, located just below the aiming reticle on the HUD. Each blue box represents one dash. Following a single dash, one of the blue boxes is depleted and slowly begins recharging. An additional dash can be performed as long as a fully replenished blue box is visible in the dash meter. If all these boxes are depleted, you must wait for them to recharge before your Titan can dash again. Resume the exercise by walking down the adjoining hallway, but watch out for incoming rockets. Time your dashes carefully to duck into alcoves on the left or right side of the hall, allowing the rockets to pass by. Before moving out of the alcove, wait for your dash meter to recharge, then continue down the hallway. You must evade two rocket barrages to reach the exit.

MODULE 12: TITAN VORTEX SHIELD

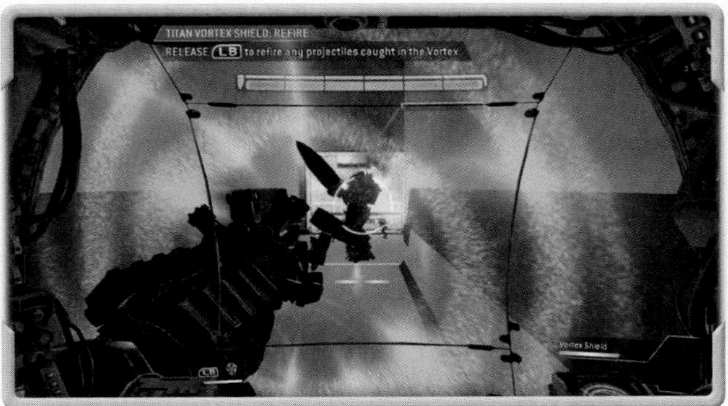

The Vortex Shield can catch incoming bullets, rockets, and missiles, and then redirect them in any direction.

To defend against ranged threats, Titans can be equipped with the Vortex Shield Tactical Ability. This ability absorbs incoming projectiles for a limited time and then refires them. Advance down the hallway and deploy the Vortex Shield—press and hold the Tactical Ability button/key. The enemy Titan at the end of the hall opens fire, but all the incoming rounds are caught by the Vortex Shield. Keep gathering rounds with the Vortex Shield until the enemy Titan pauses to reload—use this as your opportunity to strike back. Release the Tactical Ability button/key to refire the projectiles caught in the Vortex Shield, redirecting them back at the enemy Titan with devastating results. In combat, catching incoming projectiles with the Vortex Shield takes timing and practice. Also, you can only keep the Vortex Shield active for a few seconds before it needs to recharge. So when the Tactical Ability isn't available, be ready to dash out of the way or seek cover.

MODULE 13: TITAN AI CONTROL

Hack the console with your Data Knife, then put your Titan in Follow mode.

Skilled Pilots often disembark from their Titans on the battlefield. Start this exercise by exiting your Titan and entering the control room on the right. Hack the console inside the control room using your Data Knife—this opens the adjoining gate. The Data Knife can also be used to hack turrets and Spectres—kills accumulated by these hacked assets are credited to the Pilot who originally hacked them. Pilots can control their Titan's AI when they are on foot. The AI can be toggled to follow you or guard its current location. The lower-right corner of your Pilot's HUD displays your Titan's current AI mode. Put your Titan's AI into Follow mode to make it follow you through the gate. When your Titan is in Follow mode it will try to stay close to your position. Whether in Follow or Guard mode, the Auto-Titan will automatically engage nearby threats. To complete this exercise, rendezvous with your Titan outside the control room, mount up, and proceed to the exit.

MODULE 14: TITAN COMBAT SCENARIO

Survive the Titan onslaught as long as possible. Use dashes and the Vortex Shield to avoid taking damage.

Now it's time to go toe-to-toe against some enemy Titans. But before they arrive, give the Titan's ordnance a shot. In addition to a primary weapon, Titans carry off-hand weapons into combat. These weapons can be fired at times when primary weapons are unavailable, which enhances your Titan's combat effectiveness. For this exercise your Titan has been equipped with the Rocket Salvo ordnance—fire a barrage to proceed. After testing out the Rocket Salvo, your first opponent arrives. The first enemy Titan's shield has been disabled, but don't get overconfident—it can still pack a punch.

Your Titan has a shield that deflects incoming damage. Your shield bar wraps above the health bar at the top of the HUD. If you avoid taking damage for a short time, your shields will recharge. The best Pilots monitor their Titan's shields during combat, taking breaks to recharge as necessary. Always keep an eye on your Titan's shield bar—retreat or find cover before your shield is depleted.

Dash laterally to flank enemy Titans, attacking them from the side or rear—if you're not in front of them, they can't retaliate.

After eliminating the first enemy Titan, two more arrive, this time with heavier weapons. Avoid taking on both of these Titans at the same time. Instead, monitor their movements on the minimap and try to isolate them, picking them off one by one. To drop them quickly, try to score critical hits by targeting the red glowing sections on their hull. While fighting the Titans, keep an eye on their health bars, superimposed on the HUD. Take into account how much damage they've taken compared to your Titan's current shield and health status when determining whether to press the attack or retreat.

The third and subsequent waves feature Titans with active bodyshields. As a result, these fights are much tougher. Your Titan's health bar status is located at the top of the HUD. Unlike shields, when your health bar goes down, it will not replenish. Once your health bar is depleted, your Titan is doomed to die shortly. So if your health bar starts taking hits, immediately retreat and find cover, allowing your shields to recover. The same shielding and health system applies to the enemy Titans too. You must first deplete their shield before dealing permanent damage to their health. Facing off against multiple enemy Titans isn't easy, so remain mobile and try to isolate them. When you have one enemy Titan isolated, attack aggressively, firing all weapons to deplete its shield and deal permanent damage to its health. But don't overcommit. If your shield is depleted, retreat and seek cover, giving your shields a moment to recharge before exposing your Titan to more punishment. When you're outnumbered, mobility and patience are key to surviving. Whittle away at the Titans little by little until you can pick them off one by one.

When the doomed state bar appears at the top of the HUD, prepare to eject, escaping your doomed Titan before it self-destructs.

Eventually your Titan will suffer critical damage, requiring you to abandon it. Combat veterans refer to this as doomed state, indicated by the yellow-and-black dashed bar at the top of the HUD. This bar depletes over time, counting down to your Titan's inevitable self-destruction. When your Titan is in this doomed state, it is extremely vulnerable, particularly to melee attacks, which result in your Pilot's gruesome death. To escape your Titan, you must eject—press the Eject button/key three times to escape. Ejecting launches your Pilot high into the sky—use the higher vantage point to plan your next move. Even when falling from such heights, your Jump Kit prevents you from taking any fall damage, allowing you to escape and continue the fight on foot.

Your Pilot Combat Certification is complete soon after ejecting from your doomed Titan. But there's still more to learn. Continue reading this chapter to gain a broader perspective of what it takes to become an effective Pilot.

TIP

When an enemy Titan reaches its doomed state, consider backing off—it will eventually self-destruct. It's often better to seek cover and recharge your shields than it is to expose yourself to incoming fire from a doomed Titan—they have nothing to lose, but you do.

Pilot Fundamentals Completing the training is a good way to get your feet wet, but there's still more to learn about being a Pilot. Here we take a look at some of the most fundamental aspects of playing as a Pilot, complete with some helpful tips from the developers at Respawn Entertainment.

MOBILITY

Wall running and double jumping are essential for taking the high ground.

Utilizing Jump Kits, Pilots have a distinct advantage on the battlefield, capable of wall running, wall hanging, and double jumping. While the basics of movement are covered during training, putting these moves into practice during combat takes some getting used to. For starters, look for opportunities to take the high ground. Advance to rooftops and other elevated positions to gain a better perspective of your environment. If you stay on the ground you'll be at a serious disadvantage as enemy Pilots (and Titans) attack from above. Furthermore, moving on the ground (even when sprinting) is much slower than utilizing wall runs and other Jump Kit-assisted techniques.

TIP

Crouching is helpful for squeezing into tight spots. It also offers greater stability when firing a weapon—the reticle constricts while crouching, improving accuracy. So when accuracy counts, make a habit of dropping to a knee before firing.

Zip Lines

Zip lines are a fast way to move across a map, whether traveling up or down a cable.

Some environments feature zip lines, offering Pilots a speedy way to get around. When within close proximity to a zip line, attach to it by pressing the Reload button/key—you can even do this while in mid-air. The direction you're facing when you attach to a zip line dictates the direction you'll travel. But don't let the angle of the zip line fool you. All zip lines are two-way linear paths, allowing you to travel up or down zip lines at a consistent speed. Zip lines are often arranged to offer quick movement from one side of a map to the other.

Sometimes you may need to utilize multiple zip lines to cross an environment. Learning the zip line paths for each map can give you a huge advantage, allowing you quickly to flank the enemy team or a score a flag during Capture the Flag matches. While moving along zip lines is fast and efficient, you're vulnerable to incoming fire. So avoid using zip lines in hotly contested areas, as you're likely to draw fire from enemy Pilots and Titans—cloaking while speeding along a zip line makes you much tougher to spot.

DEVELOPER TIP

Respawn ENTERTAINMENT

You move faster when running along walls than you do running on the ground. Use wall running to traverse through environments quickly.

Keep an eye open for wall running paths through maps. You'll get to places faster and safer than running across open ground.

Shooting while wall running won't cause you to lose any speed.

You can move quickly by "skipping" across the ground. This will preserve whatever speed you've built up to that point as a Pilot. To try this, jump away from a wall while wall running at a full sprint. Then, as your feet touch the ground, jump again. Each time your feet are about to touch the ground, as long as you are moving at a high speed, you can jump to "skip" along the ground, until you mistime your jump and slow down too much, or you come to a stop against some object.

There are two ways to dismount from a zip line. If you jump to detach, you will carry speed through the air. If you crouch to detach, you will drop like a rock. These methods can be used to keep enemies in pursuit guessing, in addition to giving you more maneuvering options to navigate the environment.

Hanging on to a wall high up while defending an objective can help you get the drop on unsuspecting enemies. To perform a wall hang, hold your aim control while in the middle of a wall run.

Enemy Titans can see your Jump Kit's exhaust when you double jump while cloaked as a Pilot. Sometimes it's best to avoid double jumping when cloaked, so as not to draw enemy attention.

WEAPONS

Each Pilot has an impressive arsenal of weapons at their disposal, including a primary weapon, a sidearm, an Anti-Titan weapon, and ordnance, such as grenades, mines, and explosive charges.

Primary Weapons and Sidearms

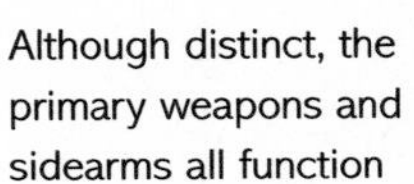

Take aim through your weapon's sight for better accuracy, particular when engaging distant targets.

Although distinct, the primary weapons and sidearms all function similarly, firing cartridge-based projectiles. If you're familiar with other FPS titles, the gunplay in *Titanfall* should feel very familiar.

For best results, always take aim before firing, using the weapon's iron sights or optical attachment to acquire your target—headshots inflict the most damage. Aimed fire is always more precise than shooting from the hip, greatly increasing your odds of hitting a target. However, there may be some instances where hip fire is preferred. Hip fire is less accurate, but allows for better tracking of moving targets in close-quarter fire fights—automatic weapons with high rates of fire and large magazine capacities are most effective when hip firing. Fire modes differ from firearm to firearm, with automatic, semi-automatic, and burst-fire weapons available. Experiment with different primary weapons and sidearms until you find a combination that works for you.

TIP

When selecting a sidearm, choose one that offsets the weaknesses of your primary weapon. For example, if choosing the EVA-8 Shotgun as your primary, consider opting for the B3 Wingman as your sidearm. While the shotgun is great for close-quarter fights, it lacks range, a deficiency the B3 Wingman makes up for.

Reloading

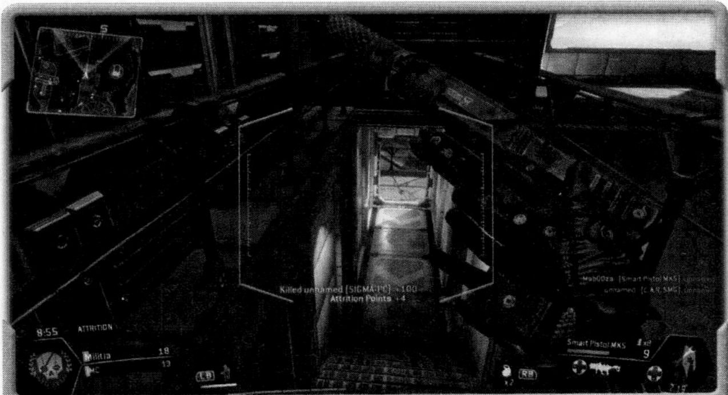

Scout your surroundings and check the minimap before reloading your primary weapon.

Eventually all firearms must be reloaded. Reloading should always be conscious decision and not a reaction. In these chaotic battles, you can't afford to reload after each kill—this is a bad habit that will get you killed. Instead, keep an eye on your magazine status and consider reloading once its capacity dips below 50%. The frequency of your reloads are largely determined by your magazine capacity. But that shouldn't be the only consideration. Only reload when you've reached cover and can safely swap out magazines. Also, overcome the urge to reload during heated close-quarter firefights. Instead, switch to your sidearm and finish the fight—it's always faster to draw your sidearm than it is to reload your primary weapon.

NOTE

For a comprehensive analysis of every Pilot weapon, flip ahead to the Pilot Gear chapter.

PILOT CERTIFICATION

Anti-Titan Weapons

Wait until an enemy Titan is distracted before engaging it with an Anti-Titan weapon.

Even when enemy Titans come raining down, Pilots have a way to directly counter this threat. There are four Anti-Titan weapons to choose from, each with their own characteristics and functionality. But they're all designed to inflict heavy damage against enemy Titans. Unlike the Titan-wielded weapons, Anti-Titan weapons inflict damage to a Titan's shield and health simultaneously. If a Titan's bodyshield is active, the bulk of the Anti-Titan weapon's damage is dealt to the shield while a small percentage bleeds through and deals permanent damage to the Titan's health. So no matter what condition a Titan is in, all hits by Anti-Titan weapons inflict permanent damage. But don't expect to drop a Titan with one of these weapons. Instead, these weapons function best when deployed in a supporting role. So while a friendly Titan is engaging an enemy Titan, consider scoring a few hits with your Anti-Titan weapon to tilt the odds in your teammate's favor.

DEVELOPER TIP

Respawn ENTERTAINMENT

You can swap out your sidearm with another primary weapon if you pick it up off of a fallen enemy or friendly.

Rounds fired by the Mag Launcher will be drawn towards Spectres as well as Titans.

Cook your grenades for added control. You can do this by holding the grenade in your hand instead of releasing it immediately. To cook a grenade, hold the grenade-throw control without letting go. Timing a grenade properly can be risky, but if done properly, it is a very effective way to make a grenade explode exactly where and when you want it to.

Arc Mines are great for defending fixed positions, such as bases in Capture the Flag or the hardpoints in Hardpoint Domination.

Your ordnance and ammunition are automatically replenished when you embark into your Titan.

HACKING: THE DATA KNIFE

Hacking turrets and Spectres with the Data Knife leaves you vulnerable for a few seconds—have a teammate watch your back.

All Pilots are equipped with a Data Knife, a specialized bladed weapon designed to hack enemy systems. In battle, the Data Knife is used to hack turrets and enemy Spectres, reprogramming these assets to fight and score kills for you. To hack a turret, look for an upright console near its base. Interact with the console to initiate the hack—it takes several seconds to complete a hack, leaving your Pilot vulnerable. So make sure the area is clear of threats before attempting a hack. Once the hack is successful, the turret will automatically engage enemy units. Spectres are hacked in a similar fashion, but you must approach them from behind. When a Spectre is hacked, it follows you around the map and attacks enemy units. Hack multiple Spectres to create a small army of loyal robots.

DEVELOPER TIP

Respawn ENTERTAINMENT

When hacking enemy Spectres, you will automatically convert any other Spectres within a short distance to join your team.

Hacking Spectres and turrets will help your team when in Attrition, and will earn you extra points.

You get kill credit for kills achieved by your hacked Spectres, turrets, Conscripted Grunts, and Auto-Titans—Grunts can be conscripted to fight for you by playing the Conscription Burn Card.

TACTICAL ABILITIES

Active Radar Pulse allows Pilots to detect enemies hidden behind walls and other obstructions.

Each Pilot can choose from three different Tactical Abilities. When activated, these abilities remain active for a few seconds, giving the Pilot a temporary tactical advantage. The Cloak ability renders a Pilot nearly invisible, allowing them to sneak around the battlefield. Titans and minions have a hard time detecting cloaked Pilots, but other Pilots can see a slight silhouette. The Stim ability boosts the Pilot's speed and health regeneration for a few seconds, aiding in fight-or-flight situations. While Stim is active, a fast-moving Pilot can jump farther, allowing for greater parkour skills, perfect for retreating or chasing down enemy Pilots. The Active Radar Pulse ability is like x-ray vision for Pilots, illustrating the locations of enemy units on the HUD, even if they're concealed behind walls and other pieces of cover. This versatile ability is perfect for getting the jump on enemies by anticipating their moves.

DEVELOPER TIP

Respawn ENTERTAINMENT

The Smart Pistol MK5 locks on to cloaked Pilots slower than uncloaked Pilots. If you know your opponents are relying on the Smart Pistol, and they catch you in the open, try using the Cloak ability as a countermeasure. This will buy you some time to break line of sight and cancel the progress of any Smart Pistol lock-ons.

RODEO

Although risky, rodeo attacks are a great way to heavily damage enemy Titans.

Pilots show no fear when facing down enemy Titans, sometimes resorting to risky rodeo attacks. During a rodeo attack, a Pilot leaps onto the top of a Titan and tears off the cranial hatch on the outer hull. With the Titan's internal systems exposed, the Pilot can then attack these critical components directly with weapons. So how do you get on top of a Titan in the first place? The easiest way is to drop from above, leaping down from a nearby rooftop or other elevated position. But even if you're on the ground, you can perform a rodeo attack. Double jump toward an enemy Titan, then press the Reload button/key as you make contact to initiate a grapple, causing your Pilot to automatically assume a position atop the Titan. Once in position, the cranial hatch is automatically torn free by your Pilot. As soon as the hatch is open, fire at the Titan's internal systems using a primary weapon or sidearm—Satchel Charges are also very effective. However, exercise extreme caution when using explosives weaponry, like the Sidewinder or Mag Launcher Anti-Titan weapons, as the splash damage will kill you. Damage dealt in a rodeo attack depletes the Titan's health, even if its bodyshield is still intact, making rodeo attacks extremely effective.

DEVELOPER TIP

Respawn ENTERTAINMENT

The best time to jump onto an enemy Titan (also called a rodeo attack) is when it is busy fighting another Titan, or when the situation is very chaotic. Pilots inside their Titans are less likely to hear you jumping onto their Titans, or notice the warning display in their cockpits that tells them you're on board.

Use rodeo to encourage the Titan's Pilot to disembark and fight you on foot. Enemy Pilots inside their Titans receive a warning display when you expose the internal systems by pulling off the cranial hatch. They also receive the same warning if the hatch is already missing and you start inflicting internal damage with your weapon.

Satchel Charges do substantial damage when placed on enemy Titans during a rodeo maneuver. Toss multiple charges inside the hatch, then jump to safety before detonating the explosives.

You can hitch rides on friendly Titans. While you are riding on a friendly Titan, its bodyshield will protect you from incoming fire. Once the bodyshield is down, you will be susceptible to damage.

Don't be afraid to ask a friend for help. Use team chat when you are being rodeo attacked by an enemy Pilot so that a friendly can easily shoot the Pilot off of your back.

When performing a rodeo attack, instead of reloading your primary weapon, switch to your sidearm instead to deliver more damage faster. You never know how much time you have on the back of an enemy Titan.

Some weapons are more effective when rodeo attacking than others. If you enjoy rodeo attacking Titans, try the Spitfire LMG with the Slammer mod.

Riding on the back of a friendly Titan will prevent enemies from being able to rodeo the Titan you're on. Consider using friendly Titans as a springboard, jumping to new heights.

TITAN BUILD TIME

Dish out damage to enemy Grunts, Spectres, Pilots, and Titans to reduce your Titan's build time.

Pilots always deploy to the battlefield first, while their customized Titan is still under construction. By default, it takes four minutes for a Titan to be constructed—this time is visible in the Build Timer, located in the lower-right corner of the HUD. However, you can reduce your Titan's build time by damaging enemies. Damaging high-value targets, like enemy Pilots and Titans, greatly reduces build time while damaging lesser targets, like minions, results in a smaller time reduction. But every bit of damage counts, so don't miss a chance to mow down enemy Grunts and Spectres. The more effective you are in combat, the less time you have to wait for your Titan.

DEVELOPER TIP

Respawn Entertainment

The Build Timer is located in the lower-right corner of your display. When you are a Pilot, this indicates the time remaining until your Titan is ready to call in. When you are a Titan, this indicates the time remaining until your Titan's Core Ability is ready to use.

The Build Timer counts down on its own, but you can reduce the build time faster by inflicting damage to Titans and other enemies. Each hit earns a time reduction. These time reductions appear briefly to the lower left of your reticle each time you score a hit on an enemy.

You start earning build time progress towards earning your next Titan as soon as you're out of your current Titan.

The damage inflicted by using Nuclear Ejection can give you a quick boost to building your next Titan when there are enemies nearby.

TITANFALL

Once Titanfall is initiated, a green holographic ring on the HUD indicates where your Titan will arrive.

Titanfall isn't just the name of the game. It's the name of the iconic event when your Titan comes rocketing down to a planet's surface. Once the Build Timer ticks down to zero, your Titan is ready for deployment. Titans can be deployed at any exterior spot on the map as long as there's no overhead obstructions. Simply aim where you want your Titan to land and it will come crashing down within a few seconds. But before initiating Titanfall, look for tactical opportunities—an incoming Titan can crush your opponents, including enemy Titans. Try dropping your Titan on unsuspecting enemies. Also, choose your deployment area carefully. It's best to deploy your Titan in a relatively safe spot of the map, allowing you to embark without incident. Or you can drop your Titan in unison with other friendly Pilots, allowing you to roam the map together—when it comes to Titan-on-Titan combat, it's best to outnumber and overwhelm your opponents.

DEVELOPER TIP

Respawn Entertainment

The lower-left corner of your display shows how many Titans are active on each team. Titan icons appear above and below the team score indicators. You can also see how many Titans are standing by, ready to be called in by your team—these Titan icons are slightly faded in appearance. Use this information to gauge when to call in your Titan. Make sure you're not too outnumbered to be effective. Try to coordinate Titan drops with your teammates to create a numerical Titan advantage against the enemy team.

You can quickly "wake" your Titan from its kneeling pose after Titanfall by putting it into Guard mode. When you do this and you hear the computer voice say, "Guard Mode", your Titan is going active as an unmanned Auto-Titan.

Distracting an enemy Titan with Pilot fire can manipulate his movement and make it easier for your Titan to fall on it after you've initiated Titanfall.

By getting your Titan to you faster when you invoke Titanfall, the Warpfall Transmitter also improves your chances of crushing unsuspecting enemies.

TITAN FUNDAMENTALS

You just initiated Titanfall—now what? Moving around as a Titan is a completely different experience than roaming the map as a Pilot. So here's some pointers on getting the most out of your Titan, complete with some insider tips from the developers at Respawn Entertainment.

THE DOME-SHIELD

Don't attack an enemy Titan until it steps outside its Dome-Shield.

Upon initiating Titanfall, your Titan comes crashing to the planet's surface, temporarily protected by an energy barrier called the Dome-Shield. This shield remains in place for a few seconds, protecting your Titan from enemy attack. This should give you more than enough time to reach your Titan. The Dome-Shield is invulnerable, capable of absorbing heavy damage without failing. But the Dome-Shield won't last forever, so get to your Titan soon— the Pilot's Dome-Shield Battery Tier 1 Kit increases the amount of time the Dome-Shield is active, giving you more time to reach and embark your Titan. The Dome-Shield also disappears when you put the Titan in Guard or Follow mode.

DEVELOPER TIP

Respawn ENTERTAINMENT

All Titans are protected by a transparent Dome-Shield when they land after Titanfall. The Dome-Shield makes the newly arrived Titan invulnerable to damage, even if enemies enter the dome and try to hurt it. Note that you will sustain damage and eventually die if you enter an enemy Titan's Dome-Shield.

After your Titan has dropped in, you can use your Titan's Dome-Shield as cover from enemy fire. Step in and out of the Dome-Shield, alternating between fighting an enemy and keeping yourself protected.

When you "wake" your Titan by putting it into Guard mode after Titanfall, the Dome-Shield will dissipate a moment after the Titan stands up and goes active.

MANEUVERING AS A TITAN

Dash in and out of cover while engaging enemy Titans.

Jumping into a Titan for the first time is an exciting yet somewhat jarring experience. Compared to the light and nimble Pilots, the heavy, lumbering Titans move at a much slower pace. The sudden change in speed and agility requires a different tactical mindset. But Titans are by no means sitting ducks. Their ability to sprint and dash allows them to maneuver around the battlefield with relative ease. Dashing is ideal for gaining a sudden boost in speed. But it's best to reserve your limited dashes for combat—dashing laterally is ideal for evading incoming fire.

While piloting a Titan, it's easy to get caught up in the moment, charging headlong into battle with weapons blazing. But more experienced Pilots play more defensively, keeping their distance from enemies while formulating engagement and escape plans based on the surrounding terrain. What can you use for cover? Can enemy Pilots attack you from surrounding rooftops? If you're ambushed, how will you escape? Are friendly Titans nearby to provide support? These are the things you should be thinking when piloting a Titan.

DEVELOPER TIP

Respawn ENTERTAINMENT

Staying within dash range of cover is important for winning Titan fights. This should affect how you navigate through levels with the different Titan chassis.

Remember to keep track of how many dashes you have left—using your dash wisely can make a big difference in combat. Sometimes you need it to get somewhere quickly, and other times you need to keep it in reserve to dodge incoming fire or to escape an ambush. You can see how many dashes you have at any time by looking at the rectangular pips just below the reticle.

Form an exit strategy before you commit to a fight with another Titan. If you get ambushed by additional Titans, or something else goes wrong, you'll be glad you did.

Always think ahead and predict potential new threats. Titan fights tend to be longer than those between Pilots, so circumstances can evolve and even reverse themselves dramatically over the course of a Titan fight.

HEALTH AND BODYSHIELD MANAGEMENT

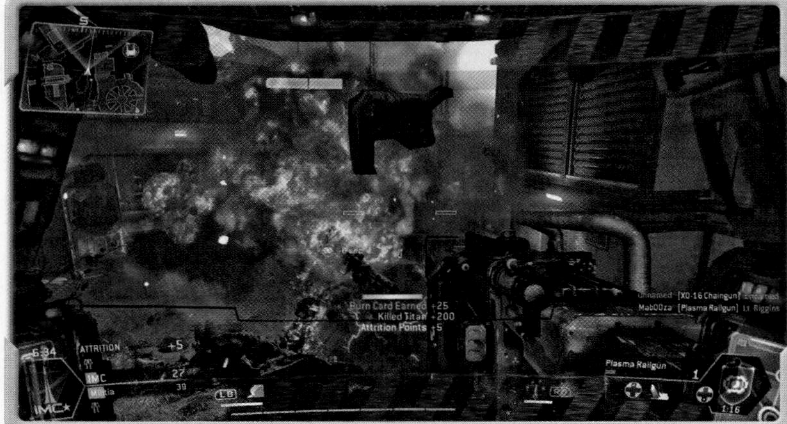

If your Titan has sustained heavy damage, seek cover fast, allowing the bodyshield to regenerate.

Despite their heavy armor and intimidating appearance, Titans aren't invulnerable. Each Titan has two lines of defense: the outer hull and the bodyshield. The bodyshield is a Titan's first line of defense. This is an invisible energy barrier surrounding the Titan that absorbs hits from incoming projectiles. Each subsequent hit weakens the bodyshield, causing it to deplete. However, the bodyshield can regenerate if the Titan avoids taking damage for a limited time—this is why it's so important to utilize cover. During combat, keep an eye on the shield bar, wrapped above the Titan's health bar at the top center of the HUD. As the shield bar nears depletion, immediately seek cover, allowing the bodyshield to regenerate.

If a Titan's bodyshield fails, all subsequent damage is dealt to the Titan's hull. Bodyshield failure exposes vulnerable parts of the Titan, allowing enemies to score high-damage critical hits—these weak spots appear as red glowing sections on a Titan's hull. As damage piles up, the Titan's health bar begins to deplete. Unlike the bodyshield, a Titan's hull cannot be regenerated once damage has occurred. Thus, all hull damage is permanent, as indicated by a diminished health bar. Externally, heavily damaged Titans spew flames and sparks, potentially making them juicy targets for enemy units. But a Titan with low health isn't necessarily out of the fight. By carefully managing the regenerative properties of the bodyshield, skilled Pilots can keep a heavily damaged Titan on the battlefield indefinitely. The key to survival is escaping danger before the bodyshield is fully depleted.

DEVELOPER TIP

Respawn Entertainment

When a bodyshield takes damage, you will see small hexagons flash momentarily in the air around the Titan as the bodyshield absorbs the hits. The bodyshield fully restores itself after a short period of time, if no further damage is sustained.

When a Titan's built-in bodyshield is depleted, its hull and critical hit locations are exposed. Critical hits do extra damage, so try to aim for these locations when they appear—look for the spots highlighted in red on the front and back of the Titan. Keep in mind that not all weapons are capable of inflicting critical hits.

If your Titan's bodyshield is depleted, try to move and dash away from your enemies until your Titan's bodyshield regenerates. If possible, deter any pursuing enemies by firing missiles from your Titan's built-in Ordnance pod as you back away. Using your defensive abilities can help buy time for your shield to regenerate.

Any shot from any Titan weapon will prevent an enemy's bodyshield from regenerating. Sometimes landing a few well-placed shots to keep an enemy's bodyshield down is a better tactic than brute force.

As a Pilot, use Arc Grenades against Titans before using your Anti-Titan weapon. A couple of Arc Grenades can bring down a Titan's bodyshield very quickly, allowing your Anti-Titan weapon to hit the hull directly. Even when a Titan's bodyshield is active, Anti-Titan weapons deal a small percentage of damage to the hull.

TITAN TACTICAL ABILITIES

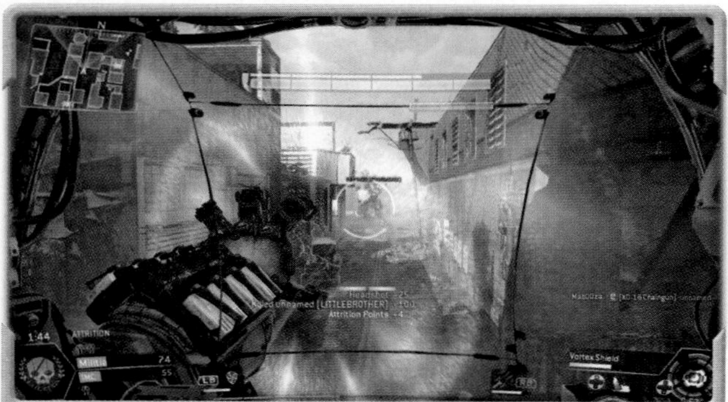

The Vortex Shield catches and refires incoming projectiles.

Like Pilots, Titans can equip one of three Tactical Abilities, each providing a unique defensive benefit. The Vortex Shield is the first Tactical Ability available to all Pilots. When active, the Vortex Shield can catch incoming bullets, missiles, and rockets and redirect them at a target—this is a great way to use an enemy Titan's weapons against them. The Particle Wall ability deploys a stationary energy barrier capable of blocking incoming projectiles. However, unlike traditional cover, the Titan who deployed the Particle Wall can shoot through it, as long as they stay behind the wall. The Electric Smoke Tactical Ability is a multi-purpose countermeasure, perfect for deterring rodeo attacks on your Titan. In addition to obscuring your Titan in smoke, the electrical properties inflict damage on enemies within the smokescreen, including enemy Pilots and Titans.

DEVELOPER TIP

Respawn Entertainment

Projectiles released by the Vortex Shield ability can be caught mid-air by another Vortex Shield.

The Vortex Shield takes a second to cool down once deployed, so if you find yourself stuck in a game of "catch" with an enemy Titan, try returning fire with your own Vortex Shield immediately after you catch your opponent's incoming attack.

If you have lots of ammo caught in your Vortex Shield but you suspect an opponent has more Vortex Shield time remaining than you, discard the contents of your Vortex Shield into the sky or to one side. This way, you avoid feeding more ammo into the enemy's Vortex Shield with no way for you to block the imminent blast of Vortex Shield fire.

The Particle Wall ability will buy you extra time to aim more carefully or charge a weapon more fully, protecting you completely from incoming fire. It works well in concert with long-range or charge-dependent Titan weapons such as the Plasma Railgun, the Arc Cannon, and the XO-16 Chaingun.

The Particle Wall only allows weapon fire to pass through in one direction, no matter what team you're on, so try chasing an enemy around to the opposite side and use his own barrier against him.

Electric Smoke is very effective against enemy Pilots that jump onto your Titan's back. It will kill them over time or force them to jump off of you. Once they are off, dash far away so that they don't easily jump back onto you.

Standing in a cloud of Electric Smoke will negate all weapon lock-ons, including your own.

CAUTION

If you've been rodeo attacked, deploy Electric Smoke—stay within the smoke until your unauthorized passenger is dead or jumps off.

CORE ABILITIES

Damaging enemy units reduces the time it takes for your Titan's Core Ability to come online.

Aside from speed, acceleration, and durability, the three Titans have another major difference: their Core Ability. When activated, these unique Core Abilities give Titans a significant tactical advantage. But that advantage differs based on the selected Titan chassis. For instance, the Atlas benefits from Damage Core, temporarily increasing damage output substantially. The Ogre's Shield Core enhances the Titan's bodyshield, allowing it to absorb more punishment for a short period of time. Dash Core temporarily gives the Stryder the ability to perform unlimited dashes.

Core Abilities aren't readily available upon receiving your Titan. Instead, they take time to charge up—reference the Build Timer in the lower-right corner of the HUD to see how much time is left until your Titan's Core Ability is available. But just like your Titan's build time, the time you have to wait for your Core Ability can be decreased by inflicting damage on enemy units—the more damage you dish out, the quicker you'll gain access to your Titan's Core Ability. Even once your Core Ability is available, wait to deploy it until you can put it to good use—each Core Ability is online for only a few seconds. After the Core Ability has expired, it must recharge before it can be deployed again.

DEVELOPER TIP

Respawn Entertainment

Each Titan has a unique Core Ability, which takes some time to charge up. The time remaining is indicated in the Build Timer. You can reduce the amount of time it takes to charge your Titan's Core Ability in the same way you earn your Titan as a Pilot—by inflicting damage on Titans and enemies. The more damage you deal, the less time it takes to charge your Titan's Core Ability.

Once you activate your Titan's Core Ability, it is available for a short time before it expires, after which it must be recharged. In each combat situation, look for the best possible moment to activate your Titan's Core Ability to get the most use out of it.

There is a brief warm-up delay when activating your Titan's Core Ability before it actually takes effect. Keep this in mind and anticipate accordingly during battle.

The Atlas' Damage Core enhances the damage of all of the Atlas' attacks. Primary weapons, ordnance, and even Electric Smoke will inflict more damage while the Damage Core is active.

The Stryder's Dash Core provides unlimited dash capacity while active. You can dash as much and as often as you want until the Dash Core shuts down.

The Ogre's Shield Core enhances the Ogre's bodyshield capacity substantially—you are not made invulnerable, but it will take a lot more hits to deplete the bodyshield.

AUTO-TITAN

When attempting to evacuate, use your Auto-Titan to distract the enemy while you make a run for the dropship.

Following Titanfall deployment, instead of embarking, Pilots have the option of initiating one of two Auto-Titan modes: Follow mode and Guard mode. While in Follow mode, your Titan will follow you around the map, automatically engaging enemy units it encounters. Obviously, a Titan cannot access all the places a nimble Pilot can, such as rooftops or building interiors. But the Titan will do its best to stay close to the Pilot's position. In Guard mode, the Titan stays put and attacks enemy contacts within its line of sight, ideal for defending fixed positions.

Application of the Auto-Titan modes differs from Pilot to Pilot. Some Pilots prefer to stay on foot, allowing their Auto-Titan to serve as a distraction. In this sense, the Auto-Titan is a true force multiplier, adding its weapons to the mix while the Pilot continues to fight on foot. This is an effective way to divide and conquer during Titan battles—have your Auto-Titan engage a threat while you fire your Anti-Titan weapon from a safe distance. Or better yet, rodeo attack an enemy Titan while your Auto-Titan engages it.

DEVELOPER TIP

Respawn Entertainment

Auto-Titans can be useful, but they are not nearly as effective as a Titan being controlled by a skilled Pilot.

If you do not take any action to "wake" your Titan after Titanfall, after some time, it will automatically wake up and go into Follow mode by default, unless you set its mode earlier in the match. In that case it will use the last mode you set.

Auto-Titans can defend places if you put them into Guard mode. Install a Guardian Chip Kit into your Titan for maximum effectiveness.

Experiment with your Auto-Titan to simultaneously attack enemies by yourself from multiple directions at once.

DOOMED TITANS

When your Titan is doomed, get ready to eject—there's nothing you can do to save your Titan when it reaches its doomed state.

Even the most durable Titans eventually fall when subjected to heavy damage. Once the Titan's health bar is fully depleted, it enters what is called doomed state, indicated by a striped yellow-and-black bar that appears at the top of the HUD. This doomed state bar slowly depletes, even when no damage is being taken, essentially counting down to the Titan's self-destruction. During doomed state the Titan is still functional, capable of moving and firing weapons. However, a Titan is also extremely vulnerable during this state, particularly to melee attacks. Instead of fighting, it's best to eject—otherwise your Pilot will die when the Titan explodes or get killed by an enemy Titan's melee attack. Ejecting launches a Pilot high into the sky, allowing them to escape and continue the fight on foot.

CAUTION

Ejecting from a Titan launches you high into the sky, allowing your Pilot to reach some unique elevated vantage points. However, some of these areas are outside the playable boundaries of the map. If you don't return to the battle within a few seconds, you will die.

DEVELOPER TIP

Respawn Entertainment

When a Titan's health bar (not bodyshield) is depleted, it becomes doomed, and its health bar changes from a solid color to a striped pattern. That Titan will soon self-destruct.

During the time that a Titan is doomed, the enemy Pilot in that Titan can still try to disembark, eject, or keep fighting. You can guarantee a kill on the Pilot of a doomed Titan if you can close the distance and melee attack it before the Pilot has a chance to activate the ejection sequence. The Atlas, for example, will punch through a doomed Titan's hull, yank out the enemy Pilot, and throw him to his death. This is known as a Titan Execution.

Equipping the Auto-Eject Kit will prevent you from being executed by enemy Titans. Auto-Eject will also cloak you automatically when you eject. However, with this kit, you will lose the ability to continue to fight in your Titan once it is doomed.

GAME MODES

There are five different game modes available in *Titanfall*, all with unique objectives and victory conditions. Here's a quick rundown of all the game modes, along with some helpful tips to help your team maintain an edge during combat.

ATTRITION

Grunts and Spectres are worth Attrition Points too, so don't overlook these easy kills.

If you've never played *Titanfall* before, Attrition is the best place to start. In this game mode, players are awarded Attrition points for scoring kills, but just not kills on other players. Attrition points are awarded for killing Grunts, Spectres, Pilots, Titans, and even dropships. The winning team is the one that hits the score limit first, or has the highest score when the time is up.

Tactics

- Each enemy provides a different amount of Attrition Points. Killing Grunts and Spectres gives your team one Attrition Point, Pilots get you four points, and defeating a Titan gives you five points.
- With the amount of minions on the map, players can choose to avoid enemy Pilots. Grunts usually run in a pack of three or four, so you get the same amount of points for taking out a Grunt squad as you would taking out an enemy Pilot.
- Hunting minions is critical in Attrition as it will help you call down your Titan quickly. One or two players should hunt the minions while the rest of the team protects these players from enemy Pilots. Getting a Titan quickly will help make light work of enemy Pilots.
- The Arc Cannon is an excellent primary weapon to have equipped to your Titan. Simply fire a lightning bolt towards a Grunt in a pack of minions and watch the lightning zap nearby enemies. Keep your Titan up and moving for as long as you can—don't set it to Auto-Titan and take full advantage of the Arc Cannon.
- Since minions are easy points, position Pilots near allied minions to ambush enemy Pilots. Let the enemy Pilots take out an allied minion squad and then ambush the enemy Pilot once they are reloading.
- When Minion Detector is equipped, focus on your minimap at all times. Not only will you see where the enemy minions are located, but you will also see your friendly minions. Keep an eye on your friendly minions. If you see them dropping like flies then there is most likely an enemy Pilot nearby killing them. So either get close and take them out or keep distance while you kill more minions.

DEVELOPER TIP — Respawn Entertainment

Don't miss the opportunity to kill Grunts and Auto-Titans in the Attrition game mode—they count towards your team's total score.

The Pilot's Minion Detector Kit, combined with a suppressed weapon, allows you to easily locate and attack enemy Grunts and Spectres without being noticed by other players. Suppressors on your Pilot weapons prevent you from appearing on your enemies' minimaps when you fire your weapons.

The Minion Detector Kit shows Grunts and Spectres on the minimap even when you're in your Titan.

CAPTURE THE FLAG

Always approach the enemy flag with extreme caution—defenders and booby traps are likely waiting for you.

In this classic game mode, steal the enemy flag and return it to your base, while stopping the enemy team from grabbing your flag. To score a capture, your team's flag must be present at your base, set into its pedestal. Then, if you have the enemy flag, capture it by running through your team's flag at your base—scoring a flag earns your team one point. The winning team is the one with the most captures when the match timer runs out. At halftime, the teams switch sides, giving each team the chance to attack/defend each base.

Tactics

- Capture the Flag consists of two rounds so Pilots will get a chance to play on both sides. Each side is played differently when playing on an asymmetrical map. But when playing on a symmetrical map, you will notice that each side is played fairly the same.
- Throw Satchel Charges around your flag. Once an enemy decides to grab the flag, quickly detonate the charges to stop the enemy in their tracks. You can detonate charges by double tapping your Reload button/key rather than pulling out the detonator to explode the charges. This saves you time and allows you to roam the map instead of just staring at the flag waiting for enemies to grab it.
- This game mode gives you the opportunity to really take advantage of your Titan. When your Titan is ready, save it until you are near the enemy's flag—it is much easier to sneak into the enemy base as a Pilot. Once you are near the enemy flag, call down your Titan and then grab the flag, quickly jump into your Titan, and ride away.
- There is sure to be an enemy Pilot with a shotgun positioned around the flag defending the objective. Equip Active Radar Pulse to pinpoint enemies hiding in corners defending their flag. This Tactical Ability will aid in picking the right route to use once you grab the enemy's flag, activate the ability, and find out where the enemies are located before exiting the enemy base.
- Electric Smoke is an excellent Tactical Ability to have equipped on your Titan. When escaping with the flag, the smoke will blur the pursuers' field of vision and force the enemy Pilots to go around the smoke to avoid being killed.
- A friendly Pilot should always shadow the flag carrier. There are many moments where you run the flag back to your base and then suddenly an enemy Pilot camping near your base jumps out, kills you, and successfully returns the flag. The player shadowing the flag carrier will be able to kill the camping opponent before they return the flag or kill them before they kill the flag carrier.

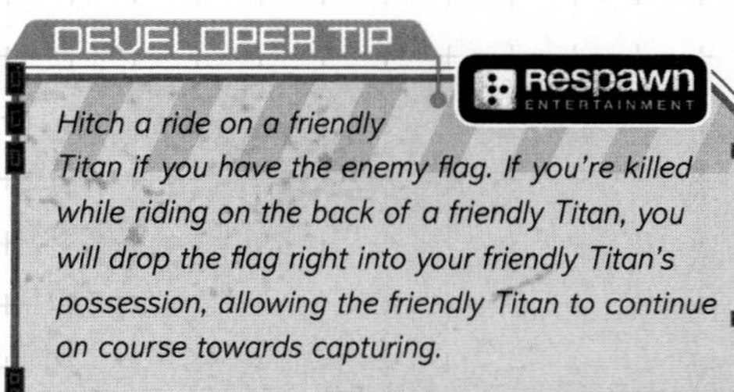

Hitch a ride on a friendly Titan if you have the enemy flag. If you're killed while riding on the back of a friendly Titan, you will drop the flag right into your friendly Titan's possession, allowing the friendly Titan to continue on course towards capturing.

HARDPOINT DOMINATION

Expect resistance at enemy-held hardpoints—capture and hold at least two hardpoints to hold out for a win.

This game mode is all about capturing and holding three system nodes, known as hardpoints. Capture and hold the three hardpoints on the map for your team to earn points—the more hardpoints you hold, the faster you accrue points. Capture neutral hardpoints by standing near them for a short period of time. Retake enemy-held hardpoints by standing near them for a longer period of time—a hardpoint must be rendered neutral before you can begin to capture it. If enemies are near a hardpoint, you must find and eliminate them before any capturing or neutralizing can occur.

Tactics

- For each Pilot inside the hardpoint, the capture speed increases. A hardpoint is contested if an enemy Pilot moves within the capture radius. If there are two IMC Pilots and one Militia Pilot, the IMC Pilots override the Militia Pilot, allowing the IMC Pilots to begin neutralizing or capturing the hardpoint.
- Minions are capable of capturing and defending hardpoints, making their starting routes much different than the other game modes. During Hardpoint Domination, the minions make their way towards the three hardpoints and engage opposing minions—whichever side that wins will then move to the hardpoint and begin capturing it.
- Arc Mines work tremendously well in this game mode, especially for the hardpoints that are only accessible to Pilots. When outfitting your Pilot, choose the Explosives Pack Kit. Then, when defending, plant multiple mines around the entrances of the hardpoint. The damage dealt by two of these mines is enough to kill a Pilot.
- Wall hanging will save your life and make enemies look all over for you while you defend the hardpoint. Equip the Enhanced Parkour Kit, allowing you to double your time of wall hanging. Combine this with Cloak and the opponent will be in daze as they check every corner of the hardpoint.
- Throw Arc Grenades or Frag Grenades before entering the hardpoint—figure out all the corners Pilots like to hide in and lob your grenade. If you don't get a kill or any hit markers, then you know the enemy is positioned in a different location.
- Entering a hardpoint with a Titan will override the other team's Pilots if they are inside the objective. In this instance, one Titan can begin neutralizing or capturing the hardpoint even if the opposing team has one, two, or three Pilots in the capture radius. Always man your Titan in this game mode instead of using Guard or Follow mode, allowing you to capture the objectives more effectively.
- Defending the hardpoint is critical to win the match—close-quarter combat is the way to go, so equip SMGs and shotguns to defend.

DEVELOPER TIP — Respawn Entertainment

Your team earns one point every two seconds for each hardpoint they control.

Take a hardpoint and then defend it. Enemies will naturally run into these hardpoints, giving you the element of surprise.

Use caution near doorways and windows when defending hardpoints. You'll be exposed to Titans and explosives when you are near a window.

Use the Active Radar Pulse ability to find enemies in hiding. This is especially useful in hardpoint matches, where enemy Pilots often defend from obscure positions within the hardpoint.

LAST TITAN STANDING

Prepare for long-range, stand-off engagements in this game mode as most Pilots are likely to play very conservatively.

In Last Titan Standing, all Pilots start in a Titan. Your team must eliminate all of the enemy team's Titans or Pilots to win. This is a round-based mode, and the team that wins the best of five rounds wins the match. Within each round, there is no respawning, and there are no replacement Titans, until the next round starts. However, if your Titan is destroyed, and you successfully eject, you can continue to play as a Pilot, helping your teammates eliminate the other team's Titans.

Tactics

- Titan weapons can be broken down into subclasses; some are versatile and capable of doing damage up close and from a distance while others should be mainly used for long-range engagements. The Arc Cannon and Plasma Railgun are much more effective from a long range as both of these weapons can be charged to optimize damage output. Use these long-range weapons with the Particle Wall—the wall blocks incoming projectiles, allowing you to fully charge your Arc Cannon or Plasma Railgun.
- Weapons like the XO-16 Chaingun and 40mm Cannon can be fired from long range or used to battle enemy Titans up close. The Accelerator mod should be equipped when using the XO-16 Chaingun, giving your primary weapon more ammo and a higher fire rate.
- Tactical Abilities play a huge role in this game mode. When grouping with friendly Titans, a Titan with the Vortex Shield should lead the charge to grab incoming projectiles that can be used to throw back at the enemy.
- Electric Smoke combined with the Cluster Missile will restrict the movements of enemy Titans in close-quarter battles. Activate your smoke when exchanging melees with the enemy Titans and then fire the Cluster Missile where you think the enemy Titan will dash to. This forces them to back down from fights, allowing you to chase the enemy Titan down and finish it off.
- All Titans have the same bodyshield, but the Orge has the most health, followed by the Atlas, and then finally the Stryder. Having a few more Orge Titans on the team assists in winning rounds, especially if you decide to play the game passively. Sit back and force the opponent to engage your Orge Titans in close quarters.
- Stryder Titans excel in matches with open fields and objects that can be used for cover. Equip Dash Quickcharger to glide around the map and annoy the opposing team because of your Titan's quick movements.
- Your Pilot's primary weapon for your Last Titan Standing loadout should always be the Spitfire LMG with the Slammer mod. If your Titan is destroyed, you can still be of use with your Anti-Titan Weapon or LMG—if the opportunity presents itself, perform a rodeo attack.

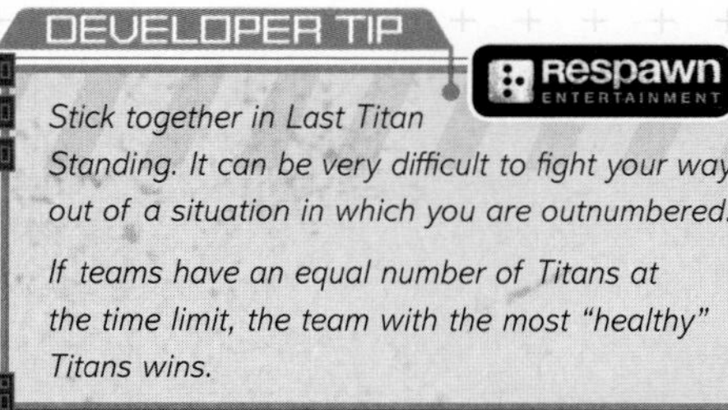

Stick together in Last Titan Standing. It can be very difficult to fight your way out of a situation in which you are outnumbered.

If teams have an equal number of Titans at the time limit, the team with the most "healthy" Titans wins.

PILOT HUNTER

In addition to hunting Pilots, hunt Grunts and Spectres in an effort to get your Titan sooner.

In Pilot Hunter, it's all about hunting or being hunted! Kill the enemy team's Pilots to reach the score limit and win—one point is awarded for each Pilot killed. Although killing Grunts and Spectres in this mode will not earn points towards your team's score, doing so will still give you build time reductions on your replacement Titans and Titan Core Ability.

Tactics

- When playing Pilot Hunter, be sneaky. Unlike Attrition, you can no longer kill a group of minions, die at the hands of an enemy Pilot, and justify it on the scoreboard. Stealth is even more important now that you're the main focus of your opponents. Utilizing a Suppressor mod, melee attacks, and ordnance to kill minions keeps you off the minimap.
- A great way to find enemy Pilots is to use Minion Detector, keeping an eye on a nearby group of friendly minions. Once you see the minions disappear, head over there and find the nearby enemy Pilot. Otherwise, just focus on killing enemy minions and get your Titan as soon as possible.
- Since the enemy team can only score points by killing Pilots, your life becomes much more valuable. When you are doomed in a Titan, eject from your Titan and retreat to safety without being shot out of the air. Equipping Auto-Eject to your Titan Tier 2 Kit slot helps you sneak away once your Titan is taken out. With this kit you'll be forced to eject once your Titan is doomed and you'll receive Cloak for a short moment, giving you enough time to retreat to safety. You can never be executed inside your Titan if you have Auto-Eject equipped.
- If you are a player that wants to duke it out for a bit longer while your Titan is doomed, equip Cloak as your Pilot's Tactical Ability and Survivor as your Titan's Tier 2 Kit. Combining these allows you to fight longer while doomed. And once you feel your Titan is going to explode, eject yourself. While you're ejecting, activate your Cloak and sneak away to safety.
- Stim is an effective Tactical Ability when playing this mode. The extra speed allows you to escape enemy Pilots when they catch you by surprise. This ability also begins regeneration of your health, allowing you to reengage enemies who have ambushed you. Countering ambushes is best done when you have cover to run in and out of or a nearby wall to gain some speed to make the enemy Pilot miss a few shots.
- Snipers are extremely effective in this game mode. They allow you to sit back at a distance and pick off enemy Pilots. Having Cloak equipped will allow you to constantly switch sniping locations, forcing the opposing team to never know where you are.

EPILOGUE

Can you reach the Evac Point before the dropship takes off? Prepare for some intense moments.

The Epilogue, occurring at the end of a round, is a fun little mini-game within the main match. The losing team has a point marked on their screen showing the Evac Point where a dropship will arrive. At the same time the winning team will have an intercept marker to stop the opposing team from escaping. During the Epilogue, each Pilot only has one life, so once you are taken out, the match is over for you—but you can watch the remainder of the match from the perspectives of other players.

Each Pilot on the losing team gets XP for making it on board the dropship. But this isn't easy because the opposing team, who just won, is looking to hunt you all down. During the main match if you feel the team is about to lose and you have a Titan ready to call in, save it for the Epilogue. This may throw off the other team because they won't expect you to call down a Titan since you just lost. Get underneath or close to the dropship with your Titan and eject towards the ship—use the Cloak Tactical Ability to avoid getting picked off while you're flying through the air.

It takes a lot of firepower to bring down a dropship—the weaponry of three Titans should be enough.

The winning team gains XP for killing each Pilot or stopping enemy Pilots from escaping. The best way to do this is by locking down the intercept point, surrounding it with Pilots and Titans. But be prepared for enemy Pilots hiding inside buildings near the Evac Point or wall running and jumping across the map. The best way to stop the enemy team from escaping is by destroying the dropship while it waits to pick up enemy Pilots. But it takes a team effort to bring down the dropship—three Titans concentrating fire on the ship is usually enough to bring it down before it can escape. Nuclear Ejections can also damage Evac Dropships.

DEVELOPER TIP

Respawn ENTERTAINMENT

If your team loses the match, don't rush to the Evac Point when the Epilogue starts—check your minimap for threats and friendlies, and try to survey the Evac Point from afar before making your escape. Be wary of enemy forces attempting to cut you off at the Evac Point.

PILOT CERTIFICATION

PERSISTENCE AND PROGRESSION

One of the most addictive elements of *Titanfall* is the persistence system. Attaining new levels, unlocks, and Burn Cards keeps players hooked for hours on end, itching to play just one more round. After all, who needs sleep?

LEVELS

A message appears on screen each time you level up. Customize your Pilot with newly unlocked weapons, abilities, and kits.

In *Titanfall*, players earn experience points, or XP, by performing a variety of actions including kills, assists, headshots, rodeo attacks, and successful hacks. As XP accumulates over time, players attain new levels—there are 50 levels in all. Leveling up earns Pilots unique rewards, like new weapons and loadout options including Tactical Abilities and kits. So as players level up, they have more options when customizing their Pilot and Titan.

Gen Status

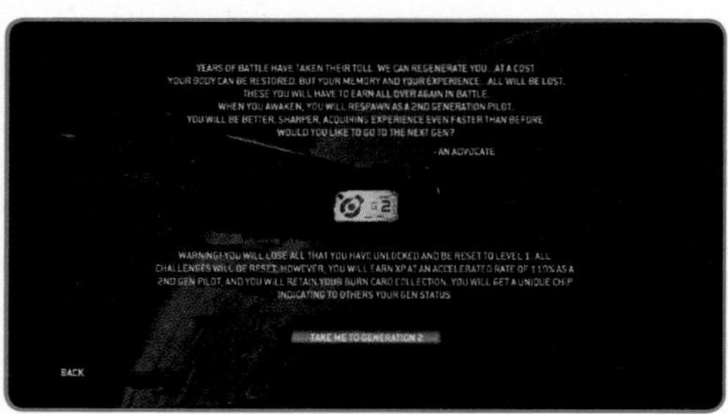

When choosing to Regenerate you essentially start from scratch, losing all levels and unlocks.

Once you reach Level 50 you're given the option to Regenerate. This essentially resets your stats, removing all experience and unlocks—the only thing you're allowed to keep are your Burn Cards. So what's the benefit? Second generation Pilots (and beyond) attain a unique chip icon that appears next to their name on the scoreboard, indicating their elite status—it's basically bragging rights. If you choose to Regenerate, you become second generation, as indicated by your chip. At that point, everything is reset, and you restart your Pilot career at Level 1. However, you will earn XP at an accelerated rate of 110%, allowing you to level up a bit faster. There are ten Gen levels, each requiring you to advance through 50 levels to complete. Tenth generation, Level 50 is the end of the line, reserved only for the most dedicated Pilots.

CHALLENGES

Complete weapon-based challenges to unlock new attachments and mods.

Challenges are optional objectives, rewarding Pilots with bonus XP, Burn Cards, and unlocks for weapons. There are five tiers within each challenge, each tier requiring Pilots to perform a specific number of actions. For example, a tier I challenge may require you to kill ten Pilots with the Smart Pistol MK5 while tier II of the same challenge requires you to kill twenty-five Pilots with the Smart Pistol MK5. Rewards are doled out for the completion of each tier. All challenges can be viewed from the Lobby screen and are divided into eleven major categories. Many challenges are earned naturally through gameplay, but others may require you to perform some obscure actions to complete.

BURN CARDS

Sort through your deck periodically and discard unwanted cards—you can only hold a maximum of twenty-five cards in your deck.

Burn Cards add a unique layer of strategy and tactical benefits to the game, altering the way Pilots approach each match. Throughout the course of your Pilot career, you'll accumulate a number of these Burn Cards by completing challenges. Each Burn Card is different, providing a specific benefit when in play. For example, the Ghost Squad Burn Card keeps your Pilot permanently cloaked, even if Cloak isn't your selected Tactical Ability. Not all Burn Cards are equal, as some provide greater benefits than others. It's a good idea to sort through your Burn Cards and sort the powerful Burn Cards from the less powerful ones. But don't get in the habit of hoarding. Your collection of Burn Cards is known as your deck. You can only have a maximum of twenty-five cards in your deck. So if your deck is full and you earn a Burn Card, that new card is simply lost. Either use or discard unwanted cards on a regular basis—take your deck down to about twenty cards before each match, leaving space for new Burn Cards.

Once you've acquired some Burn Cards, you're prompted to select up to three before each match. You can manually change which card is played next during the match, so ordering of the cards isn't critical. Every Pilot has their own strategy about when in a match a Burn Card should be played. So study the cards in your deck and select three that will benefit your Pilot throughout a match. For instance, the Thin the Ranks Burn Card is a good choice for your first card as it increases XP earned from killing Grunts and reduces your Titan's build time, helping you get your Titan sooner.

The activated Burn Card appears on the HUD momentarily when you deploy, reminding you of its benefits.

After selecting your three Burn Cards and beginning a match, a Burn Card can be activated before you deploy—this can be done in the dropship. An image of the active Burn Card appears on the HUD for a few seconds when you first deploy or when you spawn. The Burn Card is in play until you die or until the match ends. After dying, you can manually choose which of the two remaining cards is played next. Failing to select a card before respawning will put you back in the match with no active Burn Card. Once all three cards have been played, you must play the remainder of the match without a Burn Card. If you're not careful, you can waste your Burn Cards quickly by dying. So take into account the value of your activated Burn Card before determining how aggressive you should play.

DEVELOPER TIP — Respawn Entertainment

Burn Cards temporarily give you special abilities or equipment. The effects of a Burn Card will persist until you die, or when the match ends.

Remember to select and activate a Burn Card before the start of every match. You can also select and activate a Burn Card after you die. In both cases, the Burn Card will take effect when you respawn.

The effects of a Burn Card will persist across multiple rounds during round-based game modes, such as Last Titan Standing, if you manage to stay alive.

You can only carry a limited number of Burn Cards. Be sure to use them often, so that none go to waste. If your Burn Card collection is full, discard or use your existing Burn Cards so that you may earn more.

Many Challenges have Burn Card rewards. Complete various challenges to get certain Burn Cards.

Consider which game mode is best for specific Burn Cards, and try using them in the best game mode possible. For example, the card Titan Salvage is great in the game mode called Last Titan Standing because it gives you more XP for fighting Titans, and the card Adrenaline Transfusion is great for Capture the Flag, because the constant high speed of movement it provides reduces the amount of time it takes you to run across the map.

NOTE

For a complete gallery of all Burn Cards, see the Quick Reference section in the back of the guide.

ADVANCED COMBAT TACTICS

Learning the basics of Pilot mobility and Titan operation should be enough to get you started. But how do you apply this knowledge on the battlefield? Here we take a look at some practical, field-tested tactics with the aim of giving you the edge in each in each battle.

LOADOUT CUSTOMIZATION

Before starting a match, take a moment to customize your Pilot and Titan loadouts.

Initially all players have three preset Pilot and Titan loadouts available. But after playing *Titanfall* for a short period of time you'll unlock the Custom Pilot and Custom Titan loadouts. Here you can completely customize your loadouts, selecting different weapon, ability, and kit configurations to suit your style of play. Consider customizing your Pilot loadout around your Primary Weapon, selecting an ability, kits, and ordnance that complement this weapon. The same goes for customizing your Titan—weapon choice largely dictates the range at which you engage targets. So when selecting your ability and kits, ask yourself how those options complement your weapon. Of course, there are other factors to consider when making these decisions. But try to build loadouts where all elements work together to make your Pilot or Titan more effective in combat.

NOTE

Flip ahead to the Pilot Gear and Titans chapters for more information on customizing your Pilot and Titan loadouts.

COMBAT SCENARIOS

In *Titanfall*, every battle plays out differently. But by understanding the fundamentals of each possible scenario, you can gain an edge over your opponents. Whether playing as a Pilot or Titan, there are numerous combat engagements you need to prepare for. Here's a quick breakdown of each major combat scenario you're likely to face, with tips on how to overcome each one.

Pilot vs. Minion

Think of hunting minions as a way of getting your Titan faster—but watch out for enemy Pilots doing the same thing.

This is by far the most common scenario you'll face throughout your Pilot career. Enemy Grunts and Spectres make up the majority of hostile forces you encounter in every battle. Collectively known as minions, these AI-controlled units pose little threat to fast and nimble Pilots. But that doesn't mean you should ignore them. Hunting minions plays a big part in the game, earning you XP and reducing your Titan's build time.

Tactics

- Grunts are standard infantry armed with a mix of small arms and anti-armor weapons—they usually deploy in small three-man squads, arriving via dropship and drop pods.
- Spectres are durable robotic warriors designed to counter Titans with their heavy weapons—but they also carry small arms and can be dangerous in large groups. Spectres only appear once Titans are on the battlefield.
- IMC and Militia Grunts often engage each other in prolonged firefights. Look for small red dots on the minimap to find large concentrations of minions. But exercise caution when approaching these conflicts, as enemy Pilots are likely in the area also looking for easy kills.
- A Pilot's primary weapon is the best way to deal with both Grunts and Spectres. For best results, score headshots to quickly down these threats and conserve ammo. Spectres take significantly more damage than their Grunt counterparts, so be ready to expend a few more rounds on each target. Grenades are also effective against these enemies, often wiping out multiple targets with a single explosion. Minions pose the biggest threat at close range, so keep your distance, particularly when engaging multiple Spectres.
- If you happen to sneak up on an enemy Spectre from behind, hack it with your Data Knife. A hacked Spectre will follow you around the map and fight for you, crediting you with any kills it scores.

NOTE

Marvins are also considered minions, but they pose no direct threat. Instead, these robots perform a variety of non-combat tasks on certain maps. Each weapon has a Victimless Crime challenge, requiring you to kill a number of Marvins—this is the only reason to engage these harmless minions.

Pilot vs. Pilot

You never know when you'll come face to face with an enemy Pilot—be prepared.

Facing off against enemy Pilots is extremely dangerous as they benefit from the same Jump Kit-enabled mobility as you. As a result, these fights often favor the Pilot who can stay on the move while returning accurate fire—if you stand still you don't stand a chance against a skilled, veteran Pilot. Eliminating enemy Pilots nets you 100 XP, and depending on game mode, may even give your team the lead in close matches. But hunting Pilots is risky business, requiring quick reflexes, fluid mobility, and constant situational awareness.

Tactics

- When Pilots fire an unsuppressed weapon, they appear as a large red dot on the minimap. But the same goes for you as well. Consider equipping your primary weapon with a Suppressor mod to avoid giving away your position, then use the minimap as a radar, guiding you to your next enemy Pilot.
- Activating the Stim Tactical Ability during a heated firefight with an enemy Pilot may just give you the edge required to survive. Stim not only boosts your Pilot's speed, but it also improves health regeneration. This makes Stim very helpful if you're hunting Pilots.
- Due to their enhanced mobility, Pilots are very easy to spot in a battle. Look for enemies running along walls or double jumping onto buildings—a Jump Kit's thrusters are a dead giveaway. To avoid being spotted, consider activating the Cloak Tactical Ability when performing wall runs and other Pilot-specific maneuvers. Or hide amongst a group of Grunts and try to go unnoticed.
- When monitoring a Titan battle, watch for enemy Pilots ejecting from doomed Titans. Even when cloaked, Pilots are vulnerable when flying through the air following an ejection. Track their movements through the air and try to pick them off before they reach the ground—automatic weapons are most effective when trying to hit ejecting Pilots.
- Arc Grenades are the preferred ordnance when engaging enemy Pilots. In addition to dealing damage, Arc Grenades blur a Pilot's vision, making it difficult for them to maneuver and defend themselves. Arc-based weapons also disrupt a Pilot's Jump Kit, causing them to abort wall runs and wall hangs.

Pilot vs. Titan

Always approach enemy Titans from behind and blind them with an Arc Grenade before attempting a rodeo attack.

There's no getting around it—Pilots at are a serious disadvantage in these engagements. Encountering a Titan in direct combat is an intimidating experience, even for the most veteran Pilots. But that doesn't mean Pilots have to run away. Utilizing Anti-Titan weapons, rodeo attacks, and ordnance, Pilots have a shot at downing a Titan on their own, netting them a whopping 200 XP in the process. So even if you're seriously outgunned, look for opportunities to take on enemy Titans—your team will thank you for it.

Tactics

- When firing their weapons, enemy Titans appear as red arrow icons on the minimap. If an enemy Titan is nearby, make sure you have adequate cover and consider getting to high ground—you don't want to engage a Titan toe-to-toe on the ground where you stand the chance of getting crushed. Instead, look for opportunities to crush enemy Titans by initiating your own Titanfall.
- Hacking turrets and Spectres is a good way to harass enemy Titans indirectly. While these hacked assets don't dish out a ton of damage, they can serve as a distraction, allowing friendly Titans to move in and score an easy kill. Or better yet, perform a rodeo attack while the enemy Titan is distracted.
- When performing a rodeo attack on an enemy Titan, start by activating the Cloak Tactical Ability—this makes you nearly invisible to Titans, making you tougher to spot during your approach. Once cloaked, hammer the Titan with an Arc Grenade to temporarily blind it before hopping aboard. By the time the Titan has recovered from the Arc Grenade (and the enemy Pilot realizes they have a stowaway) you can dish out a ton of damage by targeting the Titan's internal systems—the Spitfire LMG equipped with the Slammer mod is the best rodeo attack weapon, capable of dropping any Titan without the need to reload.
- When you don't feel like risking a rodeo attack, keep your distance and engage enemy Titans with your Anti-Titan weapon. These weapons are designed to inflict damage on a Titan's hull, even if their bodyshield is still active. Once the Titan's bodyshield is down, target the red glowing sections on the Titan's hull to score critical hits—only the Sidewinder and Charge Rifle are capable of damaging these weak spots.
- Instead of taking on a Titan by yourself, work together with teammates to overwhelm opponents. While a friendly Titan is battling an enemy Titan, stay back and score hits with your Anti-Titan weapon and Arc Grenades. Or if a teammate is rodeo attacking an enemy Titan, provide support by engaging the enemy Pilot who disembarks from the Titan, allowing your teammate to complete the rodeo attack without interruption.

Titan vs. Minion

Blast any Grunts and Spectres you encounter to gain your Core Ability sooner.

Of all possible engagements, this scenario is the least threatening. However, don't overlook the significance of engaging minions with your Titan. Inflicting damage on Grunts and Spectres reduces the amount of time it takes for your Titan's Core Ability to come online—the more damage you dish out, the quicker you get your Core Ability. Both Grunts and Spectres are capable of launching anti-armor weapons, potentially depleting your Titan's bodyshield and health. So don't let these units gather around your Titan.

Tactics

- While piloting a Titan, minions are low-priority targets. Use the minimap to help find them, looking for the small red dots. But shift your focus when enemy Pilots and Titans appear on the minimap. Pilots and Titans pose a bigger threat and should be dealt with first.
- Due to their rapid fire, the 40mm Cannon and XO-16 Chaingun are two of the most effective weapons against minions. The 40mm Cannon's rounds benefit from splash damage, meaning you don't need to score a direct hit to inflict damage on nearby Grunts and Spectres.
- The Cluster Missile ordnance is devastating against minions. When fired, this volley of missiles sets off a series of secondary explosions over a wide area. This is a good way to take out minions inside buildings. Simply fire this weapon through a door or window and watch all the secondary explosions go off inside, killing all within the expansive blast radius.
- Minions sometimes arrive via dropship. These dropships can be shot down, but you'll probably need the help of a friendly Titan (or two) to do so. Dropships are only present for a few seconds before taking off. You'll need to focus your fire on one of these dropships to knock it out of the sky.
- While all Titan weapons are capable of killing minions, not every Titan weapon is effective in doing so. When carrying a specialized weapon, like the Plasma Railgun, rely on other options to eliminate minions. Either crush them with your Titan's feet, blast them with ordnance, or smash them with a melee attack. Dashing through a group of minions is also very effective.

Titan vs. Pilot

Enemy Pilots are most vulnerable when they're on the ground—make them pay!

In some respects, engaging enemy Pilots is just as dangerous as facing off against an enemy Titan. While Titans have a definite advantage when it comes to armor and firepower, they trail far behind Pilots when it comes to mobility. This makes Titans vulnerable to Anti-Titan weapons and rodeo attacks. As a result, Titans are best off keeping their distance from enemy Pilots and engaging them from long range. Otherwise Pilots can quickly chip away at a Titan's bodyshield and health. This cat-and-mouse dynamic leads to some intense engagements.

Tactics

- Keep a close eye on the minimap at all times while piloting a Titan. Enemy Pilots appear as a large red dot on the minimap, but only when firing an unsuppressed weapon. If you see one of these red dots near your Titan, immediately move out and put some distance between your Titan and the enemy Pilot.
- Anti-Titan weapons not only wear down your Titan's bodyshield, but they also deplete your health, even if the shields are still up, so don't take these weapons lightly. Incoming Anti-Titan weapons can be blocked with either the Vortex Shield or Particle Wall. If you can't locate or engage the enemy Pilot pelting your Titan with these weapons, simply retreat, particularly if your bodyshield is down. Pilots equipped with the Sidewinder and Charge Rifle can score critical hits, potentially crippling and destroying your Titan.
- Enemy Pilots are fast and nimble, capable of evading incoming fire. Instead of relying on accuracy and precision, weapons with a high rate of fire give you the best chance of hitting enemy Pilots. Go with the XO-16 Chaingun or 40mm Cannon. The Arc Cannon is also effective, particularly when engaging enemy Pilots who have ejected from their Titan.
- Rodeo attacks are extremely dangerous to Titans—watch for the notification atop the HUD to determine when your Titan has been boarded by an enemy Pilot. The Electric Smoke Tactical Ability is by far the best way to counter rodeo attacks. Stay within the electrified smokescreen until the enemy Pilot is dead or jumps off, then immediately dash out of the area.
- If you're rodeo attacked and don't have Electric Smoke, try to trick the enemy Pilot into jumping off. While still in the Titan, stop and make the Titan crouch down—this mimics the motion when you disembark. But instead of disembarking, remain motionless—in many cases, the enemy Pilot will hop off your Titan, thinking you're about to emerge. As soon as the enemy Pilots hops off, dash to safety. This tactic doesn't work every time, but it beats jumping out of your Titan and shooting the enemy Pilot with your primary weapon.

Titan vs. Titan

Make an effort to melee doomed Titans before the enemy Pilot can eject, killing the Titan and Pilot with one gruesome attack.

Succeeding in these epic battles requires more skill than brawn. Although protected by a bodyshield and a thick hull, Titans don't last long in a toe-to-toe slugfest with each other. As a result, Pilots must constantly monitor the tactical situation, keeping an eye on both their Titan's health and the health of the enemy Titan while weighing the pros and cons of each action. Always respect your opponent and be careful not to overcommit—otherwise you'll be ejecting from your Titan in no time, wondering what you did wrong.

Tactics

- When enemy Titans enter the battlefield, you're notified over the Titan's communication system. Take this opportunity to study the minimap for contacts—enemy Titans appear as red arrow icons on the minimap. Before rushing toward the location of an enemy Titan, enlist the help of a friendly Titan or two to assist. Titan-on-Titan battles are much easier when you have the help of a teammate.
- Upon engaging an enemy Titan, make note of their bodyshield and health bar. Before you can damage the Titan's health, you must first deplete its bodyshield. Once their bodyshield is gone, don't let the enemy Titan take cover, otherwise the bodyshield will regenerate. Keep hitting the Titan with weapon fire to deal damage to its health while preventing the bodyshield from regenerating. However, don't forget to monitor your own Titan's status too—if your bodyshield is gone, consider disengaging.
- When a Titan's bodyshield is down, it is vulnerable to critical hits. Target these red glowing weak spots on the Titan's hull to inflict heavy damage. Only the 40mm Cannon, XO-16 Chaingun, and Plasma Railgun can score critical hits.
- Instead of standing still during a Titan battle, stay on the move, dashing laterally to evade incoming fire. Lateral dashes are a great way to evade incoming dumb-fire rockets and missiles, such as those fired by the Quad Rocket, Rocket Salvo, and Cluster Missile. Or dash behind cover to break the locks of guided projectiles, like the Archer Heavy Rocket, Slaved Warheads, and Multi-Target Missiles—Electric Smoke can also negate lock-ons.
- Have you been saving up a Core Ability? Titan battles are the perfect time to deploy these powerful abilities, giving your Titan a significant advantage. The Atlas' Core Damage greatly increases damage output of all attacks—try to score critical hits to take down enemy Titans fast. Activate the Ogre's Shield Core ability to strengthen the Titan's bodyshield, allowing it to absorb much more damage. Or stay on the move using the Stryder's Dash Core ability, constantly dashing around your prey, making your Titan extremely difficult to target.

CAUTION

If a doomed Titan emits a bright, white flash of light, retreat! It's about to go nuclear! The Nuclear Ejection Kit results in a devastating self-destruction sequence, killing all enemies in a wide radius.

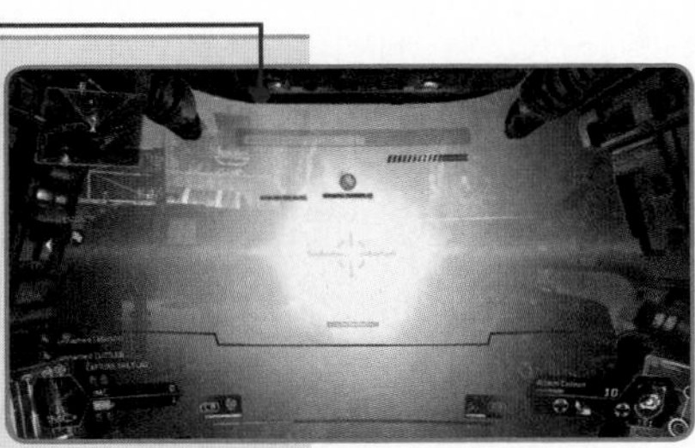

TEAMPLAY

Whether playing the campaign or any of the multiplayer game modes, *Titanfall* is a team-based game. While individual skill plays a big part in each team's success, teams are much more effective when working together, particularly when Titans enter the battle.

Communication

You can speak to all players in the game's Lobby before a match. Use this opportunity to establish a rapport with your teammates.

A team who communicates will always have a huge advantage over those who don't. *Titanfall* supports voice chat on all platforms, making setup as easy as connecting a microphone. In the Lobby screen you can talk with all players, including those on the opposing team. But once a match starts, voice channels are isolated between teams, ensuring your discussions aren't heard by the enemy. Communicating with complete strangers can be awkward at first, but as long as you keep the discussion focused on the gameplay, you'll find most players are receptive to your comments. After all, you're all on the same team, and you all want to win. Even if you are playing one of the game modes on your own, you should always communicate with the players you are teamed up with. Calling out the position of enemy Pilots allows your teammates to make the right play.

PRO TIP: STRONGSIDE

Work together with a teammate and look for opportunities to isolate opponents for two-on-one engagements. In this situation neither you nor your ally should die and the way you will succeed in staying alive is through communication. Bait and switch with your ally—catch the attention of the enemy and distract while your ally flanks and scores the kill.

Team Pilot Tactics

- When playing Capture the Flag and you're bringing the flag into your base to capture, have an allied Pilot storm the base first to make sure it is safe and there aren't any enemy Pilots hiding inside. The worst way to lose a flag capture is to die right inside your own base.
- Before the start of the match make a game plan. This will let you know where to go off the start of the match, who to work with, and where to watch for incoming enemy Pilots.
- A Pilot equipped with a sniper rifle can hang back and play a bit passive. As the Pilot with the sniper rifle, find an elevated position and provide cover for your teammates moving into battle.

Team Titan Tactics

- Teamwork becomes even more important when inside a Titan—bait and switching becomes essential. With the various Tactical Abilities, Titans excel in bait and switching. One Titan can use the Vortex Shield to stop enemy Titan fire. At the same time, an ally with Vortex Shield can attack the enemy Titan from the side.
- A Titan equipped with a Particle Wall can stay behind the barrier for cover and call out for help. The wall buys you some time while allies try to reach your location. The Particle Wall comes in handy when friendly Pilots are nearby—drop the Particle Wall and allow them to hide behind the barrier until the area is safe to move about.
- When playing Capture the Flag, allow a flag-carrying teammate to hop on your Titan's back. This will protect the Pilot from being killed as long as your Titan has shields. Dash back to your base with your Titan and drop off your teammate to capture the flag.
- As a Titan you'll want to work with other friendly Titans. If you are rodeo attacked by a enemy Pilot, communicate with your teammate quickly so your teammate can shoot the enemy off your back immediately.
- When fighting with a group of Titans, be sure to stay near the back of the pack if you are the weakest. You'll still want to deal damage, but you're much better alive than dead. Consider rotating with teammates, allowing the weaker Titans to slip to the rear while Titans with regenerated bodyshields assume front line positions.

PILOT GEAR

Fighting for both the IMC and Militia, Pilots are an elite warrior class, and their performance is a decisive factor in every battle in the Frontier. While trained to operate Titans, Pilots spend just as much time racing across the battlefield on foot, utilizing their Jump Kits to flank and outmaneuver their opponents. Although raw skill and mobility are important, so is picking the right equipment for the job. Here we take a look at all customization options available to Pilots, offering tactics and recommended loadouts to help you get the most out of each weapon, ability, and kit.

PILOT CUSTOMIZATION

Unlike Grunts or Spectres, which deploy with standard-issue weapons and gear, Pilots are capable of equipping a wide range of custom weapons, abilities, and kits to enhance their performance in combat. As an elite unit, it's up to you to find the right mix of equipment that complements your style of play. Each Pilot has seven customizable slots. Here's a brief rundown of each slot.

Primary Weapon: This is your default weapon when deploying. There are a total of ten to choose from, each with unique characteristics and specializations. Primary weapons can be equipped with optional attachments and mods, altering their performance.

Anti-Titan Weapon: These specialized weapons are designed to damage enemy Titans. Hit-and-run tactics are recommended—don't get in a duel with a Titan.

Sidearm: Pistols serve primarily as a backup to your primary weapon—when your primary runs out of ammo in a firefight, switch to your sidearm and finish strong.

Tactical Ability: There are a total of three active abilities giving Pilots the ability to blend into the environment, boost movement/health regeneration, or detect enemies hidden behind cover.

Before joining a match, or while waiting for one to start, take some time to customize your Pilot's loadout.

Ordnance: Choose from grenades, mines, or remotely detonated charges, dishing out heavy damage against Pilots, minions, and Titans.

Kits: There are two kit slots, Tier 1 and Tier 2, each with five options. These passive kits enhance Pilots in various ways. Select kits that complement your other loadout selections.

PRESET PILOT LOADOUTS

As a rookie Pilot, there are three preset loadouts available to you: Rifleman, Assassin, and CQB. Later on, as you level up, you can access the Custom Pilot loadouts, allowing you to select your own weapons, abilities, and kits. But until then you must make the most of these three preset loadouts. These loadouts should serve as an example of what kind of customization is available—study these loadouts and experiment with their strengths and weaknesses while defining your own style of gameplay.

The preset Rifleman, Assassin, and CQB loadouts offer a mere glimpse of the customization options available to experienced Pilots.

Rifleman

PRIMARY WEAPON
FULL-AUTO ASSAULT WEAPON
R-101C CARBINE
ATTACHMENT: HCOG
MOD: FACTORY ISSUE
ANTI-TITAN WEAPON
FIRES A POWERFUL HOMING ROCKET
ARCHER HEAVY ROCKET
SIDEARM
PRECISION SEMI-AUTO PISTOL
HAMMOND P2011
TACTICAL ABILITY
CLOAK
MOST EFFECTIVE AGAINST TITANS
ORDNANCE
FRAG GRENADE
EXPLOSIVE ANTI-PERSONNEL WEAPON
TIER 1 KIT
EXPLOSIVES PACK
CARRY EXTRA PILOT ORDNANCE
TIER 2 KIT
DOME-SHIELD BATTERY
TITANFALL DOME-SHIELD LASTS LONGER

Loadout Unlock: Level 1

The Rifleman loadout is well-rounded, making it a good go-to loadout for new Pilots. The full-auto R-101C Carbine is the most versatile of the primary weapons, capable of engaging targets at any range while the Hammond P2011 serves as a dependable backup. But be cautious when engaging Titans. Although the Archer Heavy Rocket inflicts impressive damage against enemy Titans, it takes a while for the weapon to attain a lock, putting you at risk during the lengthy lock-on process. Use the Cloak Tactical Ability to sneak up behind Titans, then hit them from behind with the Archer Heavy Rocket. The Explosives Pack Tier 1 Kit gives the Rifleman a total of three Frag Grenades, ideal for taking out groups of enemy Grunts, Spectres, and the occasional unsuspecting Pilot. The Dome-Shield Battery Tier 2 Kit increases the amount of time your Titan's Dome-Shield is active, giving you more time to reach your Titan before it's vulnerable to attack.

Assassin

PRIMARY WEAPON
LOCKS ONTO NEARBY TARGETS
SMART PISTOL MK5
ATTACHMENT: IRON SIGHTS
MOD: SUPPRESSOR
ANTI-TITAN WEAPON
RAPIDLY FIRES MICRO-MISSILES
SIDEWINDER
SIDEARM
.45 CAL FULL-AUTO PISTOL
RE-45 AUTOPISTOL
TACTICAL ABILITY
CLOAK
MOST EFFECTIVE AGAINST TITANS
ORDNANCE
FRAG GRENADE
EXPLOSIVE ANTI-PERSONNEL WEAPON
TIER 1 KIT
POWER CELL
YOUR PILOT'S TACTICAL ABILITY RECHARGES FASTER
TIER 2 KIT
MINION DETECTOR
REVEALS ALL GRUNTS AND SPECTRES ON YOUR MINIMAP ALL THE TIME

Loadout Unlock: Level 1

Compared to the Rifleman loadout, the Assassin rewards a stealthier style of gameplay. Equipped with a Suppressor, the Smart Pistol MK5 can silently dispatch minions and Pilots alike without revealing your position on the minimap. But due to the Smart Pistol MK5's limited effective range, it's crucial to rely on mobility and the Cloak Tactical Ability to get the jump on opponents—the Power Cell Tier 1 Kit allows you to activate Cloak with greater frequency, making you difficult to spot, particularly by Titans. This loadout also benefits from the Minion Detector Tier 2 Kit, which reveals the locations of all Grunts and Spectres on the minimap at all times—use this information to hunt down these enemies, reducing your Titan's build time. While the Sidewinder Anti-Titan weapon is capable of rapid fire, each hit does minimal damage. So instead of taking on a healthy enemy Titan, look for damaged Titans, preferably with disabled shields, and then unleash a volley of Sidewinder fire to take them down.

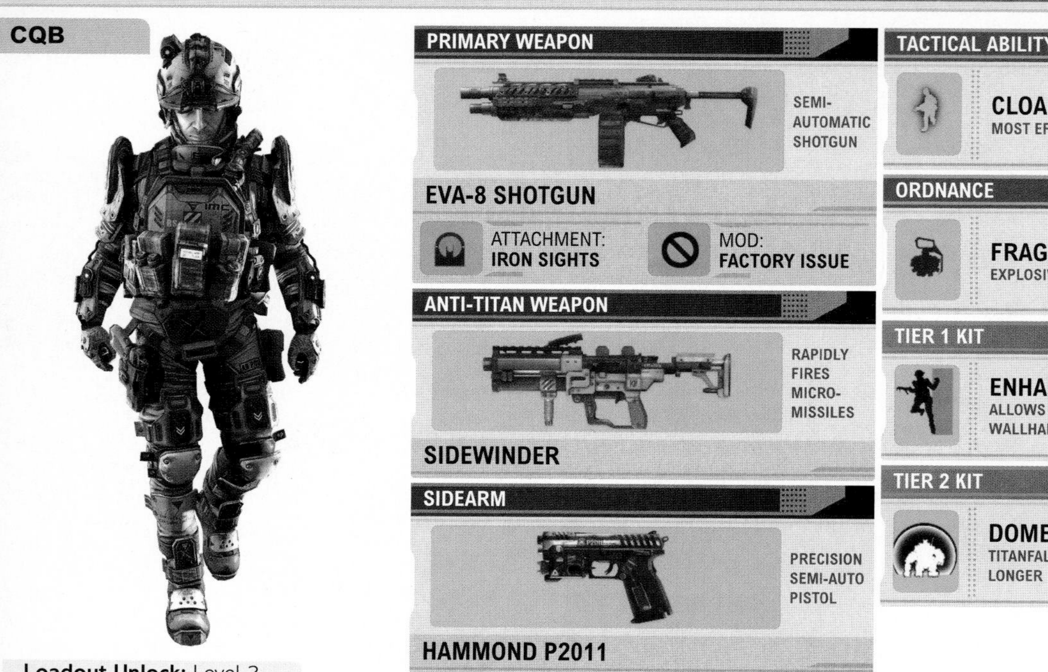

Loadout Unlock: Level 2

CQB stands for Close-Quarter Battle, and such tactics should be the focus of your gameplay while using this specialized loadout. While the EVA-8 Shotgun is capable of one-shot kills against minions and Pilots alike, it only does so at extremely close range. This puts you at a significant disadvantage when facing off against Pilots equipped with longer-range weapons—the Hammond P2011 sidearm is actually more effective when engaging targets beyond 10 meters. Therefore stick to interiors, alleys, and other cramped spaces where you can make the most of the shotgun's high-damage output. The Enhanced Parkour Tier 1 Kit gives you the ability to extend wall runs and wall hangs, allowing you to close distance faster, rushing enemy Pilots with the EVA-8. When facing off against enemy Titans, rely on the Cloak ability to remain undetected and then perform a rodeo attack or engage at close range with the Sidewinder. In a pinch, the Sidewinder can also be deployed against Pilots and minions, when your shotgun doesn't have the requisite range.

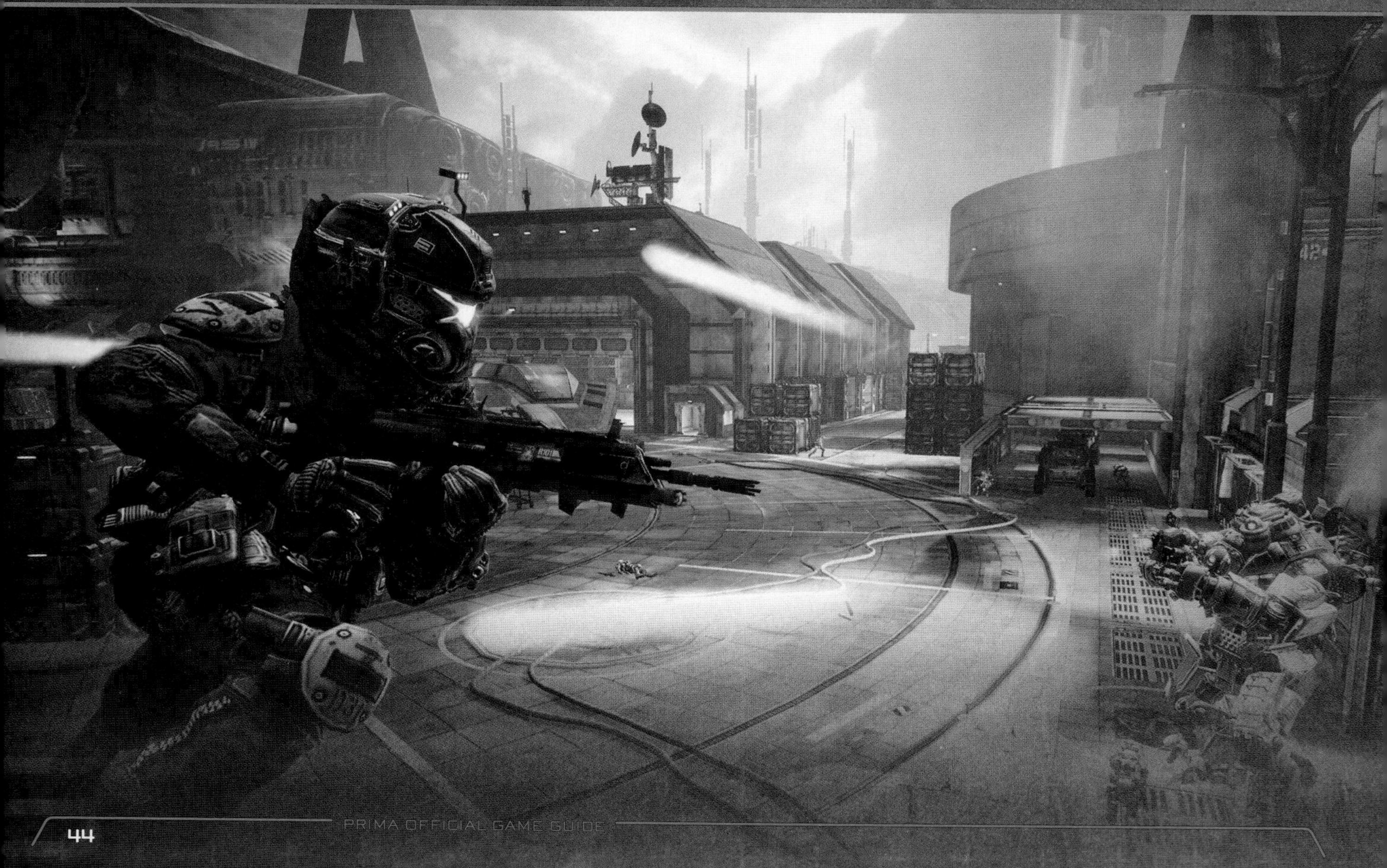

PRIMARY WEAPONS

Selecting a primary weapon is the most important choice when customizing your Pilot's loadout. The characteristics of your primary weapon determine how and at what range you engage enemy Pilots and minions—this in turn dictates your style of play. By completing challenges tied to each primary weapon, you can unlock a variety of attachments and mods. Attachments consist of different weapon sights, each offering unique sight pictures and varied magnifications—see the provided table for more details. While attachments change the way targets are acquired when aiming down sights, they have no impact on the weapon's overall performance. Mods, on the other hand, alter the way a weapon functions, sometimes increasing or decreasing a weapon's stats. Each primary weapon has one attachment slot and one mod slot. Experiment with different configurations to find a combination that works for you.

ATTACHMENTS: SIGHT PICTURES

IMAGE	NAME	DESCRIPTION
	AOG	The AOG, or Advanced Optical Gunsight, is fixed at 2.4X magnification, and includes an integrated "current magazine capacity" readout with a backup numerical display. The AOG is ideal for combat at extended range.
	HCOG	The Holographic Combat Optical Gunsight has an open sight picture, making it easier to acquire and track targets, particularly in the vertical. The gunsight is fixed at 1.85X magnification, and includes integrated ammunition readouts.
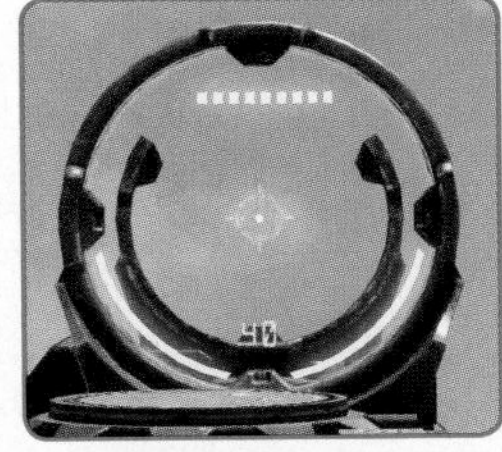	Holosight	The Holosight's optics are fixed at a 2.1X zoom factor. The sight picture is designed to induce a tighter visual perception, making it effective both at range and in close quarters. The Holosight is equipped with an integrated ammunition readout.
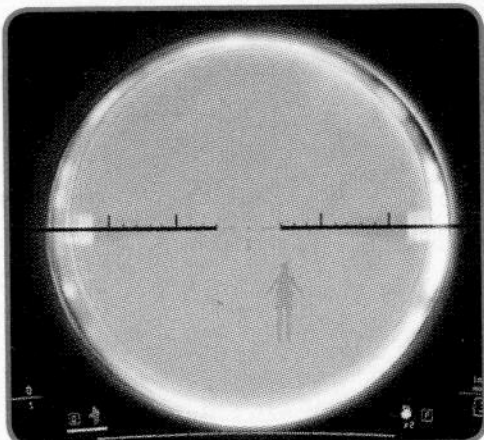	4.5X Zoom Scope	This scope provides fixed, mid-range magnification for highly fluid combat situations. It provides a balance of precision and ranged situational awareness.
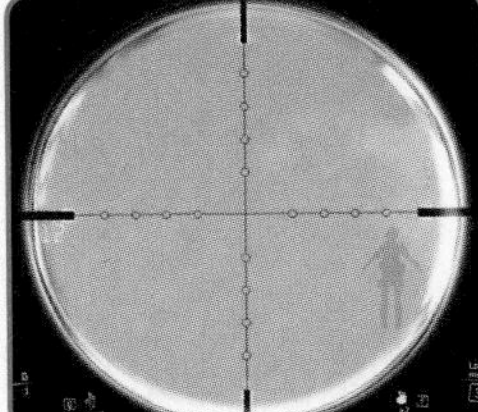	6X Zoom Scope	This scope provides fixed, long-range magnification for engaging very distant targets. However, your situational awareness may be compromised while it is in use, due to the high magnification.

R-101C CARBINE

MAGAZINE CAPACITY: 30 WEAPON UNLOCK: LEVEL 1

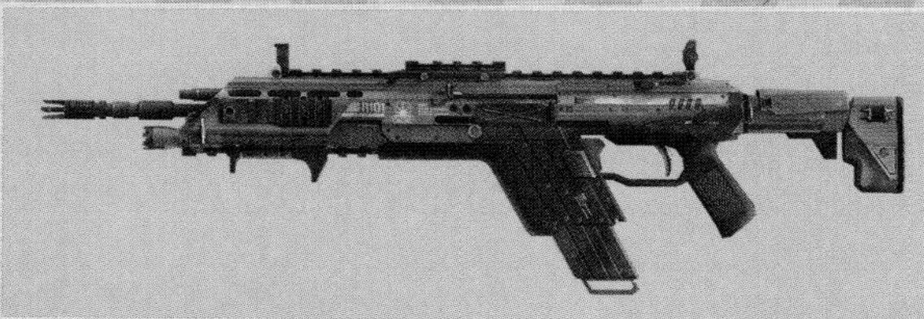

The R-101C is a fully automatic, compact assault weapon commonly used throughout the Frontier.

STRENGTHS:
- Highly versatile
- Large magazine capacity
- Ultimate mid-range weapon

WEAKNESSES:
- Outclassed at short range by EVA-8 Shotgun and SMGs
- Outclassed at long range by rifles

WEAPON PERFORMANCE

DAMAGE

ACCURACY

RANGE

FIRE RATE

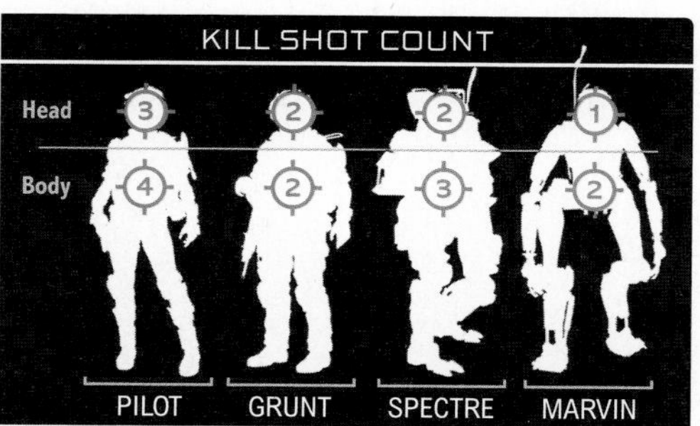

WEAPON ATTACHMENTS

IMAGE	NAME	DESCRIPTION	UNLOCK
	Iron Sights	Factory issue gunsights are cheap and reliable, but visibility through them can be somewhat limited.	Default Weapon Sight
	HCOG	The Holographic Combat Optical Gunsight has an open sight picture, making it easier to acquire and track targets, particularly in the vertical. The gunsight is fixed at 1.85X magnification, and includes integrated ammunition readouts.	The Expendables (II) Challenge: Kill 25 Grunts
	Holosight	The Holosight's optics are fixed at a 2.1X zoom factor. The sight picture is designed to induce a tighter visual perception, making it effective both at range and in close quarters. The Holosight is equipped with an integrated ammunition readout.	The Expendables (III) Challenge: Kill 50 Grunts
	AOG	The AOG, or Advanced Optical Gunsight, is fixed at 2.4X magnification, and includes an integrated "current magazine capacity" readout with a backup numerical display. The AOG is ideal for combat at extended range.	If It Moves... (III) Challenge: Kill 50 Enemies

WEAPON MODS

IMAGE	NAME	DESCRIPTION	UNLOCK
	Extended Magazine	This mod increases the ammo capacity of the weapon, making it so that you don't have to reload as often.	Machine War (II) Challenge: Kill 25 Spectres
	Suppressor	This mod reduces the firing noise and muzzle flash of the weapon, making it ideal for taking your enemies by surprise.	If It Moves... (II) Challenge: Kill 25 Enemies

Field Notes

- If you're looking for the all-around weapon, this is it. The R-101C Carbine is the most versatile weapon in the game. It has great accuracy and range while its rate of fire is quite fast and deals a solid amount of damage to take down Pilots and minions.
- Being an extremely versatile weapon, you can play aggressive or passive throughout the game. Its range enables you to pick off Pilots from a distance and its fully automatic feature allows you to fire away in those close-quarter battles. When engaging targets at long range, fire the weapon in short bursts to maintain accuracy.
- With this weapon, you're able to pick off most minions from a distance with quick headshots or a few bullets to the body. The magazine capacity allows you to pick off a group of minions and still have enough ammo left to drop a Pilot.
- The sight attachments offer different magnifications. If you're looking to sit back and defend on a open map, attach the AOG. At closer ranges attach the HCOG or Holosight. If you find yourself running out of ammo, attach the Extended Magazine to increase your magazine capacity. However adding the Suppressor allows you to be a stealthy ninja and stay hidden from the minimap when firing the weapon, but at a minor reduction in damage and range.

PRO TIP: STRONGSIDE

When using the R-101C Carbine, I like to attach the Suppressor mod to hide myself on the minimap when firing the weapon. I also use the HCOG attachment because of its versatility in most situations and quick target acquisition. The HCOG also takes up minimal screen view in the HUD.

R-101C Carbine Challenges

IF IT MOVES...

TIER	CRITERIA	REWARD
1	Kill 10 Enemies	500 XP
2	Kill 25 Enemies	1,000 XP, Suppressor Mod, Amped R-101 Burn Card
3	Kill 50 Enemies	2,500 XP, AOG Attachment, Amped R-101 Burn Card
4	Kill 100 Enemies	5,000 XP, Amped R-101 Burn Card
5	Kill 200 Enemies	10,000 XP, Amped R-101 Burn Card

THE EXPENDABLES

TIER	CRITERIA	REWARD
1	Kill 10 Grunts	500 XP
2	Kill 25 Grunts	HCOG Attachment
3	Kill 50 Grunts	Holosight Attachment
4	Kill 100 Grunts	5,000 XP, Amped R-101 Burn Card
5	Kill 200 Grunts	10,000 XP, Amped R-101 Burn Card

TOP GUN

TIER	CRITERIA	REWARD
1	Kill 5 Pilots	500 XP
2	Kill 15 Pilots	1,000 XP, Amped R-101 Burn Card
3	Kill 30 Pilots	2,500 XP, Amped R-101 Burn Card
4	Kill 50 Pilots	5,000 XP, Amped R-101 Burn Card
5	Kill 75 Pilots	10,000 XP, Amped R-101 Burn Card

THIS IS MY WEAPON

TIER	CRITERIA	REWARD
1	Use Weapon for .5 Hour	500 XP
2	Use Weapon for 1 Hour	1,000 XP, Amped R-101 Burn Card
3	Use Weapon for 1.5 Hours	2,500 XP, Amped R-101 Burn Card
4	Use Weapon for 2 Hours	5,000 XP, Amped R-101 Burn Card
5	Use Weapon for 3 Hours	10,000 XP, Amped R-101 Burn Card

MACHINE WAR

TIER	CRITERIA	REWARD
1	Kill 10 Spectres	500 XP
2	Kill 25 Spectres	1,000 XP, Extended Magazine Mod, Amped R-101 Burn Card
3	Kill 50 Spectres	2,500 XP, Amped R-101 Burn Card
4	Kill 75 Spectres	5,000 XP, Amped R-101 Burn Card
5	Kill 100 Spectres	10,000 XP, Amped R-101 Burn Card

OFF THE DOME

TIER	CRITERIA	REWARD
1	Get 5 Headshots	500 XP
2	Get 15 Headshots	1,000 XP, Amped R-101 Burn Card
3	Get 30 Headshots	2,500 XP, Amped R-101 Burn Card
4	Get 50 Headshots	5,000 XP, Amped R-101 Burn Card
5	Get 75 Headshots	10,000 XP, Amped R-101 Burn Card

AWARDED BURN CARD

Amped R-101C
Replace Primary Weapon with a more lethal R-101C Carbine
They'll call us terrorists or worse, but we can't win playing by their rules.
-MacAllan

Amped R-101

EVA-8 SHOTGUN

MAGAZINE CAPACITY: 6 WEAPON UNLOCK: LEVEL 1

This EVA-8 is a semi-automatic shotgun, originally designed for extra-vehicular activity, both in conventional and exo-atmospheric conditions.

STRENGTHS:

- Up close, fire away and the enemy is dead
- Great for controlling the building interiors

WEAKNESSES:

- Limited magazine capacity
- Ineffective at mid-long range

WEAPON PERFORMANCE

DAMAGE

ACCURACY

RANGE

FIRE RATE

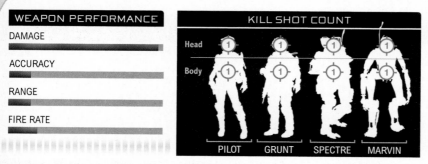

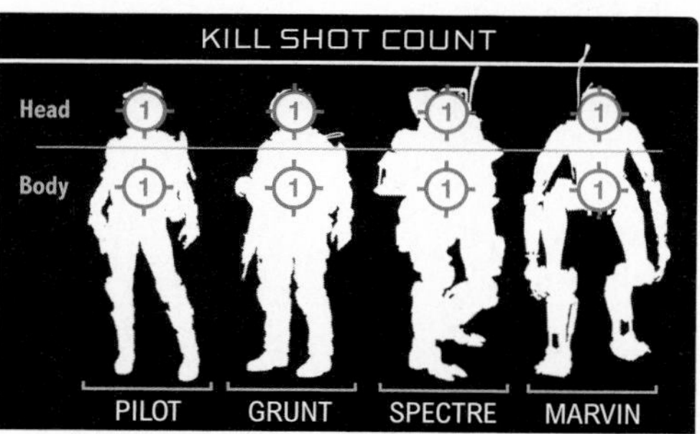

WEAPON ATTACHMENTS

IMAGE	NAME	DESCRIPTION	UNLOCK
	Iron Sights	Factory issue gunsights are cheap and reliable, but visibility through them can be somewhat limited.	Default Weapon Sight

WEAPON MODS

IMAGE	NAME	DESCRIPTION	UNLOCK
	High-Capacity Drum	This mod increases the ammo capacity of the weapon, making it so that you don't have to reload as often.	Machine War (II) Challenge: Kill 25 Spectres
	Leadwall	This mod increases the spread of the weapon, causing it to disperse its pellets over a larger area. It is ideal for attacking targets that are bunched up near each other.	Top Gun (II) Challenge: Kill 15 Pilots
	Suppressor	This mod reduces the firing noise and muzzle flash of the weapon, making it ideal for taking your enemies by surprise.	If It Moves... (II) Challenge: Kill 25 Enemies

Field Notes

- Up close, nothing can compare to this weapon. Getting caught mid- to long-range with this weapon is asking to die. Best way to play with this weapon is to stay inside the buildings with the highest amounts of traffic and force the close-range battle.
- The EVA-8 Shotgun is all about being close to the opponent. When engaged by enemy Pilots at medium or long range, don't bother trying to fight back. Instead, retreat and look for a way to take the fight to close range. A great way to draw enemy Pilots to come to you is to shoot at minions, or even shoot randomly with your pistol, to give away your position on the minimap and bait them in. They will come around the corner and be surprised when you are waiting for them with the ultimate close-range weapon.
- This weapon makes quick work of minions. However, be careful not to waste your entire magazine in case there are nearby enemy Pilots.
- Leadwall or Suppressor are a must-have for this weapon. Even though you give up a little damage, you can still one-shot enemy Pilots while taking advantage of the stealth from the Suppressor or the increased spread of the Leadwall mod. If you find yourself running low on ammo, consider using the High-Capacity Drum, which adds three more rounds.

PRO TIP: WALSHY

When equipping the EVA-8 Shotgun, consider activating the Prosthetic Legs Burn Card for faster movement. This allows you to rush into close range where the weapon is most effective.

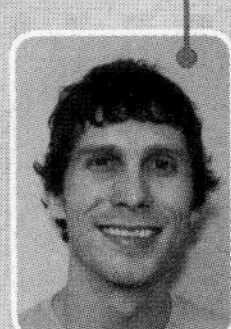

EVA-8 Shotgun Challenges

IF IT MOVES...

TIER	CRITERIA	REWARD
1	Kill 10 Enemies	500 XP
2	Kill 25 Enemies	1,000 XP, Suppressor Mod, Amped EVA-8 Burn Card
3	Kill 50 Enemies	2,500 XP, Amped EVA-8 Burn Card
4	Kill 100 Enemies	5,000 XP, Amped EVA-8 Burn Card
5	Kill 200 Enemies	10,000 XP, Amped EVA-8 Burn Card

THE EXPENDABLES

TIER	CRITERIA	REWARD
1	Kill 10 Grunts	500 XP
2	Kill 25 Grunts	1,000 XP, Amped EVA-8 Burn Card
3	Kill 50 Grunts	2,500 XP, Amped EVA-8 Burn Card
4	Kill 100 Grunts	5,000 XP, Amped EVA-8 Burn Card
5	Kill 200 Grunts	10,000 XP, Amped EVA-8 Burn Card

TOP GUN

TIER	CRITERIA	REWARD
1	Kill 5 Pilots	500 XP
2	Kill 15 Pilots	1,000 XP, Leadwall Mod, Amped EVA-8 Burn Card
3	Kill 30 Pilots	2,500 XP, Amped EVA-8 Burn Card
4	Kill 50 Pilots	5,000 XP, Amped EVA-8 Burn Card
5	Kill 75 Pilots	10,000 XP, Amped EVA-8 Burn Card

THIS IS MY WEAPON

TIER	CRITERIA	REWARD
1	Use Weapon for .5 Hour	500 XP
2	Use Weapon for 1 Hour	1,000 XP, Amped EVA-8 Burn Card
3	Use Weapon for 1.5 Hours	2,500 XP, Amped EVA-8 Burn Card
4	Use Weapon for 2 Hours	5,000 XP, Amped EVA-8 Burn Card
5	Use Weapon for 3 Hours	10,000 XP, Amped EVA-8 Burn Card

MACHINE WAR

TIER	CRITERIA	REWARD
1	Kill 10 Spectres	500 XP
2	Kill 25 Spectres	1,000 XP, High-Capacity Drum Mod, Amped EVA-8 Burn Card
3	Kill 50 Spectres	2,500 XP, Amped EVA-8 Burn Card
4	Kill 75 Spectres	5,000 XP, Amped EVA-8 Burn Card
5	Kill 100 Spectres	10,000 XP, Amped EVA-8 Burn Card

Awarded Burn Card

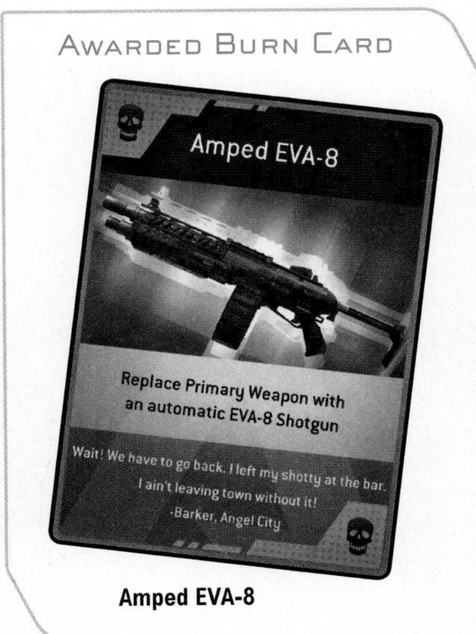
Amped EVA-8
Replace Primary Weapon with an automatic EVA-8 Shotgun
Wait! We have to go back. I left my shotty at the bar. I ain't leaving town without it!
-Barker, Angel City

Amped EVA-8

SMART PISTOL MK5

MAGAZINE CAPACITY: 12 WEAPON UNLOCK: LEVEL 1

The Smart Pistol scans for hostile targets within a short range, locking on to them automatically. Any rounds fired will then maneuver to hit the locked targets. Aiming with the iron sights allows the operator to use the pistol in manual targeting mode.

STRENGTHS:

- Has a target system that locks on to enemies
- Easily wipe out minions to reduce Titan build time

WEAKNESSES:

- Target lock takes more time on enemy Pilots
- Requires steady shot to fire in manual mode

WEAPON PERFORMANCE

DAMAGE

ACCURACY

RANGE

FIRE RATE

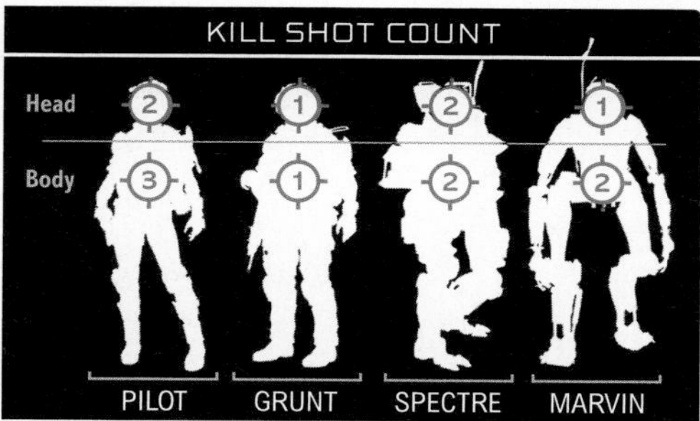

WEAPON MODS

IMAGE	NAME	DESCRIPTION	UNLOCK
	Enhanced Targeting	This mod accelerates the Smart Pistol's lock-on speed and increases its target acquisition range, at the expense of a smaller targeting area.	Top Gun (II) Challenge: Kill 15 Pilots
	Extended Magazine	This mod increases the ammo capacity of the weapon, making it so you don't have to reload as often.	Machine War (III) Challenge: Kill 50 Spectres
	Suppressor	This mod reduces the firing noise and muzzle flash of the weapon, making it ideal for taking your enemies by surprise.	If It Moves... (II) Challenge: Kill 25 Enemies

Field Notes

- The Smart Pistol MK5 is one of the most interesting weapons in *Titanfall*. This pistol doesn't have the word "Smart" in front of its name for nothing. The pistol has a target zone on the screen; when Grunts, Specters, or Pilots move into the zone, the pistol will begin to lock on to the opponent. Once locked on, the player only needs to pull the trigger and the opponent will drop to their knees. The tougher the opponent, the longer you will need to keep them in your sights to lock on. Grunts require one lock on, Specters need two lock ons, and Pilots require three lock ons as they are the toughest opponent besides the Titans.
- This weapon is incredible against Pilots—players just need to keep opponents in the target zone and you can wipe them out real quick. Since it does take some time to lock on to a Pilot, you want to be a bit more sneaky and approach the enemy from angles that allow you to lock on before they are able to react. If you do decide to play head-to-head with a Pilot, this weapon will still be effective as it only takes three bullets to the body, when firing manually, to take an opposing Pilot out.
- This pistol is a monster against AI! The lock on feature allows you to easily wipe out a squad of four Grunts. Chill back and let the pistol lock on or rush in and just cause havoc. Be cautious if you do rush in—opposing Pilots could be waiting nearby to ambush you.
- This weapon has three different mods to choose from: Enhanced Targeting, Extended Magazine, and the Suppressor. Enhanced Targeting will do exactly as it says: enhance the targeting, allowing you to lock on to opponents quicker and at a greater distance. The only down side is that the target zone is decreased. Extended Magazine will help and is recommended to players who are always in the opponent's face to be able to fire off more rounds. The Suppressor will allow players to maximize the Smart Pistol MK5's targeting ability. Players will be able to fight waves of Grunts without exposing themselves on the minimap, which allows them to catch enemy Pilots off guard.

PRO TIP: FLAMESWORD

The Smart Pistol MK5 is very powerful with its targeting system. Equipping the Suppressor allows you to freely roam the map without giving away your position when engaging the opposing team. I prefer this mod as it allows me to take out multiple Pilots without giving away my location.

Smart Pistol MK5 Challenges

IF IT MOVES...

TIER	CRITERIA	REWARD
1	Kill 10 Enemies	500 XP
2	Kill 25 Enemies	1,000 XP, Suppressor Mod, Amped Smart Pistol Burn Card
3	Kill 50 Enemies	2,500 XP, Amped Smart Pistol Burn Card
4	Kill 100 Enemies	5,000 XP, Amped Smart Pistol Burn Card
5	Kill 200 Enemies	10,000 XP, Amped Smart Pistol Burn Card

THE EXPENDABLES

TIER	CRITERIA	REWARD
1	Kill 10 Grunts	500 XP
2	Kill 25 Grunts	1,000 XP, Amped Smart Pistol Burn Card
3	Kill 50 Grunts	2,500 XP, Amped Smart Pistol Burn Card
4	Kill 100 Grunts	5,000 XP, Amped Smart Pistol Burn Card
5	Kill 200 Grunts	10,000 XP, Amped Smart Pistol Burn Card

TOP GUN

TIER	CRITERIA	REWARD
1	Kill 5 Pilots	500 XP
2	Kill 15 Pilots	1,000 XP, Enhanced Targeting Mod, Amped Smart Pistol Burn Card
3	Kill 30 Pilots	2,500 XP, Amped Smart Pistol Burn Card
4	Kill 50 Pilots	5,000 XP, Amped Smart Pistol Burn Card
5	Kill 75 Pilots	10,000 XP, Amped Smart Pistol Burn Card

THIS IS MY WEAPON

TIER	CRITERIA	REWARD
1	Use Weapon for .5 Hour	500 XP
2	Use Weapon for 1 Hour	1,000 XP, Amped Smart Pistol Burn Card
3	Use Weapon for 1.5 Hours	2,500 XP, Amped Smart Pistol Burn Card
4	Use Weapon for 2 Hours	5,000 XP, Amped Smart Pistol Burn Card
5	Use Weapon for 3 Hours	10,000 XP, Amped Smart Pistol Burn Card

MACHINE WAR

TIER	CRITERIA	REWARD
1	Kill 10 Spectres	500 XP
2	Kill 25 Spectres	1,000 XP, Amped Smart Pistol Burn Card
3	Kill 50 Spectres	2,500 XP, Extended Magazine Mod, Amped Smart Pistol Burn Card
4	Kill 75 Spectres	5,000 XP, Amped Smart Pistol Burn Card
5	Kill 100 Spectres	10,000 XP, Amped Smart Pistol Burn Card

AWARDED BURN CARD

Amped Smart Pistol
Replace Primary Weapon with a more lethal Smart Pistol MK5
So it'll do calculus now? -Sarah

Amped Smart Pistol

DEVELOPER TIP

respawn ENTERTAINMENT

The Smart Pistol locks on to cloaked Pilots slower than uncloaked Pilots. If you know your opponents are relying on the Smart Pistol, and they catch you in the open, try by using the Cloak ability as a countermeasure. This will buy you some time to break line of sight and cancel the progress of any Smart Pistol lock ons.

R-97 COMPACT SMG

MAGAZINE CAPACITY: 40 WEAPON UNLOCK: LEVEL 6

The R-97 is a compact submachine gun that excels at close-quarter combat due to its extremely high rate of fire and minimal recoil.

STRENGTHS:
- Large magazine capacity
- Extremely high rate of fire; excels in close quarters, kills fast

WEAKNESSES:
- Weak shot-for-shot damage output
- Limited effective range; outclassed by carbine and rifles

WEAPON PERFORMANCE

DAMAGE

ACCURACY

RANGE

FIRE RATE

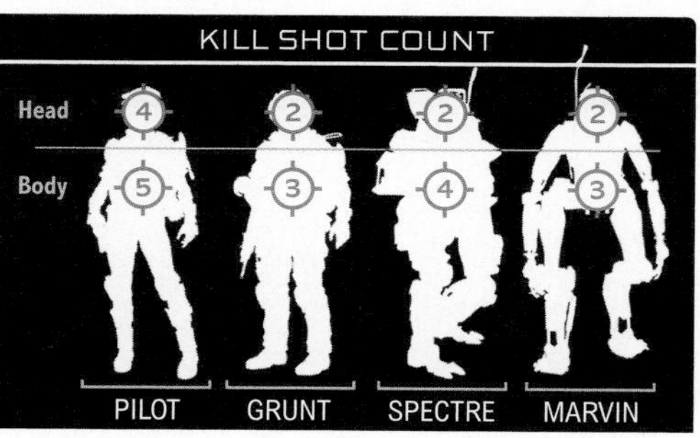

WEAPON ATTACHMENTS

IMAGE	NAME	DESCRIPTION	UNLOCK
	Iron Sights	Factory issue gunsights are cheap and reliable, but visibility through them can be somewhat limited.	Default Weapon Sight
	HCOG	The Holographic Combat Optical Gunsight has an open sight picture, making it easier to acquire targets, particularly in the vertical. The gunsight is fixed at 1.85X magnification, and includes integrated ammunition readouts.	The Expendables (III) Challenge: Kill 50 Grunts

WEAPON MODS

IMAGE	NAME	DESCRIPTION	UNLOCK
	Extended Magazine	This mod increases the ammo capacity of the weapon, so that you don't have to reload as often.	Machine War (II) Challenge: Kill 25 Spectres
	Scatterfire	This mod increases the R-97's high rate of fire even further, at the expense of accuracy.	Top Gun (II) Challenge: Kill 15 Pilots
	Suppressor	This mod reduces the firing noise and muzzle flash of the weapon, making it ideal for taking your enemies by surprise.	If It Moves... (II) Challenge: Kill 25 Enemies

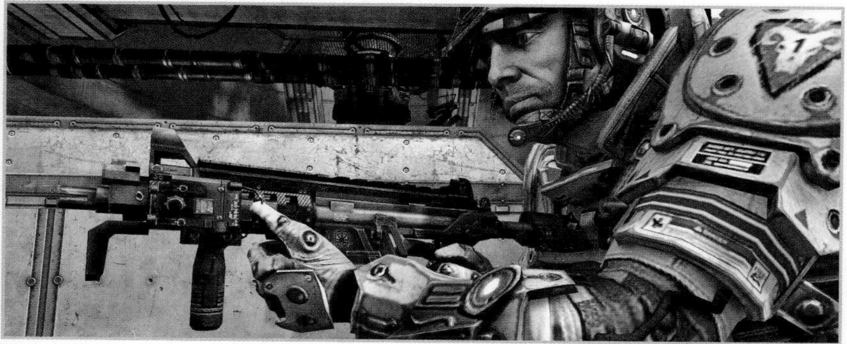

Field Notes

- Shot for shot, the R-97 Compact SMG has the lowest damage output of all the primary weapons. But what it lacks in damage output it more than makes up for in its impressive rate of fire. The weapon's blistering cyclic rate makes it an extremely formidable weapon in close-quarter encounters, easily mowing down pilots and AI alike. However, go easy on the trigger. The high rate of fire results in extreme recoil, making it difficult to keep the weapon on-target. Compensate for muzzle climb by firing in short bursts, particularly when engaging targets beyond 15-20 meters.
- The R-97 is most effective against pilots at close range, where its high rate of fire gives the shooter an edge over their opponents. While this SMG doesn't kill as fast as the EVA-8 Shotgun, its high rate of fire and 40-round magazine capacity makes it a true contender at close range. As a result, look to engage enemy pilots in buildings, alleys, and other cramped environments where you can take advantage of the weapon's strengths. Likewise, avoid open areas where this SMG is easily outclassed by most of the other primary weapons.
- This SMG is an absolute minion killer, perfect for wiping out squads of Grunts and Spectres. Look for newly arrived drop pods, then rush in for the kill. At close range the R-97 is an effective hip fire weapon, allowing you to spray targets with decent accuracy. But at ranges beyond 10 meters, always aim down the weapon's sights. While ammo conservation shouldn't be much of a concern with this weapon, you can always drop enemies faster with headshots.
- Equip the HCOG as soon as it's available, as it offers faster target acquisition than the standard iron sights. When it comes to mods, it depends on what kind of game you want to play. The Extended Magazine offers an extra 10 rounds per magazine, leading to less-frequent reloads. Scatterfire takes the weapon's rate of fire to a whole new level, allowing the SMG to pump out lethal amounts of lead in a flash. Or if you want to take a stealthy approach, opt for the Suppressor to remain hidden on the minimap.

PRO TIP: STRONGSIDE

Nothing shoots faster than the R-97 Compact SMG when it's fitted with the Scatterfire mod. Use this configuration to dominate against Pilots, Grunts, and Spectres in close quarters.

R-97 Compact SMG Challenges

IF IT MOVES...

TIER	CRITERIA	REWARD
1	Kill 10 Enemies	500 XP
2	Kill 25 Enemies	1,000 XP, Suppressor Mod, Amped R-97 Burn Card
3	Kill 50 Enemies	2,500 XP, Amped R-97 Burn Card
4	Kill 100 Enemies	5,000 XP, Amped R-97 Burn Card
5	Kill 200 Enemies	10,000 XP, Amped R-97 Burn Card

TOP GUN

TIER	CRITERIA	REWARD
1	Kill 5 Pilots	500 XP
2	Kill 15 Pilots	1,000 XP, Scatterfire Mod, Amped R-97 Burn Card
3	Kill 30 Pilots	2,500 XP, Amped R-97 Burn Card
4	Kill 50 Pilots	5,000 XP, Amped R-97 Burn Card
5	Kill 75 Pilots	10,000 XP, Amped R-97 Burn Card

MACHINE WAR

TIER	CRITERIA	REWARD
1	Kill 10 Spectres	500 XP
2	Kill 25 Spectres	1,000 XP, Extended Magazine Mod, Amped R-97 Burn Card
3	Kill 50 Spectres	2,500 XP, Amped R-97 Burn Card
4	Kill 75 Spectres	5,000 XP, Amped R-97 Burn Card
5	Kill 100 Spectres	10,000 XP, Amped R-97 Burn Card

OFF THE DOME

TIER	CRITERIA	REWARD
1	Get 5 Headshots	500 XP
2	Get 15 Headshots	1,000 XP, Amped R-97 Burn Card
3	Get 30 Headshots	2,500 XP, Amped R-97 Burn Card
4	Get 50 Headshots	5,000 XP, Amped R-97 Burn Card
5	Get 75 Headshots	10,000 XP, Amped R-97 Burn Card

THE EXPENDABLES

TIER	CRITERIA	REWARD
1	Kill 10 Grunts	500 XP
2	Kill 25 Grunts	1,000 XP,Amped R-97 Burn Card
3	Kill 50 Grunts	2,500 XP, HCOG Attachment, Amped R-97 Burn Card
4	Kill 100 Grunts	5,000 XP, Amped R-97 Burn Card
5	Kill 200 Grunts	10,000 XP, Amped R-97 Burn Card

THIS IS MY WEAPON

TIER	CRITERIA	REWARD
1	Use Weapon for .5 Hour	500 XP
2	Use Weapon for 1 Hour	1,000 XP, Amped R-97 Burn Card
3	Use Weapon for 1.5 Hours	2,500 XP, Amped R-97 Burn Card
4	Use Weapon for 2 Hours	5,000 XP, Amped R-97 Burn Card
5	Use Weapon for 3 Hours	10,000 XP, Amped R-97 Burn Card

AWARDED BURN CARD

Amped R-97
Replace Primary Weapon with a more lethal R-97 Compact SMG
Merc gear. Better keep moving, nobody hires just one bounty hunter.
-Sarah, outside Cobalt Station

Amped R-97

LONGBOW-DMR SNIPER

MAGAZINE CAPACITY: 8 WEAPON UNLOCK: LEVEL 9

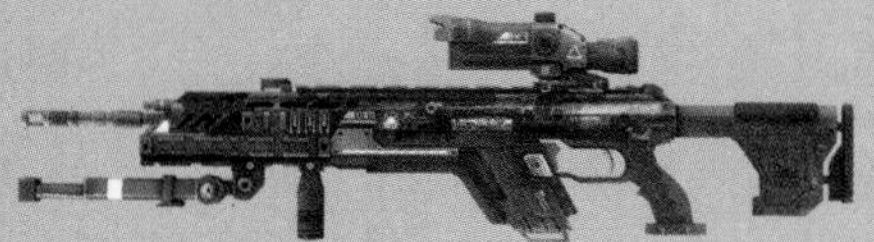

The Longbow-DMR is a semi-automatic sniper rifle. Its hyper-velocity round completely eliminates the need to lead targets, and allows the shooter to fire multiple shots quickly in succession.

STRENGTHS:

- Don't have to lead your shots at a distance
- Easily pick off Pilots that are on top of buildings

WEAKNESSES:

- Difficult to kill Pilots that are wall running and jumping around the map
- Close-range fights with this weapon are ineffective; you need to rely on your sidearm

WEAPON PERFORMANCE

DAMAGE

ACCURACY

RANGE

FIRE RATE

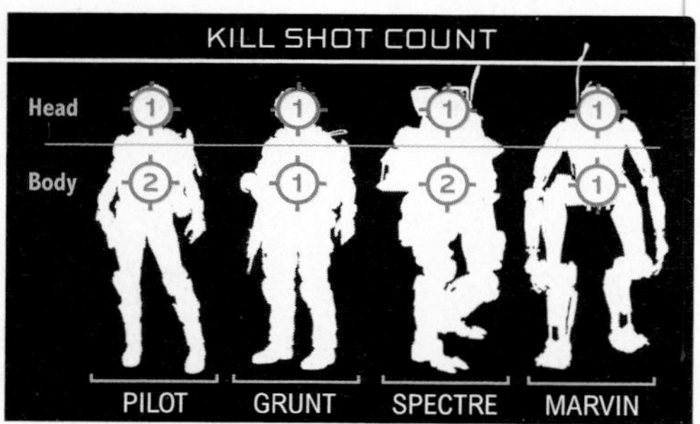

WEAPON ATTACHMENTS

IMAGE	NAME	DESCRIPTION	UNLOCK
	6X Zoom Scope	This scope provides fixed, long-range magnification for engaging very distant targets. However, your situational awareness may be compromised while it is in use, due to the high magnification.	Default Weapon Sight
	AOG	The AOG, or Advanced Optical Gunsight, is fixed at 2.4X magnification, and includes an integrated "current magazine capacity" readout with a backup numerical display. The AOG is ideal for combat at extended range.	The Expendables (I) Challenge: Kill 5 Grunts
	4.5X Zoom Scope	This scope provides fixed, mid-range magnification for highly fluid combat situations. It provides a balance of precision and ranged situational awareness.	If It Moves... (II) Challenge: Kill 25 Enemies

WEAPON MODS

IMAGE	NAME	DESCRIPTION	UNLOCK
	Extended Magazine	This mod increases the ammo capacity of the weapon, making it so that you don't have to reload as often.	Machine War (I) Challenge: Kill 5 Spectres
	Suppressor	This mod reduces the firing noise and muzzle flash of the weapon, making it ideal for taking your enemies by surprise.	If It Moves... (I) Challenge: Kill 10 Enemies
	Stabilizer	This mod reduces the amount of instability in the view when looking through the scope, making it easier to keep the crosshairs steady on a target.	Top Gun (I) Challenge: Kill 5 Pilots

Field Notes

- Not having to lead your shots makes this weapon strong for cross-map sniping of moving targets. This is not a run-and-gun type of weapon; find the best locations to set yourself up to pick off enemies from a distance.
- If the enemy Pilot is not moving, take the extra second to line up the headshot to guarantee the kill. Otherwise don't be afraid to miss a shot on a moving Pilot. This sniper rifle has a rapid rate of fire that you need to take advantage of because it takes two body shots to kill a Pilot.
- If you don't have the Suppressor equipped, you have to shoot the AI and then relocate to avoid enemy Pilots that will sneak up to your location. Otherwise, this weapon is fast at picking off a group of AI at a distance.
- When backing up your teammates, the Extended Magazine is a great way to have four more bullets in your magazine to give extra cover fire. When in doubt, use the Suppressor; it will allow you the opportunity to miss a few shots without giving away your position to the entire enemy team.

PRO TIP: WALSHY

Using the Longbow-DMR Sniper's default 6X Zoom Scope can be challenging. That's why I prefer the AOG. It offers ample magnification on most maps, and makes it easier to track (and hit) moving targets.

Longbow-DMR Sniper Challenges

IF IT MOVES...

TIER	CRITERIA	REWARD
1	Kill 10 Enemies	500 XP, Suppressor Mod
2	Kill 25 Enemies	1,000 XP, 4.5X Zoom Scope Attachment, Amped DMR Burn Card
3	Kill 50 Enemies	2,500 XP, Amped DMR Burn Card
4	Kill 100 Enemies	5,000 XP, Amped DMR Burn Card
5	Kill 150 Enemies	10,000 XP, Amped DMR Burn Card

TOP GUN

TIER	CRITERIA	REWARD
1	Kill 5 Pilots	500 XP, Stabilizer Mod
2	Kill 15 Pilots	1,000 XP, Amped DMR Burn Card
3	Kill 25 Pilots	2,500 XP, Amped DMR Burn Card
4	Kill 35 Pilots	5,000 XP, Amped DMR Burn Card
5	Kill 50 Pilots	10,000 XP, Amped DMR Burn Card

MACHINE WAR

TIER	CRITERIA	REWARD
1	Kill 5 Spectres	500 XP, Extended Magazine Mod
2	Kill 15 Spectres	1,000 XP, Amped DMR Burn Card
3	Kill 25 Spectres	2,500 XP, Amped DMR Burn Card
4	Kill 35 Spectres	5,000 XP, Amped DMR Burn Card
5	Kill 50 Spectres	10,000 XP, Amped DMR Burn Card

OFF THE DOME

TIER	CRITERIA	REWARD
1	Get 5 Headshots	500 XP
2	Get 15 Headshots	1,000 XP, Amped DMR Burn Card
3	Get 30 Headshots	2,500 XP, Amped DMR Burn Card
4	Get 50 Headshots	5,000 XP, Amped DMR Burn Card
5	Get 75 Headshots	10,000 XP, Amped DMR Burn Card

THE EXPENDABLES

TIER	CRITERIA	REWARD
1	Kill 5 Grunts	500 XP, AOG Attachment
2	Kill 15 Grunts	1,000 XP, Amped DMR Burn Card
3	Kill 50 Grunts	2,500 XP, Amped DMR Burn Card
4	Kill 100 Grunts	5,000 XP, Amped DMR Burn Card
5	Kill 150 Grunts	10,000 XP, Amped DMR Burn Card

THIS IS MY WEAPON

TIER	CRITERIA	REWARD
1	Use Weapon for .5 Hour	500 XP
2	Use Weapon for 1 Hour	1,000 XP, Amped DMR Burn Card
3	Use Weapon for 1.5 Hours	2,500 XP, Amped DMR Burn Card
4	Use Weapon for 2 Hours	5,000 XP, Amped DMR Burn Card
5	Use Weapon for 3 Hours	10,000 XP, Amped DMR Burn Card

AWARDED BURN CARD

Amped DMR
Replace Primary Weapon with a sonar scope Longbow-DMR Sniper
Synthetics has its advantages.
I can see from a cliff that you can't even imagine.
-Spyglass

Amped DMR

G2A4 RIFLE

MAGAZINE CAPACITY: 14 WEAPON UNLOCK: LEVEL 18

Despite recent advances in weapons technology, the older G2A4 semi-automatic rifle remains a favorite of special forces units due to its high damage and extremely precise fire—a testament to its high level of craftsmanship.

STRENGTHS:

- Can quickly drop Pilots and minions with one shot to the head

WEAKNESSES:

- Small magazine capacity

WEAPON PERFORMANCE

DAMAGE

ACCURACY

RANGE

FIRE RATE

KILL SHOT COUNT

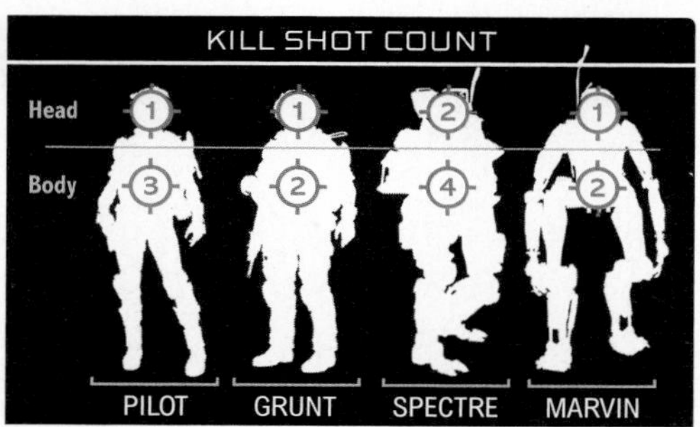

WEAPON ATTACHMENTS

IMAGE	NAME	DESCRIPTION	UNLOCK
	Iron Sights	Factory issue gunsights are cheap and reliable, but visibility through them can be somewhat limited.	Default Weapon Sight
	Holosight	The Holosight's optics are fixed at a 2.1X zoom factor. The sight picture is designed to induce tighter visual perception, making it effective both at range and in close quarters. The Holosight is equipped with an integrated ammunition readout.	The Expendables (II) Challenge: Kill 25 Grunts
	HCOG	The Holographic Combat Optical Gunsight has an open sight picture, making it easier to acquire and track targets, particularly in the vertical. The gunsight is fixed at 1.85X magnification, and includes integrated ammunition readouts.	The Expendables (III) Challenge: Kill 50 Grunts
	AOG	The AOG, or Advanced Optical Gunsight, is fixed at 2.4X magnification, and includes an integrated "current magazine capacity" readout with a backup numerical display. The AOG is ideal for combat at extended range.	If It Moves… (III) Challenge: Kill 50 Enemies

WEAPON MODS

IMAGE	NAME	DESCRIPTION	UNLOCK
	Extended Magazine	This mod increases the ammo capacity of the weapon, making it so that you don't have to reload as often.	Machine War (II) Challenge: Kill 25 Spectres
	Match Trigger	This mod allows you to fire the weapon as fast as you can pull the trigger. This lets you smoothly transition between firing precise single shots at range and firing rapidly at close quarters.	Top Gun (II) Challenge: Kill 15 Pilots
	Suppressor	This mod reduces the firing noise and muzzle flash of the weapon, making it ideal for taking your enemies by surprise.	If It Moves… (II) Challenge: Kill 25 Enemies

Field Notes

- The G2A4 Rifle is the old school weapon in the mix of weapons. It is the only semi-automatic weapon in the game and does high damage but has a low magazine capacity. With its high accuracy, this weapon is great for long-range battles.
- Against Pilots this weapon is most used for longer-range battles, so keep your distance and pick off Pilots in the distance. With its semi-automatic functionality you'll have to be extremely accurate with your aim. At close range, prepare to tap your trigger as fast as you can.
- The smaller magazine makes this weapon less effective against minions. You don't want to get ambushed by a Pilot when you're taking out minions since you'll most likely run out of ammo and have to reload. If you're going to kill Grunts or Spectres, keep your distance and watch out for incoming Pilots.
- The Match Trigger mod is an excellent way to increase your rate of fire, but it also allows you to fire rapidly in a close-quarter battle. Attaching the Suppressor is also the best way to keep your position hidden on the minimap when firing.

PRO TIP: WALSHY

The G2A4 Rifle really shines during long- and mid-range engagements. Equip it with a Suppressor and sneak around the map while silently picking off enemy Pilots and minions, delivering lethal headshots from a distance.

G2A4 Rifle Challenges

IF IT MOVES...

TIER	CRITERIA	REWARD
1	Kill 10 Enemies	500 XP
2	Kill 25 Enemies	1,000 XP, Suppressor Mod, Amped G2A4 Burn Card
3	Kill 50 Enemies	2,500 XP, AOG Attachment, Amped G2A4 Burn Card
4	Kill 100 Enemies	5,000 XP, Amped G2A4 Burn Card
5	Kill 200 Enemies	10,000 XP, Amped G2A4 Burn Card

THE EXPENDABLES

TIER	CRITERIA	REWARD
1	Kill 10 Grunts	500 XP
2	Kill 25 Grunts	1,000 XP, Holosight Attachment, Amped G2A4 Burn Card
3	Kill 50 Grunts	2,500 XP, HCOG Attachment, Amped G2A4 Burn Card
4	Kill 100 Grunts	5,000 XP, Amped G2A4 Burn Card
5	Kill 200 Grunts	10,000 XP, Amped G2A4 Burn Card

TOP GUN

TIER	CRITERIA	REWARD
1	Kill 5 Pilots	500 XP
2	Kill 15 Pilots	1,000 XP, Match Trigger Mod, Amped G2A4 Burn Card
3	Kill 30 Pilots	2,500 XP, Amped G2A4 Burn Card
4	Kill 50 Pilots	5,000 XP, Amped G2A4 Burn Card
5	Kill 75 Pilots	10,000 XP, Amped G2A4 Burn Card

THIS IS MY WEAPON

TIER	CRITERIA	REWARD
1	Use Weapon for .5 Hour	500 XP
2	Use Weapon for 1 Hour	1,000 XP, Amped G2A4 Burn Card
3	Use Weapon for 1.5 Hours	2,500 XP, Amped G2A4 Burn Card
4	Use Weapon for 2 Hours	5,000 XP, Amped G2A4 Burn Card
5	Use Weapon for 3 Hours	10,000 XP, Amped G2A4 Burn Card

MACHINE WAR

TIER	CRITERIA	REWARD
1	Kill 10 Spectres	500 XP
2	Kill 25 Spectres	1,000 XP, Extended Magazine Mod, Amped G2A4 Burn Card
3	Kill 50 Spectres	2,500 XP, Amped G2A4 Burn Card
4	Kill 75 Spectres	5,000 XP, Amped G2A4 Burn Card
5	Kill 100 Spectres	10,000 XP, Amped G2A4 Burn Card

OFF THE DOME

TIER	CRITERIA	REWARD
1	Get 5 Headshots	500 XP
2	Get 15 Headshots	1,000 XP, Amped G2A4 Burn Card
3	Get 30 Headshots	2,500 XP, Amped G2A4 Burn Card
4	Get 50 Headshots	5,000 XP, Amped G2A4 Burn Card
5	Get 75 Headshots	10,000 XP, Amped G2A4 Burn Card

Awarded Burn Card

Amped G2A4
Replace Primary Weapon with a more lethal G2A4 Rifle
Grab the rifle, boy.
There's something moving in the fields,
and it ain't natural.
-Albert Woodman, Colony hydro farmer

Amped G2A4

HEMLOK BF-R

MAGAZINE CAPACITY: 24 WEAPON UNLOCK: LEVEL 29

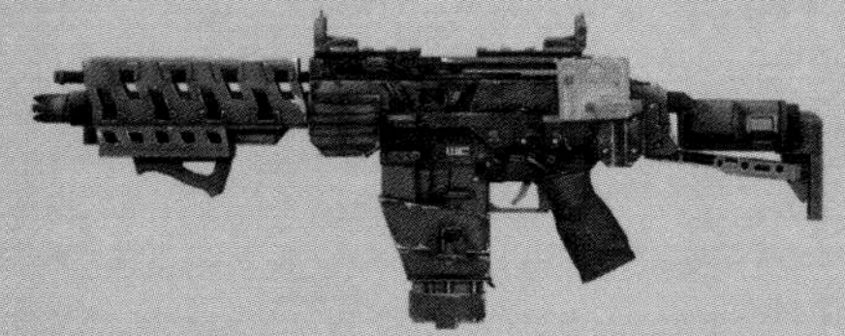

The factory issue Hemlok fires a three-round burst. While this can be a liability at short range, this tradeoff allowed the engineers at TW Ordnance to deliver a weapon with a good balance of long-range accuracy, damage, and rate of fire.

STRENGTHS:

- Accurately fires multiple rounds with impressive accuracy
- Solid mid-range weapon

WEAKNESSES:

- Poor close-quarter performance
- Diminished accuracy due to recoil

WEAPON PERFORMANCE

DAMAGE

ACCURACY

RANGE

FIRE RATE

KILL SHOT COUNT*

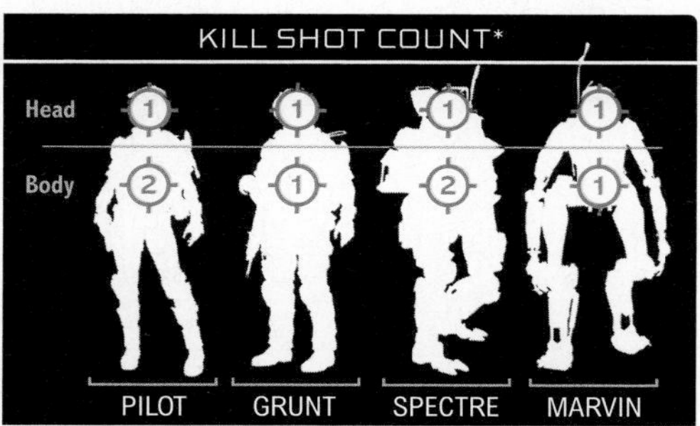

	PILOT	GRUNT	SPECTRE	MARVIN
Head	1	1	1	1
Body	2	1	2	1

* = based on three-round burst

WEAPON ATTACHMENTS

IMAGE	NAME	DESCRIPTION	UNLOCK
	Iron Sights	Factory issue gunsights are cheap and reliable, but visibility through them can be somewhat limited.	Default Weapon Sight
	HCOG	The Holographic Combat Optical Gunsight has an open sight picture, making it easier to acquire targets, particularly in the vertical. The gunsight is fixed at 1.85X magnification, and includes integrated ammunition readouts.	If It Moves... (III) Challenge: Kill 50 Enemies
	Holosight	The Holosight's optics are fixed at 2.1X zoom factor. The sight picture is designed to induce a tighter visual perception, making it effective at range and in close quarters. The Holosight is equipped with an integrated ammunition readout.	The Expendables (III) Challenge: Kill 50 Grunts
	AOG	The AOG, or Advanced Optical Gunsight, is fixed at 2.4X magnification, and includes an integrated "current magazine capacity" readout with a backup numerical display. The AOG is ideal for combat at extended range.	The Expendables (II) Challenge: Kill 25 Grunts

WEAPON MODS

IMAGE	NAME	DESCRIPTION	UNLOCK
	Extended Magazine	This mod increases the ammo capacity of the weapon, so that you don't have to reload as often.	Machine War (II) Challenge: Kill 25 Spectres
	Suppressor	This mod reduces the firing noise and muzzle flash of the weapon, making it ideal for taking your enemies by surprise.	If It Moves… (II) Challenge: Kill 25 Enemies
	Starburst	This mod converts the Hemlok's burst fire rate to five rounds per shot.	Top Gun (II) Challenge: Kill 15 Pilots

Field Notes

- The Hemlok BF-R is unique as the only burst-fire weapon available. The weapon's three-round burst offers impressive damage output, taking down most threats with a single burst. This makes it a very effective weapon when engaging targets at long and intermediate ranges. However, the Hemlok is easily outclassed at close range by all of the automatic weapons. Tap fire as fast as possible to maintain a high rate of fire during close-quarter encounters.
- When engaging Pilots with the Hemlok, keep your distance and do your best to avoid detection, preferably by equipping the Suppressor mod. Due to their quick movements, Pilots are difficult to track and hit. Fortunately the weapon can fire several bursts in quick succession, making it easier to score hits on fast-moving targets. If enemy Pilots close on you to short range, consider switching to your sidearm.
- This is the ultimate minion-killing weapon, dropping most threats with a single burst. Hold back and engage minions at mid-range, where they pose minimal risk. This allows you to down entire squads of Grunts and Spectres without reloading. But while hunting minions, watch out for enemy Pilots trying to sneak up on you.
- When carrying the Hemlok, stealth is key. Therefore consider opting for the Suppressor to keep you off the minimap. If you're less concerned with stealth, the Starburst mod upgrades the weapon, allowing it to fire a five-round burst with each pull of the trigger. Five-round bursts deal much more damage, but also consume ammo at a quicker rate. Still, hitting a Pilot (or any target) with a five-round burst pretty much guarantees a kill. But you may need to engage targets at closer ranges to ensure all five rounds hit your target; recoil leads to a wider spread.

PRO TIP: STRONGSIDE

The Hemlok BF-R balances accuracy and rate of fire. It's best deployed as a mid-range weapon where you can pick off most enemies with a single burst. In close quarters, be ready to tap fire—keep shooting until your target drops.

Hemlok BF-R Challenges

IF IT MOVES...

TIER	CRITERIA	REWARD
1	Kill 10 Enemies	500 XP
2	Kill 25 Enemies	1,000 XP, Suppressor Mod, Amped Hemlok Burn Card
3	Kill 50 Enemies	2,500 XP, HCOG Attachment, Amped Hemlok Burn Card
4	Kill 100 Enemies	5,000 XP, Amped Hemlok Burn Card
5	Kill 200 Enemies	10,000 XP, Amped Hemlok Burn Card

THE EXPENDABLES

TIER	CRITERIA	REWARD
1	Kill 10 Grunts	500 XP
2	Kill 25 Grunts	1,000 XP, AOG Attachment, Amped Hemlok Burn Card
3	Kill 50 Grunts	2,500 XP, Holosight Attachment, Amped Hemlok Burn Card
4	Kill 100 Grunts	5,000 XP, Amped Hemlok Burn Card
5	Kill 200 Grunts	10,000 XP, Amped Hemlok Burn Card

TOP GUN

TIER	CRITERIA	REWARD
1	Kill 5 Pilots	500 XP
2	Kill 15 Pilots	1,000 XP, Starburst Mod, Amped Hemlok Burn Card
3	Kill 30 Pilots	2,500 XP, Amped Hemlok Burn Card
4	Kill 50 Pilots	5,000 XP, Amped Hemlok Burn Card
5	Kill 75 Pilots	10,000 XP, Amped Hemlok Burn Card

THIS IS MY WEAPON

TIER	CRITERIA	REWARD
1	Use Weapon for .5 Hour	500 XP
2	Use Weapon for 1 Hour	1,000 XP, Amped Hemlok Burn Card
3	Use Weapon for 1.5 Hours	2,500 XP, Amped Hemlok Burn Card
4	Use Weapon for 2 Hours	5,000 XP, Amped Hemlok Burn Card
5	Use Weapon for 3 Hours	10,000 XP, Amped Hemlok Burn Card

MACHINE WAR

TIER	CRITERIA	REWARD
1	Kill 10 Spectres	500 XP
2	Kill 25 Spectres	1,000 XP, Extended Magazine Mod, Amped Hemlok Burn Card
3	Kill 50 Spectres	2,500 XP, Amped Hemlok Burn Card
4	Kill 75 Spectres	5,000 XP, Amped Hemlok Burn Card
5	Kill 100 Spectres	10,000 XP, Amped Hemlok Burn Card

OFF THE DOME

TIER	CRITERIA	REWARD
1	Get 5 Headshots	500 XP
2	Get 15 Headshots	1,000 XP, Amped Hemlok Burn Card
3	Get 30 Headshots	2,500 XP, Amped Hemlok Burn Card
4	Get 50 Headshots	5,000 XP, Amped Hemlok Burn Card
5	Get 75 Headshots	10,000 XP, Amped Hemlok Burn Card

AWARDED BURN CARD

Amped Hemlok
Replace Primary Weapon with a more lethal Hemlok BF-R
Applying the Socratic method. -Bish

Amped Hemlok

C.A.R. SMG

MAGAZINE CAPACITY: 30 WEAPON UNLOCK: LEVEL 34

The C.A.R. (Combat Advanced Round) submachine gun is designed to fire a more powerful round that provides greater damage and accuracy at range, at the cost of fire rate and capacity.

STRENGTHS:

- High rate of fire beneficial in close quarters
- Dampened recoil makes weapon accurate at intermediate range

WEAKNESSES:

- Lower rate of fire/magazine capacity than R-97 Compact SMG
- Outclassed at long range by rifles

WEAPON PERFORMANCE

DAMAGE

ACCURACY

RANGE

FIRE RATE

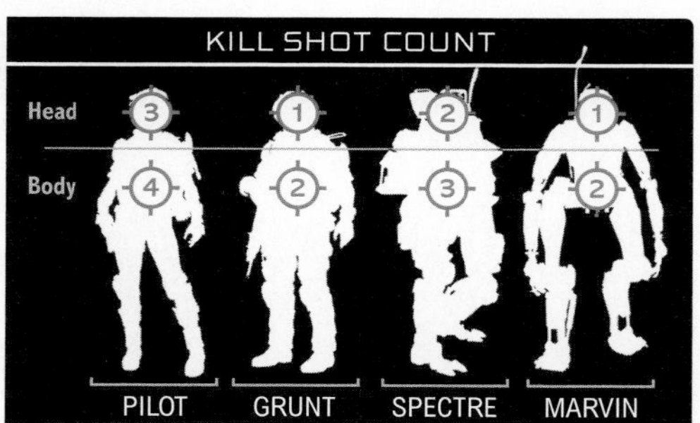

WEAPON ATTACHMENTS

IMAGE	NAME	DESCRIPTION	UNLOCK
	Iron Sights	Factory issue gunsights are cheap and reliable, but visibility through them can be somewhat limited.	Default Weapon Sight
	HCOG	The Holographic Combat Optical Gunsight has an open sight picture, making it easier to acquire and attack targets, particularly in the vertical. The gunsight is fixed at 1.85X magnification, and includes integrated ammunition readouts.	The Expendables (III) Challenge: Kill 50 Grunts

WEAPON MODS

IMAGE	NAME	DESCRIPTION	UNLOCK
	Counterweight	This mod dampens the recoil of the weapon, allowing you to maintain higher accuracy while moving, including wall running.	Top Gun (II) Challenge: Kill 15 Pilots
	Extended Magazine	This mod increases the ammo capacity of the weapon, making it so you don't have to reload as often.	Machine War (II) Challenge: Kill 25 Spectres
	Suppressor	This mod reduces the firing noise and muzzle flash of the weapon, making it ideal for taking your enemies by surprise.	If It Moves... (II) Challenge: Kill 25 Enemies

Field Notes

- The C.A.R. SMG has a lower rate of fire when compared to the R-97 Compact SMG, but what it lacks in fire rate it makes up for in damage output and accuracy. This weapon provides players with the versatility of clearing out waves of Grunts and Spectres while at the same time providing the right amount of firepower to mow down Pilots.
- With a stable and accurate shot, this weapon can make quick work of enemy Pilots. If long-distance shooting isn't your forte, don't let that worry you. This weapon has the perfect magazine capacity, allowing players to hold down the trigger in medium to close distances to make light work of the opponent. When facing off against enemy Pilots, try to close the distance to use this weapon effectively.
- This weapon is very useful against Grunts and Spectres. With thirty bullets in the magazine, players will want to quickly become friendly with the spawn locations of the minions. The C.A.R. SMG allows you to lay down steel and helps you quickly gain access to your Titan. This will then allow you to engage opposing Pilots more effectively.
- If you want to feel the real power of the C.A.R. SMG, equip the Counterweight attachment. This will reduce the recoil, allowing you to engage with enemies from a distance. Enemies will think you have a rifle in hand and will try to close the distance, only to find that you have an SMG that specializes in close quarters. The Extended Magazine adds ten extra bullets to each magazine clip, giving you a total of forty bullets per magazine. Thirty bullets seems to be the right amount for this weapon, but if you are feeling trigger happy this is a great attachment to equip.

PRO TIP: FLAMESWORD

Feel the full power of the C.A.R. SMG when fitting it with the Counterweight mod and the Run N Gun Kit. The Counterweight reduces recoil while the Run N Gun Kit allows you to fire the weapon while sprinting, perfect for chasing down enemy Pilots.

C.A.R. SMG Challenges

IF IT MOVES...

TIER	CRITERIA	REWARD
1	Kill 10 Enemies	500 XP
2	Kill 25 Enemies	1,000 XP, Suppressor Mod, Amped C.A.R. Burn Card
3	Kill 50 Enemies	2,500 XP, Amped C.A.R. Burn Card
4	Kill 100 Enemies	5,000 XP, Amped C.A.R. Burn Card
5	Kill 200 Enemies	10,000 XP, Amped C.A.R. Burn Card

TOP GUN

TIER	CRITERIA	REWARD
1	Kill 5 Pilots	500 XP
2	Kill 15 Pilots	1,000 XP, Counterweight Mod, Amped C.A.R. Burn Card
3	Kill 30 Pilots	2,500 XP, Amped C.A.R. Burn Card
4	Kill 50 Pilots	5,000 XP, Amped C.A.R. Burn Card
5	Kill 75 Pilots	10,000 XP, Amped C.A.R. Burn Card

MACHINE WAR

TIER	CRITERIA	REWARD
1	Kill 10 Spectres	500 XP
2	Kill 25 Spectres	1,0000 XP, Extended Magazine Mod, Amped C.A.R. Burn Card
3	Kill 50 Spectres	2,500 XP, Amped C.A.R. Burn Card
4	Kill 75 Spectres	5,000 XP, Amped C.A.R. Burn Card
5	Kill 100 Spectres	10,000 XP, Amped C.A.R. Burn Card

OFF THE DOME

TIER	CRITERIA	REWARD
1	Get 5 Headshots	500 XP
2	Get 15 Headshots	1,000 XP, Amped C.A.R. Burn Card
3	Get 30 Headshots	2,500 XP, Amped C.A.R. Burn Card
4	Get 50 Headshots	5,000 XP, Amped C.A.R. Burn Card
5	Get 75 Headshots	10,000 XP, Amped C.A.R. Burn Card

THE EXPENDABLES

TIER	CRITERIA	REWARD
1	Kill 10 Grunts	500 XP
2	Kill 25 Grunts	1,000 XP, Amped C.A.R. Burn Card
3	Kill 50 Grunts	2,500 XP, HCOG Attachment, Amped C.A.R. Burn Card
4	Kill 100 Grunts	5,000 XP, Amped C.A.R. Burn Card
5	Kill 200 Grunts	10,000 XP, Amped C.A.R. Burn Card

THIS IS MY WEAPON

TIER	CRITERIA	REWARD
1	Use Weapon for .5 Hour	500 XP
2	Use Weapon for 1 Hour	1,000 XP, Amped C.A.R. Burn Card
3	Use Weapon for 1.5 Hours	2,500 XP, Amped C.A.R. Burn Card
4	Use Weapon for 2 Hours	5,000 XP, Amped C.A.R. Burn Card
5	Use Weapon for 3 Hours	10,000 XP, Amped C.A.R. Burn Card

AWARDED BURN CARD

Amped C.A.R.
Replace Primary Weapon with a more lethal C.A.R. SMG
It's not all trash on the black market. -Blisk

Amped C.A.R.

PRIMARY WEAPONS

SPITFIRE LMG

MAGAZINE CAPACITY: 80 WEAPON UNLOCK: LEVEL 39

The Spitfire Light Machine Gun recoils heavily when first fired, but quickly settles into a tight firing pattern. The manufacturer strongly recommends sustained saturating fire, instead of short controlled bursts.

STRENGTHS:

- Large magazine capacity
- Accuracy increases with sustained fire

WEAKNESSES:

- First shots inaccurate due to harsh recoil
- Requires prolonged bursts before weapon settles

WEAPON PERFORMANCE

DAMAGE

ACCURACY

RANGE

FIRE RATE

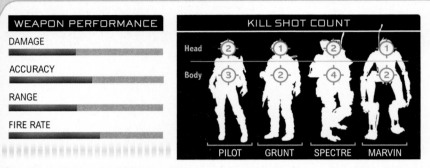

KILL SHOT COUNT

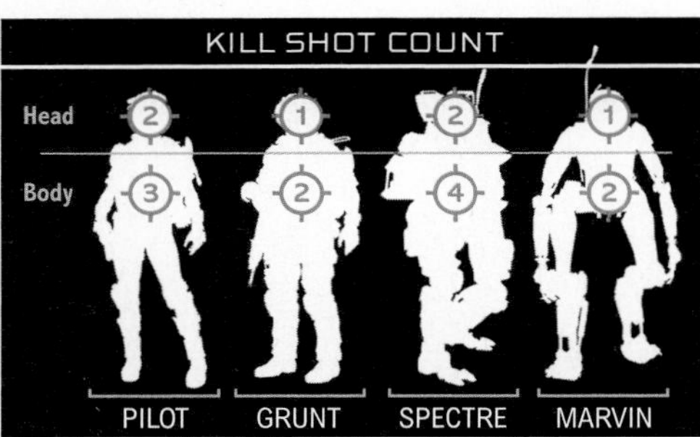

WEAPON ATTACHMENTS

IMAGE	NAME	DESCRIPTION	UNLOCK
	Iron Sights	Factory issue gunsights are cheap and reliable, but visibility through them can be somewhat limited.	Default Weapon Sight
	HCOG	The Holographic Combat Optical Gunsight has an open sight picture, making it easier to acquire and track targets, particularly in the vertical. The gunsight is fixed at 1.85X magnification, and includes integrated ammunition readouts.	The Expendables (III) Challenge: Kill 50 Grunts
	Holosight	The Holosight's optics are fixed at a 2.1X zoom factor. The sight picture is designed to induce a tighter visual perception, making it effective both at range and in close quarters. The Holosight is equipped with an integrated ammunition readout.	The Expendables (II) Challenge: Kill 25 Grunts
	AOG	The AOG, or Advanced Optical Gunsight, is fixed at 2.4X magnification, and includes an integrated "current magazine capacity" readout with a backup numerical display. The AOG is ideal for combat at extended range.	If It Moves… (III) Challenge: Kill 50 Enemies

WEAPON MODS

IMAGE	NAME	DESCRIPTION	UNLOCK
	Extended Magazine	This mod increases the ammo capacity of the weapon, making it so that you don't have to reload as often.	Machine War (II) Challenge: Kill 25 Spectres
	Slammer	When you rodeo attack an enemy Titan, this mod will significantly increase the damage your weapon inflicts to that Titan.	Top Gun (II) Challenge: Kill 15 Pilots

Field Notes

- This weapon has the largest magazine capacity of all the primary weapons. The Spitfire LMG is also the most powerful weapon to rodeo attack a Titan when using the Slammer mod.
- Try to keep the battles at a closer range rather than longer when engaging Pilots. This weapon is difficult against Pilots since the weapon recoil is much greater than the other primary weapons. If you can control the recoil, this can be a deadly weapon. This weapon is also great for spraying in those close-mid-range battles.
- Against minions this weapon is a beast. You're able to mow through minions and then jump straight into a Pilot battle without having to reload. Also, using hip fire against minions will keep you moving quick from target to target. But beware: you will be exposing yourself on the minimap and attracting enemy Pilots. There is no Suppressor for this weapon.
- The Extended Magazine gives you an additional sixteen bullets, making this high-ammo weapon even more effective against minions and for controlling a close-quarter area. The Slammer mod makes the Spitfire LMG the go-to weapon when you want to rodeo attack a Titan. The Slammer increases the damage immensely and is the strongest weapon to rodeo attack a Titan. If aimed at the enemy Titan's weak spot during a rodeo attack, it will take less than a magazine to destroy the Titan. Keep a Custom Pilot loadout with the Slammer so when you see the opportunity to rodeo, you will be ready!

PRO TIP: STRONGSIDE

Even when hip firing, the Spitfire LMG is great for laying waste to large groups of Grunts and Spectres. But the weapon is even more effective when performing a rodeo attack on an enemy Titan, particularly when equipped with the Slammer mod.

Spitfire LMG Challenges

IF IT MOVES...

TIER	CRITERIA	REWARD
1	Kill 10 Enemies	500 XP
2	Kill 25 Enemies	1,000 XP, Amped LMG Burn Card
3	Kill 50 Enemies	2,500 XP, AOG Attachment, Amped LMG Burn Card
4	Kill 100 Enemies	5,000 XP, Amped LMG Burn Card
5	Kill 200 Enemies	10,000 XP, Amped LMG Burn Card

TOP GUN

TIER	CRITERIA	REWARD
1	Kill 5 Pilots	500 XP
2	Kill 15 Pilots	1,000 XP, Slammer Mod, Amped LMG Burn Card
3	Kill 30 Pilots	2,500 XP, Amped LMG Burn Card
4	Kill 50 Pilots	5,000 XP, Amped LMG Burn Card
5	Kill 75 Pilots	10,000 XP, Amped LMG Burn Card

MACHINE WAR

TIER	CRITERIA	REWARD
1	Kill 10 Spectres	500 XP
2	Kill 25 Spectres	1,000 XP, Extended Magazine Mod, Amped LMG Burn Card
3	Kill 50 Spectres	2,500 XP, Amped LMG Burn Card
4	Kill 75 Spectres	5,000 XP, Amped LMG Burn Card
5	Kill 100 Spectres	10,000 XP, Amped LMG Burn Card

OFF THE DOME

TIER	CRITERIA	REWARD
1	Get 5 Headshots	500 XP
2	Get 15 Headshots	1,000 XP, Amped LMG Burn Card
3	Get 30 Headshots	2,500 XP, Amped LMG Burn Card
4	Get 50 Headshots	5,000 XP, Amped LMG Burn Card
5	Get 75 Headshots	10,000 XP, Amped LMG Burn Card

THE EXPENDABLES

TIER	CRITERIA	REWARD
1	Kill 10 Grunts	500 XP
2	Kill 25 Grunts	1,000 XP, Holosight Attachment, Amped LMG Burn Card
3	Kill 50 Grunts	2,500 XP, HCOG Attachment, Amped LMG Burn Card
4	Kill 100 Grunts	5,000 XP, Amped LMG Burn Card
5	Kill 200 Grunts	10,000 XP, Amped LMG Burn Card

THIS IS MY WEAPON

TIER	CRITERIA	REWARD
1	Use Weapon for .5 Hour	500 XP
2	Use Weapon for 1 Hour	1,000 XP, Amped LMG Burn Card
3	Use Weapon for 1.5 Hours	2,500 XP, Amped LMG Burn Card
4	Use Weapon for 2 Hours	5,000 XP, Amped LMG Burn Card
5	Use Weapon for 3 Hours	10,000 XP, Amped LMG Burn Card

Awarded Burn Card

Amped LMG
Replace Primary Weapon with a rapid-fire Spitfire LMG
I approve these changes.
-Charles Griffith, Pilot

Amped LMG

KRABER-AP SNIPER

MAGAZINE CAPACITY: 5 WEAPON UNLOCK: LEVEL 44

The Kraber fires a unique round that ensures "one-shot, one-kill" results against human-scale targets. However, considerable judgment in leading is required, making this a difficult weapon to use against moving targets.

STRENGTHS:
- One-shot kill damage
- Great long-range weapon

WEAKNESSES:
- Not effective close range
- Have to lead your shots at a distance

WEAPON PERFORMANCE

DAMAGE

ACCURACY

RANGE

FIRE RATE

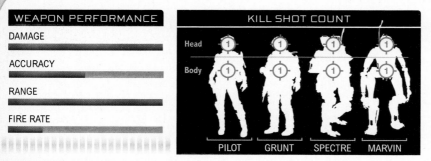

KILL SHOT COUNT

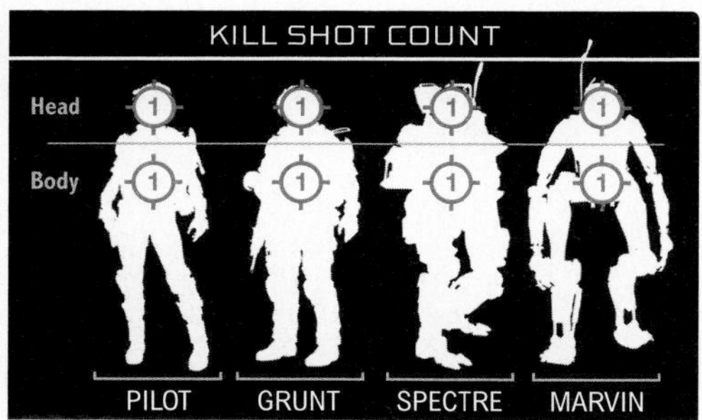

WEAPON ATTACHMENTS

IMAGE	NAME	DESCRIPTION	UNLOCK
	6X Zoom Scope	This scope provides fixed, long-range magnification for engaging very distant targets. However, your situational awareness may be compromised while it is in use, due to the high magnification.	Default Weapon Sight
	AOG	The AOG, or Advanced Optical Gunsight, is fixed at 2.4X magnification, and includes an integrated "current magazine capacity" readout with a backup numerical display. The AOG is ideal for combat at extended range.	The Expendables (I) Challenge: Kill 5 Grunts
	4.5X Zoom Scope	This scope provides fixed, mid-range magnification for highly fluid combat situations. It provides a balance of precision and ranged situational awareness.	If It Moves... (II) Challenge: Kill 15 Enemies

WEAPON MODS

IMAGE	NAME	DESCRIPTION	UNLOCK
	Extended Magazine	This mod increases the ammo capacity of the weapon, making it so that you don't have to reload as often.	Machine War (I) Challenge: Kill 1 Spectre
	Suppressor	This mod reduces the firing noise and muzzle flash of the weapon, making it ideal for taking your enemies by surprise.	If It Moves... (I) Challenge: Kill 5 Enemies
	Stabilizer	This mod reduces the amount of instability in the view when looking through the scope, making it easier to keep the crosshairs steady on a target.	Top Gun (I) Challenge: Kill 1 Pilot

Field Notes

- This one-shot-kill weapon is great for long-range fights, but if you get really confident with the weapon, you can be a threat mid-range with a well-placed shot on enemy Pilots.
- This weapon is difficult to snipe Pilots with when they are wall running and double jumping—try to catch them off-guard when they are on top of a roof. Distance is your friend when you are sniping. Get in a elevated perch away from danger so you can pick off enemy Pilots without the risk of dying. Keep in mind that you have to lead your shot due to the weapon's low bullet velocity. If enemy Pilots are sniping or holding a static position, this is the weapon to take them out with.
- If your goal is to take out minions, this is not the best weapon. With the slowest rate of fire and smallest magazine capacity, this gun is mainly an anti-Pilot weapon.
- If you want to sit back and support, be sure to use the default 6X Zoom Scope or the 4.5X Zoom Scope and find the highest perch available. If you want to move up with your team and be a mid-range threat, equip the AOG scope along with a Suppressor to conceal your position.

PRO TIP: WALSHY

Initially, play it safe when using the Kraber-AP Sniper, engaging targets from long range. Once you've unlocked the AOG attachment, consider getting closer to the action—this lower magnification sight makes it easier to operate the weapon at mid-range.

Kraber-AP Sniper Challenges

IF IT MOVES...

TIER	CRITERIA	REWARD
1	Kill 5 Enemies	500 XP, Suppressor Mod
2	Kill 15 Enemies	1,000 XP, 4.5X Zoom Scope Attachment, Amped Kraber Burn Card
3	Kill 25 Enemies	2,500 XP, Amped Kraber Burn Card
4	Kill 50 Enemies	5,000 XP, Amped Kraber Burn Card
5	Kill 100 Enemies	10,000 XP, Amped Kraber Burn Card

THE EXPENDABLES

TIER	CRITERIA	REWARD
1	Kill 5 Grunts	500 XP, AOG Attachment
2	Kill 15 Grunts	1,000 XP, Amped Kraber Burn Card
3	Kill 25 Grunts	2,500 XP, Amped Kraber Burn Card
4	Kill 35 Grunts	5,000 XP, Amped Kraber Burn Card
5	Kill 50 Grunts	10,000 XP, Amped Kraber Burn Card

TOP GUN

TIER	CRITERIA	REWARD
1	Kill 1 Pilots	500 XP, Stabilizer Mod
2	Kill 5 Pilots	1,000 XP, Amped Kraber Burn Card
3	Kill 10 Pilots	2,500 XP, Amped Kraber Burn Card
4	Kill 15 Pilots	5,000 XP, Amped Kraber Burn Card
5	Kill 25 Pilots	10,000 XP, Amped Kraber Burn Card

THIS IS MY WEAPON

TIER	CRITERIA	REWARD
1	Use Weapon for .5 Hour	500 XP
2	Use Weapon for 1 Hour	1,000 XP, Amped Kraber Burn Card
3	Use Weapon for 1.5 Hours	2,500 XP, Amped Kraber Burn Card
4	Use Weapon for 2 Hours	5,000 XP, Amped Kraber Burn Card
5	Use Weapon for 3 Hours	10,000 XP, Amped Kraber Burn Card

MACHINE WAR

TIER	CRITERIA	REWARD
1	Kill 1 Spectres	500 XP, Extended Magazine Mod
2	Kill 5 Spectres	1,000 XP, Amped Kraber Burn Card
3	Kill 10 Spectres	2,500 XP, Amped Kraber Burn Card
4	Kill 15 Spectres	5,000 XP, Amped Kraber Burn Card
5	Kill 25 Spectres	10,000 XP, Amped Kraber Burn Card

AWARDED BURN CARD

Amped Kraber
Replace Primary Weapon with a Kraber-AP Sniper that fires explosive rounds
Does everything need to explode?
-Sarah

Amped Kraber

SIDEARMS

Every Pilot needs a backup for those times when their primary weapon runs out of ammo. Although there are only three to choose from, these sidearms have distinct characteristics, giving Pilots ample tactical variety. Unlike the primary weapons, sidearms cannot be fitted with attachments or mods. However, you can complete a number of challenges with each sidearm to earn bonus XP and Burn Cards.

RE-45 AUTOPISTOL

MAGAZINE CAPACITY: **20** WEAPON UNLOCK: **LEVEL 1**

The RE-45 is a fully automatic .45-caliber pistol, sacrificing damage and accuracy at longer distances for improved effectiveness at close range.

STRENGTHS:
- Fully automatic handgun ideal for close quarters

WEAKNESSES:
- Poor damage, accuracy, and range

WEAPON PERFORMANCE

DAMAGE

ACCURACY

RANGE

FIRE RATE

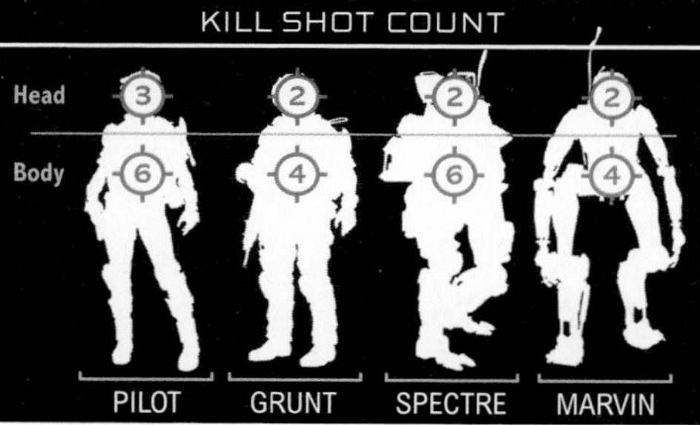

Field Notes

- Like most sidearms, the R-45 Autopistol is best utilized purely as a backup when your primary weapon is out of ammo—switching to your sidearm is always faster than reloading your primary. Due to its high rate of fire, it's easy to drop nearby threats with a quick burst, particularly if they're already injured or damaged. The weapon serves as a good complement to slow-firing, low-magazine-capacity weapons like the Kraber-AP Sniper.
- Don't try to hunt Pilots with this weapon unless you have the jump on your prey. While the RE-45 boasts a high rate of fire, it trails far behind in all other categories, putting you at a serious disadvantage while engaging enemy Pilots. That being said, the RE-45 is more than capable of finishing off an injured Pilot at close range. In this sense, the RE-45 is great for ending fights—just don't start one with it.
- While the RE-45 isn't the most effective weapon against minions, taking the fight to close range against a squad of Grunts is undeniably fun. At close range the RE-45 can tear through Grunts at a rapid pace. However, exercise caution when engaging Spectres—they take a considerable amount of damage before dropping, exposing you to potentially deadly return fire.

RE-45 Autopistol Challenges

IF IT MOVES...

TIER	CRITERIA	REWARD
1	Kill 10 Enemies	500 XP
2	Kill 25 Enemies	1,000 XP, Amped RE-45 Burn Card
3	Kill 50 Enemies	2,500 XP, Amped RE-45 Burn Card
4	Kill 100 Enemies	5,000 XP, Amped RE-45 Burn Card
5	Kill 150 Enemies	10,000 XP, Amped RE-45 Burn Card

TOP GUN

TIER	CRITERIA	REWARD
1	Kill 5 Pilots	500 XP
2	Kill 15 Pilots	1,000 XP, Amped RE-45 Burn Card
3	Kill 25 Pilots	2,500 XP, Amped RE-45 Burn Card
4	Kill 35 Pilots	5,000 XP, Amped RE-45 Burn Card
5	Kill 50 Pilots	10,000 XP, Amped RE-45 Burn Card

MACHINE WAR

TIER	CRITERIA	REWARD
1	Kill 10 Spectres	500 XP
2	Kill 25 Spectres	1,000 XP
3	Kill 50 Spectres	2,500 XP
4	Kill 100 Spectres	5,000 XP
5	Kill 200 Spectres	10,000 XP

OFF THE DOME

TIER	CRITERIA	REWARD
1	Get 5 Headshots	500 XP
2	Get 15 Headshots	1,000 XP, Amped RE-45 Burn Card
3	Get 25 Headshots	2,500 XP, Amped RE-45 Burn Card
4	Get 35 Headshots	5,000 XP, Amped RE-45 Burn Card
5	Get 50 Headshots	10,000 XP, Amped RE-45 Burn Card

THE EXPENDABLES

TIER	CRITERIA	REWARD
1	Kill 5 Grunts	500 XP
2	Kill 15 Grunts	1,000 XP, Amped RE-45 Burn Card
3	Kill 30 Grunts	2,500 XP, Amped RE-45 Burn Card
4	Kill 50 Grunts	5,000 XP, Amped RE-45 Burn Card
5	Kill 100 Grunts	10,000 XP, Amped RE-45 Burn Card

Awarded Burn Card

Amped RE-45
Replace Sidearm Weapon with a more lethal RE-45 Auto-Pistol
Presuming you don't want to become a critter's lunch, take this time to locate and secure your hollow point rounds.
-Graves, approaching Boneyard

Amped RE-45

HAMMOND P2011

MAGAZINE CAPACITY: 12 WEAPON UNLOCK: LEVEL 1

The Hammond P2011 is a semi-automatic handgun with good accuracy and damage at range. Its integrated "Match Trigger" allows it to be fired rapidly, which is useful in close quarters.

STRENGTHS:
- Rate of fire determined by trigger speed

WEAKNESSES:
- Limited range

WEAPON PERFORMANCE

DAMAGE

ACCURACY

RANGE

FIRE RATE

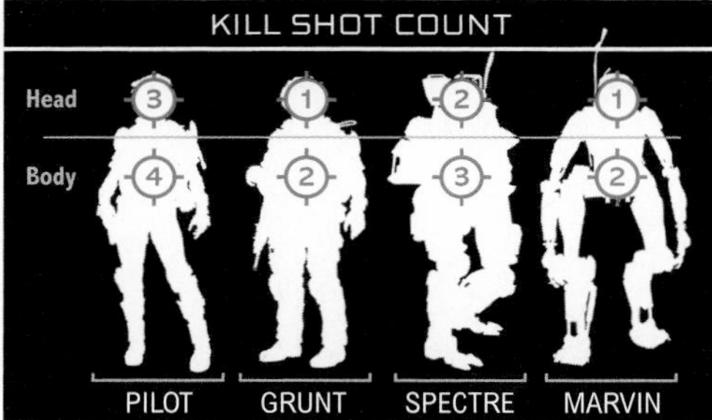

KILL SHOT COUNT	PILOT	GRUNT	SPECTRE	MARVIN
Head	3	1	2	1
Body	4	2	3	2

Field Notes

- The Hammond P2011 has a very unique feature called the Match Trigger. This feature allows the player to take full use of this sidearm, because the faster you pull the trigger the faster bullets will fire. The Match Trigger makes this sidearm very versatile, allowing a player to do damage from a distance or up close once an enemy approaches.
- With an accurate shot, the Hammond P2011 can take out a Pilot with three bullets to the head or four to the body. Players should focus on using their primaries when engaging with Pilots, but don't doubt the Hammond P2011. Force Pilots to engage you in close-quarter areas, allowing you to take full use of the weapon's Match Trigger.
- Once again, the Match Trigger makes this sidearm deadly when wiping out minions. Aim for the head to take Grunts out quickly, conserving ammo and allowing you to wipe out minion squads with one magazine.

PRO TIP: FLAMESWORD

The Hammond P2011 is my preferred sidearm. It offers a great balance of range, accuracy, and damage output. Plus, the Match Trigger allows me to maintain a high rate of fire during frantic close quarter engagements.

Hammond P2011 Challenges

IF IT MOVES...

TIER	CRITERIA	REWARD
1	Kill 10 Enemies	500 XP
2	Kill 25 Enemies	1,000 XP, Amped P2011 Burn Card
3	Kill 50 Enemies	2,500 XP, Amped P2011 Burn Card
4	Kill 100 Enemies	5,000 XP, Amped P2011 Burn Card
5	Kill 150 Enemies	10,000 XP, Amped P2011 Burn Card

TOP GUN

TIER	CRITERIA	REWARD
1	Kill 5 Pilots	500 XP
2	Kill 15 Pilots	1,000 XP, Amped P2011 Burn Card
3	Kill 25 Pilots	2,500 XP, Amped P2011 Burn Card
4	Kill 35 Pilots	5,000 XP, Amped P2011 Burn Card
5	Kill 50 Pilots	10,000 XP, Amped P2011 Burn Card

MACHINE WAR

TIER	CRITERIA	REWARD
1	Kill 5 Spectres	500 XP
2	Kill 15 Spectres	1,000 XP, Amped P2011 Burn Card
3	Kill 25 Spectres	2,500 XP, Amped P2011 Burn Card
4	Kill 35 Spectres	5,000 XP, Amped P2011 Burn Card
5	Kill 50 Spectres	10,000 XP, Amped P2011 Burn Card

OFF THE DOME

TIER	CRITERIA	REWARD
1	Get 5 Headshots	500 XP
2	Get 15 Headshots	1,000 XP, Amped P2011 Burn Card
3	Get 25 Headshots	2,500 XP, Amped P2011 Burn Card
4	Get 35 Headshots	5,000 XP, Amped P2011 Burn Card
5	Get 50 Headshots	10,000 XP, Amped P2011 Burn Card

THE EXPENDABLES

TIER	CRITERIA	REWARD
1	Kill 5 Grunts	500 XP
2	Kill 15 Grunts	1,000 XP, Amped P2011 Burn Card
3	Kill 30 Grunts	2,500 XP, Amped P2011 Burn Card
4	Kill 50 Grunts	5,000 XP, Amped P2011 Burn Card
5	Kill 100 Grunts	10,000 XP, Amped P2011 Burn Card

Awarded Burn Card

Amped P2011
Replace Sidearm Weapon with a burst fire Hammond P2011
There was a fella from the backwaters that could shoot three times before yer pinky touched the holster. I'm that fella. -Blisk

Amped P2011

SIDEARMS

B3 WINGMAN

MAGAZINE CAPACITY: 6 WEAPON UNLOCK: LEVEL 27

The B3 Wingman is an extremely powerful revolver with very high accuracy out to long ranges. Precision aim is required to mitigate the disadvantages of its very low fire rate.

STRENGTHS:
- High damage
- Long range

WEAKNESSES:
- Limited magazine capacity
- Slow rate of fire

WEAPON PERFORMANCE

DAMAGE

ACCURACY

RANGE

FIRE RATE

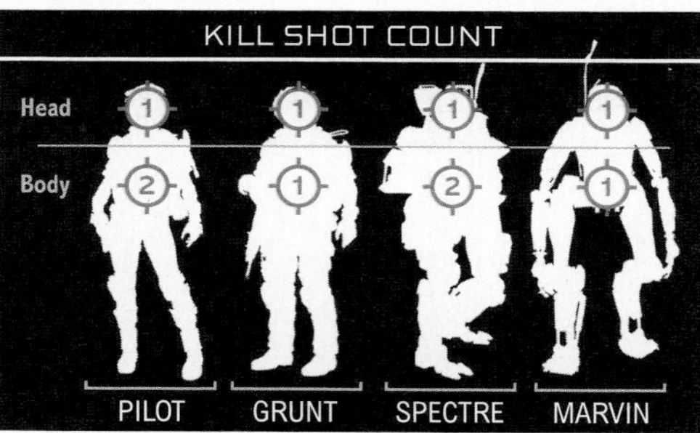

Field Notes

- The B3 Wingman is noticeably stronger than the other sidearms. This sidearm deals a lot of damage and has great accuracy and incredible range. The only weaknesses to this weapon are its small magazine and slower rate of fire. Consider equipping this sidearm when carrying a short-range primary weapon like an SMG or shotgun—you'll appreciate the range and accuracy of the Wingman even more.
- The B3 Wingman only takes two shots to the body or one to head to kill an enemy Pilot. The other sidearms take at least four shots to the body or three to the head. If you can become accurate with this weapon, it is a beastly sidearm. Use this weapon only if your primary is running low or out of ammo. It's a great one to catch a Pilot off guard in close quarters.
- Against enemy minions this weapon is powerful, but gives away your position on the minimap. Keep your distance and pick off the minions at a longer range. All minions can be killed with a single shot, but you'll need to aim for the head to one-shot a Spectre.

DEVELOPER TIP

Respawn Entertainment

You can swap out your sidearm with another primary weapon if you pick it up off of a fallen enemy or a friendly.

B3 Wingman Challenges

IF IT MOVES...

TIER	CRITERIA	REWARD
1	Kill 10 Enemies	500 XP
2	Kill 25 Enemies	1,000 XP, Amped Wingman Burn Card
3	Kill 50 Enemies	2,500 XP, Amped Wingman Burn Card
4	Kill 100 Enemies	5,000 XP, Amped Wingman Burn Card
5	Kill 150 Enemies	10,000 XP, Amped Wingman Burn Card

TOP GUN

TIER	CRITERIA	REWARD
1	Kill 5 Pilots	500 XP
2	Kill 15 Pilots	1,000 XP, Amped Wingman Burn Card
3	Kill 25 Pilots	2,500 XP, Amped Wingman Burn Card
4	Kill 35 Pilots	5,000 XP, Amped Wingman Burn Card
5	Kill 50 Pilots	10,000 XP, Amped Wingman Burn Card

MACHINE WAR

TIER	CRITERIA	REWARD
1	Kill 5 Spectres	500 XP
2	Kill 15 Spectres	1,000 XP, Amped Wingman Burn Card
3	Kill 25 Spectres	2,500 XP, Amped Wingman Burn Card
4	Kill 35 Spectres	5,000 XP, Amped Wingman Burn Card
5	Kill 50 Spectres	10,000 XP, Amped Wingman Burn Card

OFF THE DOME

TIER	CRITERIA	REWARD
1	Get 5 Headshots	500 XP
2	Get 15 Headshots	1,000 XP, Amped Wingman Burn Card
3	Get 25 Headshots	2,500 XP, Amped Wingman Burn Card
4	Get 35 Headshots	5,000 XP, Amped Wingman Burn Card
5	Get 50 Headshots	10,000 XP, Amped Wingman Burn Card

THE EXPENDABLES

TIER	CRITERIA	REWARD
1	Kill 5 Grunts	500 XP
2	Kill 15 Grunts	1,000 XP, Amped Wingman Burn Card
3	Kill 30 Grunts	2,500 XP, Amped Wingman Burn Card
4	Kill 50 Grunts	5,000 XP, Amped Wingman Burn Card
5	Kill 100 Grunts	10,000 XP, Amped Wingman Burn Card

AWARDED BURN CARD

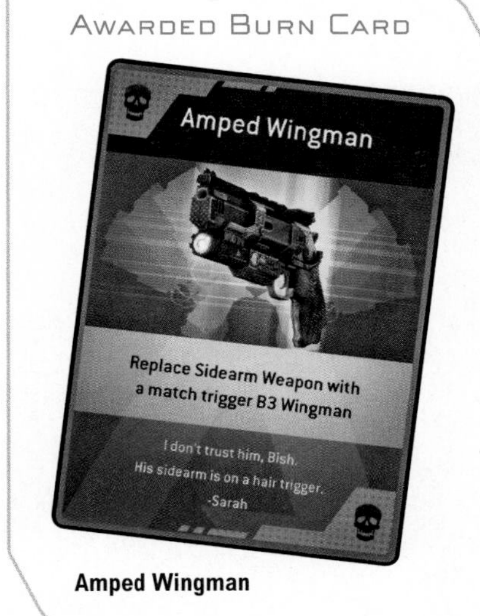
Amped Wingman
Replace Sidearm Weapon with a match trigger B3 Wingman
I don't trust him, Bish.
His sidearm is on a hair trigger.
-Sarah

Amped Wingman

ANTI-TITAN WEAPONS

There's no threat too dangerous for Pilots to handle, including enemy Titans. These devastating weapons have the ability to cripple and even destroy damaged Titans. With the exception of the Archer Heavy Rocket, these weapons can also be deployed against enemy Pilots and minions as well, giving Pilots more offensive capability. Complete challenges associated with each Anti-Titan weapon to earn bonus XP and Burn Cards.

ARCHER HEAVY ROCKET

MAGAZINE CAPACITY: 1 WEAPON UNLOCK: LEVEL 1

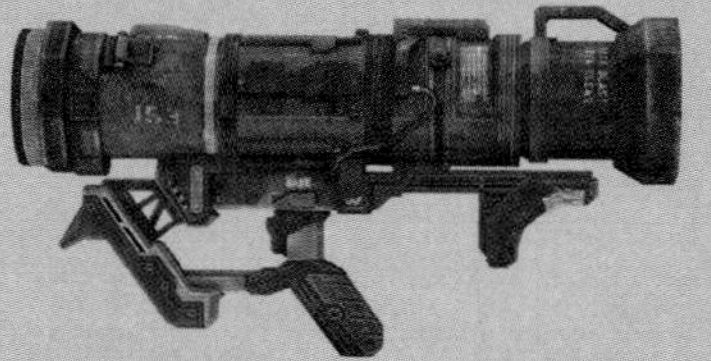

The Archer fires a powerful homing rocket. It must be locked on a target before it can be fired. When aimed, a targeting window flips out, allowing target acquisition. Hold this window over the target continuously until a lock is achieved, and then fire.

STRENGTHS:

- Guided rocket with high accuracy

WEAKNESSES:

- Lengthy lock-on procedure

WEAPON PERFORMANCE

DAMAGE

ACCURACY

RANGE

FIRE RATE

Field Notes

- This weapon is a great way to deal a massive amount of damage to an unsuspecting Titan. However, the weapon is ineffective when fighting a Titan head-on due to the lack of manual fire and having a long lock-on time—you must aim at a Titan and achieve a lock before the weapon can be fired. The most difficult part of using this weapon is following up after you score a hit with the initial rocket. Be sure to have cover nearby because the Titan can tell when the Archer locks on. The Titan will surely be gunning for you after you hit it once. Better yet, target a heavily damaged Titan to doom it, and then prepare to engage the ejecting Pilot.

DEVELOPER TIP

When using the Archer Heavy Rocket, time your shot well. For example, if the locked-on Titan is preemptively blocking with a Vortex Shield, wait for the Vortex Shield to go away before firing your Archer.

Archer Heavy Rocket Challenges

IF IT MOVES...

TIER	CRITERIA	REWARD
1	Kill 5 Enemies	500 XP
2	Kill 10 Enemies	1,000 XP, Amped Archer Burn Card
3	Kill 20 Enemies	2,500 XP, Amped Archer Burn Card
4	Kill 35 Enemies	5,000 XP, Amped Archer Burn Card
5	Kill 50 Enemies	10,000 XP, Amped Archer Burn Card

TITAN KILLER

TIER	CRITERIA	REWARD
1	Kill 1 Titans	500 XP
2	Kill 3 Titans	1,000 XP, Amped Archer Burn Card
3	Kill 5 Titans	2,500 XP, Amped Archer Burn Card
4	Kill 7 Titans	5,000 XP, Amped Archer Burn Card
5	Kill 10 Titans	10,000 XP, Amped Archer Burn Card

AWARDED BURN CARD

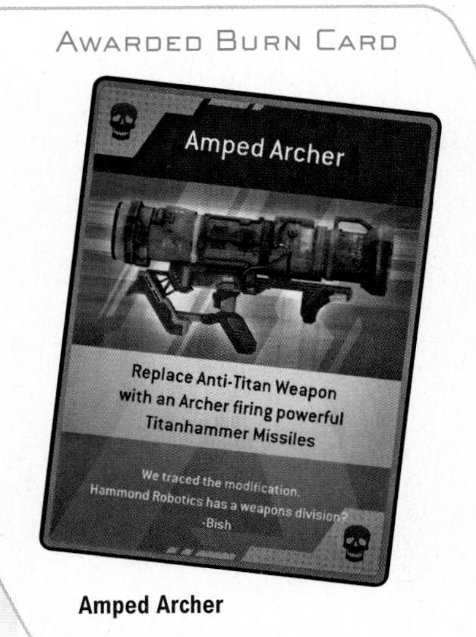

Amped Archer
Replace Anti-Titan Weapon with an Archer firing powerful Titanhammer Missiles
We traced the modification. Hammond Robotics has a weapons division?
-Bish

Amped Archer

SIDEWINDER

MAGAZINE CAPACITY: 25 WEAPON UNLOCK: LEVEL 1

The Sidewinder is a rapid-fire micro-missile launcher. It is effective against large targets, but lacks precision due to its large spread. The micro-missiles it fires do not yield a large area effect on detonation due to their shaped-charge design.

STRENGTHS:

- Rapid fire weapon with large magazine

WEAKNESSES:

- Inflicts minimal damage per hit

WEAPON PERFORMANCE

DAMAGE

ACCURACY

RANGE

FIRE RATE

Field Notes

- The Sidewinder is a great weapon to send a volley of rockets from a mid-close range distance to an enemy Titan. This weapon is most effective when coupled with an Arc Grenade for a hit and run against a dazed Titan. This weapon can also be used for a rodeo attack, but be careful—you will take splash damage from your own rockets and will kill yourself if you shoot more than a full magazine. With its fast rate of fire, you need to keep the pressure on by scoring a hit every few seconds to prevent the enemy Titan from recharging its shields. In addition to taking out Titans, the Sidewinder is a capable anti-Pilot and anti-minion weapon.

DEVELOPER TIP

respawn ENTERTAINMENT

Projectiles fired from the Sidewinder have a significant travel time. Remember to lead your targets when using this weapon, which is also capable of inflicting damage to Titans' Critical Hit locations.

Sidewinder Challenges

TITAN KILLER		
TIER	CRITERIA	REWARD
1	Kill 1 Titans	500 XP
2	Kill 3 Titans	1,000 XP, Amped Sidewinder Burn Card
3	Kill 5 Titans	2,500 XP, Amped Sidewinder Burn Card
4	Kill 7 Titans	5,000 XP, Amped Sidewinder Burn Card
5	Kill 10 Titans	10,000 XP, Amped Sidewinder Burn Card

CRITICALLY CONDITIONED		
TIER	CRITERIA	REWARD
1	Get 10 Critical Hits	500 XP
2	Get 50 Critical Hits	1,000 XP, Amped Sidewinder Burn Card
3	Get 100 Critical Hits	2,500 XP, Amped Sidewinder Burn Card
4	Get 150 Critical Hits	5,000 XP, Amped Sidewinder Burn Card
5	Get 200 Critical Hits	10,000 XP, Amped Sidewinder Burn Card

AWARDED BURN CARD

Amped Sidewinder
Replace Anti-Titan Weapon with a double ammo capacity Sidewinder
That's no ordinary Titan, Bish. It's a walking tank. We need a bigger gun. -Sarah

Amped Sidewinder

MAG LAUNCHER

MAGAZINE CAPACITY: 5 WEAPON UNLOCK: LEVEL 22

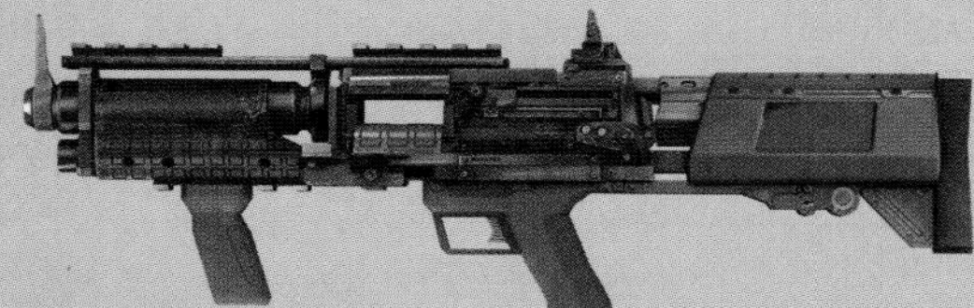

The Mag Launcher fires magnetic grenades. When fired, if they pass close enough to enemy Titans, the grenades will veer towards the hostile Titans and stick to them before detonating.

STRENGTHS:

- High-damage indirect-fire munitions stick to enemy Titans

WEAKNESSES:

- Limited accuracy and range

WEAPON PERFORMANCE

DAMAGE

ACCURACY

RANGE

FIRE RATE

Field Notes

- The Mag Launcher is a super-effective Anti-Titan weapon because of its unique ability. When you fire the grenades in the direction of the Titan, they will track the Titan and explode on impact. This makes the Mag Launcher weapon effective, because you can use your surroundings to take cover and just lob grenades over obstacles to avoid taking damage direct from the Titan. However, don't attempt to use this weapon while rodeo attacking a Titan—you'll blow yourself up. This weapon also allows you to turn around and block off doorways as you run away from enemy Pilots. They will be weak enough for you to finish them off with a primary weapon.

Mag Launcher Challenges

TITAN KILLER

TIER	CRITERIA	REWARD
1	Kill 1 Titans	500 XP
2	Kill 3 Titans	1,000 XP, Amped Mag Launcher Burn Card
3	Kill 5 Titans	2,500 XP, Amped Mag Launcher Burn Card
4	Kill 7 Titans	5,000 XP, Amped Mag Launcher Burn Card
5	Kill 10 Titans	10,000 XP, Amped Mag Launcher Burn Card

AWARDED BURN CARD

Amped
Mag Launcher
Replace Anti-Titan Weapon with a high-capacity, automatic Mag Launcher
Just because they call it the Titan Wars doesn't mean we always had Titans. Sometimes you had to improvise.
-Graves

Amped Mag Launcher

DEVELOPER TIP

Rounds fired by the Mag Launcher will be drawn towards Spectres as well as Titans.

CHARGE RIFLE

MAGAZINE CAPACITY: **500** WEAPON UNLOCK: **LEVEL 33**

The Charge Rifle fires an energy beam that inflicts massive damage. Holding the firing trigger charges the weapon. Timing is critical to its use: this weapon will only fire when it reaches full charge, and it will discharge automatically as soon as it hits full charge.

STRENGTHS:
- Extremely high damage

WEAKNESSES:
- Slow charge time

WEAPON PERFORMANCE

DAMAGE

ACCURACY

RANGE

FIRE RATE

Field Notes

- The Charge Rifle may take a while to charge, but it deals a high amount of damage to a Titan. This is also the longest range and most accurate Anti-Titan weapon. You're able to shoot across the map and deal damage from a distance. It is best used against Titans when you have cover to retreat behind. Once you've located a Titan, charge up this weapon behind cover and only expose yourself to fire the weapon. After firing the weapon, retreat behind cover and repeat the process. Try moving and attacking from different positions after each attack to keep the enemy Titan guessing the next position you'll attack from. The Charge Rifle is also the only Anti-Titan weapon you can use to rodeo attack a Titan without inflicting damage to yourself. While it's possible to kill Pilots and minions with this weapon, you're better off sticking with your primary weapon.

Charge Rifle Challenges

TITAN KILLER

TIER	CRITERIA	REWARD
1	Kill 1 Titans	500 XP
2	Kill 3 Titans	1,000 XP, Amped Charge Rifle
3	Kill 5 Titans	2,500 XP, Amped Charge Rifle
4	Kill 7 Titans	5,000 XP, Amped Charge Rifle
5	Kill 10 Titans	10,000 XP, Amped Charge Rifle

CRITICALLY CONDITIONED

TIER	CRITERIA	REWARD
1	Get 5 Critical Hits	500 XP
2	Get 10 Critical Hits	1,000 XP, Amped Charge Rifle
3	Get 15 Critical Hits	2,500 XP, Amped Charge Rifle
4	Get 20 Critical Hits	5,000 XP, Amped Charge Rifle
5	Get 30 Critical Hits	10,000 XP, Amped Charge Rifle

DEVELOPER TIP — Respawn Entertainment

Although all weapons do some damage to Titans, the most effective Pilot weapons by far are those designated as Anti-Titan weapons.

AWARDED BURN CARD

Amped Charge Rifle
Replace Anti-Titan Weapon with a faster charging Charge Rifle
Ah there you go, see? You had it set to training mode.
-Bish

Amped Charge Rifle

ANTI-TITAN WEAPONS

ORDNANCE

Rounding out each Pilot's arsenal is the Ordnance slot, reserved for grenades, mines, and charges. These hand-tossed explosives are effective against Pilots, minions, and even Titans. By default each Pilot can carry two of these explosives, but this can be increased by equipping the Explosives Pack Tier 1 Kit. Complete the challenges associated with each ordnance type to earn bonus XP and Burn Cards.

FRAG GRENADE

ORDNANCE UNLOCK: **LEVEL 1**

The Frag Grenade is an all-purpose anti-personnel weapon, useful for clearing tight spaces and areas that are out of direct line-of-sight. Its delayed fuse makes it versatile in many combat situations.

Field Notes

- The Frag Grenade is a great ordnance to quickly wipe out minions or clear out Pilots caught in small rooms. Since Pilots will be jumping around the map a lot, you will want to force them in areas that allow the Frag Grenade to apply splash damage, making the enemy weaker for you to pick off. Cooking the grenade is critical; learn the timing to be able to throw it at Pilots who are about to peek out of a window or cover.

Frag Grenade Challenges

GRENADIER

TIER	CRITERIA	REWARD
1	Kill 10 Enemies	500 XP
2	Kill 25 Enemies	1,000 XP, Bottomless Frags Burn Card
3	Kill 50 Enemies	2,500 XP, Bottomless Frags Burn Card
4	Kill 100 Enemies	5,000 XP, Bottomless Frags Burn Card
5	Kill 150 Enemies	10,000 XP, Bottomless Frags Burn Card

NO-HITTER

TIER	CRITERIA	REWARD
1	Kill 5 Pilots	500 XP
2	Kill 10 Pilots	1,000 XP, Bottomless Frags Burn Card
3	Kill 20 Pilots	2,500 XP, Bottomless Frags Burn Card
4	Kill 30 Pilots	5,000 XP, Bottomless Frags Burn Card
5	Kill 50 Pilots	10,000 XP, Bottomless Frags Burn Card

DODGE-BALL

TIER	CRITERIA	REWARD
1	Kill 5 Grunts	500 XP
2	Kill 15 Grunts	1,000 XP, Bottomless Frags Burn Card
3	Kill 30 Grunts	2,500 XP, Bottomless Frags Burn Card
4	Kill 50 Grunts	5,000 XP, Bottomless Frags Burn Card
5	Kill 100 Grunts	10,000 XP, Bottomless Frags Burn Card

DEVELOPER TIP — Respawn Entertainment

Cook your grenades for added control. You can do this by holding the grenade in your hand instead of releasing it immediately. To cook a grenade, hold the grenade-throw control without letting go. Timing a grenade properly can be risky, but if done properly, it is a very effective way to make a grenade explode exactly where and when you want it to.

Awarded Burn Card

Bottomless Frags
Replace Ordnance Weapon with infinite, more lethal Frag Grenades
In case of ticking sound, evacuate immediately and contact emergency services.
-Warning Label

Bottomless Frags

ARC GRENADE

ORDNANCE UNLOCK: **LEVEL 7**

Arc Grenades inflict limited damage compared to Frag Grenades, but heavily distort the vision systems of Titans and Pilots that are caught in the blast radius.

Field Notes

- Arc Grenades are the best ordnance against Titans because they explode on contact and render a Titan useless for a few seconds where you and your team can take down the disoriented Titan. If you don't have a Suppressor on your primary weapon and want to eliminate a group of AI, this grenade will do the trick without exposing you on the minimap. Lastly, this grenade has a large blast radius, making sure that it will hit your target, even if your aim is slightly off.

Arc Grenade Challenges

CONDUCTOR

TIER	CRITERIA	REWARD
1	Kill 5 Enemies	500 XP
2	Kill 15 Enemies	1,000 XP, Shock Rocks Burn Card
3	Kill 30 Enemies	2,500 XP, Shock Rocks Burn Card
4	Kill 50 Enemies	5,000 XP, Shock Rocks Burn Card
5	Kill 100 Enemies	10,000 XP, Shock Rocks Burn Card

BUG ZAPPER

TIER	CRITERIA	REWARD
1	Kill 5 Grunts	500 XP
2	Kill 15 Grunts	1,000 XP, Shock Rocks Burn Card
3	Kill 30 Grunts	2,500 XP, Shock Rocks Burn Card
4	Kill 50 Grunts	5,000 XP, Shock Rocks Burn Card
5	Kill 100 Grunts	10,000 XP, Shock Rocks Burn Card

ELECTROCUTIONER

TIER	CRITERIA	REWARD
1	Kill 1 Pilot	500 XP
2	Kill 5 Pilots	1,000 XP, Shock Rocks Burn Card
3	Kill 10 Pilots	2,500 XP, Shock Rocks Burn Card
4	Kill 15 Pilots	5,000 XP, Shock Rocks Burn Card
5	Kill 25 Pilots	10,000 XP, Shock Rocks Burn Card

ASSAULT WITH BATTERY

TIER	CRITERIA	REWARD
1	Kill 5 Spectres	500 XP
2	Kill 10 Spectres	1,000 XP, Shock Rocks Burn Card
3	Kill 20 Spectres	2,500 XP, Shock Rocks Burn Card
4	Kill 30 Spectres	5,000 XP, Shock Rocks Burn Card
5	Kill 50 Spectres	10,000 XP, Shock Rocks Burn Card

DEVELOPER TIP — respawn ENTERTAINMENT

Pilot Ordnance with the "Arc" designation such as the Arc Mines and Arc Grenades will temporarily slow down and blind enemy Titans. Depending on the situation, you can use this advantage to rodeo attack Titans or escape to safety. Arc Ordnance will also disrupt a Pilot during a wall run or wall hang.

AWARDED BURN CARD

Shock Rocks
Replace Ordnance Weapon with infinite, magnetic Arc Grenades
Give it a rub on the trim here before ya toss. Gives it a wicked curve.
-Blisk, above Angel City

Shock Rocks

ORDNANCE

SATCHEL CHARGE

ORDNANCE UNLOCK: **LEVEL 17**

Satchel Charges stick to any surface and are manually detonated, causing massive explosive damage to anything nearby.

Field Notes

› Satchel Charges are great for setting booby traps for Pilots as well as dealing heavy damage to Titans. Drop or place Satchel Charges in high-traffic areas such as near objectives or choke points—placing charges next to Hardpoints and flags may not be sporting, but one can't deny the effectiveness of such tactics. Once a charge is placed, it must be detonated manually, so it's best to maintain line of sight with your trap to ensure proper timing. Satchel Charges are extremely effective against Titans when performing rodeo attacks. Stick a few charges to a Titan, then jump off before detonating them. The Dead Man's Trigger Tier 2 Kit automatically detonates all charges when you die, useful for those times when you're killed before setting off the charges manually.

Satchel Charge Challenges

GRENADIER

TIER	CRITERIA	REWARD
1	Kill 10 Enemies	500 XP
2	Kill 25 Enemies	1,000 XP, Surplus Satchels Burn Card
3	Kill 50 Enemies	2,500 XP, Surplus Satchels Burn Card
4	Kill 100 Enemies	5,000 XP, Surplus Satchels Burn Card
5	Kill 150 Enemies	10,000 XP, Surplus Satchels Burn Card

NO-HITTER

TIER	CRITERIA	REWARD
1	Kill 1 Pilot	500 XP
2	Kill 5 Pilots	1,000 XP, Surplus Satchels Burn Card
3	Kill 15 Pilots	2,500 XP, Surplus Satchels Burn Card
4	Kill 30 Pilots	5,000 XP, Surplus Satchels Burn Card
5	Kill 50 Enemies	10,000 XP, Surplus Satchels Burn Card

DODGE-BALL

TIER	CRITERIA	REWARD
1	Kill 5 Grunts	500 XP
2	Kill 15 Grunts	1,000 XP, Surplus Satchels Burn Card
3	Kill 30 Grunts	2,500 XP, Surplus Satchels Burn Card
4	Kill 50 Grunts	5,000 XP, Surplus Satchels Burn Card
5	Kill 100 Grunts	10,000 XP, Surplus Satchels Burn Card

AWARDED BURN CARD

Surplus Satchels
Replace Ordnance Weapon with infinite, more lethal Satchels
Take as many as you can carry, the Titans are coming down like rain out there.
-Vlad, late in the Titan Wars

Surplus Satchels

ARC MINE

ORDNANCE UNLOCK: **LEVEL 31**

The Arc Mine is a proximity-detonated charge that sticks to any surface. In addition to nominal explosive damage, it causes massive interference to nearby Titan and Pilot vision systems on detonation.

Field Notes

› The Arc Mine is similar to the Arc Grenade, but the Arc Mine is placed in a fixed position and activated by enemy movement. This ordnance is not only great for causing massive interference to Titans and Pilots, but by placing two together behind a doorway or on a ceiling near an objective will kill an unsuspecting enemy Pilot.

Arc Mine Challenges

BLASTER

TIER	CRITERIA	REWARD
1	Kill 10 Enemies	500 XP
2	Kill 25 Enemies	1,000 XP, Personal Alarm System Burn Card
3	Kill 50 Enemies	2,500 XP, Personal Alarm System Burn Card
4	Kill 100 Enemies	5,000 XP, Personal Alarm System Burn Card
5	Kill 150 Enemies	10,000 XP, Personal Alarm System Burn Card

SON OF A...

TIER	CRITERIA	REWARD
1	Kill 1 Pilot	500 XP
2	Kill 5 Pilots	1,000 XP, Personal Alarm System Burn Card
3	Kill 15 Pilots	2,500 XP, Personal Alarm System Burn Card
4	Kill 30 Pilots	5,000 XP, Personal Alarm System Burn Card
5	Kill 50 Pilots	10,000 XP, Personal Alarm System Burn Card

GIBBER

TIER	CRITERIA	REWARD
1	Kill 5 Grunts	500 XP
2	Kill 15 Grunts	1,000 XP, Personal Alarm System Burn Card
3	Kill 30 Grunts	2,500 XP, Personal Alarm System Burn Card
4	Kill 50 Grunts	5,000 XP, Personal Alarm System Burn Card
5	Kill 100 Grunts	10,000 XP, Personal Alarm System Burn Card

DEVELOPER TIP — respawn ENTERTAINMENT

Arc Mines are great for defending fixed positions, such as bases in Capture the Flag or the Hardpoints in Hardpoint Domination.

Your ordnance and ammunition are automatically replenished when you embark into your Titan.

AWARDED BURN CARD

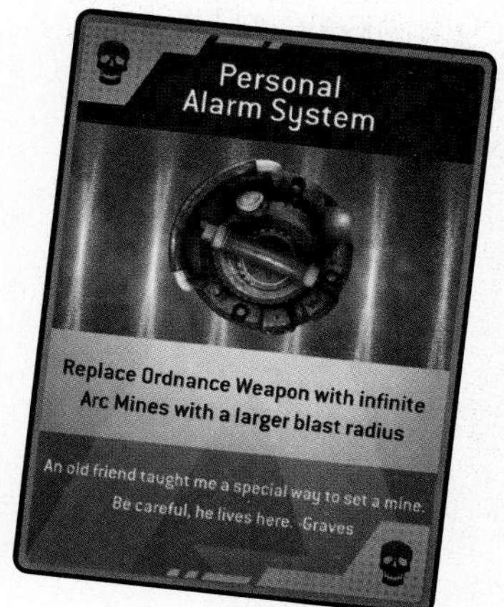

Personal Alarm System
Replace Ordnance Weapon with infinite Arc Mines with a larger blast radius
An old friend taught me a special way to set a mine. Be careful, he lives here. -Graves

Personal Alarm System

PILOT TACTICAL ABILITIES

Pilots have one Tactical Ability slot, giving them the ability to blend into their surroundings, increase speed and health regeneration, or detect enemies behind walls. Once assigned, these abilities are manually activated at a Pilot's discretion, giving them a temporary advantage. But abilities only remain active for a few seconds before they must recharge. However, the Power Cell Tier 1 Kit helps these abilities to recharge at a quicker rate, allowing them to be deployed with greater frequency.

TACTICAL ABILITY

CLOAK

ABILITY UNLOCK: **LEVEL 1**

Cloak makes you almost completely invisible to Titans and minions (Grunts, Spectres, and Marvins). However, it is not quite as effective against Pilots.

Field Notes

- When using this Tactical Ability, keep in mind that when you activate Cloak, you will lose your Cloak once you have fired a weapon. You are able to throw grenades and melee without losing the ability. A good time to use Cloak is when you are spotted by a Titan and want to make a clean getaway. The Cloak will immediately make you invisible and give you some time to retreat to cover. Keep in mind that Pilots are able to see the Cloak much easier than a Titan.

PRO TIP: STRONGSIDE

A great time to use the Cloak Tactical Ability is when you want to rodeo attack an enemy Titan. This will allow you to sneak up on the enemy Titan and jump on!

DEVELOPER TIP

Respawn ENTERTAINMENT

Enemy Titans can see your Jump Kit's exhaust when you double jump while cloaked as a Pilot. Sometimes it's best to avoid double jumping when cloaked, so as not to draw enemy attention.

TACTICAL ABILITY

STIM

ABILITY UNLOCK: **LEVEL 8**

Chemically derived from a Pilot's own adrenaline, Stim boosts movement speed and health regeneration for a short period of time.

Field Notes

- This ability increases your Pilot's speed, allowing you to do jumps that weren't possible before. The extra speed also allows you to outwit your opponent and escape a losing battle. Stay around cover to always take full use of this ability. When an enemy engages you, activate the Stim ability to recover health while taking cover and then use the speed to outmaneuver the opponent.

PRO TIP: FLAMESWORD

Always have an escape route in mind. Stim will allow you to escape a losing battle as your movement speed is increased. Think about double backing when escaping. Double backing is when you begin to run away and then you come back, catching your pursuer off guard. This takes practice—be sure to time when the opponent will begin to sprint and chase you, then double back and make them pay.

TACTICAL ABILITY

ACTIVE RADAR PULSE

ABILITY UNLOCK: **LEVEL 19**

The Active Radar Pulse triggers a scan that allows you to see enemies through walls for a short amount of time.

Field Notes

- With a range of about 50 meters, the Active Radar Pulse allows you to plan the perfect route to catch nearby enemies off guard. When active, enemies appear on the HUD as red silhouettes, even if they're hidden behind walls and other pieces of cover. Knowing where enemies are allows you to get the jump on them. This is best used in Capture the Flag or Hardpoint where you can find the nearby enemy Pilot and get a crucial kill that will lead to a capture. Although helpful in most situations, Active Radar Pulse is incapable of detecting an enemy Pilot using the Cloak ability.

TIER 1 KITS

Unlike the Tactical Abilities, Tier 1 Kits are passive, requiring no interaction on behalf of the Pilot to benefit from their bonuses. There are a total of six Tier 1 Kits, each with their own benefits. Before selecting one, take into account your other loadout selections and find a kit that complements them.

TIER 1 KIT

ENHANCED PARKOUR KIT

KIT UNLOCK: LEVEL 1

The Enhanced Parkour Kit allows you to wall run and wall hang for increased periods of time.

Field Notes

- This kit allows you to maneuver throughout each map the way a Pilot is supposed to. Increased wall running allows you to get from point A to point B in seconds and evade pursuers if being chased. The increased wall hang will allow you to ambush enemies and catch foes by surprise.

PRO TIP: FLAMESWORD

Become familiar with the Enhanced Parkour Kit. It will come in handy and save you in many situations. When being pursued, run off building tops and grab the wall before dropping. You can catch your pursuer jumping right past you, putting you in a better position to take them out. Be sure to let go of the wall once your pursuer passes you—aiming down your weapon's sight is a lot more accurate than hip firing.

TIER 1 KIT

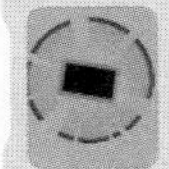

EXPLOSIVES PACK

KIT UNLOCK: LEVEL 1

The Explosives Pack increases your ordnance ammo capacity as a Pilot.

Field Notes

- The Explosives Pack is extremely useful if you are a player who tosses a lot of grenades, mines, or Satchel Charges. This kit will give you one additional piece of ordnance, boosting your offensive capability.

PRO TIP: STRONGSIDE

Using the Explosives Pack when equipping the Arc Grenade is extremely useful if you find yourself fighting Titans a lot. You'll have three Arc Grenades to stun a Titan. First throw the Arc Grenade to stun the enemy Titan and then unload with your Anti-Titan weapon for about five seconds. Repeat this process with your other two Arc Grenades. You will have done a considerable amount of damage to the enemy Titan and, if you have a teammate assisting you during this fight, you'll most likely kill the enemy Titan.

TIER 1 KIT

POWER CELL

KIT UNLOCK: LEVEL 1

The Power Cell accelerates the recharging of your Pilot's Tactical Ability.

Field Notes

- This reduces the recharge time of your Tactical Ability by about half. However, this is only an advantage if you use it consistently. First, get in the habit of always using your Tactical Ability when it is available. Once you find yourself needing your Stim, Cloak, or Active Radar Pulse a few seconds earlier, then you will be ready to use this effectively. This is strongest when coupled with the Active Radar Pulse since it shaves off a few vulnerable seconds where the opponent can sneak up on you.

TIER 1 KIT

RUN N GUN KIT

KIT UNLOCK: LEVEL 31

The Run N Gun Kit allows you to fire small arms such as pistols and SMGs while sprinting.

Field Notes

- This kit allows players with SMGs and pistols to run through minions while keeping their speed, allowing them to traverse the map. Players can also chase down enemy Pilots while keeping their top speed and being able to fire at the same time. Its greatest use is when you can sprint from building to building while you engage the enemy.

TIER 1 KIT

QUICK RELOAD KIT

KIT UNLOCK: LEVEL 42

The Quick Reload Kit accelerates the reload speeds of all your Pilot weapons.

Field Notes

- The Quick Reload Kit is exactly what is sounds like. This kit is especially effective with some of the powerful slow reloading weapons like the Kraber-AP Sniper and the Archer Heavy Rocket. Also, if you are a run and gun type of player, this is a great kit to stay in the action while decreasing the chances of getting caught off guard.

TIER 1 KIT

STEALTH KIT

KIT UNLOCK: LEVEL 48

The Stealth Kit makes your footsteps silent, and makes your Jump Kit exhaust nearly invisible.

Field Notes

- The Stealth Kit comes in handy if you specialize in aggressive game play. The kit makes your footsteps silent, allowing you to creep on enemies and assassinate them. This kit also makes your Jump Kit less noticeable, allowing you to flank enemies more efficiently and escape as opponents will not be able to hear your movements.

TIER 2 KITS

The Tier 2 Kits function just like the Tier 1 Kits, offering greater variety and customization for your Pilot's loadout. As with the Tier 1 Kits, carefully study the benefits of each, then select one that complements your overall loadout and style of play.

TIER 2 KIT

DOME-SHIELD BATTERY

KIT UNLOCK: LEVEL 1

This kit extends the duration of your Titan's Dome-Shield after Titanfall.

Field Notes

- The Dome-Shield Battery extends the duration of your Titan's Dome-Shield by ten seconds. This is a good kit to equip if you find yourself always dropping your Titan in or near battle. Your Titan cannot be damaged while in the Dome-Shield, although your Titan will take damage if you activate Guard mode or Follow mode. If enemy Titans or Pilots enter your Dome-Shield, the Dome-Shield will inflict damage to them—if they don't exit quickly they'll be killed. Since your Dome-Shield will last for approximately 23 seconds, this Tier 2 Kit is also a good distraction if dropped into a high-traffic area. Nearby enemy Titans or Pilots may flock to attack your Titan while you as a Pilot sneak attack the enemies.

DEVELOPER TIP

Respawn ENTERTAINMENT

After your Titan has dropped in, you can use your Titan's Dome-Shield as cover from enemy fire. Step in and out of the Dome-Shield region, alternating between fighting an enemy and keeping yourself protected.

TIER 2 KIT

MINION DETECTOR

KIT UNLOCK: LEVEL 1

The Minion Detector displays both friendly and enemy Grunts and Spectres on your minimap at all times.

Field Notes

- This Tier 2 Kit is great if you're always looking to quickly pick off enemy AI. Your minimap will show you the positions of the enemy AI to take them out and receive your Titan or Core ability quicker.

PRO TIP: STRONGSIDE

Since the Minion Detector also shows you friendly AI on the minimap, you can use this to locate enemy Pilots. Watch for groups of friendly AI disappearing from the minimap and you'll find an enemy Pilot nearby.

TIER 2 KIT

WARPFALL TRANSMITTER

KIT UNLOCK: LEVEL 16

The Warpfall Transmitter accelerates your Titanfall substantially, using short-range jump technology.

Field Notes

- The Warpfall Transmitter is a great way to score Titanfall kills on enemy Titans. This kit allows your Titan to fall in three seconds rather than five. With the shortened amount of time you'll be able to line up some awesome Titanfall kills.

PRO TIP: STRONGSIDE

If you notice an enemy Titan sitting in a position and not moving too much, that is the time to deploy your Titan. When an enemy Titan is running in a direct line, call in your Titan a bit in front of him. This will take some practice as you have to predict where he will be when your Titan lands. Also, if you're feeling lucky, you can bait an enemy Titan towards you and lay the Titanfall where the enemy Titan will be chasing you.

TIER 2 KIT

DEAD MAN'S TRIGGER

KIT UNLOCK: LEVEL 37

The Dead Man's Trigger auto-detonates all your planted explosives when you are killed.

Field Notes

- This is a helpful Anti-Titan kit and best used with Satchel Charges. Many times when rodeo attacking an enemy Titan, they are able to kill you before you can detonate the Satchel Charges. This kit rewards that hard work and explodes on the enemy Titan when your Pilot is taken out, allowing your teammates to finish the Titan off. Avoid using this kit with the Arc Mines; they are more effective when they stay on the map instead of just exploding once you are killed.

TIER 2 KIT

THE "ICEPICK"

KIT UNLOCK: LEVEL 43

The "Icepick" is a modified Data Knife that increases the speed with which you can hack Spectres and turret control panels.

Field Notes

- The "Icepick" cuts your time to hack a turret or Spectre in half. This allows you to capture a turret fast and immediately get back into the action. This Tier 2 Kit is best used on maps that are heavily based around turrets, like Training Ground.

TIER 2 KIT

GUARDIAN CHIP

KIT UNLOCK: LEVEL 49

This upgraded targeting system allows your Auto-Titan to engage enemies with much greater accuracy.

Field Notes

- This Tier 2 Kit upgrades your Auto-Titan greatly. Your Auto-Titan will kill many more enemy AI and even kill enemy Pilots in pursuit of the Auto-Titan or enemy Pilots that expose themselves in the open for too long.

PRO TIP: STRONGSIDE

When equipping the Guardian Chip, equip the Arc Cannon to maximize its use. This weapon will take out enemy AI and Pilots that expose themselves too much. This weapon can also eliminate enemy Pilots in mid air after they have ejected from their Titan.

ADVANCED PILOT CUSTOMIZATION

Now that you know how all the Pilot weapons, abilities, and kits function, it's time to put it all together. Your ability to customize your Pilot is largely determined by your progression—the more you level up, the more customization options are available. By the time you've reached level 38, you should have access to most weapons, abilities, and kits, allowing for deeper and more specialized loadouts. Here we take a look at some sample loadouts. While you may find some of these loadouts beneficial, feel free to tailor them to your own specific needs. These loadouts should only serve as a starting point, provided to inspire your own Pilot configurations.

SPECIALIZED LOADOUTS

What's your role? These loadouts give you some options to think about when customizing your Pilot. Do you want to rush the enemy and engage at close range? Or perhaps you'd rather skirt around the perimeter of the map and pick off enemies with stealth and precision. Here's a few loadouts capable of filling specific roles on your team. Feel free to tweak and further customize them to match your style of play.

Attacker

PRIMARY WEAPON
FULL-AUTO ASSAULT WEAPON
R-101C CARBINE
ATTACHMENT: HCOG
MOD: EXTENDED MAGAZINE
ANTI-TITAN WEAPON
FIRES MAGNETIC GRENADES
MAG LAUNCHER
SIDEARM
HIGH-POWERED REVOLVER
B3 WINGMAN
TACTICAL ABILITY
STIM
SPEED AND HEALTH REGENERATION BOOST
ORDNANCE
FRAG GRENADE
EXPLOSIVE ANTI-PERSONNEL WEAPON
TIER 1 KIT
POWER CELL
YOUR PILOT'S TACTICAL ABILITY RECHARGES FASTER
TIER 2 KIT
WARPFALL TRANSMITTER
YOUR TITAN WARPS INTO BATTLE

This is a great go-to loadout for any game mode where you want to take the fight to the enemy with speed and aggression. The R-101C Carbine is arguably the most versatile primary weapon in the game, making it a true contender in any firefight, regardless of range. Add an Extended Magazine to minimize reloads, allowing you to easily wipe out a squad of Grunts and a couple of enemy Pilots with one magazine. The Power Cell Tier 1 Kit decreases the recharge time for the Stim ability, providing more frequent speed boosts and health regeneration—if you take fire, activate Stim to evade and heal. Using this loadout, kill minions and enemy Pilots to decrease your Titan's build time. Then when it's time for Titanfall, the Warpfall Transmitter Tier 2 Kit speeds up the process—try to drop your Titan on top of an enemy Titan for a humiliating Titanfall kill.

Defender

When playing Hardpoint or Capture the Flag, sometimes it's best to stay put and defend an objective, particularly in close matches. Most flags and Hardpoints are located inside buildings where you can dominate close-range battles using the R-97 Compact SMG equipped with the Scatterfire mod. This weapon configuration may not be accurate, but at close range it doesn't matter—chew through your opponents with the weapon's intense high rate of fire. The RE-45 Autopistol (and even Sidewinder) can serve as good backups when your R-97 runs out of ammo. When you're not patrolling the objective, strategically place Arc Mines on ceilings or walls near the most common entry points. Once your Titan is ready, deploy it outside and put it on Guard or Follow mode. The Guardian Chip helps your Titan engage incoming threats more efficiently while the Active Radar Pulse ability allows you to intercept approaching enemy minions and Pilots.

Hacker

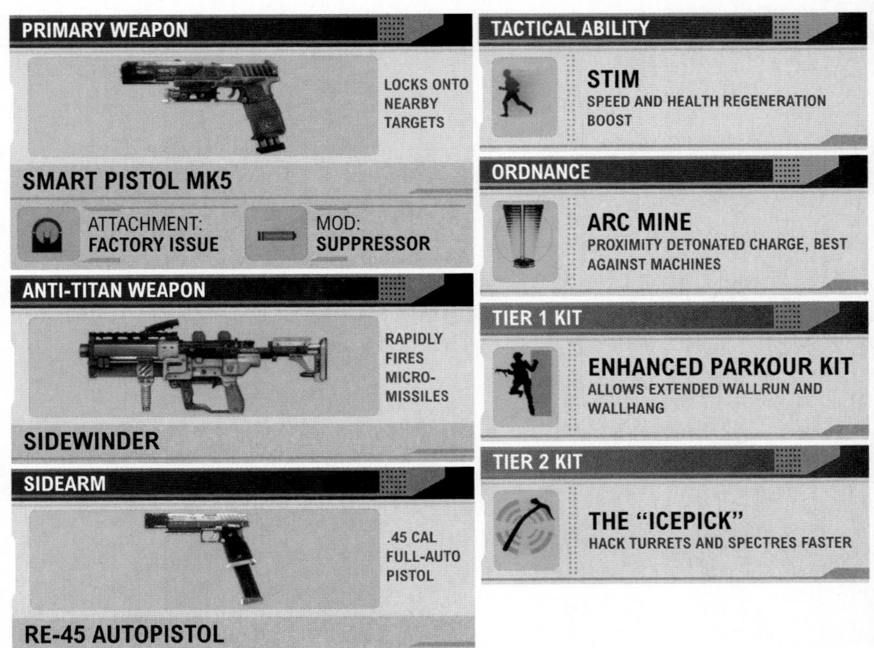

PRIMARY WEAPON
LOCKS ONTO NEARBY TARGETS
SMART PISTOL MK5
ATTACHMENT: FACTORY ISSUE
MOD: SUPPRESSOR
ANTI-TITAN WEAPON
RAPIDLY FIRES MICRO-MISSILES
SIDEWINDER
SIDEARM
.45 CAL FULL-AUTO PISTOL
RE-45 AUTOPISTOL
TACTICAL ABILITY
STIM
SPEED AND HEALTH REGENERATION BOOST
ORDNANCE
ARC MINE
PROXIMITY DETONATED CHARGE, BEST AGAINST MACHINES
TIER 1 KIT
ENHANCED PARKOUR KIT
ALLOWS EXTENDED WALLRUN AND WALLHANG
TIER 2 KIT
THE "ICEPICK"
HACK TURRETS AND SPECTRES FASTER

This is a good loadout if you're looking to hack turrets and Spectres with your Data Knife. Use the Stim ability and the Enhanced Parkour Kit to rush toward turrets early in the round. Once hacked, place Arc Mines near the console to prevent enemy Pilots from tampering with your turret. The "Icepick" Tier 2 Kit allows you to quickly hack enemy Spectres and turrets, making you less vulnerable during the hacking process. Start the round by hacking turrets, then rush enemy Spectres—most enemy Spectres arrive when your team deploys Titans. Gaining control of turrets and Spectres gives your team a significant advantage—plus you're credited with any kills they get, reducing your Titan's build time. Having your own personal army of Spectres following you around the map is never a bad thing either.

Rodeo Champion

If you like rodeo attacking enemy Titans, this is the loadout for you. When equipped with the Slammer mod, the Spitfire LMG is the most effective primary weapon during rodeo attacks, completely depleting a Titan's health within a few seconds. But don't let the enemy Titan see you coming. Use the Cloak ability to mask your movements, then daze the enemy Titan with an Arc Grenade before hopping aboard. While recovering from the Arc Grenade, the enemy Titan is vulnerable, buying you just enough time to perform a successful rodeo attack. The Charge Rifle is also effective when performing rodeo attacks—one charged shot may be enough to take out a damaged Titan. But the Spitfire LMG is without a doubt the fastest way to drop a Titan at full strength—you don't even have to reload. Even once you get your Titan, consider putting it on Follow mode to serve as a distraction. When equipped with the Guardian Chip, your unoccupied Titan is more effective at engaging targets—rodeo an enemy Titan while your own Titan helps dish out damage.

Sniper

PRIMARY WEAPON
SCOPED HEAVY RIFLE
KRABER-AP SNIPER
ATTACHMENT: 4.5X ZOOM SCOPE
MOD: STABILIZER
ANTI-TITAN WEAPON
LONG CHARGE PRECISION BEAM
CHARGE RIFLE
SIDEARM
.45 CAL FULL-AUTO PISTOL
RE-45 AUTOPISTOL
TACTICAL ABILITY
CLOAK
MOST EFFECTIVE AGAINST TITANS
ORDNANCE
ARC MINE
PROXIMITY DETONATED CHARGE, BEST AGAINST MACHINES
TIER 1 KIT
ENHANCED PARKOUR KIT
ALLOWS EXTENDED WALLRUN AND WALLHANG
TIER 2 KIT
MINION DETECTOR
REVEALS ALL GRUNTS AND SPECTRES ON YOUR MINIMAP ALL THE TIME

The Kraber-AP Sniper rifle is one of the most difficult primary weapons to master due to its slow rate of fire. But its one-shot kill capability makes it an enticing choice. The 4.5X Zoom Scope or AOG provide ample magnification for most maps, while the Stabilizer helps steady the rifle, making target acquisition much faster. But unless using the Suppressor mod, you'll appear on the minimap each time you fire. Therefore move around the map, using Cloak to avoid detection and the RE-45 Autopistol to engage any close-range threats. If you find a position too good to move from, scatter a few Arc Mines behind you to neutralize enemy Pilots attempting to sneak up on you. In addition to your rifle, engage Titans at long range too, using the powerful Charge Rifle to score critical hits from a safe distance.

If you want to decrease the build time of your Titan, consider hunting enemy Grunts and Spectres with this loadout. The Hemlok BF-R's burst fire is perfect for quickly dropping minions at close and intermediate ranges—you can wipe out entire squads with a few pulls of the trigger. Engage threats from windows and other elevated positions where you can remain concealed—avoid rooftops, as you'll be silhouetted and easy to spot. The Suppressor mod keeps you off the minimap, preventing enemy Pilots from detecting you. Meanwhile, the Minion Detector Tier 2 Kit keeps the minimap updated with new minion contacts, allowing you to hunt down Grunts and Spectres as soon as they arrive. But don't miss the chance to hunt down unsuspecting enemy Pilots too. The Cloak ability, your weapon's Suppressor, and Stealth Tier 1 Kit give you a chance to get the jump on your prey, dropping them with a couple of bursts from the suppressed Hemlok BF-R or a precise headshot using the B3 Wingman.

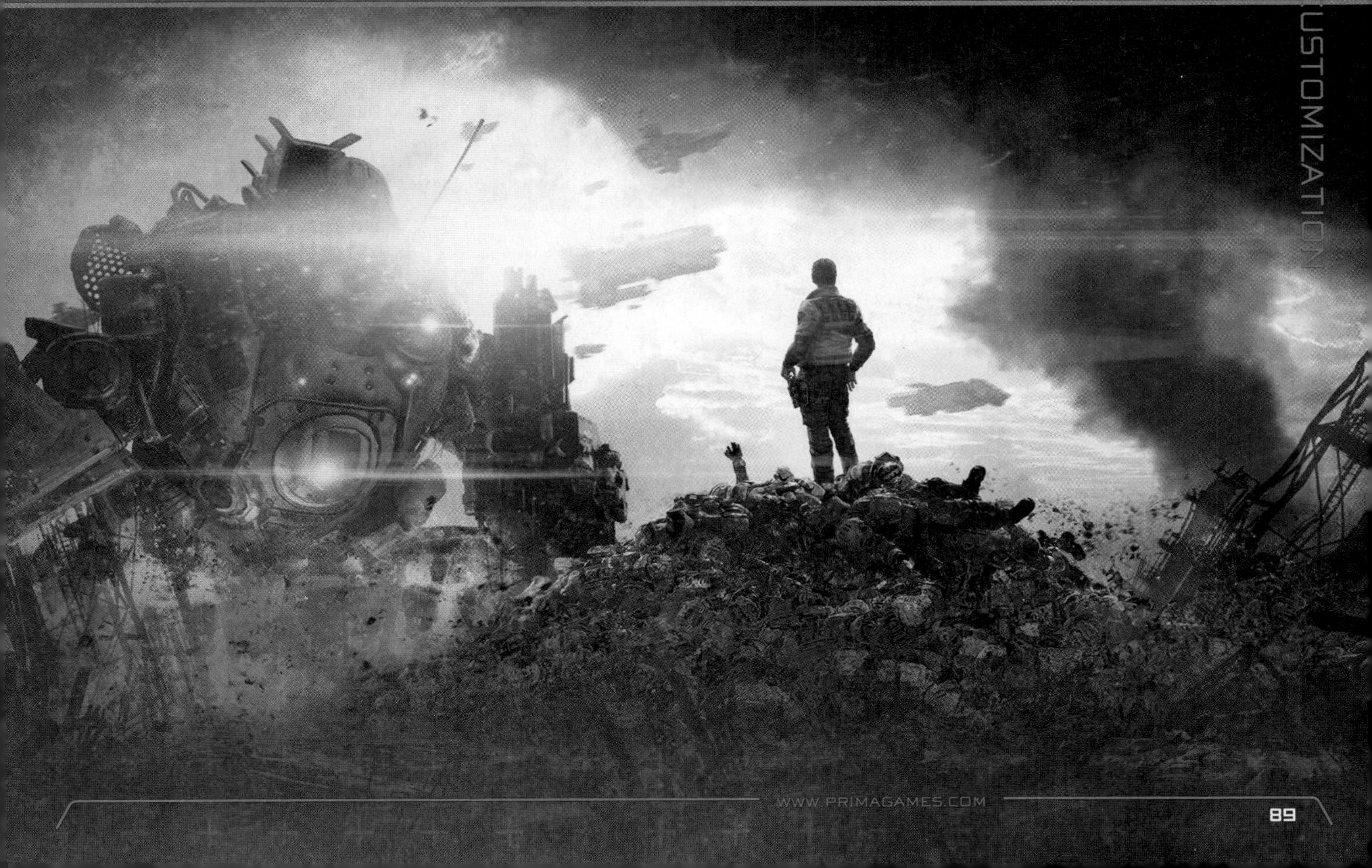

PRO LOADOUTS

Pro gamers StrongSide, Flamesword, and Walshy offer a sneak peak at a few of their go-to loadouts. Feel fee to give them a shot or tweak them slightly to make them your own. Or better yet, meet the pros online and try to beat them with their own loadout!

StrongSide's Well-Rounded Loadout

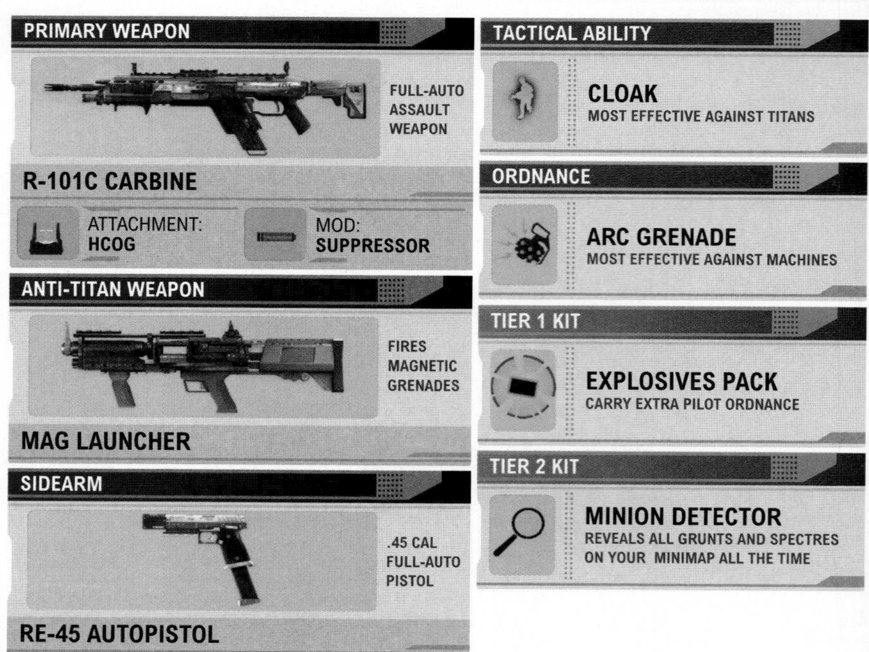

PRIMARY WEAPON
FULL-AUTO ASSAULT WEAPON
R-101C CARBINE
ATTACHMENT: HCOG
MOD: SUPPRESSOR
ANTI-TITAN WEAPON
FIRES MAGNETIC GRENADES
MAG LAUNCHER
SIDEARM
.45 CAL FULL-AUTO PISTOL
RE-45 AUTOPISTOL
TACTICAL ABILITY
CLOAK
MOST EFFECTIVE AGAINST TITANS
ORDNANCE
ARC GRENADE
MOST EFFECTIVE AGAINST MACHINES
TIER 1 KIT
EXPLOSIVES PACK
CARRY EXTRA PILOT ORDNANCE
TIER 2 KIT
MINION DETECTOR
REVEALS ALL GRUNTS AND SPECTRES ON YOUR MINIMAP ALL THE TIME

This is my go-to loadout. It is extremely versatile for all situations. I am able to stay hidden on the minimap with the Suppressor attached and I'm able to shoot at mid-long range distances with the HCOG attached. While I'm moving through a hallway, I'll pull out my RE-45 Autopistol just in case I run into any enemy Pilots. I use Cloak so I am able to sneak close to a weak enemy Titan and rodeo attack the Titan to finish it off. The Arc Grenade equipped with the Explosives Pack allows you to bombard enemy Titans and deal massive damage while they are disoriented by the Arc Grenade. Lastly, attaching Minion Detector gives you a early look where all minions are located, allowing you to kill minions quicker.

PRIMARY WEAPON
MEDIUM RANGE SUBMACHINE GUN
C.A.R. SMG
ATTACHMENT: HCOG
MOD: COUNTERWEIGHT
ANTI-TITAN WEAPON
FIRES MAGNETIC GRENADES
MAG LAUNCHER
SIDEARM
PRECISION SEMI-AUTO PISTOL
HAMMOND P2011
TACTICAL ABILITY
STIM
SPEED AND HEALTH REGENERATION BOOST
ORDNANCE
ARC GRENADE
MOST EFFECTIVE AGAINST MACHINES
TIER 1 KIT
RUN N GUN KIT
PISTOLS AND SMGS CAN BE FIRED WHILE SPRINTING
TIER 2 KIT
MINION DETECTOR
REVEALS ALL GRUNTS AND SPECTRES ON YOUR MINIMAP ALL THE TIME

One of my favorite loadouts is the C.A.R. SMG attached with the HCOG scope and Counterweight mod. I prefer this loadout for any game mode because its purpose is to quickly call down my Titan. The Minion Detector allows me to see where all the minions are on the map, and with the addition of the Run N Gun Kit I am able to sprint through minions as I lay down steel. This is primarily a Titan building loadout, so I always try to avoid long-distance fights with Pilots. Keep the fights close quarter since the SMG excels in this department. Stim is my preferred Tactical Ability and I like to save it for when I engage enemy Pilots or need extra speed to make a jump. Arc Grenades allow me to disorient enemy Titans or take out a squad of minions. Overall this is a great loadout that will play well for any game mode—its strong suit is Attrition.

My loadout has the G2A4 Rifle because I consider it to be the best mid-range weapon—I can pick off minions and Pilots with one headshot. When playing against good players that get the first shot on me, I find myself able to win a few of these battles by pulling off a headshot. I chose the HCOG because I feel that most of my fights are mid-close range and this scope's zoom is perfect for these battles. With the Suppressor mod equipped, the weapon still kills with one shot to the head and three shots to the body and, most importantly, it keeps you hidden off the minimap. For my sidearm, I pick the B3 Wingman for its power. My Anti-Titan weapon, the Mag Launcher, is the perfect weapon coupled with three Arc Grenades due to the Explosives Pack. Just throw an Arc Grenade and unload a clip of your Mag Launcher. Repeat until the Titan is dead. For my Tactical Ability, I use the Active Radar Pulse and look at the high ground, where Pilots usually are, or for irregular minion movement like jumping to spot Pilots. For my Tier 2 Kit, I use the Minion Detector to find and kill more minions each game.

StrongSide's Defensive Loadout

PRIMARY WEAPON
SEMI-AUTOMATIC SHOTGUN
EVA-8 SHOTGUN
ATTACHMENT: IRON SIGHTS
MOD: SUPPRESSOR
ANTI-TITAN WEAPON
FIRES MAGNETIC GRENADES
MAG LAUNCHER
SIDEARM
.45 CAL FULL-AUTO PISTOL
RE-45 AUTOPISTOL
TACTICAL ABILITY
CLOAK
MOST EFFECTIVE AGAINST TITANS
ORDNANCE
ARC MINE
PROXIMITY DETONATED CHARGE, BEST AGAINST MACHINES
TIER 1 KIT
EXPLOSIVES PACK
CARRY EXTRA PILOT ORDNANCE
TIER 2 KIT
MINION DETECTOR
REVEALS ALL GRUNTS AND SPECTRES ON YOUR MINIMAP ALL THE TIME

This is my close-quarter loadout when I'm trying to hold down a position or Hardpoint inside a building. I like to throw Arc Mines around a doorway or on the ceiling near an entryway. I am then free to watch any other entry points knowing the Arc Mines will kill any enemy that enters from that location. The Suppressor also keeps me hidden on the minimap, making it harder for the enemy to exactly locate me in the building. Adding Cloak to this loadout just makes you that much harder to kill. If you see an enemy Pilot approaching, activate Cloak to further assist your stealthiness.

Flamesword's Mid-Range Loadout

With the G2A4 Rifle, I look to take down enemies from a distance and provide support fire for my allies. I enjoy attaching the HCOG scope with the Suppressor mod so I can remain off the minimap. The combination of Stim and the Enhanced Parkour Kit allow me to traverse the map freely. I always have an escape route ready when playing with this class, and the Stim ability comes up clutch when I engage enemies close up, providing a speed boost and health regeneration. For my Tier 2 Kit, I enjoy equipping the Guardian Chip so my Auto-Titan is more effective and I can still roam the map.

Walshy's Long-Range Loadout

I use this loadout on open maps, such as Fracture and Lagoon, where I can position myself far from the action and catch Pilots away from cover. When sniping with the Longbow DMR-Sniper, I only go for the headshot when the opponent is staying up on a roof or is running on the ground. When the opponent is jumping or wall running, I go for the body shots. Even though I am sniping long-range, I still prefer the AOG scope with my lower default sensitivity. It feels easier for me to keep track of the enemies when they are jumping and most importantly is easier to land my shots. Even though there are sniper trails on the bullets, I use the Suppressor mod to keep my position concealed while I constantly use Stim to relocate after I get a kill or two. I have the RE-45 Autopistol as my sidearm because I feel it is the best close-range pistol. While using this loadout, I avoid all mid-range engagements with Pilots. I don't actively seek out fights with Titans, but I have three Arc Grenades, thanks to the Explosives Pack, and the Mag Launcher just waiting to deal damage to Titans that come near me. Lastly, I use the Minion Detector Tier 2 Kit so I don't have to leave my advantageous sniping positions to find minions.

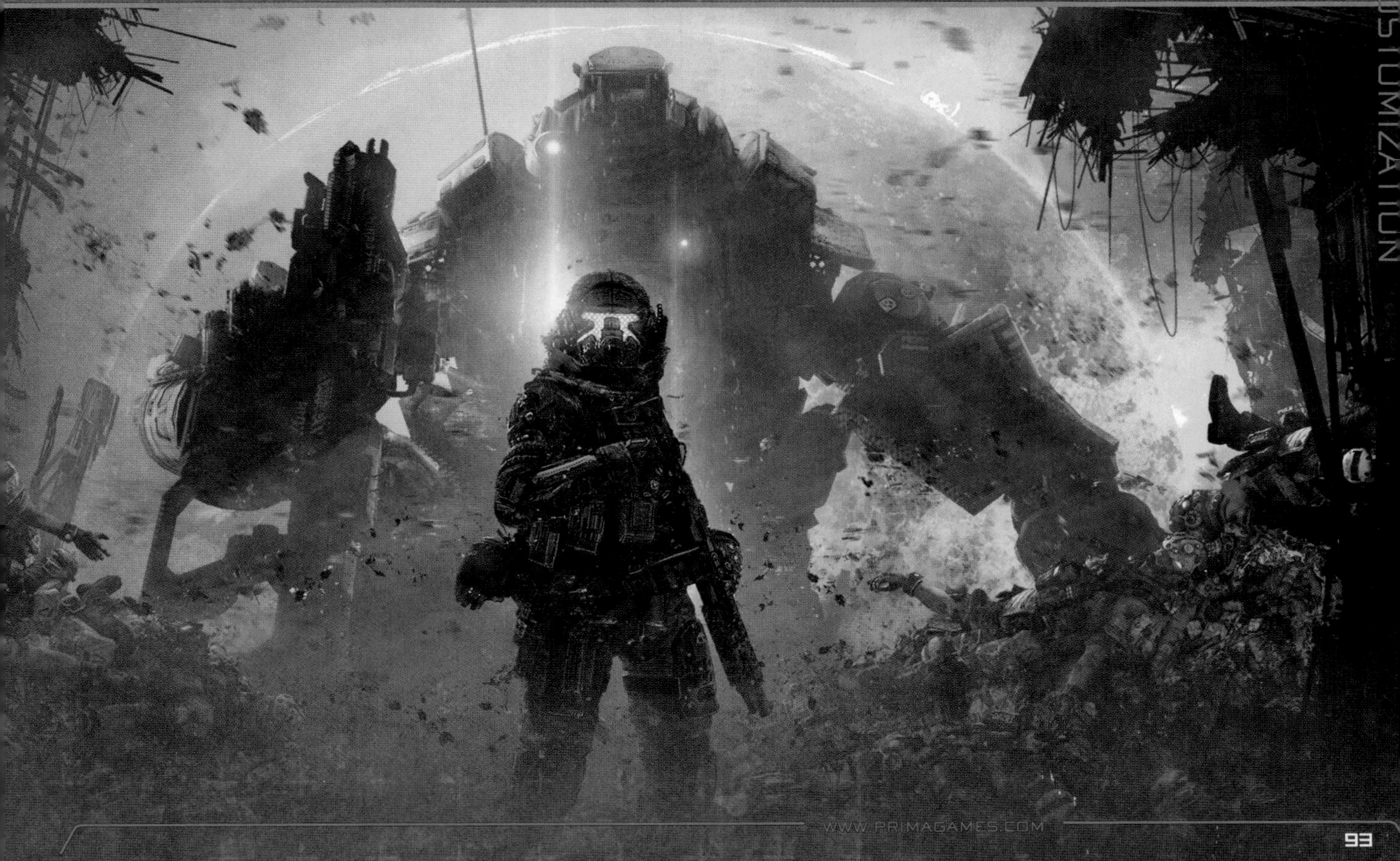

TITANS

Titans were originally designed by Hammond Robotics to perform a variety of tasks, ranging from cargo transport to deep space search and rescue. But in the Frontier, Titans have proven to be extremely effective in combat. Both the IMC and Militia rely on Titans to do the heavy lifting on the battlefield, outfitting them with heavy weapons as well as abilities and modular kits designed to give Titan Pilots a tactical advantage. Like the elite Pilots who operate them, Titans are highly customizable, allowing them to excel in a variety of combat roles.

TITAN CUSTOMIZATION

Customization doesn't end with outfitting your Pilot. Titans can also be customized to a Pilot's specifications, allowing for greater versatility or specialization. Once the Custom Titan options are unlocked, you can begin creating your own Titan loadouts. There are six options to choose from, allowing you to tailor your Titan's chassis, weapons, ability, and kits. Here's a breakdown of the different options available.

- **Chassis:** Start by choosing from the Atlas, Ogre, or Stryder Titans. These three chassis options are the platforms on which your Titan is built.
- **Primary Weapon:** This is your Titan's weapon when deploying. There are six to choose from, each with unique characteristics and functionality. Primary weapons can be equipped with optional mods, altering their performance.
- **Tactical Ability:** There are three active abilities giving Titans the ability to block/redirect incoming projectiles, emit electrically charged smoke, or deploy a defensive energy barrier.
- **Ordnance:** These shoulder-mounted missile and rocket launchers give Titans more offensive capability.
- **Kits:** As with Pilots, there are two kits slots, Tier 1 and Tier 2, each with five options. These passive kits enhance Titans in various ways. Select kits that complement your other loadout selections.

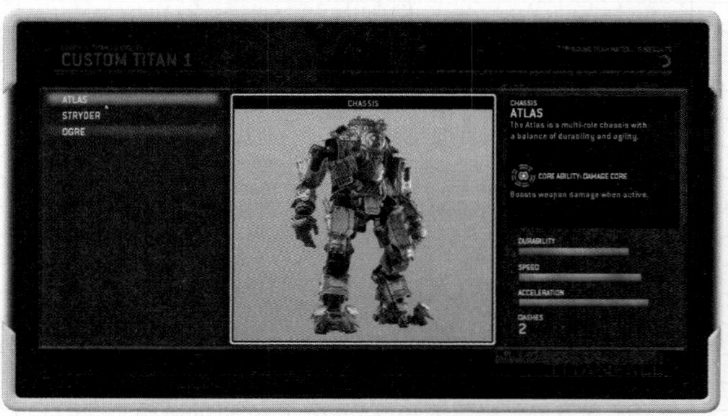

The first Custom Titan slot is unlocked at level 10, giving you the chance to build your very own Titan—start by selecting a chassis.

PRESET TITAN LOADOUTS

Titan customization isn't readily available to rookie Pilots. Instead, new Pilots must choose from three preset Titan loadouts: Assault, Tank, and Artillery. Each of these loadouts is built around a different chassis, allowing new Pilots to try out the Atlas, Ogre, and Stryder Titans. As indicated by their names, each preset Titan loadout is built to fulfill a special role on the battlefield. Experiment with these loadouts to help find the right mix of weapons, abilities, and kits. You may find some loadouts work better than others depending on your style of play and the current game mode.

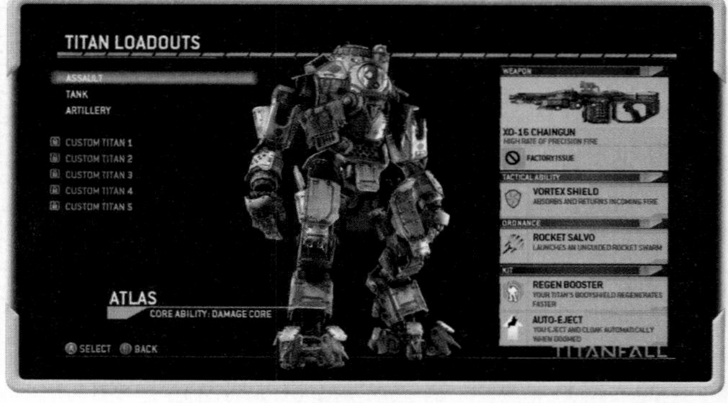

Until you reach level 10, you'll have to go into battle with one of the three preset Titan loadouts.

Assault

CHASSIS
ATLAS

Loadout Unlock: Level 1

Of the three preset Titan loadouts, this Atlas configuration is the best choice for new Pilots, offering a fine balance of durability, mobility, and firepower. The XO-16 Chaingun is very easy to use, operating like a standard machine gun—albeit much larger. Use this primary weapon to chip away at the bodyshields and armor of enemy Titans—target those red spots to score critical hits. Once the Titan's Damage Core ability is active, the XO-16 Chaingun and Rocket Salvo can dish out some extreme damage. But don't stand still and take hit after hit during Titan battles. Use the Vortex Shield to catch and redirect incoming projectiles at your enemies. When necessary, retreat behind cover and let your bodyshield recharge—the Regen Booster Kit helps reduce the recharge time. If your Titan sustains heavy damage and enters its doomed state, the Auto-Eject Kit ensures you'll escape without a scratch, temporarily cloaking your airborne Pilot in the process.

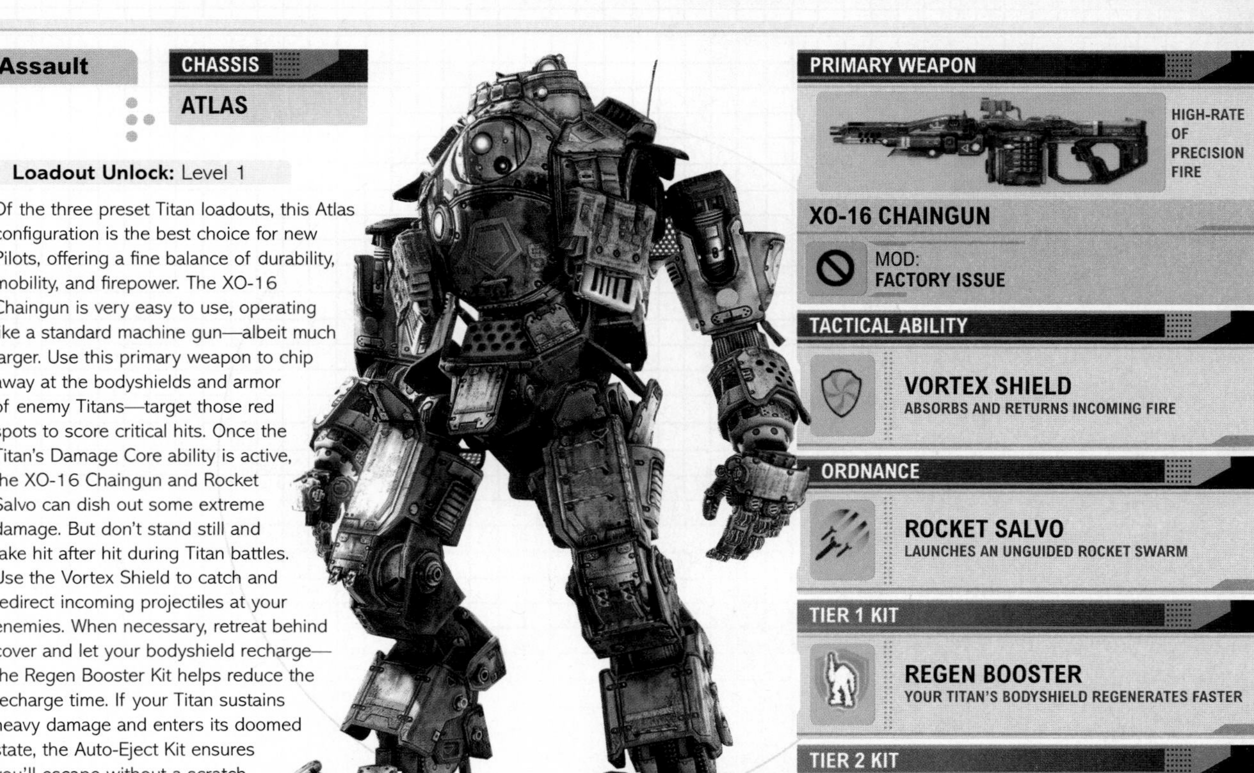

PRIMARY WEAPON

HIGH-RATE OF PRECISION FIRE

XO-16 CHAINGUN

MOD:
FACTORY ISSUE

TACTICAL ABILITY

VORTEX SHIELD
ABSORBS AND RETURNS INCOMING FIRE

ORDNANCE

ROCKET SALVO
LAUNCHES AN UNGUIDED ROCKET SWARM

TIER 1 KIT

REGEN BOOSTER
YOUR TITAN'S BODYSHIELD REGENERATES FASTER

TIER 2 KIT

AUTO-EJECT
YOU EJECT AND CLOAK AUTOMATICALLY WHEN DOOMED

Tank

CHASSIS
OGRE

Loadout Unlock: Level 1

Armed with the powerful 40mm Cannon, this Tank loadout for the Ogre is all about dishing out heavy damage, best suited for engaging enemy Titans. The 40mm Cannon is effective at both intermediate and close range, so don't worry about rushing in to point-blank range. Instead, keep your distance and pound away at your opponents while blocking and redirecting incoming fire with the Vortex Shield. Once active, the Shield Core ability can help absorb some of those incoming projectiles too. This particular loadout excels in desperate close-quarter duels thanks to its Survivor Tier 2 Kit—this allows the Titan to survive longer in its doomed state, giving you more time to fight before ejecting. But before you eject, make sure you're as close as possible to enemy units—the Nuclear Ejection Tier 1 Kit emits a massive blast, capable of wiping out Pilots, minions, and even damaged Titans in wide radius.

PRIMARY WEAPON

SEMI-AUTO 40MM HE ROUNDS

40MM CANNON

MOD:
FACTORY ISSUE

TACTICAL ABILITY

VORTEX SHIELD
ABSORBS AND RETURNS INCOMING FIRE

ORDNANCE

ROCKET SALVO
LAUNCHES AN UNGUIDED ROCKET SWARM

TIER 1 KIT

NUCLEAR EJECTION
YOUR TITAN GOES NUCLEAR WHEN YOU EJECT

TIER 2 KIT

SURVIVOR
YOUR TITAN DEGRADES SLOWER WHEN DOOMED

Artillery

CHASSIS

STRYDER

Loadout Unlock: Level 3

If you prefer fast hit-and-run tactics, this is the loadout for you. This Stryder loadout is most effective when attacking at close range. The Quad Rocket primary weapon is capable of inflicting heavy damage, but its limited range and magazine capacity can leave the Titan vulnerable in some situations. So use the Stryder's dashes and Dash Core to close the distance, attack with the Quad Rocket and Rocket Salvo, and then retreat before your target can retaliate. The Regen Booster Tier 1 Kit comes in handy for quickly recharging the Titan's bodyshield, but you need to find cover first. But unlike the Ogre, don't try any last-minute heroics in the Stryder—it doesn't have the armor to last long. While the Survivor Tier 2 Kit buys you more time during the doomed state, use that time to eject and scurry to safety.

PRIMARY WEAPON

FIRES 4 ROCKETS PER VOLLEY

QUAD ROCKET

MOD: FACTORY ISSUE

TACTICAL ABILITY

VORTEX SHIELD
ABSORBS AND RETURNS INCOMING FIRE

ORDNANCE

ROCKET SALVO
LAUNCHES AN UNGUIDED ROCKET SWARM

TIER 1 KIT

REGEN BOOSTER
YOUR TITAN'S BODYSHIELD REGENERATES FASTER

TIER 2 KIT

SURVIVOR
YOUR TITAN DEGRADES SLOWER WHEN DOOMED

CHASSIS

Choosing a chassis is the most fundamental decision Pilots face when customizing their Titan. Before selecting a chassis, take into account the kind of role you wish to play on the battlefield. There are two major factors to take into consideration: speed and durability. While the Ogre is the most durable chassis, it's also the slowest. The Stryder, on the other hand, offers speed, but at the cost of less armor. Meanwhile, the Atlas fills the middle ground, offering a balance of speed and durability. Each Titan chassis also has a unique Core Ability, further defining their combat role. Carefully weigh the pros and cons of each chassis before starting your Titan's loadout.

ATLAS

The Atlas is the workhorse of the various Titan chassis. It has served in the form of countless variants throughout the Frontier for decades, and will likely remain a common sight for many more to come. Despite the age of the design, its robust Damage Core allows it to remain competitive in battle with more modern Titans.

On the Frontier, the Atlas has always performed when needed. From the first conflicts to the latest deployments, the Atlas stands the test of time. As the workhorse of the IMC Titan fleet, it has survived every encounter and mission scenario and continues to outperform competing technologies on every battlefield.

CORE ABILITY

DAMAGE CORE: Boosts weapon damage when active.

TITAN PERFORMANCE

DURABILITY

SPEED

ACCELERATION

DASHES: 2

Field Notes

› The Atlas is the most versatile of all three Titans. This Titan isn't the fastest, but it can still move around the map quickly. And while this Titan doesn't have the strongest armor, it is still very durable. The Atlas prevails with its Core Ability, Damage Core. While active, you can quickly deal massive damage to enemy Titans. When attaching the Core Extender, you're able to deal massive damage for a longer amount of time. This Titan has two dashes and works really when combined with the Dash Quickcharger Tier 1 Kit, which charges your dashes quicker. Using the Arc Cannon you'll be able to pick off groups of minions and still be ready to fight a Pilot or Titan. Look for opportunities to melee attack doomed Titans—the Atlas punches into the enemy Titan's hull, then grabs and hurls the enemy Pilot.

DEVELOPER TIP — Respawn Entertainment

The Atlas' Damage Core enhances the damage of all of the Atlas' attacks. Primary Weapons, Ordnance, and even Electric Smoke will inflict more damage while the Damage Core is active.

OGRE

The Ogre-class Titan is often referred to as Hammond Robotics' "800 pound gorilla". Although the Ogre's weight and size make it a slow mover, it is very well armored and shielded—with armor plating this thick, you won't need to run.

In field testing, Hammond Robotics' newest model uses its heavy armor design to destroy the competition in ballistic and martial testing. And in the Ogre's initial deployment it truly delivered. In total it was responsible for 67% of enemy force depletion. It suffered only superficial damage to the outer hull while mitigating damage to friendly units by nearly 40% and inflicting over 50% more damage to enemy units.

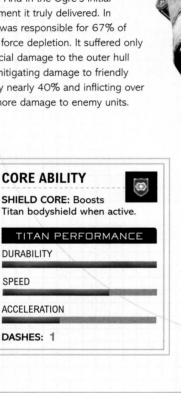

CORE ABILITY

SHIELD CORE: Boosts Titan bodyshield when active.

TITAN PERFORMANCE

DURABILITY

SPEED

ACCELERATION

DASHES: 1

Field Notes

- While this Titan is the slowest and has the least amount of dashes, it makes up for it by having the most armor. This Titan is tough to take down. When your team is on the defensive, like on Capture the Flag or defending a Hardpoint, and you have to fight your way out, this is the perfect Titan to deal tons of damage and at the same time serve as a distraction while your teammates flank. The Ogre's Core Ability is a Shield Core that gives you a stronger "boosted bodyshield" to let you take more damage over the next few seconds. Ogres excel in melee attacks, ripping the arms off of doomed enemy Titans and beating them with their own dismembered appendages.

DEVELOPER TIP — Respawn Entertainment

The Ogre's Shield Core enhances the Ogre's bodyshield capacity substantially—you are not made invulnerable, but it will take a lot more hits to deplete the bodyshield.

STRYDER

The Stryder represents Hammond Robotics' leading design in fast-attack combat systems. The Stryder is unmatched in speed and agility, but carries minimal shields and armor. Using its Dash Core aggressively, a skilled Stryder Pilot can outflank enemies in a very short time, completely taking them by surprise.

In field testing, the Stryder outperformed all other Titans in speed, acceleration, and agility, but direct action missions is where the Stryder excels. As the first to strike, Stryder destroys Class A defenses with a 63% higher success rate and it can secure rapid deployment objectives faster than any other Titan on the Frontier.

CORE ABILITY

DASH CORE: Dash is inexhaustible when active.

TITAN PERFORMANCE

DURABILITY

SPEED

ACCELERATION

DASHES: 3

Field Notes

› The Stryder is the fastest Titan in the game. This Titan has three dashes, making it extremely mobile. At the expense of speed, the Stryder does have less armor, making it weaker than the other two Titans. Don't let this bother you—this Titan's speed allows you to either play aggressively or passive. When you play aggressively, you will want to have two dashes saved up in case you need to back out of a fight or an enemy Titan tries to ambush you. When playing passive, equip a weapon that has range, providing support fire for your allies on the front lines. This Titan's Core Ability is Dash Core. Once activated, your Stryder Titan's dash is instantly recharged, allowing you to dash for a set amount of time. When melee attacking a doomed Titan, the Stryder punches through the enemy Titan's hull, grabs the Pilot, and squeezes until there's nothing left but vapor.

DEVELOPER TIP Respawn ENTERTAINMENT

The Stryder's Dash Core provides unlimited dash capacity while active. You can dash as much and as often as you want until the Dash Core shuts down.

PRIMARY WEAPONS

After choosing a chassis, selecting a primary weapon is the next most crucial step when customizing your Titan. Similar to the Pilot's primary weapons, the weapons available to Titans are all distinct, with their own strengths and weaknesses. As a result, your choice of primary weapon dictates how your Titan engages hostile forces. Do you prefer attacking from long range, scoring critical hits with precision weapons? Or maybe you savor close-quarter duels, where accuracy and range take a back seat to brute force and damage output. Whatever your preference, there's a Titan weapon to meet your needs.

40MM CANNON

MAGAZINE CAPACITY: 20 WEAPON UNLOCK: LEVEL 1

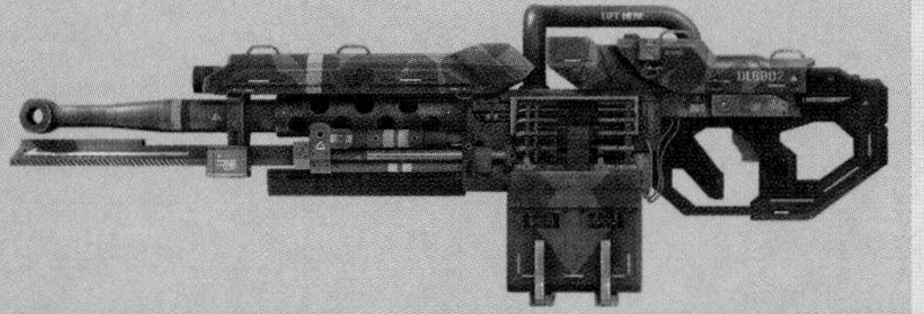

The factory-issue 40mm Cannon is a semi-automatic weapon that fires a high-explosive round with good accuracy.

STRENGTHS:

- Powerful rounds that can take out Pilots and Titans
- Large magazine capacity

WEAKNESSES:

- Hard to hit fast-moving Pilots
- Limited effective range

WEAPON PERFORMANCE

DAMAGE

ACCURACY

RANGE

FIRE RATE

WEAPON MODS

IMAGE	NAME	DESCRIPTION	UNLOCK
	Burst Fire	This mod allows you to fire three-round bursts. However, your magazine will deplete faster as a result.	Titan Killer (II) Challenge: Kill 20 Titans
	Extended Magazine	This mod increases the ammo capacity of the weapon, making it so that you don't have to reload as often.	If It Moves... (II) Challenge: Kill 25 Enemies

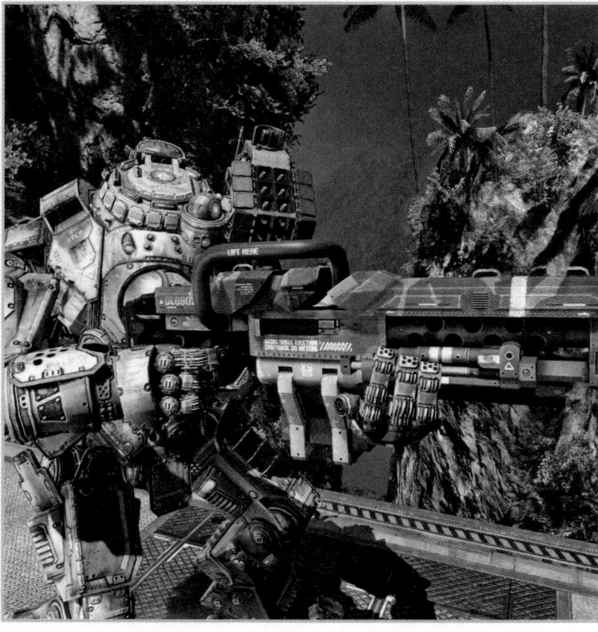

Field Notes

- This weapon packs a punch with every bullet. It has the perfect balance of being able to deal a fair amount of damage to Titans along with taking out any minions or Pilots with one round.
- This gun is very difficult to use against Pilots that are on roofs or jumping around. Be sure to take advantage of the splash damage and try to shoot enemy Pilots when they are on the ground or next to a wall. If a Pilot is high up on a roof or jumping above your head, it is better to dash away and try the fight from another angle.
- This weapon, without any mods, can take out a couple of minions that are close together. But coupled with the Burst Fire, the 40mm Cannon can easily dispose of an entire group of minions with one or two bursts.
- This is one of the strongest weapons against enemy Titans in mid-close-range battles. It has a large magazine capacity and fast rate of fire, which allows you to deal continuous damage, and you aren't punished if you miss a few shots.
- The Burst Fire mod is great when playing on a map with lots of cover, so that you can shoot a couple bursts and dash away to safety. If you like the single-round semi-automatic fire, be sure to equip the Extended Magazine to get five extra rounds per mag. When head-to-head against another Titan, if this weapon doesn't kill the enemy, it will undoubtedly leave it weak enough to be finished off by your teammates.

40mm Cannon Challenges

IF IT MOVES...

TIER	CRITERIA	REWARD
1	Kill 10 Enemies	500 XP
2	Kill 25 Enemies	1,000 XP, Extended Magazine Mod
3	Kill 50 Enemies	2,500 XP
4	Kill 100 Enemies	5,000 XP
5	Kill 200 Enemies	10,000 XP

THE EXPENDABLES

TIER	CRITERIA	REWARD
1	Kill 10 Grunts	500 XP
2	Kill 25 Grunts	1,000 XP
3	Kill 50 Grunts	2,500 XP, Thin the Ranks Burn Card
4	Kill 100 Grunts	5,000 XP, Thin the Ranks Burn Card
5	Kill 200 Grunts	10,000 XP, Thin the Ranks Burn Card

TOP GUN

TIER	CRITERIA	REWARD
1	Kill 5 Pilots	500 XP
2	Kill 15 Pilots	1,000 XP
3	Kill 30 Pilots	2,500 XP, Most Wanted List Burn Card
4	Kill 50 Pilots	5,000 XP, Most Wanted List Burn Card
5	Kill 75 Pilots	10,000 XP, Most Wanted List Burn Card

THIS IS MY WEAPON

TIER	CRITERIA	REWARD
1	Use Weapon for .5 Hour	500 XP
2	Use Weapon for 1 Hour	1,000 XP
3	Use Weapon for 1.5 Hours	2,500 XP
4	Use Weapon for 2 Hours	5,000 XP
5	Use Weapon for 3 Hours	10,000 XP

MACHINE WAR

TIER	CRITERIA	REWARD
1	Kill 10 Spectres	500 XP
2	Kill 25 Spectres	1,000 XP
3	Kill 50 Spectres	2,500 XP, Urban Renewal Burn Card
4	Kill 75 Spectres	5,000 XP, Urban Renewal Burn Card
5	Kill 100 Spectres	10,000 XP, Urban Renewal Burn Card

TITAN KILLER

TIER	CRITERIA	REWARD
1	Kill 10 Titans	500 XP
2	Kill 20 Titans	1,000 XP, Burst Fire Mod
3	Kill 30 Titans	2,500 XP, Titan Salvage Burn Card
4	Kill 40 Titans	5,000 XP, Titan Salvage Burn Card
5	Kill 50 Titans	10,000 XP, Titan Salvage Burn Card

CRITICALLY CONDITIONED

TIER	CRITERIA	REWARD
1	Get 5 Critical Hits	500 XP
2	Get 15 Critical Hits	1,000 XP
3	Get 30 Critical Hits	2,500 XP
4	Get 50 Critical Hits	5,000 XP
5	Get 75 Critical Hits	10,000 XP

Awarded Burn Cards

Most Wanted List | Titan Salvage | Urban Renewal | Thin the Ranks

QUAD ROCKET

MAGAZINE CAPACITY: 6 WEAPON UNLOCK: LEVEL 1

The factory-issue Quad Rocket launcher fires four rockets at once in its primary firing mode. In alternate fire mode, it fires slow-moving swirls of rockets that are effective at temporarily denying territory to the enemy.

STRENGTHS:

- Easily wipe out squads of minions
- Alternate fire mode delays enemy advances

WEAKNESSES:

- Titans and Pilots can easily evade
- Low magazine capacity

WEAPON PERFORMANCE

DAMAGE

ACCURACY

RANGE

FIRE RATE

WEAPON MODS

IMAGE	NAME	DESCRIPTION	UNLOCK
	Extended Magazine	This mod increases the ammo capacity of the weapon, making it so that you don't have to reload as often.	If It Moves... (II) Challenge: Kill 25 Enemies
	Rapid Fire	This mod converts the weapon to a semi-automatic rocket launcher with a high rate of fire. The ammo feed modifications caused by this mod will restrict your fire to one missile per trigger pull.	Titan Killer (II) Challenge: Kill 20 Titans

Field Notes

- This weapon shoots four rockets in a condensed circular pattern. When fired in its alternate mode, the rockets' pattern expands into a larger circle. This is extremely helpful when backing away and firing at enemies coming around corners; open fire just before the enemy comes around the corner to surprise them with a volley of rockets.
- The Quad Rocket is most effective against Pilots when they are on the ground or trying to climb a wall vertically. Pilots have so much mobility that once they start wall jumping, this weapon becomes less effective.
- The Quad Rockets are effective when engaging minions. The normal shot will easily wipe out a squad of minions and can be fired from a distance. Be sure to fire one round in the alternate mode in case an enemy Titan comes around the corner. Having one rocket impact the opposing Titan can be key to winning the fight.
- When engaging enemy Titans, do so at close-mid range to ensure a hit—the rockets are very inaccurate at long range. For best results, flank an enemy Titan, fire the Quad Rockets at close range, and then either melee (as an Ogre) or retreat (as a Stryder) before your target can retaliate.
- The Rapid Fire mod decreases damage because you now only shoot one rocket at a time. The fire rate is increased, however, allowing you to shoot at a faster pace so you can target Pilots easier once they start wall jumping.

Quad Rocket Challenges

IF IT MOVES...

TIER	CRITERIA	REWARD
1	Kill 10 Enemies	500 XP
2	Kill 25 Enemies	1,000 XP, Extended Magazine Mod
3	Kill 50 Enemies	2,500 XP
4	Kill 100 Enemies	5,000 XP
5	Kill 150 Enemies	10,000 XP

THE EXPENDABLES

TIER	CRITERIA	REWARD
1	Kill 25 Grunts	500 XP
2	Kill 50 Grunts	1,000 XP
3	Kill 100 Grunts	2,500 XP
4	Kill 250 Grunts	5,000 XP
5	Kill 500 Grunts	10,000 XP

TOP GUN

TIER	CRITERIA	REWARD
1	Kill 5 Pilots	500 XP
2	Kill 15 Pilots	1,000 XP
3	Kill 30 Pilots	2,500 XP, Most Wanted List Burn Card
4	Kill 50 Pilots	5,000 XP, Most Wanted List Burn Card
5	Kill 75 Pilots	10,000 XP, Most Wanted List Burn Card

THIS IS MY WEAPON

TIER	CRITERIA	REWARD
1	Use Weapon for .5 Hour	500 XP
2	Use Weapon for 1 Hour	1,000 XP
3	Use Weapon for 1.5 Hours	2,500 XP
4	Use Weapon for 2 Hours	5,000 XP
5	Use Weapon for 3 Hours	10,000 XP

MACHINE WAR

TIER	CRITERIA	REWARD
1	Kill 10 Spectres	500 XP
2	Kill 25 Spectres	1,000 XP, Urban Renewal Burn Card
3	Kill 50 Spectres	2,500 XP, Urban Renewal Burn Card
4	Kill 100 Spectres	5,000 XP, Urban Renewal Burn Card
5	Kill 200 Spectres	10,000 XP, Urban Renewal Burn Card

TITAN KILLER

TIER	CRITERIA	REWARD
1	Kill 10 Titans	500 XP
2	Kill 20 Titans	1000XP, Rapid Fire Mod
3	Kill 30 Titans	2,500 XP, Titan Salvage Burn Card
4	Kill 40 Titans	5,000 XP, Titan Salvage Burn Card
5	Kill 50 Titans	10,000 XP, Titan Salvage Burn Card

XO-16 CHAINGUN

MAGAZINE CAPACITY: 60 WEAPON UNLOCK: LEVEL 1

The XO-16 Chaingun is a fully automatic ballistic weapon that fires 1.6-inch slugs with high precision at considerable range.

STRENGTHS:

- Great for clearing groups of minions
- Go trigger happy with large magazine capacity

WEAKNESSES:

- Relatively weak against Titans in toe-to-toe fight
- Poor stealth; target will know they're getting pelted

WEAPON PERFORMANCE

DAMAGE

ACCURACY

RANGE

FIRE RATE

WEAPON MODS

IMAGE	NAME	DESCRIPTION	UNLOCK
	Accelerator	The Accelerator causes the weapon to fire very slowly at first and over time accelerate to a much higher fire rate than normal.	Titan Killer (II) Challenge: Kill 20 Titans
	Extended Magazine	This mod increases the ammo capacity of the weapon, so that you don't have to reload as often.	If It Moves... (II) Challenge: Kill 25 Enemies

Field Notes

- Even though it has one of the lowest amounts of damage per bullet, it makes up for it with the largest magazine capacity. You can miss a few shots and still take down enemies with this weapon. The key to using this weapon is staying alive and picking off minions to get your Core Ability faster than your opponent.
- This weapon destroys Pilots that are out in the open. Even if they are wall running or jumping around, this weapon's fully automatic fire gives you the ammo to shoot until the Pilot is dead.
- This weapon takes out a group of minions easily while leaving you with enough bullets to pick off any Pilots that might be nearby. Since the XO-16 Chaingun clears out waves of minions so quickly, it is best to use a faster Titan (like the Stryder) to move around the map and find the easy kills.
- The XO-16 Chaingun is surprisingly accurate, making it ideal for scoring critical hits on enemy Titans. Aim for the red glowing segment on your target to dish out heavy damage. The weapon's high rate of fire allows you to quickly chip away at an enemy Titan's armor, particularly when the weapon is fitted with the Accelerator mod—this is ideal for taking down enemy dropships too.
- The Accelerator is the way to go with this gun with a gain of 90 extra rounds in your magazine at the expense of some hard to control recoil. When using the Accelerator, try to have a pre-planned route so that you can use up your full magazine and then retreat to a safe position to reload and recharge your shields. You do not want to get caught out in the open reloading this weapon. If you don't like the style of playing with the Accelerator, you can't go wrong with the Extended Magazine, giving you 30 extra rounds. Try using the Atlas or the Stryder with this weapon so you can dash in and out of fights more often.

XO-16 Chaingun Challenges

IF IT MOVES...

TIER	CRITERIA	REWARD
1	Kill 10 Enemies	500 XP
2	Kill 25 Enemies	1,000 XP, Extended Magazine Mod
3	Kill 50 Enemies	2,500 XP
4	Kill 100 Enemies	5,000 XP
5	Kill 200 Enemies	10,000 XP

THE EXPENDABLES

TIER	CRITERIA	REWARD
1	Kill 10 Grunts	500 XP
2	Kill 25 Grunts	1,000 XP
3	Kill 50 Grunts	2,500 XP, Thin the Ranks Burn Card
4	Kill 100 Grunts	5,000 XP, Thin the Ranks Burn Card
5	Kill 200 Grunts	10,000 XP, Thin the Ranks Burn Card

TOP GUN

TIER	CRITERIA	REWARD
1	Kill 5 Pilots	500 XP
2	Kill 15 Pilots	1,000 XP
3	Kill 30 Pilots	2,500 XP, Most Wanted List Burn Card
4	Kill 50 Pilots	5,000 XP, Most Wanted List Burn Card
5	Kill 75 Pilots	10,000 XP, Most Wanted List Burn Card

THIS IS MY WEAPON

TIER	CRITERIA	REWARD
1	Use Weapon for .5 Hour	500 XP
2	Use Weapon for 1 Hour	1,000 XP
3	Use Weapon for 1.5 Hours	2,500 XP
4	Use Weapon for 2 Hours	5,000 XP
5	Use Weapon for 3 Hours	10,000 XP

MACHINE WAR

TIER	CRITERIA	REWARD
1	Kill 10 Spectres	500 XP
2	Kill 25 Spectres	1,000 XP
3	Kill 50 Spectres	2,500 XP, Urban Renewal Burn Card
4	Kill 75 Spectres	5,000 XP, Urban Renewal Burn Card
5	Kill 100 Spectres	10,000 XP, Urban Renewal Burn Card

TITAN KILLER

TIER	CRITERIA	REWARD
1	Kill 10 Titans	500 XP
2	Kill 20 Titans	1,000 XP, Accelerator Mod
3	Kill 30 Titans	2,500 XP, Titan Salvage Burn Card
4	Kill 40 Titans	5,000 XP, Titan Salvage Burn Card
5	Kill 50 Titans	10,000 XP, Titan Salvage Burn Card

OFF THE DOME

TIER	CRITERIA	REWARD
1	Get 5 Headshots	500 XP
2	Get 15 Headshots	1,000 XP
3	Get 30 Headshots	2,500 XP
4	Get 50 Headshots	5,000 XP
5	Get 75 Headshots	10,000 XP

CRITICALLY CONDITIONED

TIER	CRITERIA	REWARD
1	Get 50 Critical Hits	500 XP
2	Get 100 Critical Hits	1,000 XP
3	Get 200 Critical Hits	2,500 XP
4	Get 300 Critical Hits	5,000 XP
5	Get 400 Critical Hits	10,000 XP

Awarded Burn Cards

Most Wanted List | Titan Salvage | Urban Renewal | Thin the Ranks

PLASMA RAILGUN

MAGAZINE CAPACITY: 4 WEAPON UNLOCK: LEVEL 12

The Plasma Railgun fires a traveling charged pulse with high accuracy out to long range. When zoomed, the weapon's power is charged up through several stages until it reaches full power. The charge can be held indefinitely before being fired.

STRENGTHS:

- Extremely high-damage weapon
- Long range; great for picking apart Titans from a distance

WEAKNESSES:

- Limited magazine capacity/rate of fire
- No splash damage; requires direct hit

WEAPON PERFORMANCE

DAMAGE

ACCURACY

RANGE

FIRE RATE

WEAPON MODS

IMAGE	NAME	DESCRIPTION	UNLOCK
	Extended Magazine	This mod increases the ammo capacity of the weapon, making it so that you don't have to reload as often.	If It Moves... (II) Challenge: Kill 15 Enemies
	Instant Shot	This mod converts the weapon so that it fires immediately without requiring a charging phase, but at the expense of its factory-issue, higher maximum damage output.	Titan Killer (I) Challenge: Kill 10 Titans

Field Notes

- Having the slowest rate of fire, this is a great weapon for sharpshooters. Take aim, charge up the weapon, and make each shot count. The longer you aim the weapon, the more it charges, resulting in devastating damage output upon the release of its precision projectile.
- The theme for this weapon is "Make each shot count". You can easily dispose of a Pilot in one shot if you wait for the enemy Pilot to use their second jump. This way they can't juke out of your line of sight. There's no need to charge the weapon when engaging Pilots or minions.
- This weapon is the least effective against minions because of the small magazine capacity and slow rate of fire. When killing minions, be sure that no enemy Titans are nearby and try to pick off the Spectres first to get your Core Ability faster. If minions are out in the open, save your ammo and just crush or melee them.
- At a distance, this is the best Titan vs. Titan weapon. The ability to charge up allows you to deal a ton of damage and take off all of the enemy Titan's shields before they know what hit them. Being a great long-range weapon, the Plasma Railgun excels when paired with the fastest Titan, the Stryder, so you can cruise around the map and avoid the close-range slugfests.
- Extended Magazine is the safest choice for this weapon because it negates one of its biggest drawbacks, limited magazine capacity. Can't seem to ever get the full charge with the gun? Try the Instant Shot. It has a dramatic decrease in damage but eliminates the charging time so you aren't vulnerable while waiting to fire off your shot.

Plasma Railgun Challenges

IF IT MOVES...

TIER	CRITERIA	REWARD
1	Kill 5 Enemies	500 XP
2	Kill 15 Enemies	1,000 XP, Extended Magazine Mod
3	Kill 25 Enemies	2,500 XP
4	Kill 50 Enemies	5,000 XP
5	Kill 100 Enemies	10,000 XP

THE EXPENDABLES

TIER	CRITERIA	REWARD
1	Kill 5 Grunts	500 XP
2	Kill 15 Grunts	1,000 XP
3	Kill 25 Grunts	2,500 XP
4	Kill 50 Grunts	5,000 XP
5	Kill 100 Grunts	10,000 XP

TOP GUN

TIER	CRITERIA	REWARD
1	Kill 1 Pilots	500 XP
2	Kill 5 Pilots	1,000 XP
3	Kill 10 Pilots	2,500 XP, Most Wanted List Burn Card
4	Kill 15 Pilots	5,000 XP, Most Wanted List Burn Card
5	Kill 25 Pilots	10,000 XP, Most Wanted List Burn Card

THIS IS MY WEAPON

TIER	CRITERIA	REWARD
1	Use Weapon for .5 Hour	500 XP
2	Use Weapon for 1 Hour	1,000 XP
3	Use Weapon for 1.5 Hours	2,500 XP
4	Use Weapon for 2 Hours	5,000 XP
5	Use Weapon for 3 Hours	10,000 XP

MACHINE WAR

TIER	CRITERIA	REWARD
1	Kill 5 Spectres	500 XP
2	Kill 15 Spectres	1,000 XP
3	Kill 20 Spectres	2,500 XP, Urban Renewal Burn Card
4	Kill 30 Spectres	5,000 XP, Urban Renewal Burn Card
5	Kill 50 Spectres	10,000 XP, Urban Renewal Burn Card

TITAN KILLER

TIER	CRITERIA	REWARD
1	Kill 10 Titans	500 XP, Instant Shot Mod
2	Kill 20 Titans	1,000 XP
3	Kill 30 Titans	2,500 XP, Titan Salvage Burn Card
4	Kill 40 Titans	5,000 XP, Titan Salvage Burn Card
5	Kill 50 Titans	10,000 XP, Titan Salvage Burn Card

CRITICALLY CONDITIONED

TIER	CRITERIA	REWARD
1	Get 5 Critical Hits	500 XP
2	Get 10 Critical Hits	1,000 XP
3	Get 20 Critical Hits	2,500 XP
4	Get 30 Critical Hits	5,000 XP
5	Get 50 Critical Hits	10,000 XP

Awarded Burn Cards

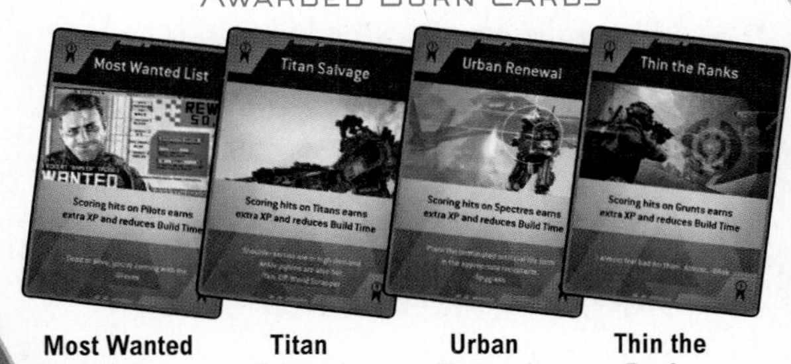

Most Wanted List — Titan Salvage — Urban Renewal — Thin the Ranks

PRIMARY WEAPONS

ARC CANNON

MAGAZINE CAPACITY: **1,000** WEAPON UNLOCK: **LEVEL 21**

The factory-issue Arc Cannon fires a bolt of lightning that propagates across multiple targets. It can be fired quickly or charged up over time for an increase in firepower.

STRENGTHS:
- Good against Titans and Pilots
- Never have to reload

WEAKNESSES:
- Limited effective range
- Charged shot takes a long time

WEAPON PERFORMANCE

DAMAGE

ACCURACY

RANGE

FIRE RATE

WEAPON MODS

IMAGE	NAME	DESCRIPTION	UNLOCK
	Capacitor	This mod stores a greater charge than normal, allowing the weapon to deal increased damage. However, with this mod, the weapon must be fully charged before it will fire.	Titan Killer (II) Challenge: Kill 20 Titans

Field Notes

- This weapon shoots a bolt of lightning. Yes, a bolt of lightning! The lightning bolt can take out multiple targets if used correctly. To shoot the Arc Cannon, you simply charge it. You will never have to reload or have a cooldown time after each shot. This weapon is extremely versatile. It is good against enemy Titans, Pilots, and minions. With this weapon, you're able to quickly kill minions and switch to an enemy Titan or Pilot without having to take time to reload. Keep in mind the Arc Cannon will automatically shoot once it reaches its full charge.
- Be sure to charge the Arc Cannon at least halfway to kill a enemy Pilot with one shot. To be on the safe side, you can charge the Arc Cannon a little more than halfway to guarantee it will kill a enemy Pilot. You'll have to be quite accurate with this weapon when attempting to kill a Pilot. It helps to stay unzoomed if the enemy Pilot is nearby.
- This weapon is incredible against minions—it has a chain effect when fired upon them. But you must charge the Arc Cannon a bit for this arc effect. You're still able to pick off single minions with the smallest charge though.
- During Titan battles, the Arc Cannon is a good supporting weapon when moving around with a group of friendly Titans. The weapon does optimal damage when fully charged, so keep your distance while charging and then unleash a lightning bolt at your target to inflict high damage. This is not a precision weapon, so don't expect to score critical hits.
- The Capacitor mod allows your weapon to deal greater damage, however the Arc Cannon must be fully charged to fire. This attachment can really hinder your ability to quickly kill groups of minions and Pilots, although it will definitely help you deal more damage in battles against enemy Titans. Just make sure you're aiming at your intended target once the weapon reaches its full charge—the Arc Cannon fires automatically. Alternatively, continuously pump the trigger, keeping the weapon about 75% charged at all times. Then when you encounter an enemy, aim and hold the trigger down to fire the powerful charged shot.

Arc Cannon Challenges

IF IT MOVES...

TIER	CRITERIA	REWARD
1	Kill 10 Enemies	500 XP
2	Kill 25 Enemies	1,000 XP
3	Kill 50 Enemies	2,500 XP
4	Kill 100 Enemies	5,000 XP
5	Kill 200 Enemies	10,000 XP

THE EXPENDABLES

TIER	CRITERIA	REWARD
1	Kill 10 Grunts	500 XP
2	Kill 25 Grunts	1,000 XP
3	Kill 50 Grunts	2,500 XP
4	Kill 100 Grunts	5,000 XP
5	Kill 200 Grunts	10,000 XP

TOP GUN

TIER	CRITERIA	REWARD
1	Kill 5 Pilots	500 XP
2	Kill 15 Pilots	1,000 XP
3	Kill 30 Pilots	2,500 XP, Most Wanted List Burn Card
4	Kill 50 Pilots	5,000 XP, Most Wanted List Burn Card
5	Kill 75 Pilots	10,000 XP, Most Wanted List Burn Card

THIS IS MY WEAPON

TIER	CRITERIA	REWARD
1	Use Weapon for .5 Hour	500 XP
2	Use Weapon for 1 Hour	1,000 XP
3	Use Weapon for 1.5 Hours	2,500 XP
4	Use Weapon for 2 Hours	5,000 XP
5	Use Weapon for 3 Hours	10,000 XP

MACHINE WAR

TIER	CRITERIA	REWARD
1	Kill 10 Spectres	500 XP
2	Kill 25 Spectres	1,000 XP
3	Kill 50 Spectres	2,500 XP, Urban Renewal Burn Card
4	Kill 75 Spectres	5,000 XP, Urban Renewal Burn Card
5	Kill 100 Spectres	10,000 XP, Urban Renewal Burn Card

TITAN KILLER

TIER	CRITERIA	REWARD
1	Kill 10 Titans	500 XP
2	Kill 20 Titans	1,000 XP, Capacitor Mod
3	Kill 30 Titans	2,500 XP, Titan Salvage Burn Card
4	Kill 40 Titans	5,000 XP, Titan Salvage Burn Card
5	Kill 50 Titans	10,000 XP, Titan Salvage Burn Card

PRO TIP: STRONGSIDE

If you see an enemy Pilot near an enemy Titan, charge the Arc Cannon and focus on just shooting the enemy Titan. The lightning bolt will deal damage to the Titan and have the chain effect to injure a nearby enemy Pilot. It can even kill a weak enemy Pilot or one riding atop a Titan.

Awarded Burn Cards

Most Wanted List
WANTED
Scoring hits on Pilots earns extra XP and reduces Build Time
Titan Salvage
Scoring hits on Titans earns extra XP and reduces Build Time
Urban Renewal
Scoring hits on Spectres earns extra XP and reduces Build Time

Most Wanted List — Titan Salvage — Urban Renewal

TRIPLE THREAT

MAGAZINE CAPACITY: 9 WEAPON UNLOCK: LEVEL 28

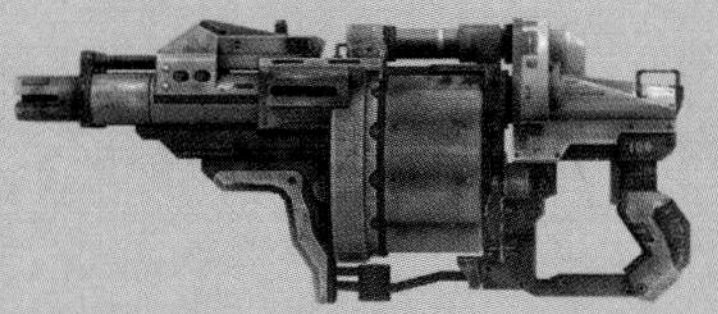

The Triple Threat is a grenade launcher that fires three grenades at once. It excels at clearing interiors, and its grenades explode on armored contact, making it effective at close range against other Titans.

STRENGTHS:

- Effective against minions
- Great defensive Titan weapon

WEAKNESSES:

- Weak against Pilots
- Limited magazine capacity

WEAPON PERFORMANCE

DAMAGE

ACCURACY

RANGE

FIRE RATE

WEAPON MODS

IMAGE	NAME	DESCRIPTION	UNLOCK
	Extended Magazine	This mod increases the ammo capacity of the weapon, making it so that you don't have to reload as often.	If It Moves… (II) Challenge: Kill 25 Enemies
	Mine Field	This mod converts the weapon to fire ballistic mines, which plant into the ground when fired and then detonate using built-in proximity.	Titan Killer (II) Challenge: Kill 20 Titans

Field Notes

- The Triple Threat is a defensive weapon and most effective when used near cover. The weapon lobs the grenades when fired, making it easy for you to shoot over objects. Take advantage of this when you find your Titan's shield is low as you can continue to fight when staying behind cover. The Triple Threat can be aimed horizontally when hip firing or vertically when zoomed.
- The Triple Threat should be used to deny enemies territory. The Pilots' mobility makes them a hard target for the Triple Threat. Instead of engaging head-on with Pilots, just shoot a barrage of grenades to keep the enemy at bay.
- Minions crumble when faced with the Triple Threat. These grenades are fired in a horizontal spread when hip firing or in a vertical spread when aiming. This allows you to wipe out minions on the ground and building tops.
- This weapon can be tricky to use against enemy Titans due to its limited range. Consider utilizing hit-and-run tactics to score some damage, then retreat to reload while your Titan's bodyshield recharges. You don't want to be caught out in the open reloading the Triple Threat.
- Equip the Triple Threat with the Mine Field mod and begin laying traps. The Mine Field allows you to lay down a total of nine grenades. This increases your chances of escaping lopsided battles with enemy Titans and score you some easy points when enemies run over the mines. The Mine Field mod is particularly effective when defending on Hardpoint or Capture the Flag.

Triple Threat Challenges

TOP GUN

TIER	CRITERIA	REWARD
1	Kill 5 Pilots	500 XP
2	Kill 15 Pilots	1,000 XP
3	Kill 30 Pilots	2,500 XP, Most Wanted List Burn Card
4	Kill 50 Pilots	5,000 XP, Most Wanted List Burn Card
5	Kill 75 Pilots	10,000 XP, Most Wanted List Burn Card

THE EXPENDABLES

TIER	CRITERIA	REWARD
1	Kill 10 Grunts	500 XP
2	Kill 25 Grunts	1,000 XP
3	Kill 50 Grunts	2,500 XP
4	Kill 100 Grunts	5,000 XP
5	Kill 200 Grunts	10,000 XP

MACHINE WAR

TIER	CRITERIA	REWARD
1	Kill 10 Spectres	500 XP
2	Kill 25 Spectres	1,000 XP
3	Kill 50 Spectres	2,500 XP, Urban Renewal Burn Card
4	Kill 75 Spectres	5,000 XP, Urban Renewal Burn Card
5	Kill 100 Spectres	10,000 XP, Urban Renewal Burn Card

THIS IS MY WEAPON

TIER	CRITERIA	REWARD
1	Use Weapon for .5 Hour	500 XP
2	Use Weapon for 1 Hour	1,000 XP
3	Use Weapon for 1.5 Hours	2,500 XP
4	Use Weapon for 2 Hours	5,000 XP
5	Use Weapon for 3 Hours	10,000 XP

TITAN KILLER

TIER	CRITERIA	REWARD
1	Kill 10 Titans	500 XP
2	Kill 20 Titans	1,000 XP, Mine Field Mod
3	Kill 30 Titans	2,500 XP, Titan Salvage Burn Card
4	Kill 40 Titans	5,000 XP, Titan Salvage Burn Card
5	Kill 50 Titans	10,000 XP, Titan Salvage Burn Card

Awarded Burn Cards

Most Wanted List
Titan Salvage
Urban Renewal
Scoring hits on Pilots earns extra XP and reduces Build Time
Scoring hits on Titans earns extra XP and reduces Build Time
Scoring hits on Spectres earns extra XP and reduces Build Time

Most Wanted List | Titan Salvage | Urban Renewal

PRO TIP: FLAMESWORD

When on the winning team, the Triple Threat is effective in stopping the opposing team in the Epilogue. Have the Mine Field mod attached and plant the area under the evacuation ship with grenades. This will either take out the enemy Pilots or delay them from escaping.

PRIMARY WEAPONS

TITAN ORDNANCE

All Titans have a shoulder-mounted missile pod. This is called Titan Ordnance. Make sure your choice of Titan Ordnance makes up for the limitations of your primary weapon. For instance, if you select a long-range Titan weapon, such as the Plasma Railgun, you'll want a missile system that can be used against threats that get close, as well as Pilots.

SLAVED WARHEADS

ORDNANCE UNLOCK: **LEVEL 11**

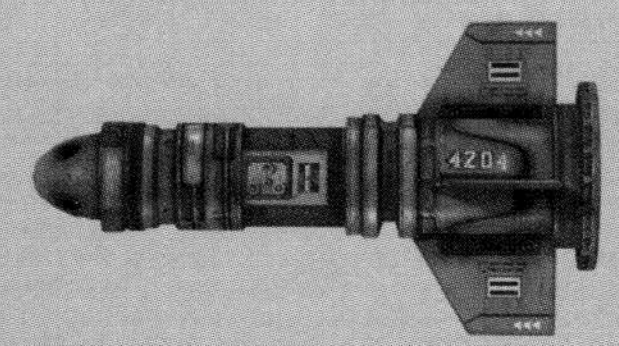

This Titan Ordnance pod requires a lock-on before you can fire. When you fire, a barrage of homing missiles will launch four at a time towards your target.

Field Notes

› This is perfect for fighting Titans that are out in the open to get some guaranteed damage (unless they dash away, which is difficult). In clustered maps, like Colony, this ordnance is not effective since the enemy Titan can duck behind cover. With this ordnance, patience is key—don't fire this off unless you know the rockets will hit.

Slaved Warhead Challenges

IF IT MOVES...

TIER	CRITERIA	REWARD
1	Kill 25 Enemies	500 XP, Most Wanted List Burn Card
2	Kill 100 Enemies	1,000 XP, Most Wanted List Burn Card
3	Kill 250 Enemies	2,500 XP, Most Wanted List Burn Card
4	Kill 500 Enemies	5,000 XP, Most Wanted List Burn Card
5	Kill 1,000 Enemies	10,000 XP, Most Wanted List Burn Card

THIS IS MY WEAPON

TIER	CRITERIA	REWARD
1	Use Weapon for .5 Hour	500 XP
2	Use Weapon for 1 Hour	1,000 XP
3	Use Weapon for 1.5 Hours	2,500 XP
4	Use Weapon for 2 Hours	5,000 XP
5	Use Weapon for 3 Hours	10,000 XP

TITAN KILLER

TIER	CRITERIA	REWARD
1	Kill 5 Titans	500 XP
2	Kill 15 Titans	1,000 XP
3	Kill 30 Titans	2,500 XP
4	Kill 60 Titans	5,000 XP
5	Kill 100 Titans	10,000 XP

AWARDED BURN CARD

Most Wanted List

Most Wanted List
WANTED
Scoring hits on Pilots earns extra XP and reduces Build Time

ROCKET SALVO

ORDNANCE UNLOCK: **LEVEL 1**

This Titan Ordnance pod rapidly fires a swarm of unguided rockets. It is ideal for wiping out clustered targets, and is useful in situations calling for direct, manually aimed fire.

Field Notes

- This ordnance is best used when an enemy Titan isn't looking or is in a narrow hallway where they can't dodge the manual rockets. Be sure to fire this ordnance off first thing during a Titan vs. Titan fight. The battle should last long enough for you to get your second volley of missiles off if you shoot your ordnance immediately.

Rocket Salvo Challenges

IF IT MOVES...

TIER	CRITERIA	REWARD
1	Kill 10 Enemies	500 XP
2	Kill 25 Enemies	1,000 XP
3	Kill 50 Enemies	2,500 XP
4	Kill 100 Enemies	5,000 XP
5	Kill 150 Enemies	10,000 XP

THE EXPENDABLES

TIER	CRITERIA	REWARD
1	Kill 5 Grunts	500 XP
2	Kill 15 Grunts	1,000 XP
3	Kill 30 Grunts	2,500 XP
4	Kill 50 Grunts	5,000 XP
5	Kill 100 Grunts	10,000 XP

TOP GUN

TIER	CRITERIA	REWARD
1	Kill 5 Pilots	500 XP
2	Kill 15 Pilots	1,000 XP
3	Kill 30 Pilots	2,500 XP, Most Wanted List Burn Card
4	Kill 50 Pilots	5,000 XP, Most Wanted List Burn Card
5	Kill 75 Pilots	10,000 XP, Most Wanted List Burn Card

THIS IS MY WEAPON

TIER	CRITERIA	REWARD
1	Use Weapon for .5 Hour	500 XP
2	Use Weapon for 1 Hour	1,000 XP
3	Use Weapon for 1.5 Hours	2,500 XP
4	Use Weapon for 2 Hours	5,000 XP
5	Use Weapon for 3 Hours	10,000 XP

MACHINE WAR

TIER	CRITERIA	REWARD
1	Kill 5 Spectres	500 XP
2	Kill 15 Spectres	1,000 XP
3	Kill 30 Spectres	2,500 XP, Urban Renewal Burn Card
4	Kill 50 Spectres	5,000 XP, Urban Renewal Burn Card
5	Kill 75 Spectres	10,000 XP, Urban Renewal Burn Card

TITAN KILLER

TIER	CRITERIA	REWARD
1	Kill 5 Titans	500 XP
2	Kill 15 Titans	1,000 XP
3	Kill 20 Titans	2,500 XP, Titan Salvage Burn Card
4	Kill 30 Titans	5,000 XP, Titan Salvage Burn Card
5	Kill 50 Titans	10,000 XP, Titan Salvage Burn Card

AWARDED BURN CARDS

Most Wanted List
Titan Salvage
Urban Renewal
Scoring hits on Pilots earns extra XP and reduces Build Time
Scoring hits on Titans earns extra XP and reduces Build Time
Scoring hits on Spectres earns extra XP and reduces Build Time

Most Wanted List | Titan Salvage | Urban Renewal

ORDNANCE

CLUSTER MISSILE

ORDNANCE UNLOCK: **LEVEL 24**

The Cluster Missile pod fires a missile which, on impact, deploys a shower of secondary explosive charges that continue to explode and saturate an area for a considerable time.

Field Notes

- This ordnance is great against enemy Titans and enemy Pilots because it leaves a secondary explosion of charges that explode over the general area where the Cluster Missile first made contact. These charges deal even more damage to the enemy Titan or can even kill a enemy Pilot. You'll want to be at a close- to mid-range distance when firing this weapon at an enemy because it does not lock on. The missile can spiral around and miss your target if you aren't close enough. Watch out for this splash damage as it can inflict damage to yourself.

Cluster Missile Challenges

IF IT MOVES...

TIER	CRITERIA	REWARD
1	Kill 10 Enemies	500 XP
2	Kill 25 Enemies	1,000 XP
3	Kill 50 Enemies	2,500 XP
4	Kill 100 Enemies	5,000 XP
5	Kill 150 Enemies	10,000 XP

THE EXPENDABLES

TIER	CRITERIA	REWARD
1	Kill 5 Grunts	500 XP
2	Kill 15 Grunts	1,000 XP
3	Kill 30 Grunts	2,500 XP
4	Kill 50 Grunts	5,000 XP
5	Kill 100 Grunts	10,000 XP

TOP GUN

TIER	CRITERIA	REWARD
1	Kill 5 Pilots	500 XP
2	Kill 15 Pilots	1,000 XP
3	Kill 30 Pilots	2,500 XP, Most Wanted List Burn Card
4	Kill 50 Pilots	5,000 XP, Most Wanted List Burn Card
5	Kill 75 Pilots	10,000 XP, Most Wanted List Burn Card

THIS IS MY WEAPON

TIER	CRITERIA	REWARD
1	Use Weapon for .5 Hour	500 XP
2	Use Weapon for 1 Hour	1,000 XP
3	Use Weapon for 1.5 Hours	2,500 XP
4	Use Weapon for 2 Hours	5,000 XP
5	Use Weapon for 3 Hours	10,000 XP

MACHINE WAR

TIER	CRITERIA	REWARD
1	Kill 5 Spectres	500 XP
2	Kill 15 Spectres	1,000 XP
3	Kill 30 Spectres	2,500 XP, Urban Renewal Burn Card
4	Kill 50 Spectres	5,000 XP, Urban Renewal Burn Card
5	Kill 75 Spectres	10,000 XP, Urban Renewal Burn Card

TITAN KILLER

TIER	CRITERIA	REWARD
1	Kill 5 Titans	500 XP
2	Kill 15 Titans	1,000 XP
3	Kill 20 Titans	2,500 XP, Titan Salvage Burn Card
4	Kill 30 Titans	5,000 XP, Titan Salvage Burn Card
5	Kill 50 Titans	10,000 XP, Titan Salvage Burn Card

AWARDED BURN CARDS

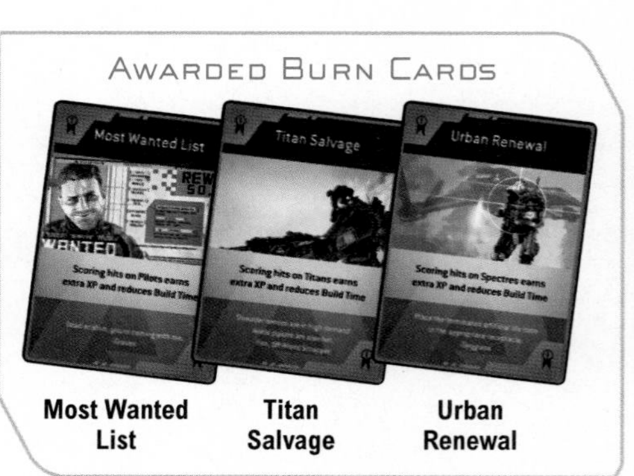

Most Wanted List — Titan Salvage — Urban Renewal

MULTI-TARGET MISSILE SYSTEM

ORDNANCE UNLOCK: 32

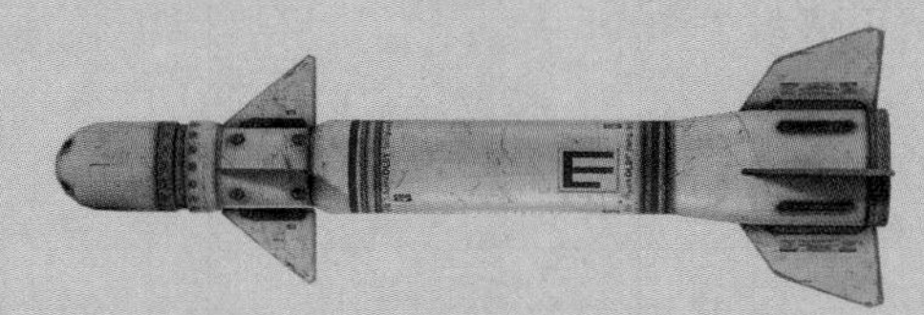

The Multi-Target System enables you to engage multiple targets at once. Hold down the Ordnance Ability control and sweep your view over your target to paint them. Then release to fire the missiles at the painted targets.

Field Notes

- The Multi-Target System can cause massive damage if you are able to paint and hit the enemy Titan with all your missiles. This ordnance requires you to engage enemy Titans in more open areas so they can't use their surroundings to evade the lock-on. Don't feel like you have to have every missile lock on, but be sure to always fire missiles before enemy Titans take cover. The Stryder Titan makes full use of this ordnance due to the Titan's fast movements. The Stryder Titan will be able to move in and out of cover, allowing you to paint the enemy while evading incoming fire.

Multi-Target Missile System Challenges

TITAN KILLER

TIER	CRITERIA	REWARD
1	Kill 5 Titans	500 XP
2	Kill 15 Titans	1,000 XP
3	Kill 20 Titans	2,500 XP, Titan Salvage Burn Card
4	Kill 30 Titans	5,000 XP, Titan Salvage Burn Card
5	Kill 50 Titans	10,000 XP, Titan Salvage Burn Card

THIS IS MY WEAPON

TIER	CRITERIA	REWARD
1	Use Weapon for .5 Hour	500 XP
2	Use Weapon for 1 Hour	1,000 XP
3	Use Weapon for 1.5 Hours	2,500 XP
4	Use Weapon for 2 Hours	5,000 XP
5	Use Weapon for 3 Hours	10,000 XP

ORDNANCE

PRO TIP: STRONGSIDE

The Cluster Missile works great against those enemy Pilots who just hide from you in a building. The ordnance can be shot through a window or door of a building, causing the massive secondary explosion of charges and killing anything inside.

AWARDED BURN CARD

Titan Salvage

Titan Salvage
Scoring hits on Titans earns extra XP and reduces Build Time

TACTICAL ABILITIES

Like Pilots, Titans can also be fitted with one Tactical Ability. Once equipped, the ability is manually activated at the Pilot's discretion, giving the Titan a temporary advantage. But abilities only remain active for a few seconds before they must recharge. There are three Tactical Abilities to choose from, all defensive in nature. Select an ability and use it to prolong your Titan's lifespan during combat.

TACTICAL ABILITY

VORTEX SHIELD

ABILITY UNLOCK: **LEVEL 1**

The Vortex Shield captures incoming projectiles and projects them back at enemies upon release.

Field Notes

- One of the Titans' most useful Tactical Abilities is the Vortex Shield, most effective when engaging another Titan. Whether it is minions, Pilots, or enemy Titans firing towards you, the Vortex Shield will stop incoming projectiles in their place. Timing this ability is critical and the timing to activate it is when the opposing team is double teaming you. Let them fire their most powerful projectiles only to stop those projectiles in mid air and send them flying back. The Vortex Shield will only block the bolt fired off by the Arc Cannon; it will not send it back.

DEVELOPER TIP

Respawn ENTERTAINMENT

Projectiles released by the Vortex Shield ability can be caught in mid-air by another Vortex Shield. The Vortex Shield takes a second to cool down once deployed, so if you find yourself stuck in a game of "catch" with an enemy Titan, try returning fire with your own Vortex Shield immediately after you catch your opponent's incoming attack.

If you have lots of ammo caught in your Vortex Shield but you suspect an opponent has more Vortex Shield time remaining than you, discard the contents of your Vortex Shield into the sky or to one side. This way you avoid feeding more ammo into the enemy's Vortex Shield with no way for you to block the imminent blast of Vortex Shield fire.

TACTICAL ABILITY

ELECTRIC SMOKE

ABILITY UNLOCK: **LEVEL 13**

The Electric Smoke system deploys a dense, electrically charged smoke cloud that damages enemy Titans and Pilots. It can be used in many ways—one of the most common is to use it to deter boarding attempts by enemy Pilots.

Field Notes

- Electric Smoke is a great way to get those pesky enemy Pilots off your back. If you are attacked by a rodeo attack, Electric Smoke is the best way to get them off your back without having to exit your Titan. Once you deploy Electric Smoke, move back and forth within the smoke to kill the enemy Pilot on your back. You can also use this defensively against an enemy Titan by deploying the smoke while your shields are down. This will allow you to sneak around a building or object while the enemy Titan's view is hindered. If the enemy Titan were to chase you, the smoke would deal damage to the Titan, possibly giving you the upper hand in the battle. Using Electric Smoke while in a close-quarter battle with an enemy Titan will help inflict even greater damage to the Titan, along with your primary weapon and ordnance.

PRO TIP: STRONGSIDE

Another great time to use Electric Smoke is at the end of the game if your team has won and the enemy team is trying to board the Evacuation Dropship. Place your Titan in front of the dropship's entrance and deploy your smoke when an enemy Pilot is near. The enemy Pilot will not be able to pass through it without being killed.

DEVELOPER TIP

Respawn ENTERTAINMENT

Electric Smoke is very effective against enemy Pilots that jump onto your Titan's back. It will kill them over time or force them to jump off of you. Once they are off, dash far away so that they don't easily jump back onto you. Standing in a cloud of Electric Smoke will negate all weapon lock-ons, including your own.

TACTICAL ABILITY

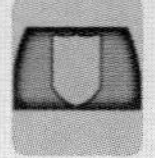

PARTICLE WALL

ABILITY UNLOCK: **LEVEL 26**

The Particle Wall is stationary force-field, blocking all incoming fire from one side. Enemy weapons can damage it, and eventually take it down.

Field Notes

- The Particle Wall is an effective ability to use when engaging enemy Titans head on. The wall will block all incoming fire and, at the same time, let the user shoot through one side of the wall, damaging the opponent. Use this ability in confined areas where the enemy can only approach from one direction. The Particle Wall can be placed to cover friendlies on the ground which, in turn, will make it easier when fighting large waves of enemies.

PRO TIP: WALSHY

To use this ability effectively, wait for an enemy Titan to fire off its ordnance before deploying the Particle Wall.

DEVELOPER TIP

Respawn ENTERTAINMENT

The Particle Wall ability will buy you extra time to aim more carefully or charge a weapon more fully, protecting you completely from incoming fire. It works well in concert with long-range or charge-dependent Titan weapons such as the Plasma Railgun, the Arc Cannon, and the XO-16 Chaingun. The Particle Wall only allows weapon fire to pass through in one direction, no matter what team you're on, so try chasing an enemy around to the opposite side and use the enemy's own barrier against it.

TIER 1 KITS

There are five Tier 1 Kits available to each Titan. These passive modules automatically enhance Titans in various ways. When choosing a Tier 1 Kit, take into account your loadout as a whole and find one that complements your other selections.

TIER 1 KIT

NUCLEAR EJECTION

ABILITY UNLOCK: LEVEL 1

After you eject, your Titan briefly charges and then detonates its nuclear core, dealing massive amounts of damage to all nearby enemies.

Field Notes

- Even the best Titan Pilots will be forced to eject once their Titan has reached its limit. The Nuclear Ejection allows you to wipe out enemies and massively damage nearby enemy Titans. If you find your Titan is usually on the front lines, this is an incredible kit to have as many times it will be just what you need to finish off enemies that you have inflicted damage upon.

DEVELOPER TIP — Respawn Entertainment

The damage inflicted by using Nuclear Ejection can give you a quick boost towards building your next Titan when there are enemies nearby.

TIER 1 KIT

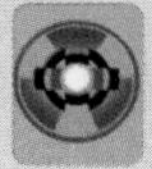

REGEN BOOSTER

ABILITY UNLOCK: LEVEL 1

Your Titan is able to regenerate its bodyshield at a faster rate than normal.

Field Notes

- Combine this kit with taking cover once your shields are down and you will find your Titan winning over half of its battles. Having your Titan shield recharge quicker allows you to pressure the opponent as they will have to retreat much sooner. Apply hit-and-run tactics, inflict damage, and then retreat to recharge your shields before reengaging.

TIER 1 KIT

FAST AUTOLOADER

ABILITY UNLOCK: LEVEL 14

This advanced autoload mechanism replenishes your Titan's ordnance faster, making it available more frequently.

Field Notes

- This Tier 1 Kit will have your ordnance up a few seconds faster. If you find that you are barely losing Titan one-on-one battles and need your ordnance quicker, this is the kit for you. This kit is ideal for hit and runs with a faster Titan like the Stryder.

TIER 1 KIT

DASH QUICKCHARGER

ABILITY UNLOCK: LEVEL 38

Your Titan's dash system recharges at a faster rate, allowing you to dash more frequently.

Field Notes

- This Tier 1 Kit will keep you moving around the map as quickly as possible. Having your dashes more frequently allows you to get away from a battle to let your shields recharge or make a quick getaway to join nearby friendly teammates.

PRO TIP: STRONGSIDE

You'll see the best results using this kit with the Stryder. The Stryder is fast and this makes the Stryder Titan even faster. This is especially effective when running a flag in Capture the Flag with the Stryder.

TIER 1 KIT

TACTICAL REACTOR

ABILITY UNLOCK: LEVEL 46

This kit makes your Titan's Tactical Ability recharge faster. The Tactical Abilities are Vortex Shield, Electric Smoke, and Particle Wall.

Field Notes

- Tactical Abilities can be the key to victory when Titans engage one another. This kit will recharge your Tactical Ability quicker, allowing you to use these abilities more often. Since all of the Tactical Abilities are defensive, equipping this kit can significantly increase your Titan's lifespan.

TIER 2 KITS

Like the Tier 1 Kits, the Tier 2 Kits are passive, requiring no interaction on behalf of the Pilot. Instead, these kits automatically enhance the Titan with a variety of tactical benefits. For best results, select a kit that complements the other selections in your Titan's loadout.

TIER 2 KIT

AUTO-EJECT

ABILITY UNLOCK: LEVEL 1

The Auto-Eject system automatically ejects you as soon as your Titan is doomed. You will also cloak briefly on ejection, whether or not you have the Cloak ability as a Pilot.

Field Notes

- With the Auto-Eject equipped, you can fight and inflict as much damage as possible to enemy Titans or Pilots knowing that you will never die inside your Titan. You will always be ejected right as your Titan is doomed. Also, if you're tired of getting killed in mid-air after you eject from your Titan, this kit is for you. You will briefly be cloaked upon ejection, giving you a small amount of time to find cover and retreat. You can also use the cloaking ability aggressively to stealthily take out enemy Pilots or rodeo attack a nearby enemy Titan.

DEVELOPER TIP

Respawn ENTERTAINMENT

Equipping the Auto-Eject Kit will prevent you from being executed by enemy Titans. Auto-Eject will also cloak you automatically when you eject. However, with this kit, you will lose the ability to continue to fight in your Titan once it is doomed.

TIER 2 KIT

SURVIVOR

ABILITY UNLOCK: LEVEL 1

Your Titan will lose health at a slower rate when doomed, allowing you to fight longer before having to abandon the Titan.

Field Notes

- This Tier 2 Kit is excellent when you want to survive that little bit longer to doom an enemy Titan or pick off a few more minions or even possibly an enemy Pilot. Although Survivor will cause you to lose health at a slower rate when doomed, don't forget to eject when the time is right. If you find yourself using Auto-Titan quite a bit, this is a good kit to equip so your Titan will kill a few more enemies.

TIER 2 KIT

CORE EXTENDER

ABILITY UNLOCK: LEVEL 23

The Core Extender allows any Titan's Core Ability to remain active for an extended period of time.

Field Notes

- This will allow you to use your Shield Core, Dash Core, or Damage Core ability for a few extra seconds. This is most effective with the Atlas' Damage Core or Stryder's Dash Core abilities so you can dish out more damage or navigate around the map longer. The Ogre's Shield Core, when used at the correct time, will get destroyed by enemies slow enough without needing to equip the Core Extender.

TIER 2 KIT

CORE ACCELERATOR

ABILITY UNLOCK: LEVEL 47

The Core Accelerator makes your Titan's Core Ability charge more quickly.

Field Notes

- This allows you to receive your Shield Core, Dash Core, or Damage Core ability quicker. This is good to equip if you don't find yourself hunting minions. Regardless of your success at scoring kills, your Core Ability will come online sooner.

TIER 2 KIT

BIG PUNCH

ABILITY UNLOCK: LEVEL 41

Your Titan's melee attack power is significantly increased, inflicting greater damage than normal, and knocking enemies back further.

Field Notes

- Big Punch gives you a good amount of extra damage for your Titan melee attacks. This is good to have if you are engaging in multiple close-quarter Titan battles. Having this equipped will literally give you the upper hand in these close-quarter duels.

PRO TIP: STRONGSIDE

Equip Big Punch when using the Ogre Titan to deal some serious damage with a punch.

ADVANCED TITAN CUSTOMIZATION

Learning how all the Titan weapons, abilities, and kits function is key to creating effective loadouts. Now that you have a grasp of all the customization options, start thinking about what kind of Titan loadouts you'd like to create. Not all customization options are immediately available—level up and complete challenges to unlock more options. Here we take a look at some sample Titan loadouts. Although effective, some of these loadouts might not suit your style of play. So simply reference these loadouts as an example of what's possible and study how the different components complement one another.

SPECIALIZED LOADOUTS

A large part of customizing your Titan is determining what kind of role you want to play on the battlefield. Are you mainly interested in hunting Grunts or Spectres? Or do you want to take the fight directly to enemy Titans? Your answers will help influence the kind of Titan loadout you want to create. These sample loadouts offer a glimpse at the possibilities awaiting you. Try them out as shown, or further customize them, making them your own.

Lightning Master

CHASSIS
ATLAS

Equipped with the powerful Arc Cannon, this Atlas configuration excels at wiping out enemy Grunts and Spectres—the electricity from each shot can arc across multiple targets. But this loadout is also very effective when attacking enemy Titans. When confronting a Titan, deploy the Particle Wall and begin charging the Arc Cannon, firing when it when it reaches its full charge. The Particle Wall will keep you safe until you get the first charged shot off. Assuming you scored a hit, you'll have a serious advantage in the ensuing battle, where you can rely on dashes to evade incoming projectiles while firing Cluster Missiles and the Arc Cannon to deal more damage. When possible, take cover or deploy another Particle Wall to let your shields recharge—the Regen Booster will decrease the amount of time it takes for your bodyshield to replenish. Meanwhile, the Core Extender increases the duration of the Atlas' Damage Core. When paired with the Arc Cannon, Damage Core is extremely powerful, even when you're outnumbered.

PRIMARY WEAPON
ZAPS ACROSS MULTIPLE TARGETS 
ARC CANNON
MOD: FACTORY ISSUE

TACTICAL ABILITY
PARTICLE WALL
DEPLOYS A ONE-WAY FORCE-FIELD

ORDNANCE
CLUSTER MISSILE
SUSTAINED EXPLOSIONS ON IMPACT

TIER 1 KIT
REGEN BOOSTER
YOUR TITAN'S BODYSHIELD REGENERATES FASTER

TIER 2 KIT
CORE EXTENDER
YOUR TITAN CORE ABILITY LASTS LONGER

Brawler

CHASSIS

OGRE

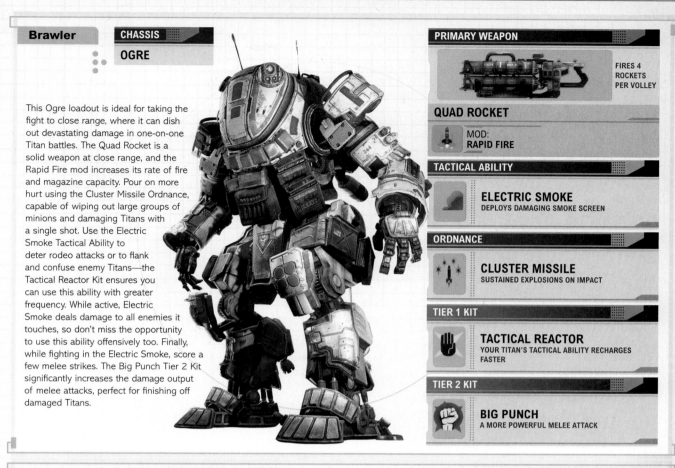

This Ogre loadout is ideal for taking the fight to close range, where it can dish out devastating damage in one-on-one Titan battles. The Quad Rocket is a solid weapon at close range, and the Rapid Fire mod increases its rate of fire and magazine capacity. Pour on more hurt using the Cluster Missile Ordnance, capable of wiping out large groups of minions and damaging Titans with a single shot. Use the Electric Smoke Tactical Ability to deter rodeo attacks or to flank and confuse enemy Titans—the Tactical Reactor Kit ensures you can use this ability with greater frequency. While active, Electric Smoke deals damage to all enemies it touches, so don't miss the opportunity to use this ability offensively too. Finally, while fighting in the Electric Smoke, score a few melee strikes. The Big Punch Tier 2 Kit significantly increases the damage output of melee attacks, perfect for finishing off damaged Titans.

PRIMARY WEAPON

FIRES 4 ROCKETS PER VOLLEY

QUAD ROCKET

MOD: **RAPID FIRE**

TACTICAL ABILITY

ELECTRIC SMOKE
DEPLOYS DAMAGING SMOKE SCREEN

ORDNANCE

CLUSTER MISSILE
SUSTAINED EXPLOSIONS ON IMPACT

TIER 1 KIT

TACTICAL REACTOR
YOUR TITAN'S TACTICAL ABILITY RECHARGES FASTER

TIER 2 KIT

BIG PUNCH
A MORE POWERFUL MELEE ATTACK

Sharpshooter

CHASSIS

STRYDER

This loadout is all about avoiding direct contact with enemy Titans. Instead, use the Stryder's speed and agility to keep your distance from chaotic close-quarter Titan battles and engage from long range using the Plasma Railgun. Upon spotting a distant Titan, take aim, charge up the Plasma Railgun, and fire the first shot—this will likely get the enemy Titan's attention. Deploy the Particle Wall to deflect incoming projectiles while continuing to fire fully charged shots from the Plasma Railgun—scoring critical hits with this weapon is absolutely devastating. If enemy Titans get too close, simply retreat and reengage from a different long-range perspective. The Dash Quickcharger and Core Accelerator Kits ensure optimal mobility, perfect for staging high-damage hit-and-run attacks. This loadout works best when working with other Titans—stay back and score long-range hits while your buddies move in and draw most of the fire.

PRIMARY WEAPON

CHARGES UP WHILE ZOOMED

PLASMA RAILGUN

MOD: **EXTENDED MAGAZINE**

TACTICAL ABILITY

PARTICLE WALL
DEPLOYS A ONE-WAY FORCE-FIELD

ORDNANCE

MULTI-TARGET MISSILE SYSTEM
YOU CAN MANUALLY PAINT MULTIPLE TARGETS

TIER 1 KIT

DASH QUICKCHARGER
YOUR DASH RECHARGES FASTER

TIER 2 KIT

CORE ACCELERATOR
YOUR TITAN CORE ABILITY CHARGES FASTER

PRO LOADOUTS

Want to know how the pros play? When jumping into a match, StrongSide, Walshy, and Flamesword have their go-to Titan loadouts ready. Here's a look at some of their favorite Titan loadouts.

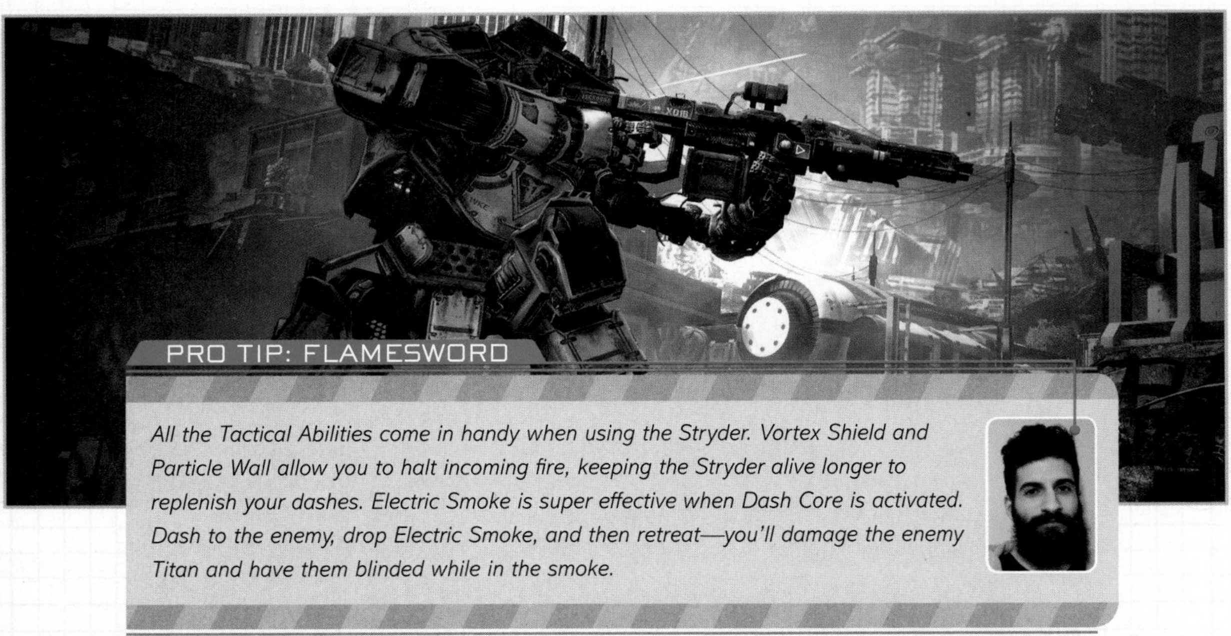

PRO TIP: FLAMESWORD

All the Tactical Abilities come in handy when using the Stryder. Vortex Shield and Particle Wall allow you to halt incoming fire, keeping the Stryder alive longer to replenish your dashes. Electric Smoke is super effective when Dash Core is activated. Dash to the enemy, drop Electric Smoke, and then retreat—you'll damage the enemy Titan and have them blinded while in the smoke.

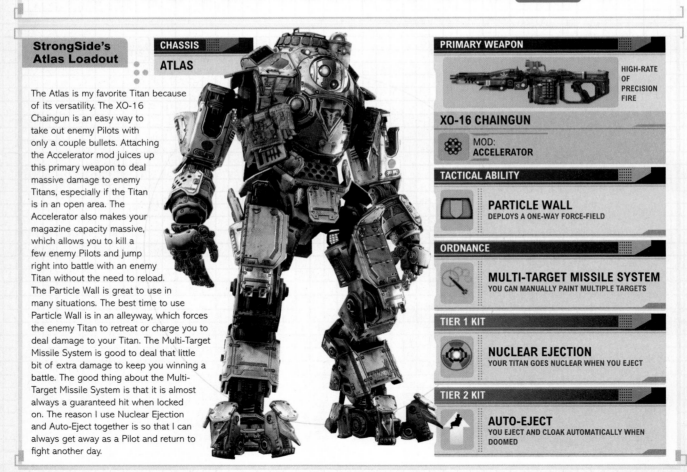

StrongSide's Atlas Loadout

The Atlas is my favorite Titan because of its versatility. The XO-16 Chaingun is an easy way to take out enemy Pilots with only a couple bullets. Attaching the Accelerator mod juices up this primary weapon to deal massive damage to enemy Titans, especially if the Titan is in an open area. The Accelerator also makes your magazine capacity massive, which allows you to kill a few enemy Pilots and jump right into battle with an enemy Titan without the need to reload. The Particle Wall is great to use in many situations. The best time to use Particle Wall is in an alleyway, which forces the enemy Titan to retreat or charge you to deal damage to your Titan. The Multi-Target Missile System is good to deal that little bit of extra damage to keep you winning a battle. The good thing about the Multi-Target Missile System is that it is almost always a guaranteed hit when locked on. The reason I use Nuclear Ejection and Auto-Eject together is so that I can always get away as a Pilot and return to fight another day.

CHASSIS
ATLAS

PRIMARY WEAPON
XO-16 CHAINGUN
HIGH-RATE OF PRECISION FIRE
MOD: ACCELERATOR

TACTICAL ABILITY
PARTICLE WALL
DEPLOYS A ONE-WAY FORCE-FIELD

ORDNANCE
MULTI-TARGET MISSILE SYSTEM
YOU CAN MANUALLY PAINT MULTIPLE TARGETS

TIER 1 KIT
NUCLEAR EJECTION
YOUR TITAN GOES NUCLEAR WHEN YOU EJECT

TIER 2 KIT
AUTO-EJECT
YOU EJECT AND CLOAK AUTOMATICALLY WHEN DOOMED

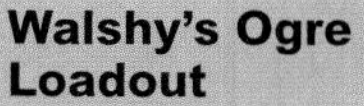

Walshy's Ogre Loadout

CHASSIS
OGRE

My loadout is great for dishing out damage while protecting my Titan from incoming damage. I use the 40mm Cannon and force fights at mid-range because it can handle Pilots and Titans at this distance. I prefer my Tactical Ability to be Particle Wall. I use it when an enemy Titan is out in the open and can't avoid the fight or the enemy Titan shoots its ordnance at me. For my ordnance, I choose the Multi-Target Missile System because it plays similar to the 40mm Cannon where I just deal out small amounts of damage that quickly adds up when I lock on a few missiles at a time. For my Tier 1 Kit, I use Dash Quickcharger. Using my dashes and Particle Wall, I can usually run from fights where I am at a disadvantage—most people make the mistake of fighting to the death when you don't have to. However, when I do know I am going to die and can't avoid it, I have the perk of my Tier 2 Kit, where I can keep dishing out damage to nearby Titans until I eject myself at the last possible second. All around I find this loadout to be a safe choice because I can one-shot minions and Pilots along with going toe-to-toe against any Titan loadout.

PRIMARY WEAPON

SEMI-AUTO 40MM HE ROUNDS

40MM CANNON

MOD: EXTENDED MAGAZINE

TACTICAL ABILITY

PARTICLE WALL
DEPLOYS A ONE-WAY FORCE-FIELD

ORDNANCE

MULTI-TARGET MISSILE SYSTEM
YOU CAN MANUALLY PAINT MULTIPLE TARGETS

TIER 1 KIT

DASH QUICKCHARGER
YOUR DASH RECHARGES FASTER

TIER 2 KIT

SURVIVOR
YOUR TITAN DEGRADES SLOWER WHEN DOOMED

Flamesword's Stryder Loadout

CHASSIS
STRYDER

This loadout and Titan Chassis fits my play style perfectly. I am a very aggressive player, so I always equip the Dash Quickcharger to enhance the Stryder's greatest asset-its speed. The XO-16 Chaingun equipped with the Accelerator mod is the perfect weapon at all ranges, allowing me to provide cover fire until I make my way to the front lines. This is where having Cluster Missile and Particle Wall comes in handy. I often dash into an enemy Titan and punch it from the side. Once it turns around and engages me, I drop the Particle Wall and begin firing my Chaingun, forcing the enemy Titan to either run away or dash through my wall. If it comes through the Particle Wall, at that exact moment, I fire a Cluster Missile on my side of the wall, inflicting heavy damage. Finally, the Core Extender allows me to freely dash around the map and help friendly Pilots or Titans. When I engage an enemy Titan with my Dash Core ability activated, they don't stand a chance.

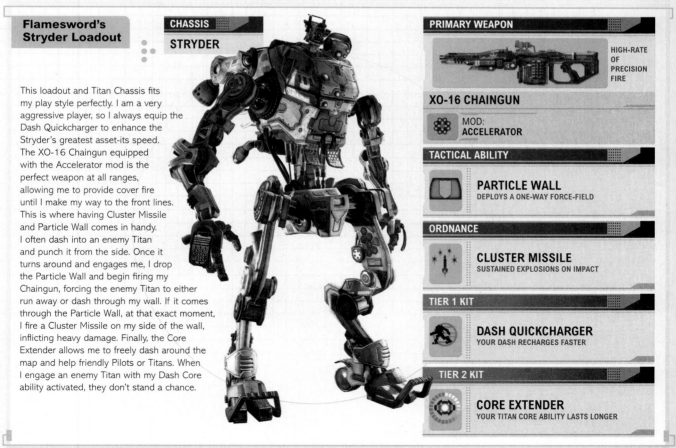

PRIMARY WEAPON

HIGH-RATE OF PRECISION FIRE

XO-16 CHAINGUN

MOD: ACCELERATOR

TACTICAL ABILITY

PARTICLE WALL
DEPLOYS A ONE-WAY FORCE-FIELD

ORDNANCE

CLUSTER MISSILE
SUSTAINED EXPLOSIONS ON IMPACT

TIER 1 KIT

DASH QUICKCHARGER
YOUR DASH RECHARGES FASTER

TIER 2 KIT

CORE EXTENDER
YOUR TITAN CORE ABILITY LASTS LONGER

MAPS

ARE YOU READY TO TEST YOUR PILOT SKILLS IN THE SERVICE OF THE MILITIA OR IMC? THERE ARE A TOTAL OF 15 ENVIRONMENTS ON WHICH TO PROVE YOURSELF WORTHY OF ADVANCEMENT AMONG THE RANKS OF ELITE PILOTS. EACH MAP IS UNIQUE, PRESENTING PILOTS WITH A VARIETY OF ENVIRONMENTS TO MASTER, RANGING FROM DERELICT SHIPWRECKS TO HEAVILY DEFENDED IMC INSTALLATIONS. DO YOU HAVE WHAT IT TAKES TO LEAD YOUR TEAM TO VICTORY? STUDY THE PROVIDED MAPS AND GAIN A TACTICAL ADVANTAGE OVER YOUR OPPONENTS IN EVERY BATTLE. EACH MAP OFFERS AN IN-DEPTH ANALYSIS OF ALL FIVE GAME MODES, PROVIDING FIELD-TESTED TACTICS DEVISED BY PROFESSIONAL GAMERS.

MAP NOTES

- Screens with a white "play" icon indicate the presence of video content in the eGuide version. Access your eGuide to watch instructional video content.
  - Look for colored "ribbons" on some screenshots, illustrating advantageous wallruns and jumps. Utilize these paths to traverse the map quickly.
- Key landmarks have been selected and named by the Prima author team of professional gamers, helping identify key locations on each map.

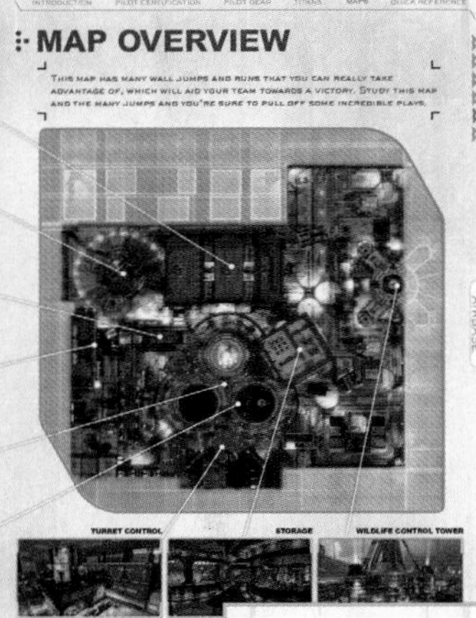

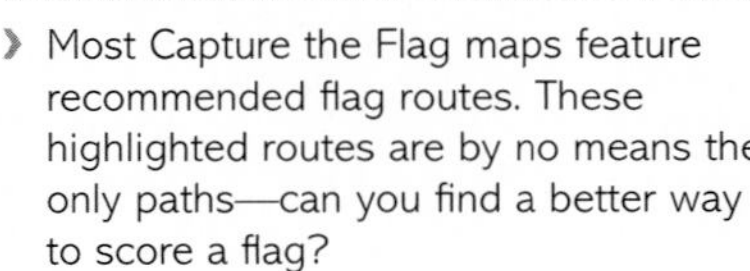

- Most Capture the Flag maps feature recommended flag routes. These highlighted routes are by no means the only paths—can you find a better way to score a flag?
- On Capture the Flag maps, all deployment areas, flags, and routes shown represent the initial round. At halftime the factions switch sides.

- The provided heat maps are a composite of all game modes and represent the highest concentrations of minion deaths—warm colors indicate high-action areas, while cool colors represent less action.

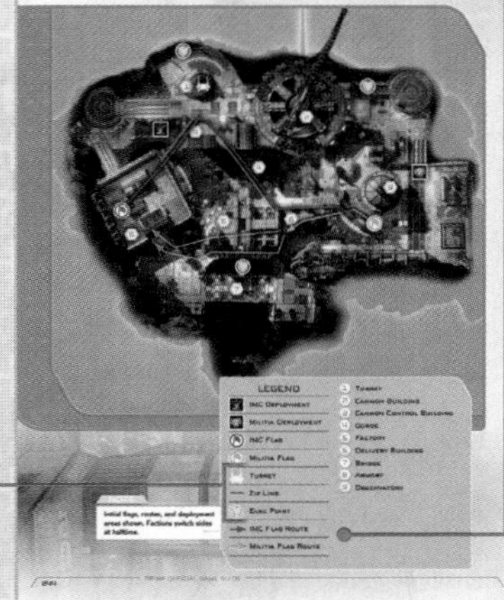

- Some maps feature turrets which can be hacked to give your team an advantage.
- Zip lines, appearing as red lines, offer a quick way to move around the map.
- With the exception of Last Titan Standing, each map has multiple preset Evac Points. During a match's Epilogue, a Dropship will appear at one of these preset Evac Points.

THE FALL

ODYSSEY

AIRBASE

IMC Airbase Sierra is one of the largest installations ever built on the Frontier, situated on a planet where giant Leviathans roam the landscape. To protect its base from the super-sized local wildlife, the IMC has installed three huge Wildlife Repulsor Towers, also referred to as "dog whistle" towers by base personnel. Built to service the largest ships in the fleet, the base structures are huge, creating large encapsulated regions of combat. Pilots often fight fiercely over the turret at the edge of the Airbase, where the adjoining building can serve as a very defensible firebase with good sight lines.

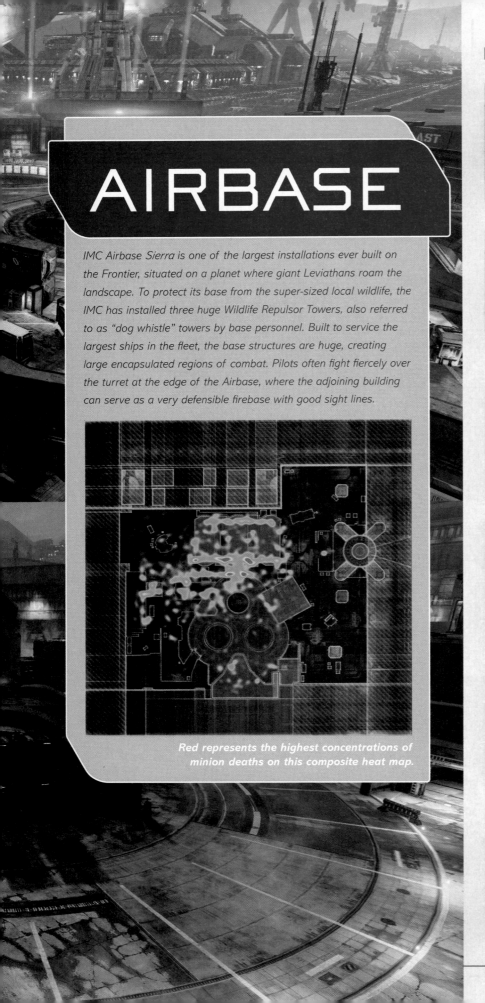

Red represents the highest concentrations of minion deaths on this composite heat map.

KEY LANDMARKS

AIR TRAFFIC CONTROL TOWER

STEALTH BOMBER

BIG RAMP

HANGAR

LANDING PAD

FUEL HUB

MAP OVERVIEW

This map has many wall jumps and runs that you can really take advantage of, which will aid your team towards a victory. Study this map and the many jumps and you're sure to pull off some incredible plays.

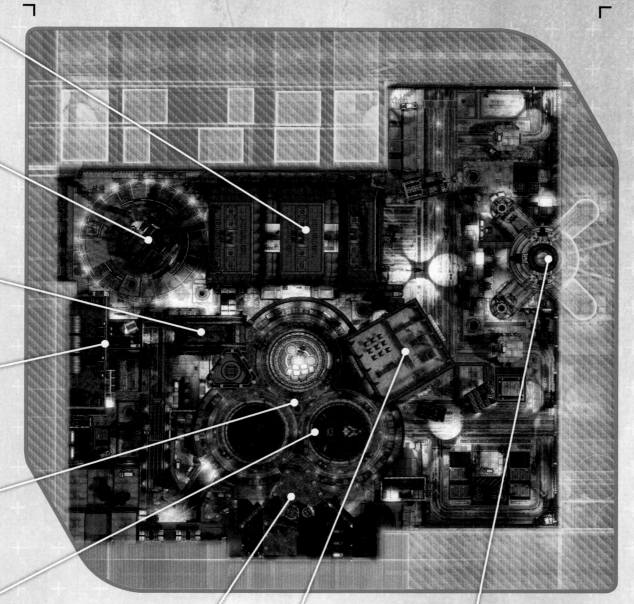

TURRET CONTROL

CIRCULAR HANGAR

WILDLIFE CONTROL TOWER

TITANFALL

ATTRITION

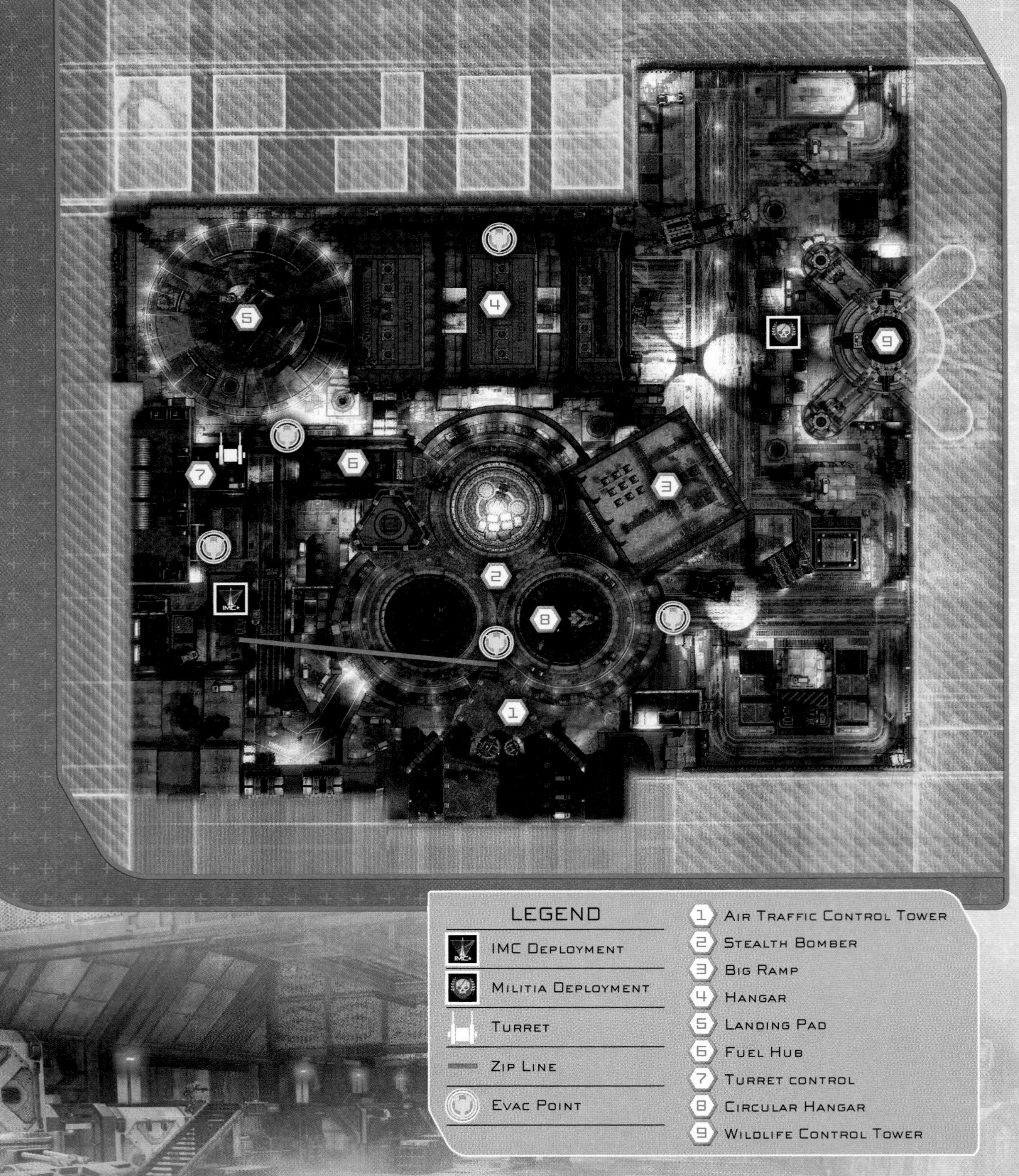

LEGEND
IMC Deployment
Militia Deployment
Turret
Zip Line
Evac Point
1 Air Traffic Control Tower
2 Stealth Bomber
3 Big Ramp
4 Hangar
5 Landing Pad
6 Fuel Hub
7 Turret control
8 Circular Hangar
9 Wildlife Control Tower

TACTICS

- Off the start of the game, minions of both teams will move towards the Hangar and have a firefight. This causes Pilots from both teams to gravitate towards this area off the beginning of the game as well. Have your Ordnance grenades ready and throw them across the Hangar to pick off a few minions.
- Off the start of the match, get to the top of the Hangar or on top of the crates that have a line of sight across the way. An enemy Pilot is most likely jumping up to crates or the roof of the Hangar on the enemy's side of the map. Have a sniper rifle equipped to get a quick Pilot kill.
- Don't get caught off guard when heading towards the Hangar—clear out the north side of the Hangar first. An enemy Pilot will usually head this way, so be prepared for a battle. Take out the enemy Pilot and then continue forward through the Hangar. If no enemies come, you are able to easily move up and shoot into the Hangar through the windows to pick off enemy minions and Pilots.

PRO TIP: FLAMESWORD

When I first spawn, if playing on the Militia team, I like to head to the turret close by and activate it. The turret's kills add to your Attrition score, so this lets me move to other areas and kill more enemies. Once the turret is activated, I quickly wall jump off the billboard to make it to the top of the Fuel Hub. From up here I look towards the Hangar to pick off any wandering enemy Pilots.

- In between the Hangar and Landing Pads is a high-traffic minion area with a ton of open crates that allows you to move in and out of the area. These crates become critical to use for cover as enemy Pilots will try to ambush you as you continue killing their minions.
- The catwalks inside the Hangar is a great location to patrol. Minions constantly engage each other in this area. Put down fire from above on the catwalks and pick up some easy kills that will reduce your time for Titanfall. Pilots can shoot through the catwalks, so take advantage of this when an enemy is directly below you or above you.
- When in a Titan, head towards the Landing Pads. This area will have plenty of minions to reduce the time on your Titan's Core Ability. If you get ambushed by enemy Pilots or a Titan, keep in mind you can drop down the open Landing Pads to get away.
- Titans are great for hit-and-run tactics inside the Hangar, with three total entrances that can be used to escape. Sweep through here periodically to kill enemies. Don't get stuck inside for too long as a group of enemy Pilots or Titans can easily take you down if you are cornered.

CAPTURE THE FLAG

NOTE

Initial flags, routes, and deployment areas shown. Factions switch sides at halftime.

TACTICS

Reference these videos in your free mobile friendly eGuide.

- Each flag is placed within structures promoting close-quarter combat. One flag is inside the Turret Control while the other is inside the Wildlife Control Tower. Since they are placed in these structures, throw Arc Mines around the area to weaken or kill enemies who sneak in. Remember, it takes two Arc Mines to kill a enemy Pilot, but if an enemy Pilot is sprinting by, a Pilot will survive the blast sometimes.
- A great location to defend the flag inside the Turret Control is the top of the Fuel Hub. The roof of the Fuel Hub has metal slants that provide you with cover and a view to spot enemy Pilots entering or exiting the flag area. If you move to the very top, you can spot enemies at a distance and take them out before they get close to the Turret Control.

PRO TIP: STRONGSIDE

While having Enhanced Parkour equipped, using these wall runs will lead to an extremely fast flag route to run the flag from the Turret Control back to your base. Start out by wall running onto the yellow sign and then running into the Fuel Hub. Now make your way out the other balcony facing the Hangar. Make your next wall run on the wall of the Fuel Hub towards the Landing Pads. Jump and wall run onto the wall of the Landing Pads and wall run all the way to the Big Ramp. Once you're wall running on the Big Ramp, wait until the last second to jump off, allowing you to get more distance towards your base. Your team should be near the base to assist you if any enemies are nearby.

PRO TIP: FLAMESWORD

Position your Pilot on the roof of the Big Ramp with a sniper when going for the flag in the Wildlife Control Tower. A Pilot will be able to get easy kills and communicate to the team where enemies are moving to. Locking down this area allows your team to move in and grab a flag. Enemy Pilots will forget about you to kill the player with the flag. Take advantage of this and shoot the enemies as they turn their backs to you.

- Having a Titan nearby when grabbing the flag inside the Turret Control can lead to a very fast capture. Grab the flag, immediately board your Titan, and take the passage underneath the Landing Pads. Underneath the Landing Pads provides a covered area and that is a good location for a one-on-one Titan battle if you have Particle Wall equipped. Kill any pursuing enemies and then continue back to your base for the capture. If you get caught underneath the Landing Pads in the Storage area, take your Titan underneath the landing pad with an opening. Here you'll want to eject from your Titan out through the opening of the landing pad and land on top of the roof of the Big Ramp. On top of the Big Ramp, you'll be able to wait for your teammates who will then assist you back to your base.
- When defending the flag within the Wildlife Control Tower, a Titan equipped with the XO-16 Chaingun can easily guard the objective. Keep your focus towards the Hangar and the Big Ramp to ensure no enemy Pilots sneak by. Patrol back and forth from these locations to pick off enemies at the top of the Big Ramp or running through the Hangar.

HARDPOINT DOMINATION

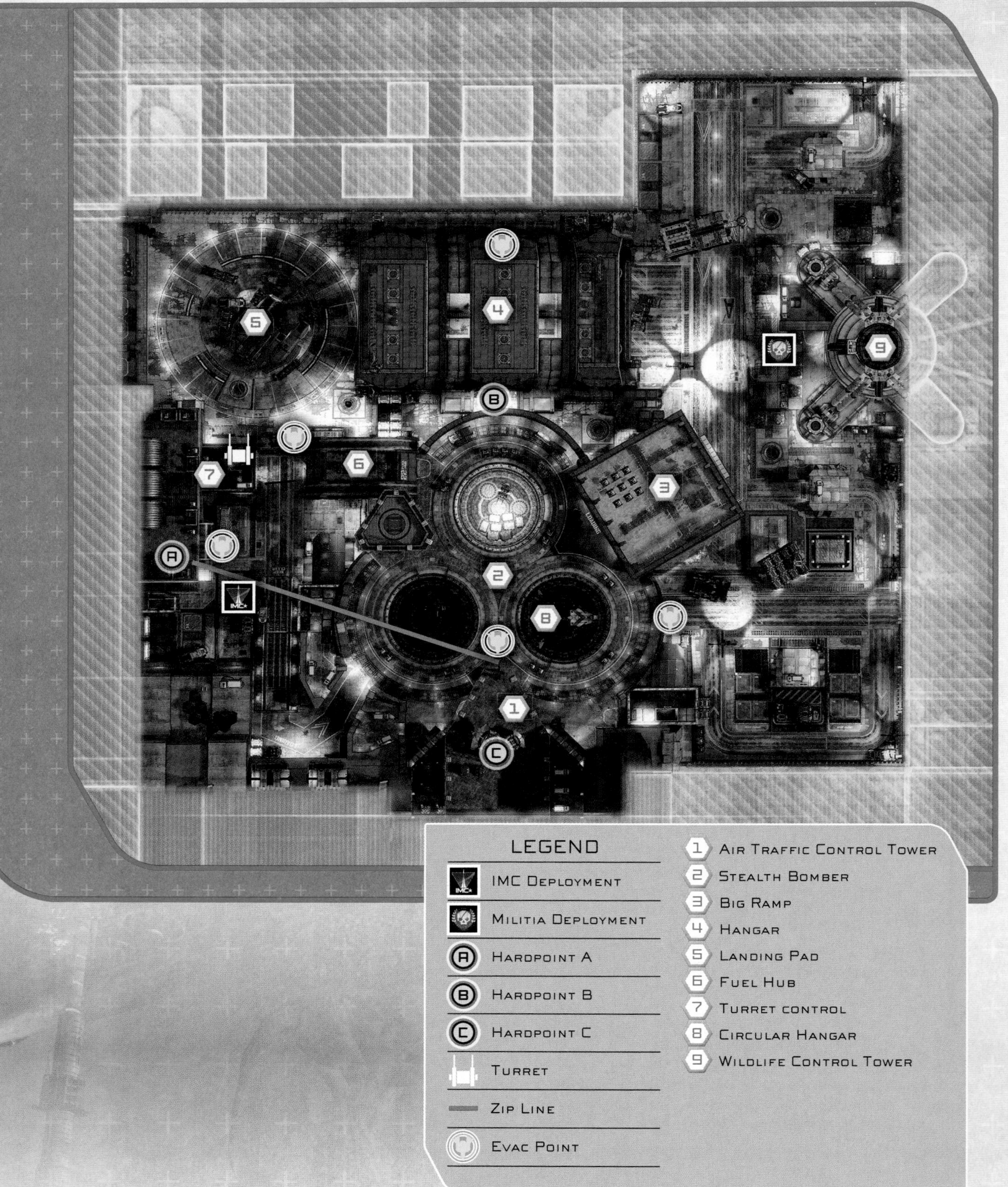

TACTICS

Reference these videos in your free mobile friendly eGuide.

- Hardpoint A is located within the Turret Control building. Equipping a shotgun or SMG allows you to make quick work of enemy Pilots who enter. A Pilot will want to stay inside the Turret Control the entire game when defending. This allows your teammates to keep their focus towards controlling the other hardpoints. Communicate with your teammates if you are being attacked by many enemies, alerting your teammates to either come back to the hardpoint you're controlling and defend it or give up the hardpoint you are controlling and move to another hardpoint to take control of it.

PRO TIP: WALSHY

Having the Active Radar Pulse Tactical Ability with the Satchel Charge Ordnance will make you the ultimate defender when guarding Hardpoint A. Place the charges inside the capture radius near an entrance while you defend a different entrance. Use your Tactical Ability every time you can to see if enemies are approaching the area. If you notice an enemy approach the entrance where you have Satchel Charges set, double tap your reload button to detonate the charges immediately.

PRO TIP: STRONGSIDE

When defending Hardpoint B, a great escape route is the jump in between the Hangar and Landing Pads. There are many ways to do this jump, but this is one way from the ground. First, start out by wall running and then jumping off the crate towards the yellow sign. Second, jump off of the sign towards the wall. Third, jump off the wall and back to the sign and either pull yourself up to the top of the sign or land on top of the sign. Finally, jump back towards the wall and double jump up and over. This can be hard at first, but give it some practice and you'll have it down in no time.

- Hardpoint B is accessible by Titans, making it a difficult objective to defend if your team has fewer Titans. When this is the case, head to areas saturated with minions to get a Titan quicker. When the time is right, trap the opposing Titans inside and recapture the hardpoint.
- A quick way to get to Hardpoint C is to take the zip line from the Turret Control. Having Cloak as your Tactical Ability is a good choice when trying to sneak inside the Air Traffic Control Tower. Take the zip line with a shotgun while cloaked and then quickly clear out the Air Traffic Control Tower of enemies to easily capture the objective.
- Controlling Hardpoints B and C is the best and most efficient way to win the match. As stated before, Hardpoint B is accessible by Titan, but instead of having your Titan underneath the Landing Pads, keep it above and guard Hardpoint C. The opening on the Landing Pads will allow you to rain fire from above with your Titan without dropping down to Hardpoint B.

LAST TITAN STANDING

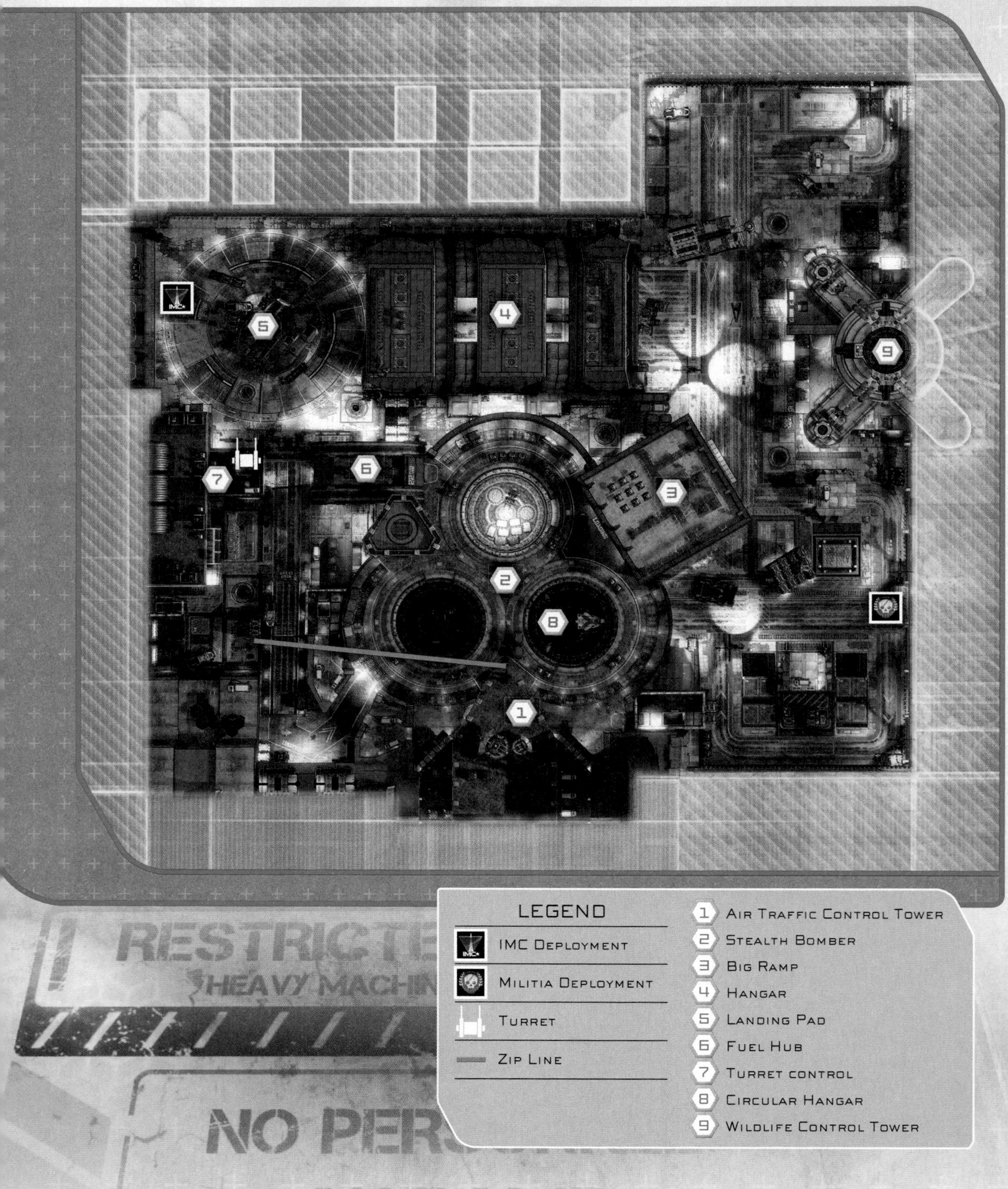

LEGEND

	IMC Deployment
	Militia Deployment
	Turret
	Zip Line

1. Air Traffic Control Tower
2. Stealth Bomber
3. Big Ramp
4. Hangar
5. Landing Pad
6. Fuel Hub
7. Turret control
8. Circular Hangar
9. Wildlife Control Tower

TACTICS

- Titans will want to stick close to one another throughout the entire match. How the match starts will be the key to success. When spawning on the Militia side, have two or more Titans head into the Hangar towards the IMC side. A Stryder in the front with Vortex Shield as its Tactical Ability will be able to stop incoming fire. This allows your team to gain control of the Hangar so you can make moves either through the Hangar or the bottom of the Landing Pads.
- When starting on the IMC side, take the Big Ramp up towards the Landing Pads and immediately look across towards the ramp near the Control Tower. This ramp is the only spot the enemies can come from at the start, so stay aimed on it, ready to damage and kill enemy Titans.

PRO TIP: WALSHY

I like to keep my Titan on the top of the Big Ramp where I can just see across the Landing Pads while still taking cover. Here I am able to assist friendly Titans engaging enemies coming from the other entrance to the Landing Pads.

- When spawning on the side with the turret, quickly disembark your Titan and activate the turret. If your team decides to overload the Hangar and bottom of the Landing Pads, the turret will be able to shoot enemy Titans that overlook the Landing Pads.
- Titan battles on Airbase are short to medium range. Equipping the XO-16 Chaingun or 40mm Cannon will excel in many of the battles, especially since battles commence quickly off the start. The Plasma Railgun will be effective for one Titan to have. Landing fully charged shots aids tremendously in taking out enemy Titans.
- Control the Landing Pads because it is the highest ground on the map. There are only two ways to enter this area. You'll be able to watch these two choke points and cut off any enemies with your entire team. If your team is overthrown on the Landing Pads, drop down and escape through the Landing Pads with a opening.

PILOT HUNTER

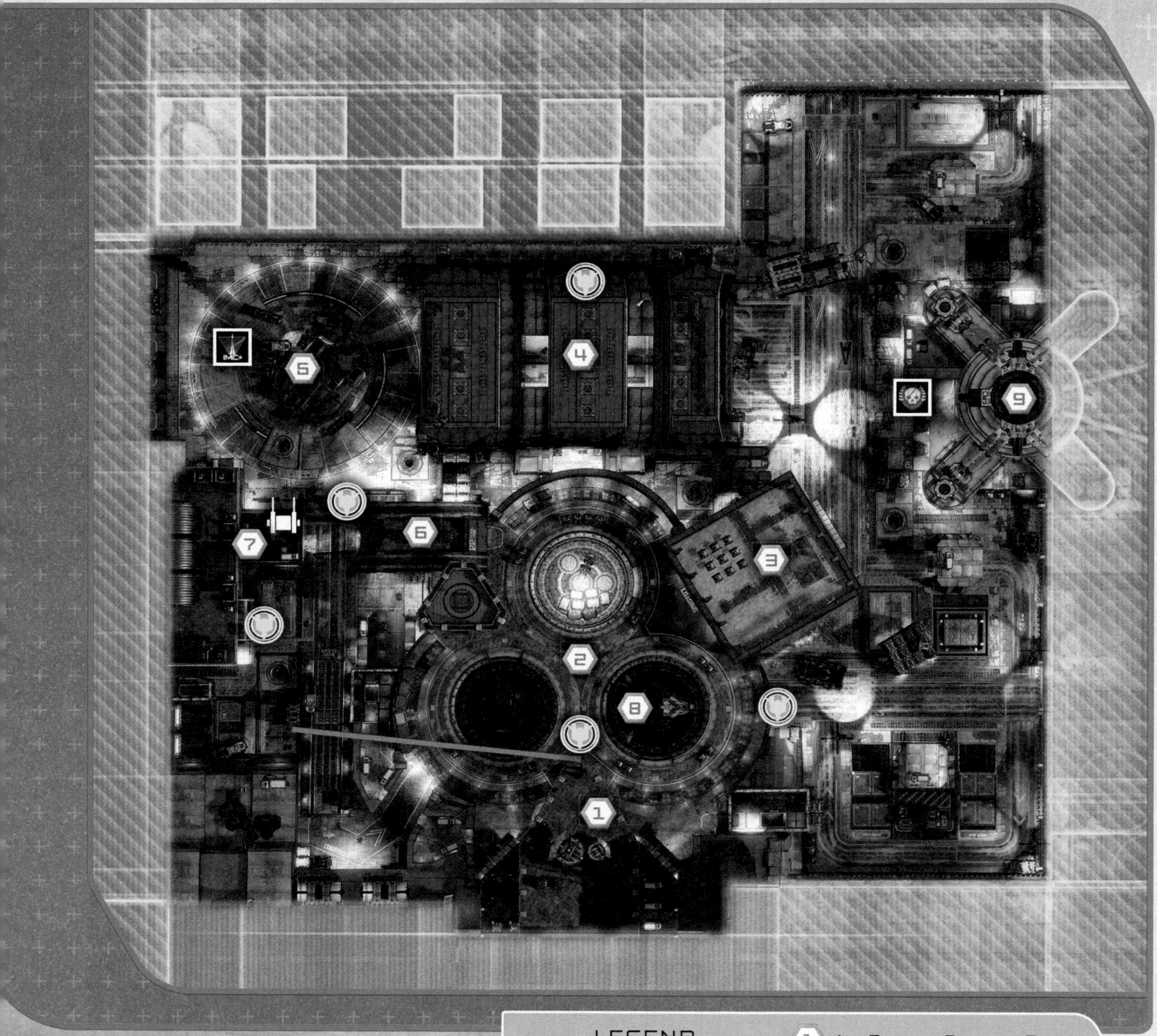

LEGEND

IMC Deployment

Militia Deployment

Turret

Zip Line

Evac Point

1. Air Traffic Control Tower
2. Stealth Bomber
3. Big Ramp
4. Hangar
5. Landing Pad
6. Fuel Hub
7. Turret control
8. Circular Hangar
9. Wildlife Control Tower

TACTICS

Reference these videos in your free mobile friendly eGuide.

- Height advantage is the key to success when playing this match, and the top of the Hangar is the perfect spot to go to. Enemy Pilots are forced to scale the Hangar from the side, putting them at a disadvantage as you will be prepared for them.
- Killing minions is still important even though it doesn't count toward your game score. Hunting minions is still the easiest way to gain Titanfall. Don't stick in one location for too long as enemy Pilots will try to ambush you.

PRO TIP: FLAMESWORD

The last place enemy Pilots would look at, a favorite spot of mine to snipe from, is on the support beam inside of the Big Ramp. A Pilot is provided with a great line of sight towards the Landing Pads and the open area outside of the Hangar leading to the Wildlife Control Tower. To get to this position you must wall run from the top of the Big Ramp towards the support beam.

PRO TIP: STRONGSIDE

When running through the crates between the Hangar and Landing Pads, head towards the indent that connects the Landing Pads and Fuel Hub. The two walls allow you to shimmy all the way to the top of the Landing Pads or Fuel Hub. This jump is very useful to escape enemy Pilots or to change locations on the fly to find enemies.

- Near the Fuel Hub is a structure that provides both incredible cover and a great overlook of the Landing Pads and Hangar. The only way up is to jump up, so be on the lookout for cloaked enemy Pilots who try to sneak up. Pick off enemy minions and Pilots roaming the Landing Pads.

PRO TIP: WALSHY

A great strategy to use with your Titan is to activate the turret near the Stealth Bomber. Have an XO-16 Chaingun equipped and sit behind the Stealth Bomber looking towards the Hangar and Fuel Hub. The turret will shoot in the direction of enemies, which will aid you in spotting out enemy Pilots. Hold down that trigger and mow down enemies.

ANGEL CITY

When the IMC instituted martial law in Angel City, massive walls were built and a system of security checkpoints was created to divide the city into many smaller districts. The unfortunate residents of the Harbor District, now unable to move freely throughout the city, are only able to view the glittering skyline from afar. Pilots fighting in the city gravitate to the highly accessible rooftops, using them to cross entire city districts without ever touching the ground.

Red represents the highest concentrations of minion deaths on this composite heat map.

KEY LANDMARKS

STORAGE

RED STAR RESTAURANT

BACKYARD

COURTYARD

KODAI BUILDING

ANGEL APARTMENTS

MAP OVERVIEW

YOUR POSITION ON THIS MAP WILL DIRECTLY REFLECT ON THE SCOREBOARD. CONTROL THE ROOFTOPS AND YOU WILL WIN THE GAME.

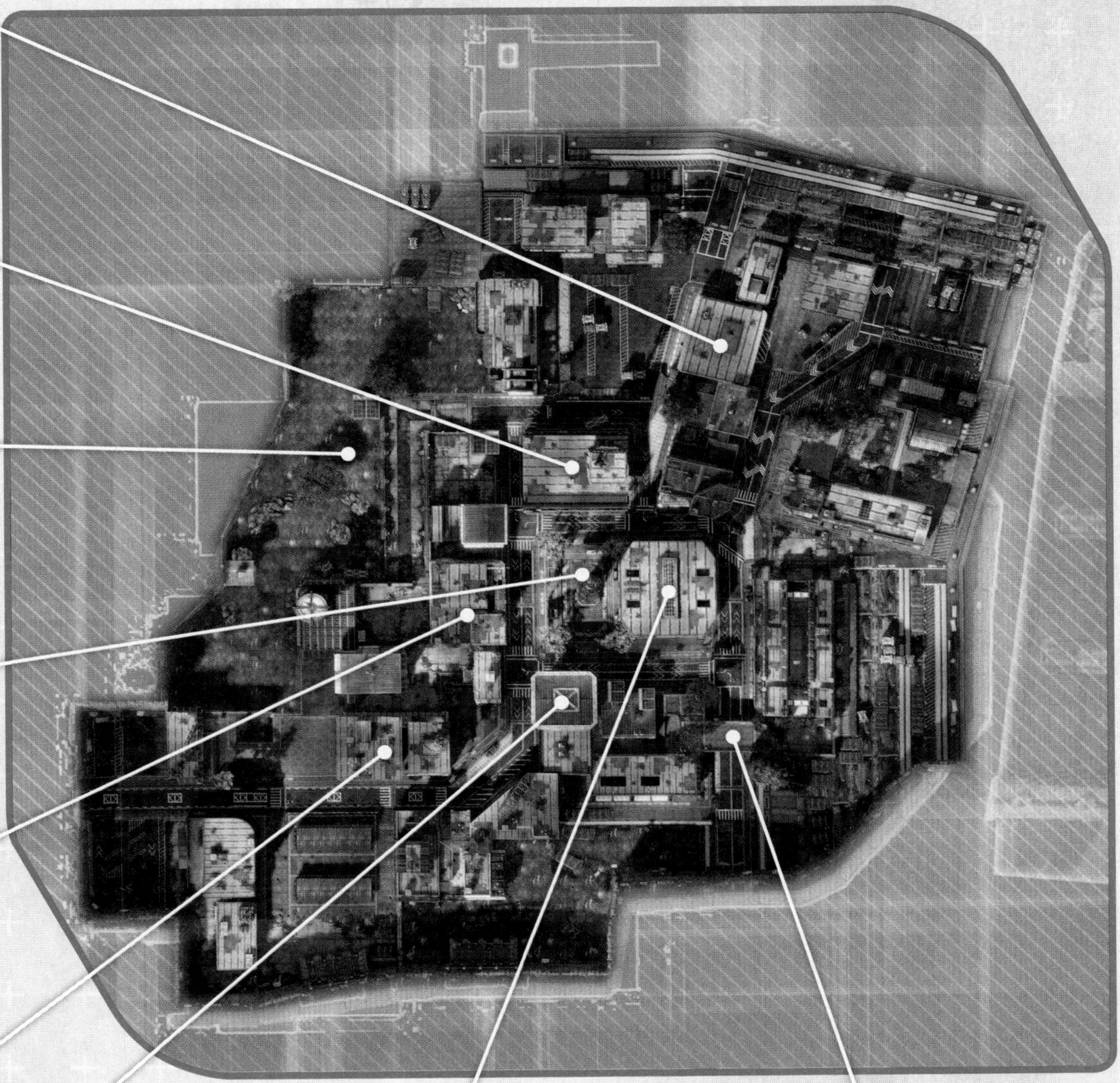

UP MART

MARKET

WALKWAY

ANGEL CITY

ATTRITION

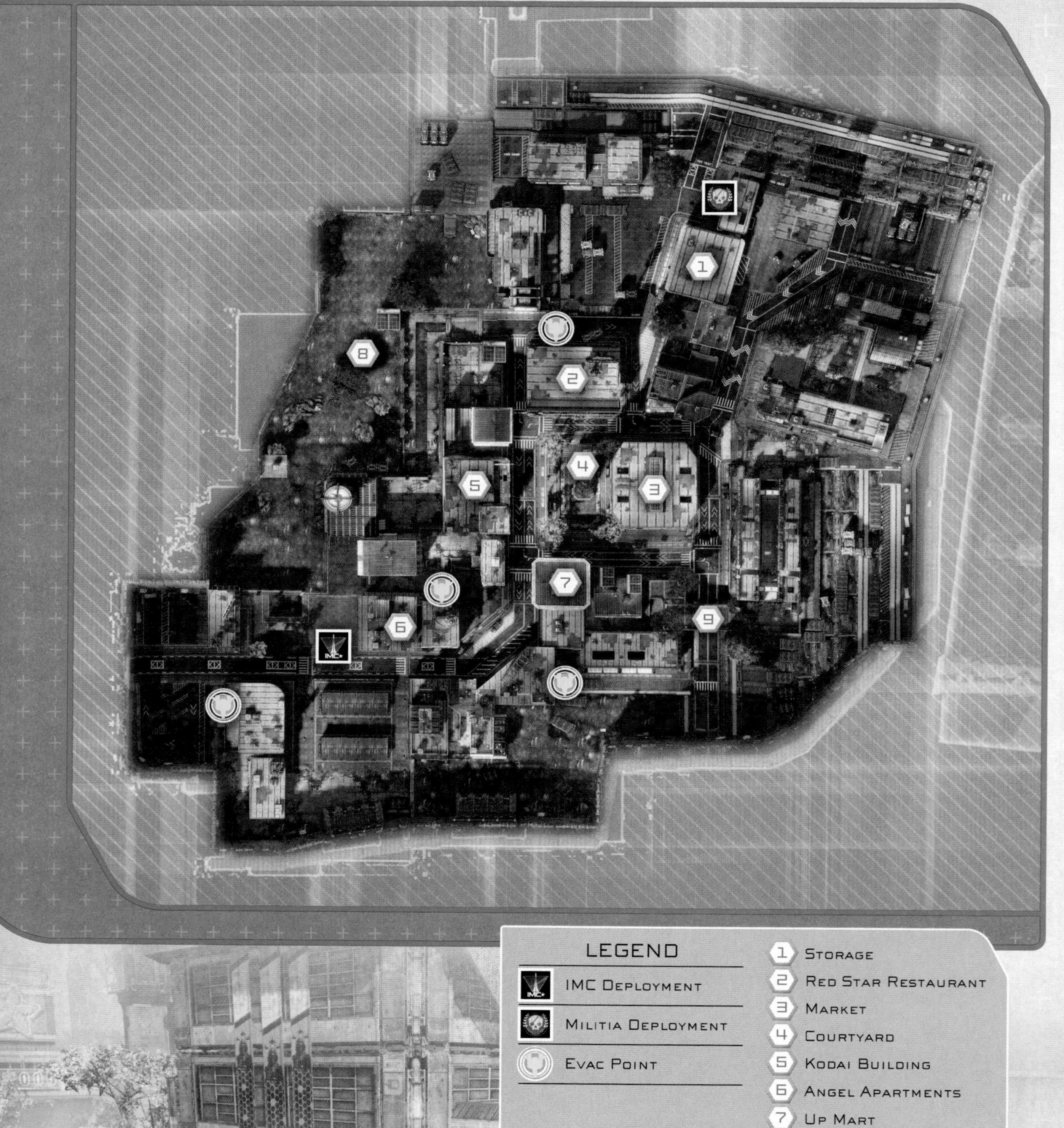
1
2
3
4
5
6
7
8
9
LEGEND
IMC Deployment
Militia Deployment
Evac Point
1 Storage
2 Red Star Restaurant
3 Market
4 Courtyard
5 Kodai Building
6 Angel Apartments
7 Up Mart
8 Backyard
9 Walkway

TACTICS

Reference these videos in your free mobile friendly eGuide.

- This wall run in the Courtyard to access the third level of the Market is a great escape route as the Courtyard is a high-traffic area. This wall run also works extremely well to attack an enemy Pilot in the third level of the Market and to get to the roof quickly.
- Controlling the roof of the Market allows you to oversee the Courtyard and the road around it. Keep an eye on these choke points to pick off fighting minions and enemy Pilots. It is also a great location to fire upon enemy Titans from above, because you can retreat down any of the four openings leading to the third level of the Market for cover.
- The Up Mart is another favorable spot for Pilots to kill minions down below in the streets while also having a great overview of the map to spot enemy Pilots. The Up Mart has many ways to wall jump to the top of the roof, so keep moving around and never stay in one location.
- The Market is a great spot to use the EVA-8 Shotgun and Active Radar Pulse. You can clear out minions that frequently roam the bottom floor, as well as use your Tactical Ability to find Pilots above and wall jump up in the center of the Market to get as close as possible for the kill.
- With all the buildings near the center of the city, this area is easily seen from many rooftops on the map and is asking to be attacked by Anti-Titan weapons and Arc Grenades. Be cautious of using your Titan's dashes—save your dashes to escape the city once enemy Pilots begin dealing damage to you.
- Pilots need to patrol the Storage for enemies. This area can spawn many minions, allowing you to set up an ambush on an unsuspecting enemy Pilot.
- When playing as the Militia, controlling the Angel Apartments near the IMC initial spawn will provide you with many minion kills. You will find enemy Pilots spawning in this area quite often unless your team pushes to close to their spawn.

CAPTURE THE FLAG

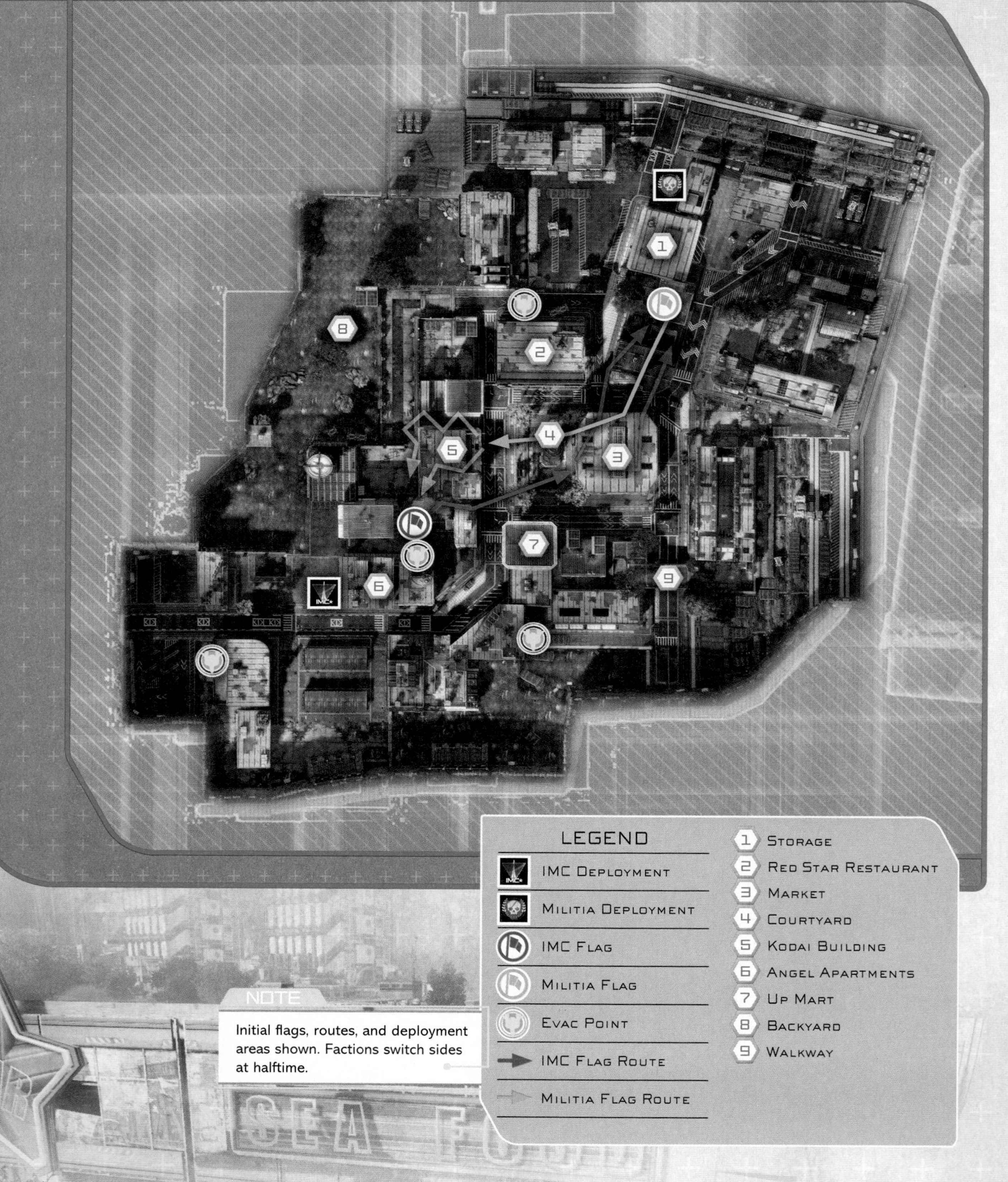
1
2
3
4
5
6
7
8
9
LEGEND
IMC Deployment
Militia Deployment
IMC Flag
Militia Flag
Evac Point
IMC Flag Route
Militia Flag Route
1 Storage
2 Red Star Restaurant
3 Market
4 Courtyard
5 Kodai Building
6 Angel Apartments
7 Up Mart
8 Backyard
9 Walkway
NOTE
Initial flags, routes, and deployment areas shown. Factions switch sides at halftime.

TACTICS

Reference these videos in your free mobile friendly eGuide.

- A solid flag route from the Kodai building is taking the flag through the Backyard. Drop your Titan behind the Kodai building and then move in to grab the flag. Once you have the flag, jump into your Titan and travel through the Backyard to avoid all the enemies that are sure to be in the center of the map.
- When defending the flag near the Storage, the Red Star Restaurant rooftop is a great location to post up on. At this position you have cover due to the building's design. While you're able to defend your flag near the Storage you're also able to apply pressure in the middle of the map and kill minions in the streets.

PRO TIP: STRONGSIDE

When grabbing the flag by the Kodai building, take advantage of the quick wall run that leads you inside the Market. You will be exposed while jumping across the main street, but once in the Market you will be provided with cover to make your way out the back of the Market and back to your base near the Storage.

Once you have grabbed the flag near the Storage, take this exceptional wall run to make it into the Market. Once inside you can perform another wall run, leading you towards the Kodai building.

- Players will want to gain control of the Market and Red Star Restaurant before pushing up to the objective near the Storage. Controlling these two points will force the opposing team to only attack you from one direction once you have them trapped in the back.
- Titans always lead to an incredible defense. Be sure to kill the minions that converge towards the Courtyard to call a Titan quickly. Titans can be easily destroyed in Angel City, so keep a distance and try to draw in enemy Pilots or Titans when guarding your flag.

HARDPOINT DOMINATION

LEGEND

IMC Deployment	1 Storage
Militia Deployment	2 Red Star Restaurant
Hardpoint A	3 Market
Hardpoint B	4 Courtyard
Hardpoint C	5 Kodai Building
Evac Point	6 Angel Apartments
	7 Up Mart
	8 Backyard
	9 Walkway

TACTICS

- The most effective strategy to win is controlling Hardpoints B and C. Hardpoint C is accessible by Titans, making it easy to capture. Once both are captured, move a Titan to help defend Hardpoint B. Since Hardpoint C is accessible by Titans, you have time to retreat back when you notice the opposing team is trying to capture it.
- Inside the third level of the Market where you capture Hardpoint B is a box that can be used to defend against the opposing team when the objective is under your control. Crouch behind the box and get an easy kill when an enemy Pilot walks by. Don't stay here if you take down an enemy Pilot—move from spot to spot, keeping the enemy guessing where you are going to be next.
- Before running into Hardpoint B, scale the building to make it to the roof. On top you will notice openings to drop down towards the objective. Pay attention to your hit markers as you throw grenades in corners to injure or kill enemies before dropping in.
- Hardpoint B's capture radius is large and gives you many places to hide and move while capturing the area. Watch a specific set of windows and stairway instead of moving around from one side of the building to the other. If you see the Hardpoint is contested, then turn around and find the lurking Pilot.
- Careful when pushing to Hardpoint A with a Titan. This narrow street can be a death trap if you don't have a friendly Titan on the streets or a friendly Pilot backing you up on the roofs.
- When defending Hardpoint A, equip the Tier 1 kit Explosives Pack and equip Frag Grenades. Spot the direction your enemies will come from and throw your grenades at the windows when they try to jump in. If they survive the explosion they will be so weak that you can easily finish them off.

PRO TIP: WALSHY

Hide in the long, open crate inside Hardpoint C to capture the point and catch enemies off guard. Watch the garage door closest to you until the Hardpoint on your HUD says the area is contested, indicating the enemy entered from a different entrance. Then move from one side of the open crate to the other side until the enemy Pilot is exposed.

LAST TITAN STANDING

LEGEND

IMC Deployment

Militia Deployment

1 Storage
2 Red Star Restaurant
3 Market
4 Courtyard
5 Kodai Building
6 Angel Apartments
7 Up Mart
8 Backyard
9 Walkway

TACTICS

PRO TIP: FLAMESWORD

Work with a teammate Titan to bait an enemy in for a 2vs1. You or your Titan friend can hide behind a building or structure while the other Titan looks vulnerable and weak to draw in the enemy Titan, letting it think it has the upper hand. When the enemy Titan gets near the structure, you and your teammate aggressively attack the enemy Titan to dominate it in 2vs1.

- Spreading out is a must. Gain control of the Market's cross streets and make the enemy Titans funnel in through the narrow entrances.
- Cluster Missile and Rocket Salvo are ideal for dishing out as much damage as possible to all the enemy Titans that are sure to be next to each other on these confined streets.
- This map allows for multiple primary weapons to shine. Choose the one that best fits your style. If you want to sit back, go with the Plasma Railgun. If you are the aggressive type, you can't go wrong with the 40mm Cannon.
- Although it is tempting, refrain from attempting a rodeo attack on an enemy Titan. Other enemy Titans are sure to be close by to shoot you off. Go for a rodeo attack on an enemy Titan if it is alone or is the last enemy Titan left.
- A great time to deploy an Auto-Titan is when you are near a building. As a Pilot, you're able to jump to the top of a building and attack alongside your Auto-Titan, dealing double the damage to enemy Titans.

PILOT HUNTER

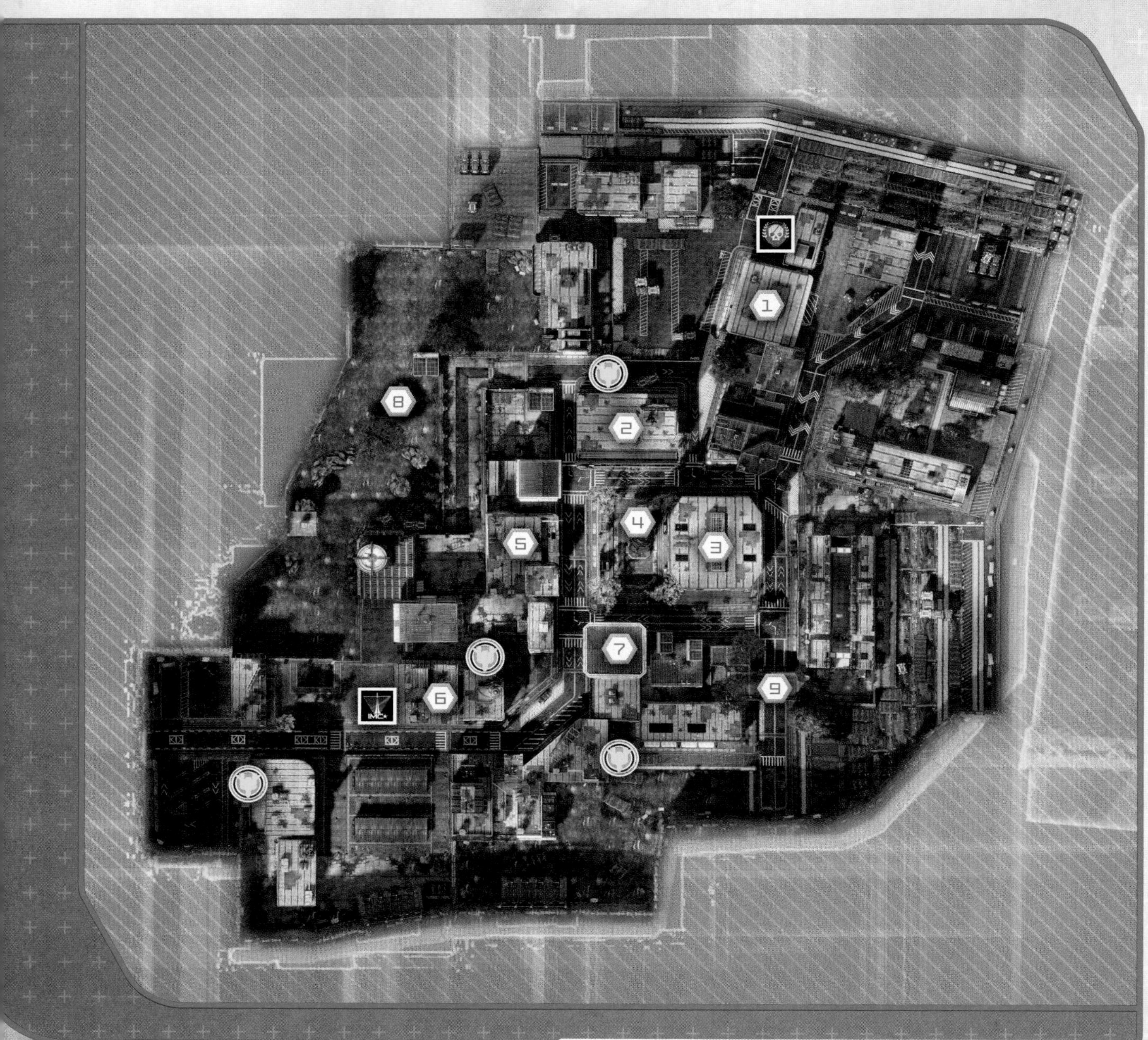

LEGEND

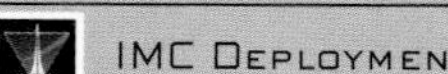

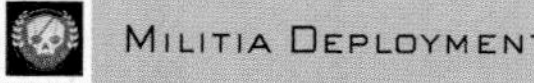

IMC Deployment

Militia Deployment

Evac Point

1. Storage
2. Red Star Restaurant
3. Market
4. Courtyard
5. Kodai Building
6. Angel Apartments
7. Up Mart
8. Backyard
9. Walkway

TACTICS

- When on the rooftops, don't shoot the minions down low for too long. You will just give away your position to other Pilots that are sure to be making their way up to you. If you are looking to kill a few minions to get your Titanfall faster, do it from a lower level or window.
- The Courtyard is a tempting shortcut, but do not use it unless you are jumping into the Market. Going across the street from the Courtyard exposes you completely and you will be killed or called out by the enemy.
- With your life being more valuable in Pilot Hunter, go inside the Up Mart and shoot from the windows rather than shooting from the roof of the Up Mart. With more cover you're still able to see out to the Courtyard and also pick off enemy Pilots jumping from building to building.
- To get the highest vantage point, go to the top tower of the Red Star Restaurant. Use the pole for cover if being shot at, but don't get greedy and try to hold this position until you die. Move after you get a few kills.
- If the enemy team is sitting back and waiting, rack up a bunch of minion kills to get your Titanfall faster. The best place to do this is at the Market where you can clean up minions on the first floor, in the Courtyard, and on the surrounding streets.

PRO TIP: FLAMESWORD

When you are losing a game, stay calm. If you can force the opposing team to play defensively, your team will be able to kill minions and call in Titanfalls. Then you can make your comeback.

BONEYARD

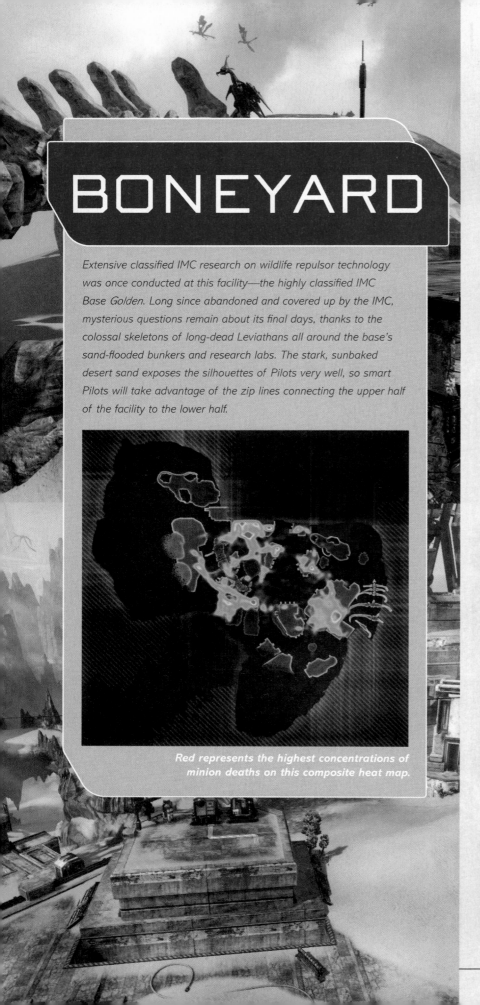

Extensive classified IMC research on wildlife repulsor technology was once conducted at this facility—the highly classified IMC Base Golden. Long since abandoned and covered up by the IMC, mysterious questions remain about its final days, thanks to the colossal skeletons of long-dead Leviathans all around the base's sand-flooded bunkers and research labs. The stark, sunbaked desert sand exposes the silhouettes of Pilots very well, so smart Pilots will take advantage of the zip lines connecting the upper half of the facility to the lower half.

Red represents the highest concentrations of minion deaths on this composite heat map.

KEY LANDMARKS

AMMUNITION BUNKER

BOTTOM TURRET

LANDING PAD

RESEARCH LAB

SPINE

TRAIL

MAP OVERVIEW

Most of the action takes place in the center of the map in between the Research Lab, Ammunition Bunker, and the Marvin Building. Control these areas and you're sure to find success.

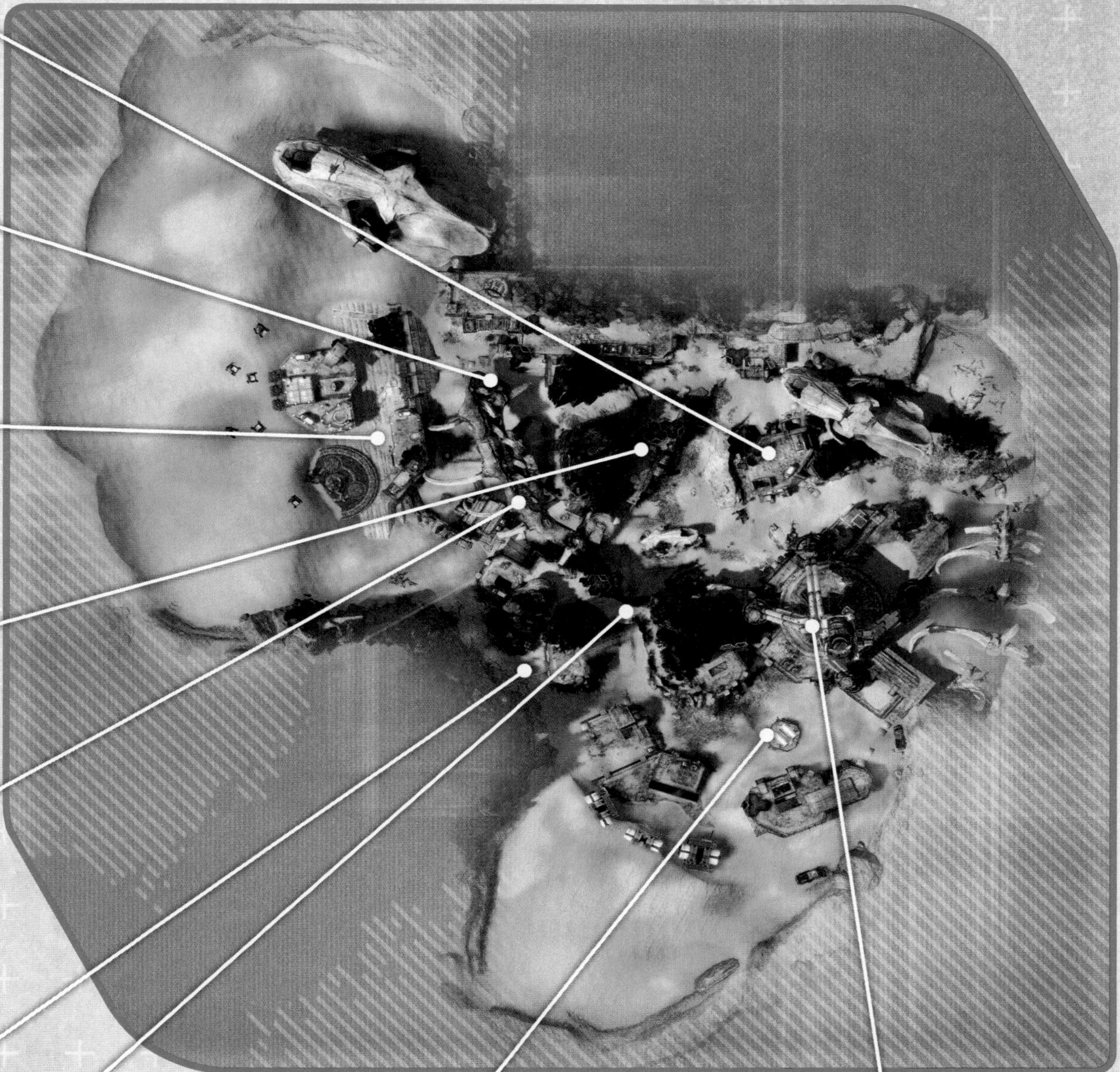

ARCH

TOP TURRET

MARVIN BUILDING

ATTRITION

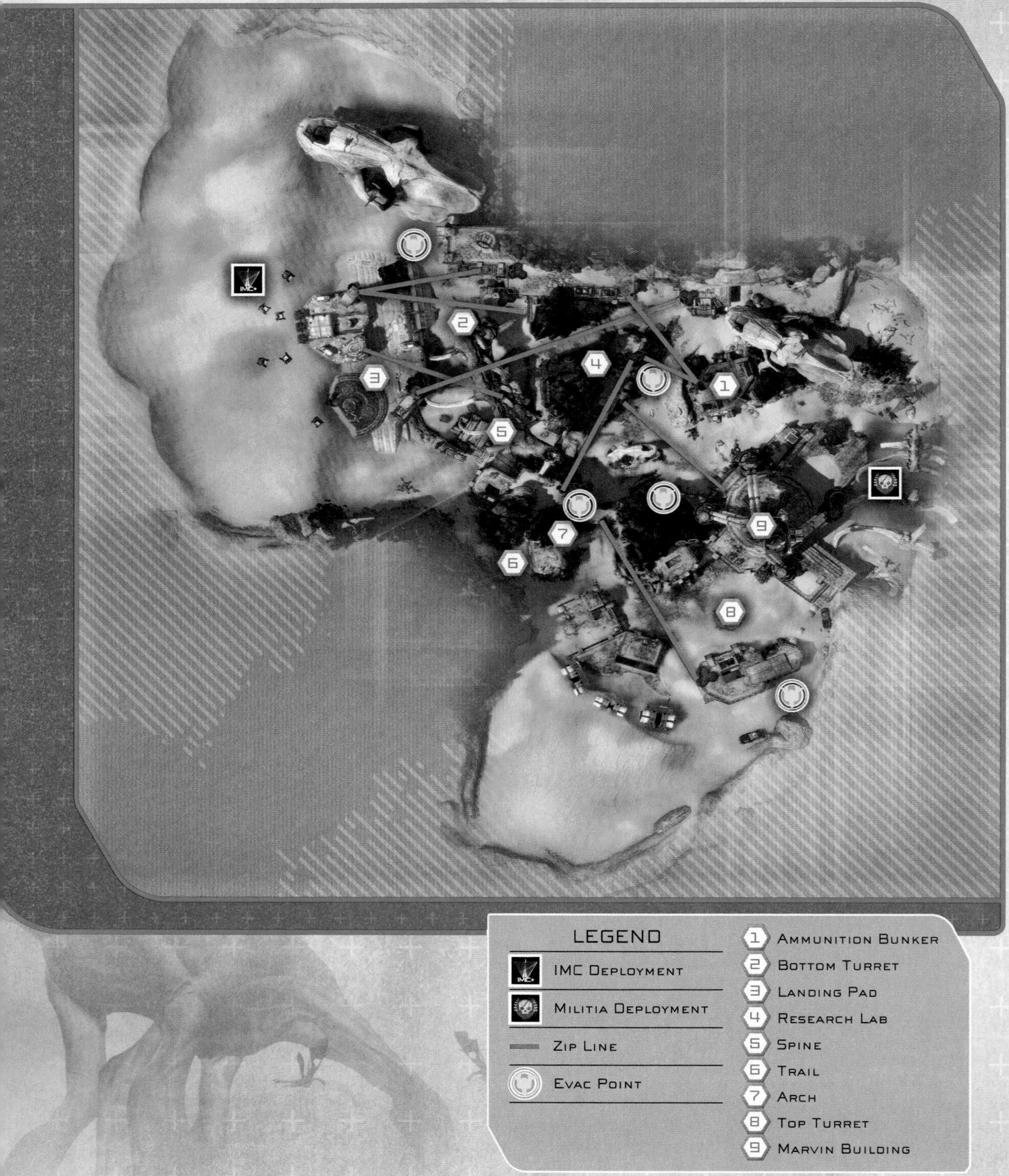

LEGEND

IMC Deployment

Militia Deployment

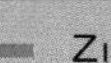
Zip Line

Evac Point

1. Ammunition Bunker
2. Bottom Turret
3. Landing Pad
4. Research Lab
5. Spine
6. Trail
7. Arch
8. Top Turret
9. Marvin Building

TACTICS

- The top of the Arch is great for picking off minions and Pilots with a Suppressor. Use a R-101C Carbine or G2A4 Rifle to best control these mid-long-range fights. Even though it seems like a great sniping spot, it can be difficult to hit your shots with a sniper rifle at such a steep angle.

PRO TIP: WALSHY

When holding the lower Research Lab, be sure to stay inside where you have more cover and put shots on the Ammunition Bunker. This roof should only be used for the wall run connecting the two zip lines, which allows you to zip line away, or to ambush an enemy inside of the Research Lab.

- The Ammunition Bunker is a great location to run back and forth from each door. You will find this area to be saturated with minions, allowing you to score easy points while reducing your build time for Titanfall.
- When roaming the map with a Titan, it is best if you have a friendly Titan nearby. This map has many narrow paths that encourage enemy Pilots to rodeo attack you and fire Anti-Titan weapons from a distance. An allied Titan nearby will provide you and your teammate more angles to fire from and force enemy Pilots to deal with you. This will allow you to have control of your Titan and destroy every enemy Pilot attacking you.
- No buildings are safe on this map. The map design promotes many close-quarter battles, both with minions and Pilots. Players with SMGs that stay inside the buildings will be able to shoot minions at a distance and then destroy enemy Pilots that decide to challenge you head on while inside.

- Take advantage of the zip lines around the map when needed. Use them when cloaked or to escape from losing battles, but don't just freely jump on them without scoping the area. A lot of the action happens in the middle, so blindly jumping on zip lines can lead to death.
- There are two turrets located on the map. Activate or hack these whenever you get the chance—the kills the turrets get will count towards your Attrition score.

CAPTURE THE FLAG

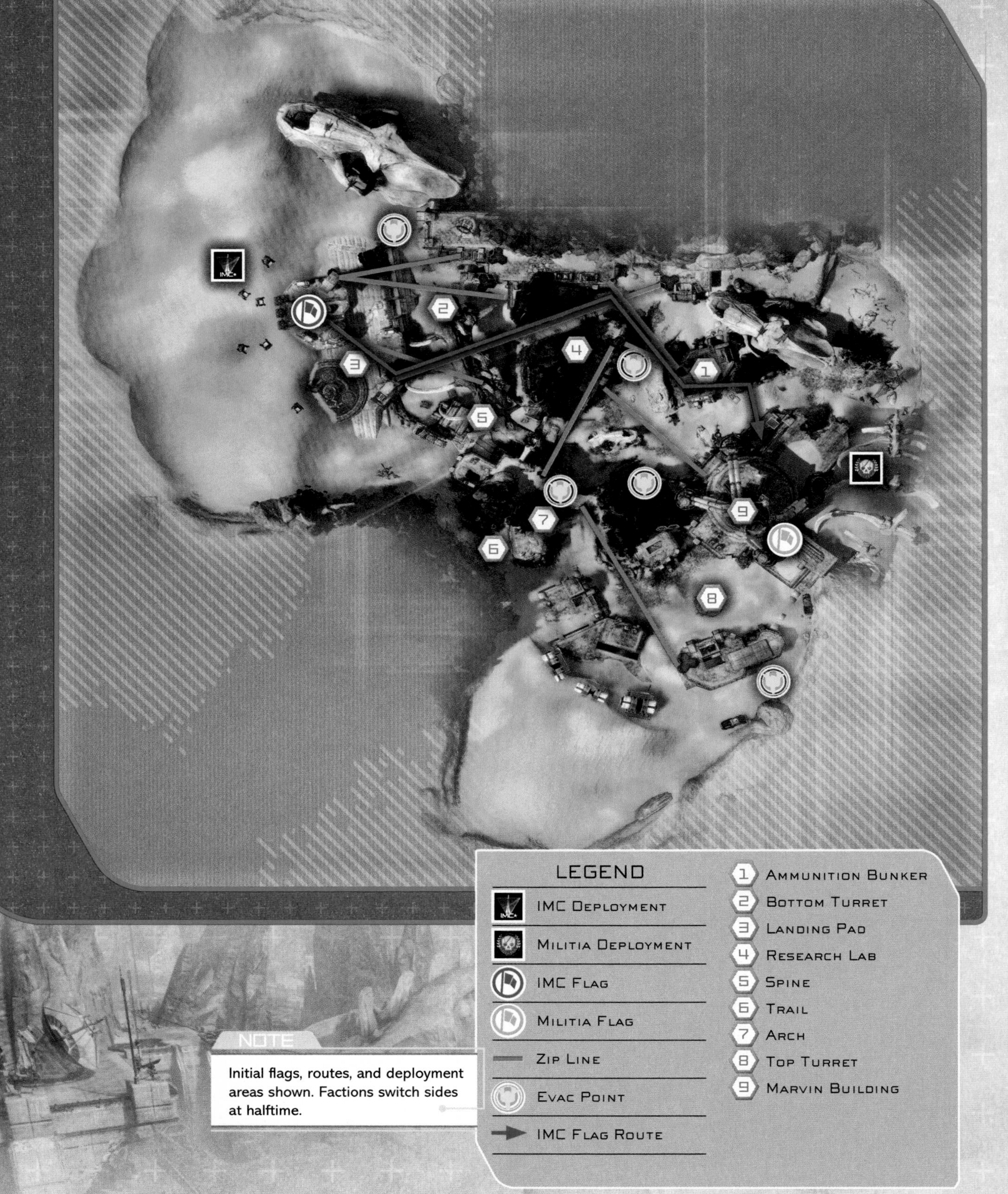

NOTE

Initial flags, routes, and deployment areas shown. Factions switch sides at halftime.

TACTICS

- When running the flag from the Marvin Building, don't use the zip line that leads out the front unless you have a friendly Titan waiting to pick you up. You'll be exposed so much that any enemy could pick you off.
- When running the flag from the Landing Pad with a Titan, use the Trail. This path provides the most cover and lets you run the flag safely in the back door for a capture.

- Holding the Spine and Arch will allow you to control the pace of the game. It sets up opportunities for pushing on the enemy's flag or defending your own flag.
- With a turret near each flag, players will want to activate these right off the start. The turrets assist in covering a side and alerting you that an enemy Pilot or Titan may be nearby.

PRO TIP: FLAMESWORD

Once you grab the flag in the Landing Pad area, take the southeast zip line that leads all the way back to the Research Lab. You will see another zip line along your way, near the middle of the map. Hit crouch at the right time to drop to the lower zip line, which will bring you above the Ammunition Bunker. Then it is just a little run to capture the flag.

- This is great spot for cover—enemies will be unaware of your location. This position provides a great line of sight towards the flag, allowing you to gun down an enemy if your foe decides to pull the flag.

Reference these videos in your free mobile friendly eGuide.

BONEYARD

HARDPOINT DOMINATION

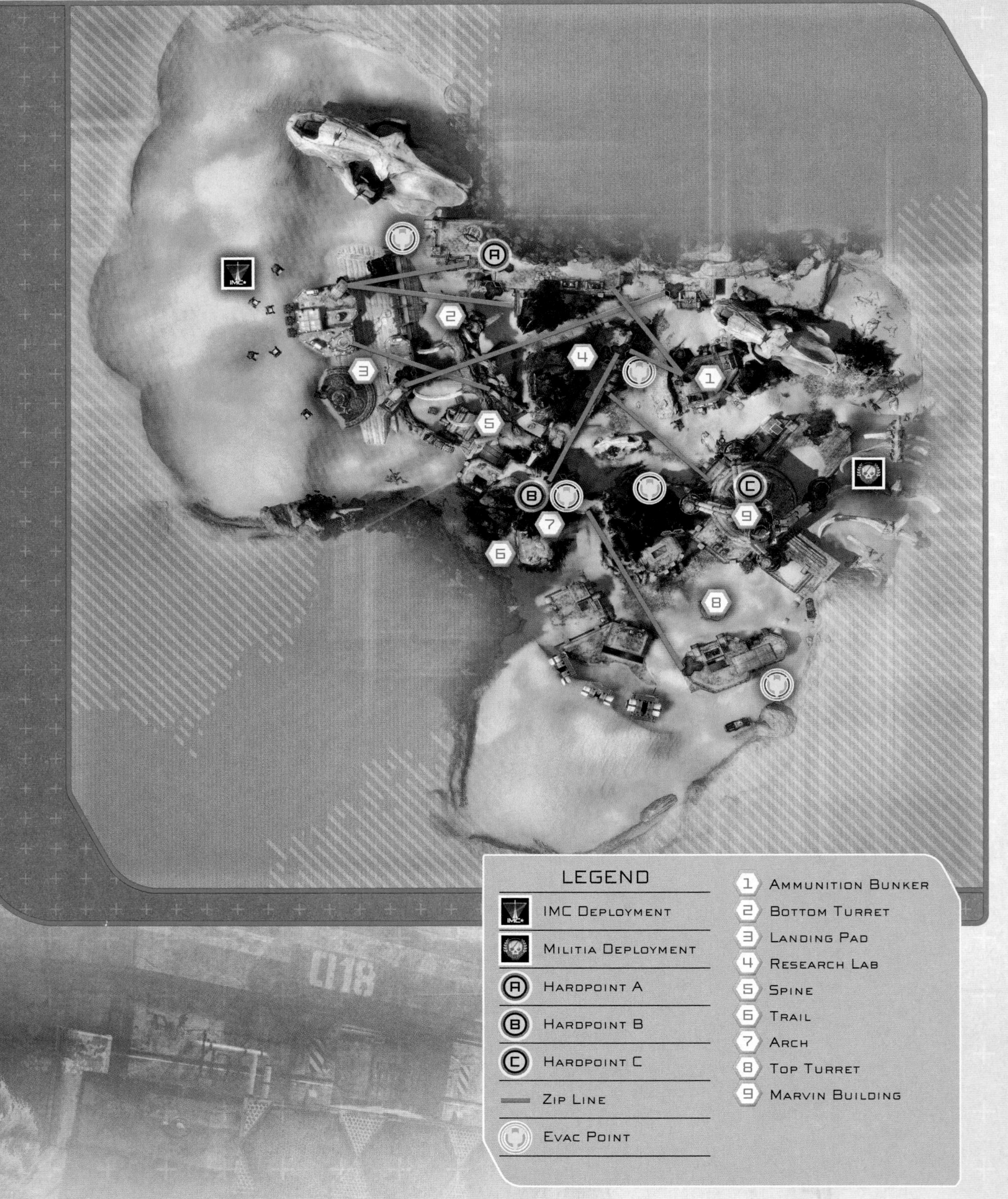
IMC
LEGEND
IMC Deployment
Militia Deployment
Hardpoint A
Hardpoint B
Hardpoint C
Zip Line
Evac Point
1 Ammunition Bunker
2 Bottom Turret
3 Landing Pad
4 Research Lab
5 Spine
6 Trail
7 Arch
8 Top Turret
9 Marvin Building

TACTICS

- When holding Hardpoint B, your biggest threats will be Titans coming from the Trail or Pilots coming from the Arch. Instead of hiding inside of Hardpoint B with your Pilot, be the aggressor and take control of the Arch. If you have a Titan, put it at the end of the Trail near the Arch where you can cut off enemies trying to take the Trail or go on the Arch.
- The Ammunition Bunker is a good place to catch enemies off guard and watch Hardpoints A and B. Most Pilots will sprint through this building, unprepared to fight, making them easy kills.
- Hardpoint C is located inside the Marvin Building and has many tricky spots that can be used to capture the objective and take cover from enemies. Once captured there are two areas above that you can hide on until you see an enemy Pilot trying to capture your objective. Once you see the bar move, be sure to ambush the unaware enemy.
- The most effective strategy on this map is to hold Hardpoints A and B. Hardpoint C is accessible by a Titan, but is far away from the other two, while Hardpoints A and B are close to one another. If you are a medium- to long-range shooter, posting up on the Spine or the front of the Research Lab is a great location to spot enemy Pilots.
- A great tactical ability for this map is Active Radar Pulse. When you notice your teammates are down, retreat back to one of your objectives inside and use the ability. You will be able to spot incoming attackers and get the jump on them.

LAST TITAN STANDING

TACTICS

- The turrets on this map are usually away from the battles. However, you can bring the fight to a friendly turret by running to it when you are weak and letting the turret turn the fight in your favor.
- The Atlas is the all-around Titan to go with for this map. Boneyard has open areas that you need a couple dashes to safely cross and the Atlas provides the armor you need to win the heads-up battles.
- With so many open areas, this map is great for sitting back and delivering long-range damage with the Plasma Railgun. If you are the aggressive type, push forward with your team and use the Quad Rockets to guarantee some close- to mid-range damage.
- Don't get yourself trapped in the center of the map near the skull. Your Titan will be exposed from multiple areas and can be destroyed within seconds. Try to only swing by this spot when your team has more Titans standing.

PRO TIP: FLAMESWORD

Place your Titan in Auto-Titan mode in a safe place off the start. Equip a sniper rifle of your choice and look towards the enemy's initial spawn point to see where the enemy Titans and Pilots are moving towards. Be sure to communicate to your team what you see. If the enemy also has a Pilot running around trying to scout the area, pick the Pilot off with your sniper and then return to your Titan to finish the fight with your team.

- If your team is feeling sneaky, flank with three of your team's Titans through the Trail while holding back the other three Titans on the team near your spawn. The Titans sneaking through the Trail need to communicate when they are closing in behind the enemy Titans so the other three Titans waiting near your spawn can push up and sandwich the other team. Communicate with your team to focus on shooting one enemy Titan at a time to take down the pack quickly.

PILOT HUNTER

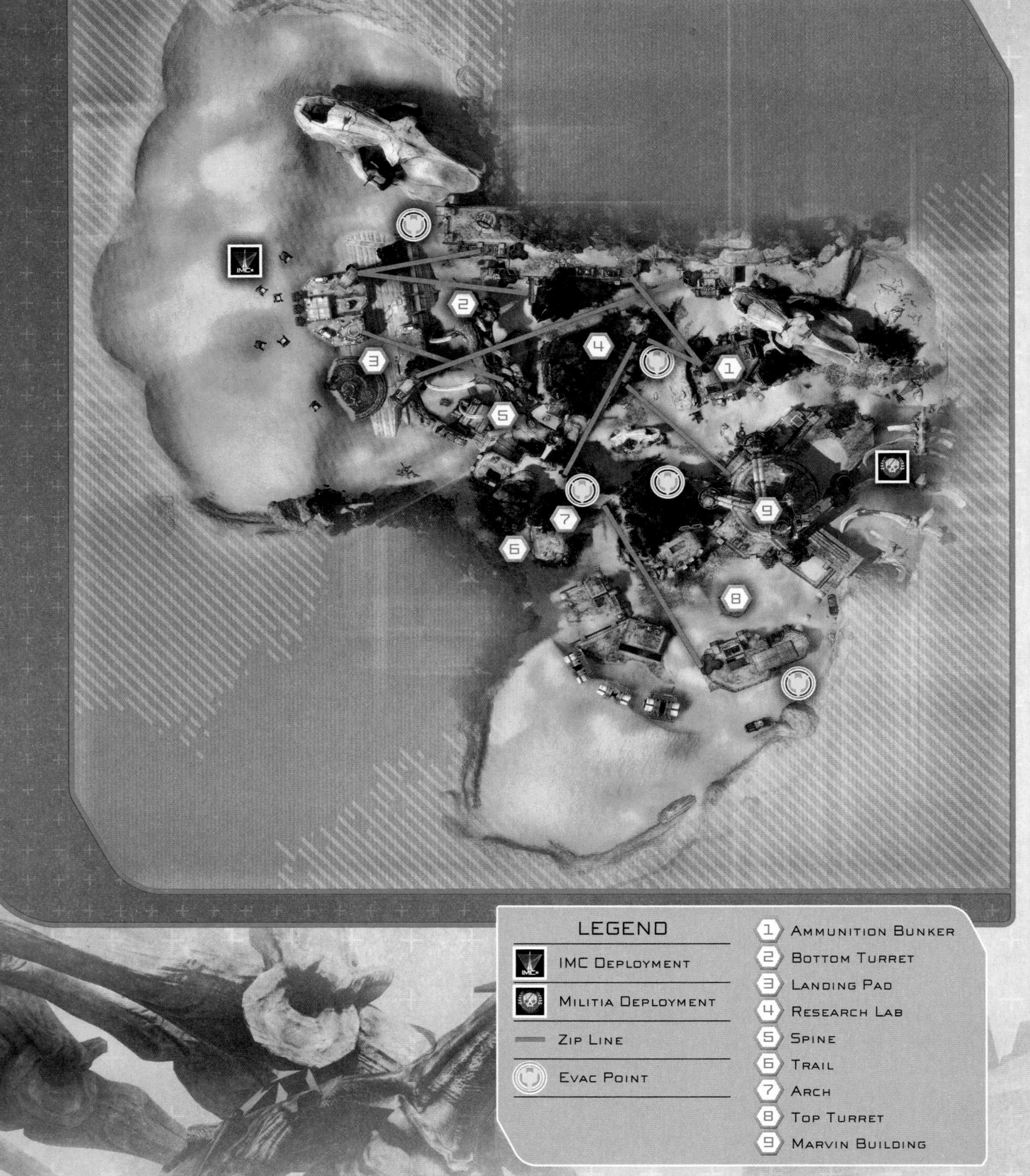
LEGEND
IMC Deployment
Militia Deployment
Zip Line
Evac Point
1 Ammunition Bunker
2 Bottom Turret
3 Landing Pad
4 Research Lab
5 Spine
6 Trail
7 Arch
8 Top Turret
9 Marvin Building

TACTICS

- Be aware of where all the zip lines are located. This map is so large that if you get killed, it is worthwhile to backtrack to a nearby zip line, which you can usually find close to any spawn on the map. This will allow you to jump right back in the action.
- The Ammunition Bunker is heavily saturated with minions. Keep an eye on this location if you see an enemy Pilot killing a ton of them. With the right timing, you will be able to take the enemy Pilot out without letting the enemy return any fire.
- If you are continuously getting picked off when moving from building to building, you are likely running out in the open too much. Taking a slightly longer route with more cover is a good way to switch it up if you find yourself dying often.
- This position is a great overview of the map and an incredible location to snipe from. The Kraber-AP is the best choice to snipe with because you will not have to lead your shots for these mid-range kills. Still having trouble landing your shots? The Longbow-DMR sniper rifle will allow you to rapidly shoot and apply more suppressive fire.
- Controlling the Marvin Building is a very effective tactic. Players have plenty of areas to take cover when being shot at. The Marvin Building also allows you to provide cover fire towards the Ammunition Bunker and Research Lab.
- A player running Cloak and the EVA-8 Shotgun can do heavy damage on this map. Run along the outskirts of the map and use your Cloak when approaching buildings. Remember to switch locations after you have killed an enemy Pilot to keep the enemy guessing at all times.

COLONY

This Colony was built by former IMC personnel in the valley beneath the crashed carrier IMS Odyssey, using the only materials available to them—the wreckage of their destroyed starship. Because of construction logistics, most of the Colony was built quite close together, creating a busy warren of rooftops, flank routes, and interiors favorable to Pilots. Titans should use extreme caution when taking a route through the town center, where they are at risk from close-range Anti-Titan weapons fire and Pilot rodeo attacks.

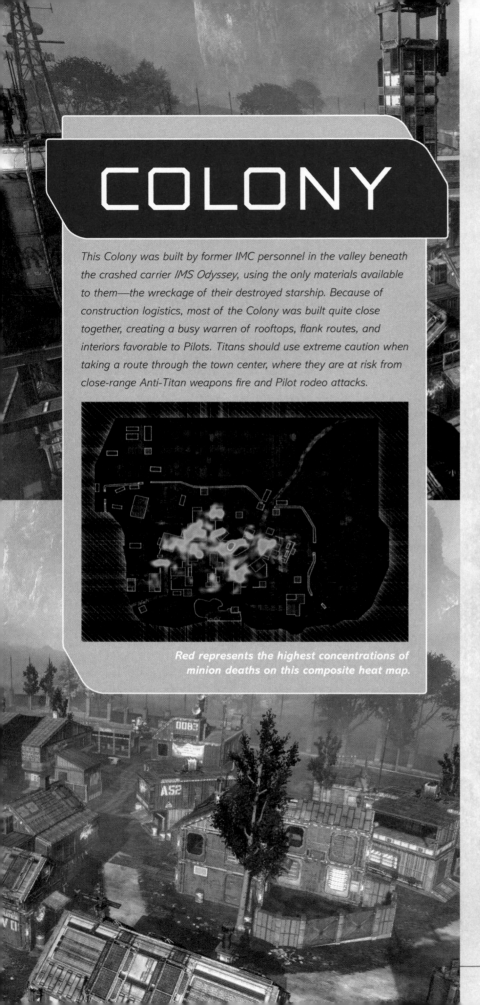

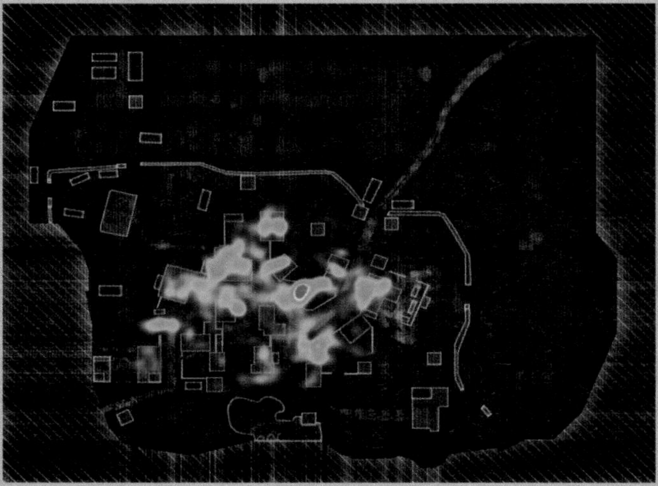

Red represents the highest concentrations of minion deaths on this composite heat map.

KEY LANDMARKS

QUICKSTOP

POWER STATION

BLACKWELL STORE

TOWN HALL

THE FALL BAR

SUPPLY RATIONS

MAP OVERVIEW

On this map you'll find yourself sneaking through the many buildings and picking off Pilots on the rooftops. The rooftops will be a major part of this map since it is the quickest way to travel and they have a great overview of the entire Colony.

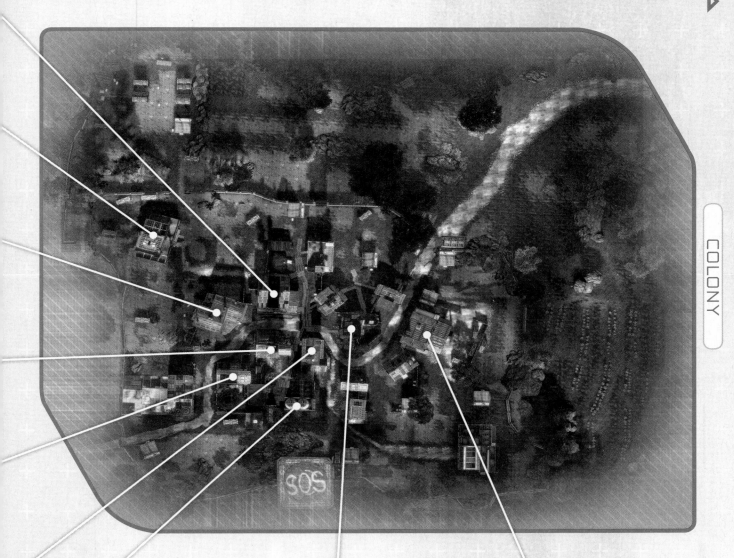

ANDERSON GRAINING

FAMILY HOUSE

GRIDION GARAGE

ATTRITION

LEGEND

IMC Deployment

Militia Deployment

Evac Point

1. QuickStop
2. Power Station
3. Blackwell Store
4. Town Hall
5. The Fall Bar
6. Supply Rations
7. Anderson Graining
8. Family House
9. Gridion Garage

TACTICS

Reference these videos in your free mobile friendly eGuide.

- At the start of the match, the minions meet around the Supply Rations and around the QuickStop. You'll want to rush this area or reach a higher vantage point that overlooks this area to pick off enemy Pilots killing your minions. Traveling through the buildings and shooting from the windows can also be great because it will make you blend in with your minions.
- Minions like to travel through buildings on this map, making you have to hunt for them—sometimes through a building. Staying inside a building can prove useful to pick off the enemies inside your building as well as to kill the enemies roaming the streets. Don't get too greedy and expose yourself by running from building to building, however. Take your time and scan the perimeter before you make your move to another location.
- As a Titan, you'll be able to take advantage of your dash to dash through the streets of the Colony and crush all the minions roaming the streets. This allows you to save your ammo for a Titan battle or to pick off an enemy Pilot running on the rooftops.
- The rooftops are incredibly useful on this map, but stay on the rooftops around the perimeter of the Colony to have an overview of all the rooftops in the center of the map. When you stay back on a roof around the perimeter of the Colony, attach a sniper rifle with the AOG scope to easily take down enemies in the distance.

PRO TIP: STRONGSIDE

There are many balconies and windows throughout the buildings of the map. Be sure to become comfortable with all the little jumps that take you from the open streets to inside the buildings with cover. When near the Town Hall, double jump up to begin wall running—you will want to hit your double jump at the peak of your first jump. From here, wall run off the Town Hall and then jump into the Blackwell Store. Simple jumps like this allow you to escape many situations.

- A loadout with Frag Grenades for an Ordnance and Explosives Pack as your Tier 1 Kit will come in handy. Move throughout the buildings and try to get behind enemy Pilots. Time your grenade so that once you throw it towards the enemy, it will explode immediately instead of warning the enemy Pilot to escape.

CAPTURE THE FLAG

NOTE

Initial flags, routes, and deployment areas shown. Factions switch sides at halftime.

TACTICS

- Guarding the flag within the Gridion Garage will be best with a Titan. You can sit back behind the wall in the back of the Gridion Garage. From this position you have a great view to defend your flag and be able to crouch down behind the wall for cover.
- When grabbing the flags from either base, you'll want to head straight into a building with cover. As a Pilot, take advantage of the many wall runs and jumps you can use to get back to your base. As a Titan, you don't want to get caught in the Colony between any buildings because you can get cut off by enemy Titans. Take the long route along the outside of the Colony and dash back quickly.

PRO TIP: FLAMESWORD

When grabbing the flag from the Gridion Garage, use this wall run route to quickly make it back to your base. Have Stim on to quickly run out the front of the garage and begin wall running off the building attached to the Family House. Immediately jump to the building ahead of the Family House and then jump again to the Town Hall. After this you will jump to the QuickStop and then immediately double jump in the direction of your flag.

- When defending the flag from the starting Militia spawn, go to the building behind the flag base and you'll be able to look out a window directly at your flag. Stand back a bit in the window so you are not spotted. This position is a great defense against the enemy Pilots trying to sneak by and grab your flag.
- No matter what side you're on, getting to the top tower of Town Hall will always be useful. At this position you can see the entire map and call out to your team what you see the enemy doing. You can also easily stop enemy Pilot flag runners from the top of this tower with a sniper rifle.

Reference these videos in your free mobile friendly eGuide.

HARDPOINT DOMINATION

LEGEND

	IMC Deployment
	Militia Deployment
A	Hardpoint A
B	Hardpoint B
C	Hardpoint C
	Evac Point

1. QuickStop
2. Power Station
3. Blackwell Store
4. Town Hall
5. The Fall Bar
6. Supply Rations
7. Anderson Graining
8. Family House
9. Gridion Garage

PRO TIP: WALSHY

Since Titans completely run this map for this game mode, as a Pilot you'll want to play stealthy when capturing a hardpoint. Use Cloak to sneak around the map and get behind the enemy or take a longer route around the perimeter of the map.

TACTICS

› All the hardpoints on this map cannot be captured by Titans, but a Titan can have a view into every hardpoint to kill any enemies attempting to capture any of the points. The hardpoint locations on this map are all on upper-level floors with windows. These windows allow a Titan to look in and kill enemy Pilots. Equip the Cluster Missile as this will come in handy to shoot into the buildings through the windows and the secondary explosions are sure to kill any enemies inside near the hardpoint. With all this said, tread carefully if you are inside a building and an enemy Titan is near. You'll most likely want to move to another location for cover.

PRO TIP: STRONGSIDE

With all three hardpoints in such small areas, Arc Mines are going to be your best friend. Place Arc Mines near a stairway or window to kill or stun an enemy Pilot. Remember, to kill an enemy Pilot with an Arc Mine, you need to place two Arc Mines near each other so that they both deal damage to the enemy Pilot.

PRO TIP: FLAMESWORD

Hardpoint A is difficult to capture when enemies are around due to all the open windows. Make the enemy look for you by wall hanging in the corner of the building. The wall will cover you and allow you to see when the enemy is coming across. Once you see them, jump off and aim in to take them out. Then go back to capturing once the area is clear.

› When moving in for Hardpoint B, head to the staircase corner to capture the hardpoint. At this position you are hidden and cannot be seen through the windows. If you crouch while in the corner, your Pilot will be hidden even more. Before going into the corner of the staircase, move into the capture radius for a second and then move into the staircase corner to keep capturing. If you move in the staircase corner first, you will not initiate a capture on Hardpoint B.

› Taking control of Hardpoint C should feel easier then the other two. A Pilot should only need to focus on the front two windows that let you overlook The Fall Bar. The back window shouldn't see any action since it would require an enemy Pilot to take a long flank. By the time an enemy Pilot could do that, you will have already captured the objective.

› As a Pilot, be sure to equip Arc Grenades and the Explosives Pack to give you three Arc Grenades. Use these grenades against enemy Titans outside the building of the hardpoint you are capturing. Once you've captured the hardpoint, move to the lower level and make the enemy Pilot exit the Titan to attack you. Active Radar Pulse comes in great use on this game mode since you'll be inside a building capturing hardpoints most of the game.

LAST TITAN STANDING

TACTICS

- This map has many buildings and cement walls that you can use for cover within the Colony. As a team, you'll want to take advantage of all the cover and use the buildings and walls to peek shoot and drop behind cover to weaken the enemy Titans before charging.
- At the start of the match, your team will want to get control of the center of the map as quickly as possible. You do not want your team to get stuck back in your base where you can get cornered and trapped by the enemy Titans.

PRO TIP: WALSHY

If your Titan is destroyed, you'll want to move throughout the buildings as a Pilot and save your Arc Grenades until your friendly Titans enter battle. As a Pilot you don't want to initiate any battles. You want to join in to assist your team once both team's Titans are battling. If you initiate a battle as a Pilot, you will most likely be killed.

- Have the Charge Rifle or Archer Heavy Rocket equipped as your Pilot's Anti-Titan Weapon. If your Titan is destroyed, make your way to the top of the Town Hall and focus on firing on enemy Titans that your teammates are engaging. You don't need a Titan to be effective in Last Titan Standing.
- This battle throughout Colony can be a very slow one because there is so much cover. Be patient and wait for the right moment when your team has severely injured an enemy Titan from long range. The Plasma Railgun, Arc Cannon, and 40mm Cannon are great weapons to use on this map to deal small bits of damage to the enemy Titans.
- When playing this game mode, you'll want to equip the Spitfire LMG with the MOD Slammer attached. This will allow you to deal massive damage to an enemy Titan when you rodeo attack it.

PILOT HUNTER

LEGEND
IMC Deployment
Militia Deployment
Evac Point
1 QuickStop
2 Power Station
3 Blackwell Store
4 Town Hall
5 The Fall Bar
6 Supply Rations
7 Anderson Graining
8 Family House
9 Gridion Garage
SOS

TACTICS

Reference these videos in your free mobile friendly eGuide.

- If you make your way to the top of the Town Hall by wall jumping, you'll find this tower is great for sniping a couple enemy Pilots, but only for a short time. Once you kill an enemy Pilot here, the enemy Pilot is sure to see your location and let teammates know where you are or come back to hunt you down personally. If the enemy Pilot comes to hunt you down, it can lead to another easy kill by placing Arc Mines along the walls and jumping up to the top of Town Hall. Enemy Pilots are most likely not going to be paying attention to the walls, so you'll get an easy kill. After the second kill you get up here, it's probably time you moved positions.
- All the buildings in the center of the map promotes a lot of wall running and jumping. Use these to quickly maneuver around the map and to get away from a losing battle when you are outnumbered.
- The interior of the buildings also provide for sneaky play. Make your way into a building and use Active Radar Pulse near a wall or window to see if any enemies are near. While Active Radar Pulse is activated, be sure to look towards rooftops as many Pilots travel these areas.

PRO TIP: STRONGSIDE

Equip Cloak if you are going to be traveling on the rooftops or sniping back on a rooftop around the perimeter of the Colony. Although Cloak doesn't completely hide you from enemy Pilots, it still makes you tough to see from a far distance. Cloak also makes you especially hard to hit if you are wall running and jumping while you have Cloak activated.

- The rooftops play a big role on this map. You'll get an overview of most of the map from almost every rooftop, but you'll want to stay clear of the rooftops on the center of the map near Supply Rations as you'll been seen from every rooftop surrounding this area and you are most noticeable here. Use a sniper rifle and position yourself on the rooftops around the perimeter of the Colony to look into the Colony and kill enemy Pilots running from rooftop to rooftop or traveling throughout the streets.
- Position yourself on top of the Town Hall rooftop and equip a sniper rifle with the AOG attachment. At this position you're able to view most of the map and use the cubby hole for cover. Here you can peek shoot across the map and pick off enemy Pilots jumping from rooftop to rooftop or pick off enemy Pilots sitting back trying to snipe.
- With your Titan, you'll have a lot of access throughout the Colony, but many Pilots can hide in buildings and jump out to rodeo attack you easily. Make use of the Tactical Ability Electric Smoke to keep those pesky enemy Pilots off your back. The Electric Smoke is also good to use if you want to halt an enemy Titan charging you through the Colony. Deploy your Electric Smoke in the middle of the street and make your escape to your teammates or to get your shield back.
- While in your Titan, you'll have a good view of most of the rooftops in the Colony. This view allows you to pick off many enemy Pilots running from rooftop to rooftop. Attach the XO-16 Chaingun to pick off enemy Pilots quickly and still have ammo to turn and fight an enemy Titan if needed.

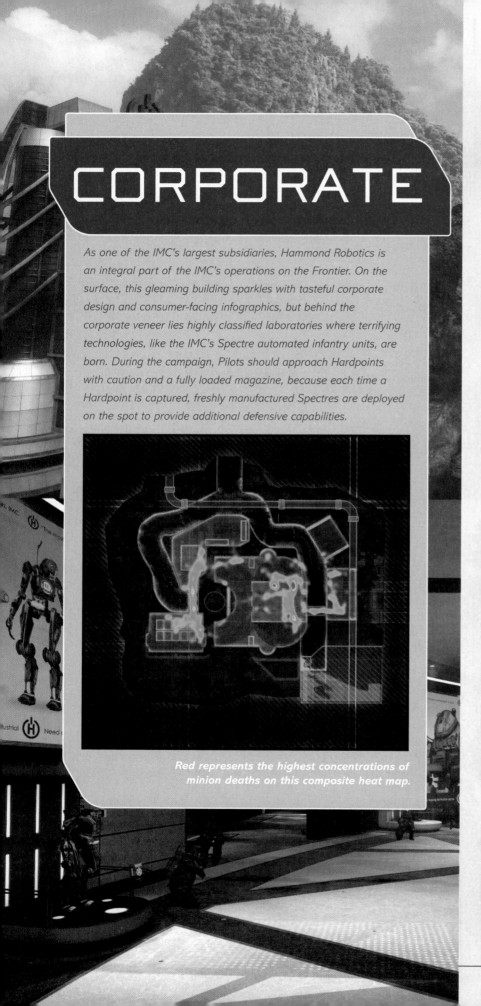

CORPORATE

As one of the IMC's largest subsidiaries, Hammond Robotics is an integral part of the IMC's operations on the Frontier. On the surface, this gleaming building sparkles with tasteful corporate design and consumer-facing infographics, but behind the corporate veneer lies highly classified laboratories where terrifying technologies, like the IMC's Spectre automated infantry units, are born. During the campaign, Pilots should approach Hardpoints with caution and a fully loaded magazine, because each time a Hardpoint is captured, freshly manufactured Spectres are deployed on the spot to provide additional defensive capabilities.

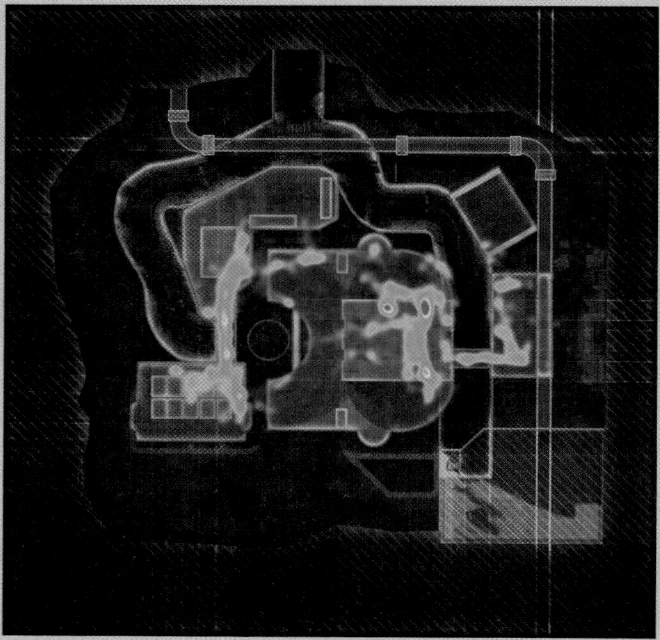

Red represents the highest concentrations of minion deaths on this composite heat map.

KEY LANDMARKS

CAFE

DESIGN OFFICE

MAIN STREET

STATUE SKYBRIDGE

ROUNDABOUT

APPLIED ROBOTICS

MAP OVERVIEW

THIS MAP MOSTLY REVOLVES AROUND CLOSE-QUARTER BATTLES INSIDE BUILDINGS. YOU'LL WANT TO MOVE QUICKLY AND NEVER STICK AROUND TOO LONG IN ONE SPOT.

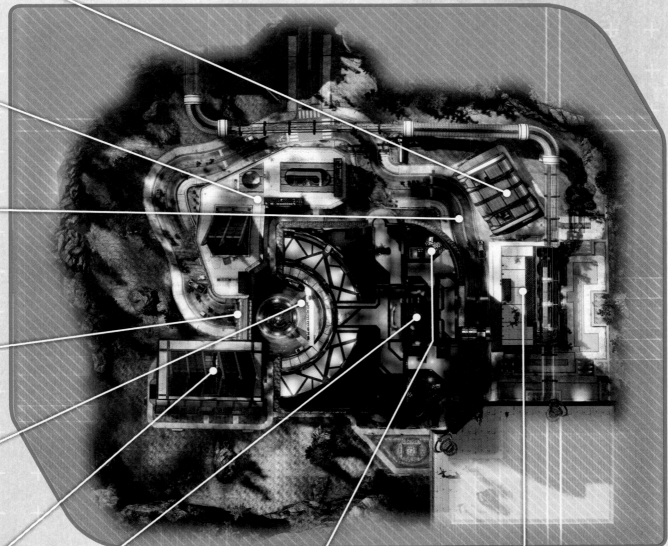

MAIN LOBBY

BOARD ROOM

QUALITY CONTROL

ATTRITION

LEGEND

- IMC Deployment
- Militia Deployment
- Zip Line
- Evac Point

1. Cafe
2. Design Office
3. Main Street
4. Statue Skybridge
5. Roundabout
6. Applied Robotics
7. Main Lobby
8. Board Room
9. Quality Control

TACTICS

- The Roundabout will be a top priority throughout the entire match because a lot of action occurs here. Minions mostly swarm the Roundabout and Main Street throughout the entire match. You will want to patrol the buildings, halls, and most importantly the rooftops while constantly staying on the move.
- Use the jump shown here to swiftly escape and take cover inside the Cafe. While you're on the run, activate Cloak if you have it equipped to make it even harder for the enemy chasing you to kill you. Turn around once in the Cafe to see if any enemy Pilots continued their pursuit after you.

PRO TIP: FLAMESWORD

A Pilot can take a position in the open skywalk overseeing the fountain in the Roundabout. Keep an eye towards the Main Lobby—there will be plenty of minions for you to pick off, increasing your score significantly. I like close-quarter battles and if an enemy Pilot challenges me, I reduce his movements since the skywalk is constricted. An SMG or the R-101C Carbine with Stim as your Tactical Ability allows you win consecutive fights.

- The Board Room is a great area to roam in and out of. Within this room is a staircase and a sunroof that can be used for escape when being attacked. The Board Room provides a window that has great lines of sight for killing enemies.
- The Active Radar Pulse is a great Tactical Ability to have equipped. Take control of the rooftops and activate the ability to see where enemies are at. Calculate which enemies would be the easiest to take out and go after them.
- Every Titan is effective on this map. Equip them with a high rate of fire weapon and dominate enemy minions, Pilots, and Titans. As a Titan, be sure to stay outside of any buildings and attack from a distance. Don't bring your Titan inside a building unless a teammate also has a Titan and wants to drop in for a quick sweep. Going in a building with a Titan by yourself is asking to be lit up by the enemy team and quickly taken out.
- Once inside a Titan, position yourself near the Cafe on the Main Street looking in the direction of the Sky Bridge connecting the Quality Room and the Waterfall Room. Normally a Pilot could patrol this area and pick up many minion kills. With you in a Titan, enemy Pilots will have to think twice when patrolling this area. Picking off the many minions allows you to greatly reduce time on your Core Ability. Save your Core Ability for encountering an enemy Titan.

CAPTURE THE FLAG

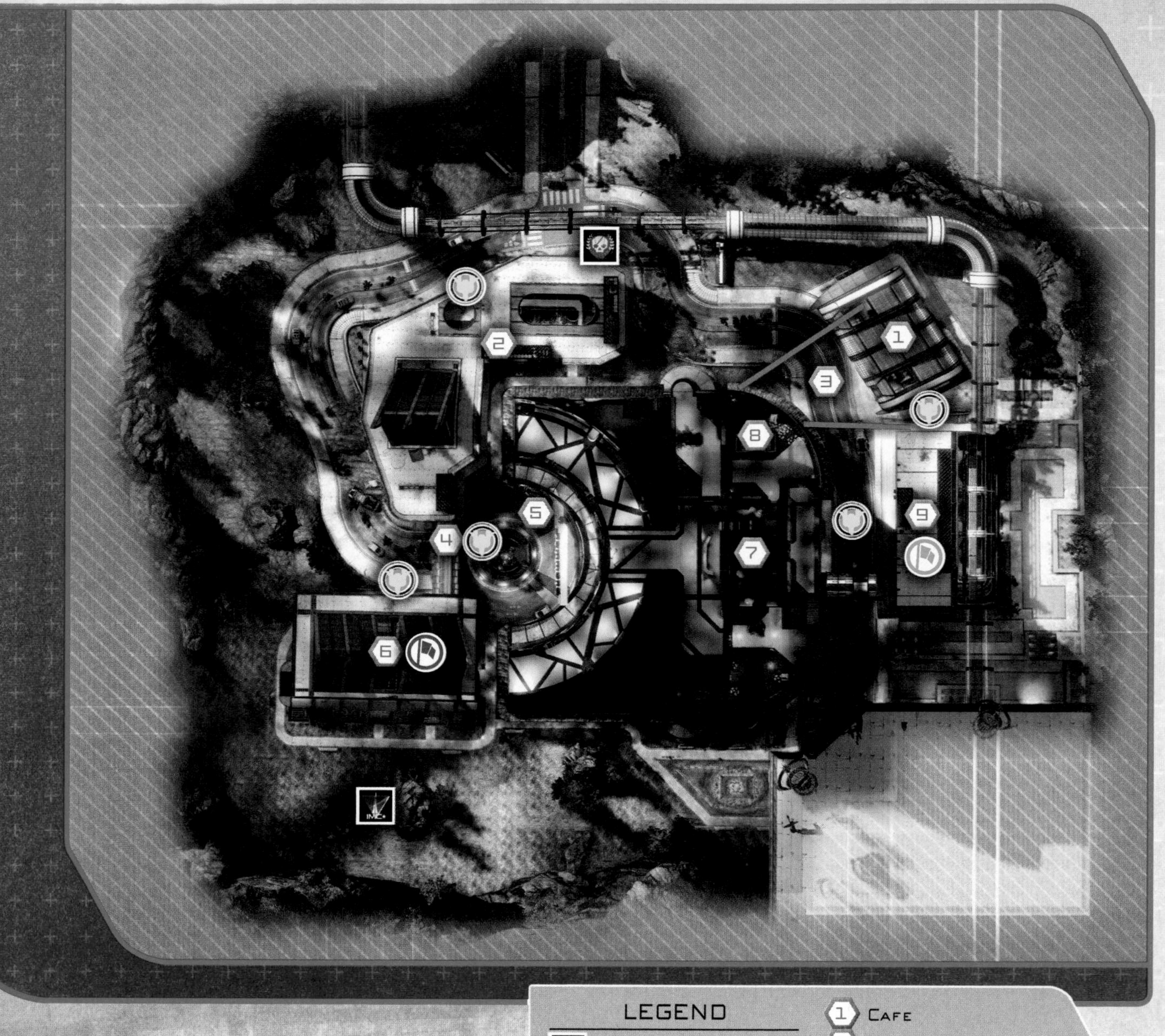

LEGEND

- IMC Deployment
- Militia Deployment
- IMC Flag
- Militia Flag
- Zip Line
- Evac Point

1. Cafe
2. Design Office
3. Main Street
4. Statue Skybridge
5. Roundabout
6. Applied Robotics
7. Main Lobby
8. Board Room
9. Quality Control

NOTE

Initial flags, routes, and deployment areas shown. Factions switch sides at halftime.

TACTICS

Reference these videos in your free mobile friendly eGuide.

- Each flag is located on the upper levels of their respected buildings. One flag will be held inside of the Applied Robotics and the other flag is positioned inside of Quality Control. Get behind the enemy and sneak into their base to get a flag grab. Once you have the flag, drop a Titan outside the building and quickly make your way back towards your base. Wait to pull the flag until you see a few enemies die or until a couple of your teammates have Titans. This will increase your chances of making it back to your base.
- When defending the flag inside of the Applied Robotics, a sniper posted up on the rooftop of the Design Office will be extremely productive. The sniper can spot enemies and provide suppressive fire. The sniper should always communicate and let the team know where the enemies are attacking from.
- Pilots who get inside of Quality Control have a few ways to escape quickly. Once you grab the flag, begin wall running and get to the roof. From here you will be more aware of the enemies' locations, and then able to analyze the situation and move in the safest direction to score the enemy's flag.
- Quality Control has many different points to enter to grab the flag. Don't get bunched inside defending your flag. Instead have a Pilot move towards the Cafe to spot enemy Pilots flanking or charging in from the skywalk or windows. A player patrolling the Main Lobby will be able to pick off enemies who try to enter Quality Control through the skywalk.
- Titans aren't the most effective means of transporting flags due to the all the buildings being so close to one another. Sometimes running the flag through a building or on the roof can be the best route to use. These buildings promote plenty of enemy rodeo attacks, so keep your eyes peeled when escorting a flag carrier.
- When running flags with a Titan, the safest route is sticking to the outskirts of the map and slowly making your way back to home base. If you are pressed for time, this route allows you to quickly move the flag in a Stryder Titan from the Applied Robotics back to Quality Control.
- A Titan patrolling the Main Lobby and halls will be a huge headache for the opposing team. Keep this Titan alive as long as possible and repeatedly perform hit-and-run tactics. Killing one enemy Pilot every sweep will be just enough to delay the opposing team from stealing your flag.

HARDPOINT DOMINATION

LEGEND

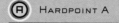

- IMC Deployment
- Militia Deployment
- (A) Hardpoint A
- (B) Hardpoint B
- (C) Hardpoint C
- Zip Line
- Evac Point

1. Cafe
2. Design Office
3. Main Street
4. Statue Skybridge
5. Roundabout
6. Applied Robotics
7. Main Lobby
8. Board Room
9. Quality Control

PRO TIP: STRONGSIDE

When defending or attacking Hardpoint B with a Titan, be sure to equip Electric Smoke. This is a close-quarter area, encouraging enemy Pilots to rodeo attack you. The Electric Smoke not only gets them off your back, but blasts the entire area, killing anything nearby. This allows you to control Hardpoint B easier.

TACTICS

- Hardpoint A involves a lot of close-quarter combat. A Pilot who excels in this field will want to defend this area once the objective is captured. This objective doesn't provide an angle to support allied Pilots going for Hardpoint B. When defending this area, a Pilot equipped with an EVA-8 Shotgun should control this objective for the majority of the game while teammates work to capture another point.
- The Main Lobby is the location of Hardpoint B. This area is accessible by Titans, but should be used with extreme caution. Near this objective are two windows. One is located in the Board Room facing the other window. Enemy Pilots can poke out of these windows to unload their Anti-Titan Weapons and Arc Grenades, causing massive damage on your Titan. Only move your Titan in this area when you want to cause a distraction, allowing friendly Pilots to sneak up on the enemies.

PRO TIP: STRONGSIDE

Cloak is an incredible Tactical Ability for capturing Hardpoint B. This objective usually has a Titan nearby. Cloak will make you vanish right in front of an enemy Titan's eyes, allowing you to move around freely while Cloak is activated.

- The final Hardpoint is C and it is right behind Hardpoint B. This objective is located in the upper level of Quality Control. Above the terminal in the Hardpoint is a window connected with a zip line. When defending this objective, keep an eye on this window as you will catch many enemy Pilots zipping in.

- This map layout lets players pick and choose which two Hardpoints they want to control. Hardpoints B and C are favorites since they are so close to each other. Hardpoint B allows you to move in and out of the Main Lobby with a Titan that will assist in defending Hardpoint C as well. The Titan can kill any enemy Pilots jumping around or zip lining into Hardpoint C. Pilots are able to easily run from Hardpoint C to B and repel enemies going for Hardpoint B.
- Controlling Hardpoints A and C is a viable option as well, but requires great communication with the team. Players will want to watch each entrance of Hardpoint C and use teamwork to wipe out anyone who enters. Players guarding Hardpoint A should spread out past the skywalk, use the objective as an alarm and, once you see it is being stolen or contested, ambush the enemy Pilots.
- When the opponent keeps killing you or your teammates zip lining into Hardpoint C, use this jump and approach the objective from a different angle. Catch your opponent off guard and begin neutralizing the opponent's objective.

Reference these videos in your free mobile friendly eGuide.

LAST TITAN STANDING

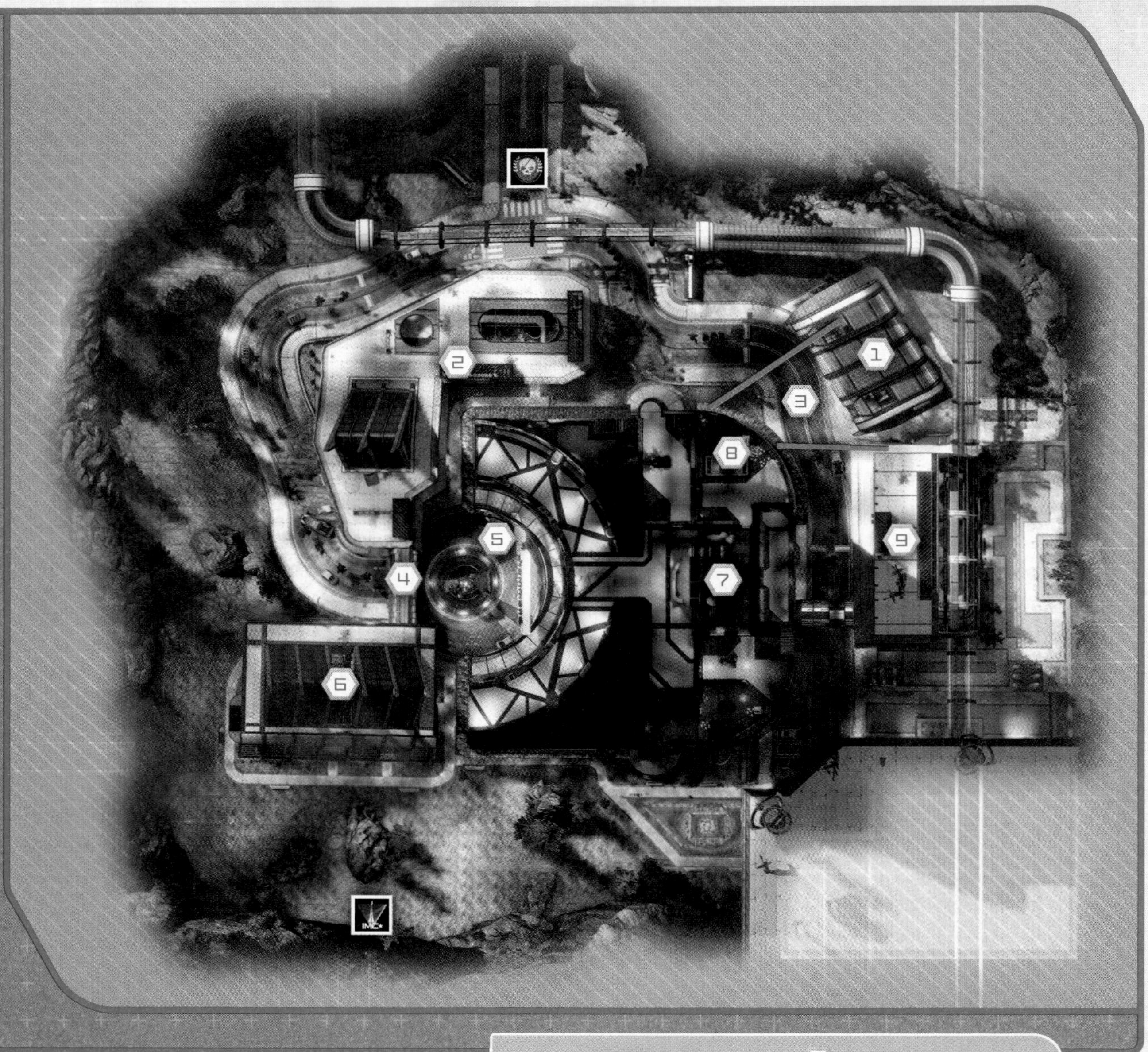

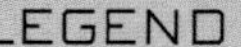

LEGEND

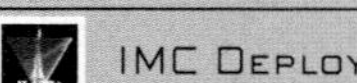

IMC Deployment

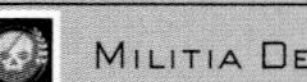

Militia Deployment

Zip Line

1. Cafe
2. Design Office
3. Main Street
4. Statue Skybridge
5. Roundabout
6. Applied Robotics
7. Main Lobby
8. Board Room
9. Quality Control

TACTICS

- This map is extremely limited for your Titan's movement—it is confined and has few open areas. You'll want to really stick together in a pack on this map when going into battle.
- Stay clear of the Roundabout if you're traveling alone—it is a deathtrap. If you get caught in this area by yourself, you are asking to be killed by enemy Titans and Pilots. Only go into the Roundabout if you have a few friendly Titans assisting you.
- At the start of the match, one Pilot should put a Titan in Auto-Titan and the Pilot should head straight towards the rooftops of the Design Office and above the Roundabout. This will give you a great view to alert your team where all the enemy Titans are headed. Be sure to equip Cloak so you aren't spotted on the roof by the enemy team. As a Pilot, roam around the rooftops, but be sure to not get spotted. Don't shoot any enemy Titans either, until you see a Titan battle initiating. Once you see the battle, start throwing some Arc Grenades at the enemy Titans and fire away to assist your friendly Titans.
- Move around the perimeter of the map on the streets with a few teammates. Try finding the enemy Titans who are running solo and destroy them quickly.
- With this map having so many close-quarter areas, equip the Triple Threat primary weapon. Triple Threat excels on this map with all the narrow paths. This weapon also works really well when attacking a group of Titans because it will deal heavy damage to all the Titans in the area of its explosion.

PILOT HUNTER

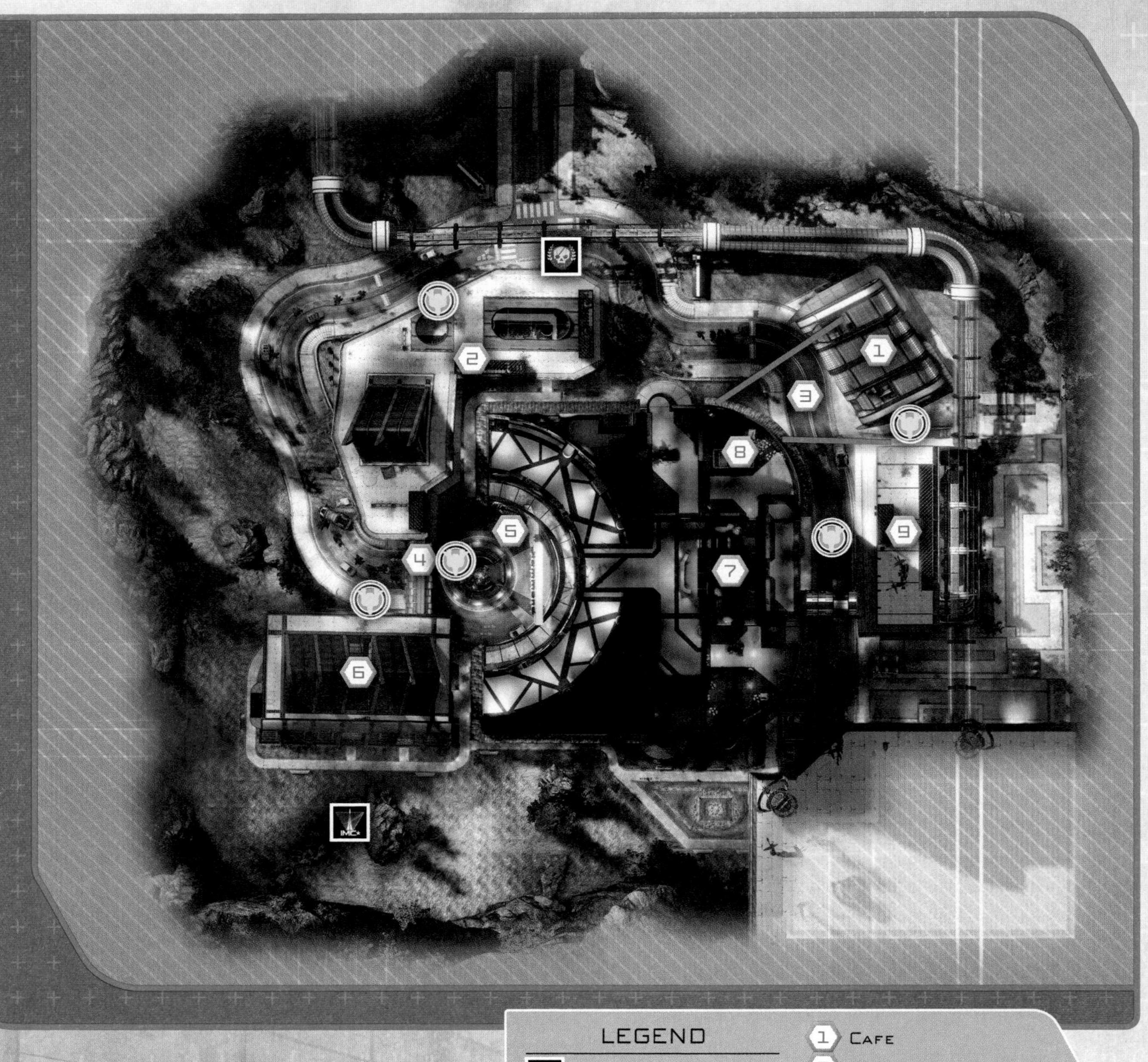

LEGEND

- IMC Deployment
- Militia Deployment
- Zip Line
- Evac Point

1. Cafe
2. Design Office
3. Main Street
4. Statue Skybridge
5. Roundabout
6. Applied Robotics
7. Main Lobby
8. Board Room
9. Quality Control

TACTICS

- Minions are very important to find to reduce Titanfall build time. You'll want to be the first to have a Titanfall so you can start picking off enemy Pilots quickly and get an early lead. Position your Pilot on the roof above the Roundabout to slay the many minions running around below.
- Running on the ground, especially around the Roundabout, is not recommended. Enemy Pilots are sure to be on the rooftops waiting for you and your allies to blindly run out in the open so they can pick you off. Always have an object or wall near you, allowing you to gain momentum and escape death by maneuvering away.

PRO TIP: WALSHY

Attaching a Suppressor to your primary weapon is a must when playing Pilot Hunter. Having the ability to hunt minions while staying off an enemy Pilot's minimap is crucial. You don't want to zone out when killing minions without a Suppressor because enemy Pilots will see you on their minimap and will move to your location. Stay stealthy and always have a Suppressor class for Pilot Hunter.

- A Longbow-DMR Sniper with an AOG scope attached deals tons of damage. The map is designed with long halls and various lines of sight so that snipers can constantly be on the move. The reason for attaching the AOG scope is that it allows you to hit those medium-range battles since you will constantly be moving as opposed to setting up on a rooftop.

PRO TIP: FLAMESWORD

Even though the Minion Detector is primarily used in Attrition to spot minions, it can be used effectively in Pilot Hunter. Have the Minion Detector attached to your Tier 1 Kit and keep an eye on your minimap. If you see your minions are vanishing quickly, odds are that an enemy Pilot is killing them. Move in this direction and take out the enemy.

- An Ogre Titan will excel during this match. The extra health on the Titan allows it move around the Main Lobby, forcing enemy Pilots to either engage your Titan or run outside of the building in the open where your friendlies will be waiting for them. Be sure to equip Electric Smoke in this area as you are more prone to get rodeo attacked.

DEMETER

Demeter is a critical fueling station for IMC forces making the jump into the Frontier. The station is full of pipes, maintenance shafts, bridges, and other unique features that allow Pilots great freedom of movement. Pilots frequently use the bridge between Hardpoints B and C to stay in control of the two stations in Hardpoint operations. Demeter's sky is dominated by a dying red giant star. Combatants can use this to their advantage, orienting themselves in such a way that their attackers' vision is obscured by the sun's brilliant red glow.

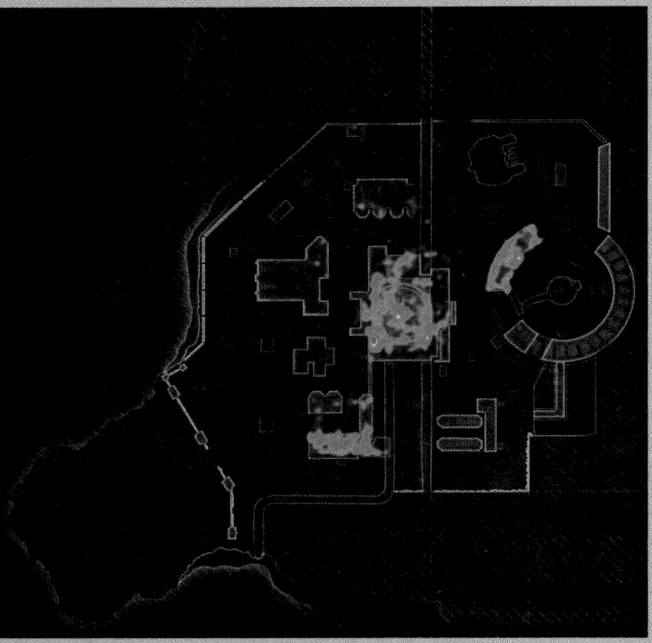

Red represents the highest concentrations of minion deaths on this composite heat map.

KEY LANDMARKS

SINGLE PIPE

STEALTH BOMBER

GARAGE

SUB STATION

LOADING BAY

REACTOR CORE

MAP OVERVIEW

The action on this map takes place mostly inside and around the Reactor Core. You'll find both teams fighting over this hot spot on the map throughout the entire game. You'll find the Single Pipe and Double Pipe extremely useful when traveling towards the Reactor Core.

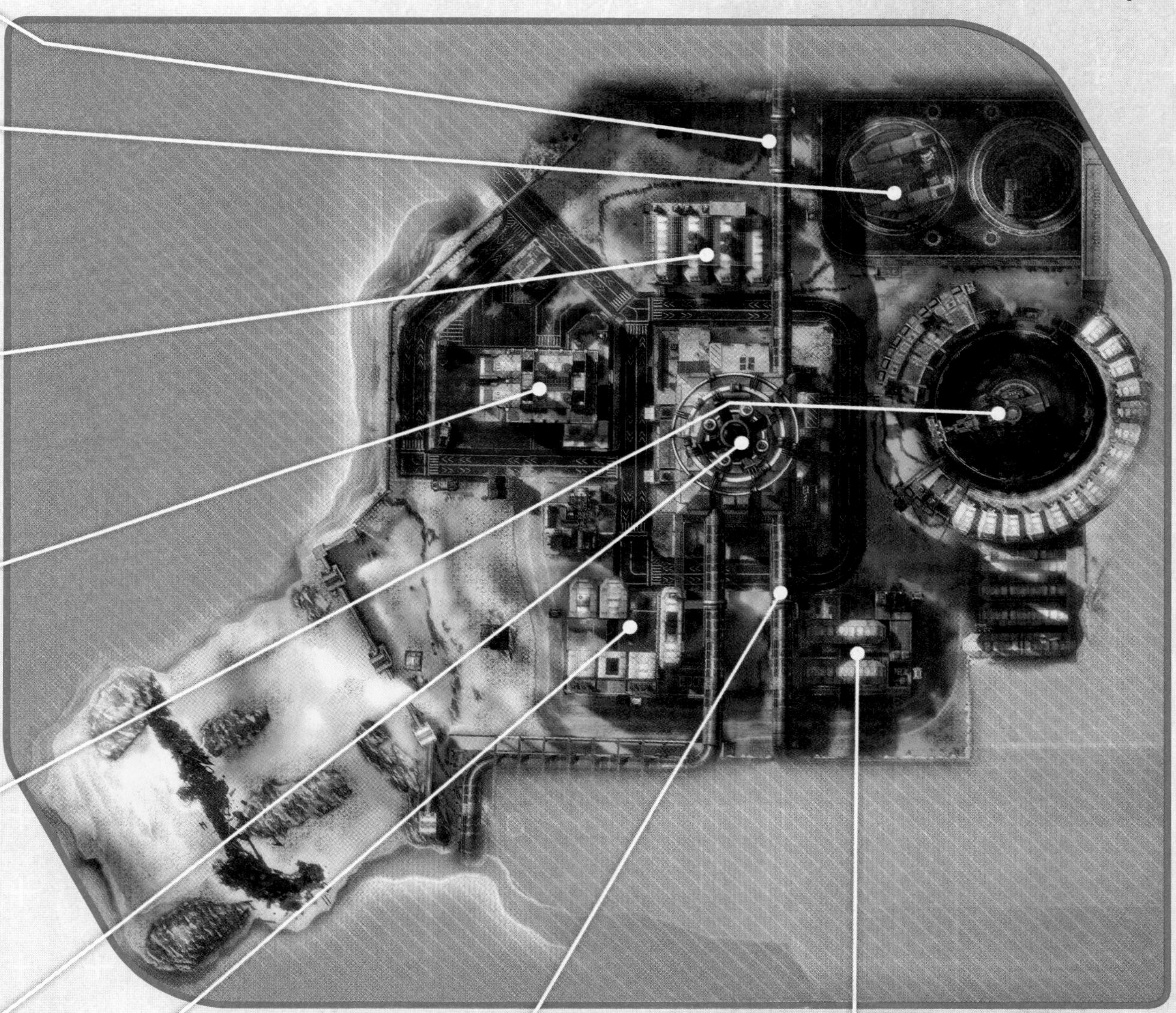

MARVIN REPAIR

DOUBLE PIPE

PIPE ARRAY

DEMETER

ATTRITION

LEGEND

IMC Deployment

Militia Deployment

Evac Point

1. Single Pipe
2. Stealth Bomber
3. Garage
4. Sub Station
5. Loading Bay
6. Reactor Core
7. Marvin Repair
8. Double Pipe
9. Pipe Array

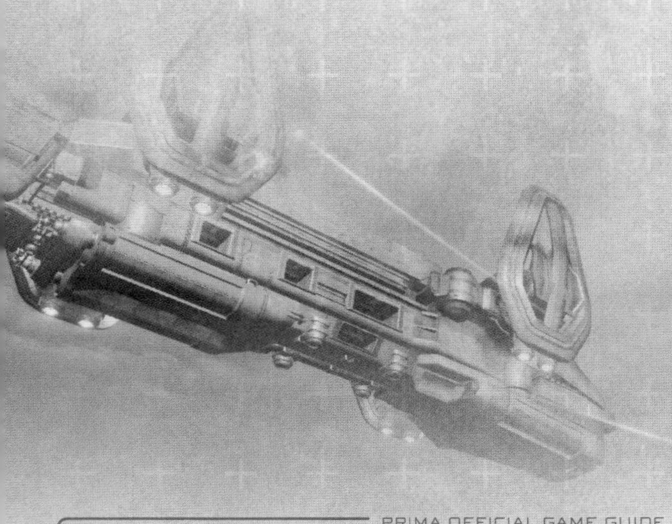

TACTICS

- Between the Sub Station and Garage, players will find drop pods of minions constantly throughout the game. This is a good area to hunt minions to reduce your build time.
- A sniper can pick up kills by sitting back on the roof of the Marvin Repair building. You will be able to pick off minions near the Sub Station and pick off any enemy Pilots jumping around the Reactor Core.
- Running around the walkway on the outside of the Reactor Core is a sound plan to spot where the action is going on. Run back and forth to kill minions and spot enemy Pilots off guard from time to time. Don't stay at one location on the walkway because you are exposed a lot.
- Raining steel down from the Single Pipe is a great tactic. The Single Pipe presents a great overview of the map and is easy to defend. There are only a couple ways to make it up here so all you will need to check periodically is the top of the Garage and Reactor Core building. If you are shot at, crouch down on the opposite side of the pipe.
- Titans prove very useful on this map and are provided many objects around the map that can be used for cover. Stryders will be able to do laps around the map and be a thorn in the enemy's side the entire game.

PRO TIP: WALSHY

The EVA-8 Shotgun is a powerful weapon to have in hand during this game mode. Combine the weapon with Cloak and you will be able to hold down the inside of the Reactor Core for the majority of the game.

CAPTURE THE FLAG

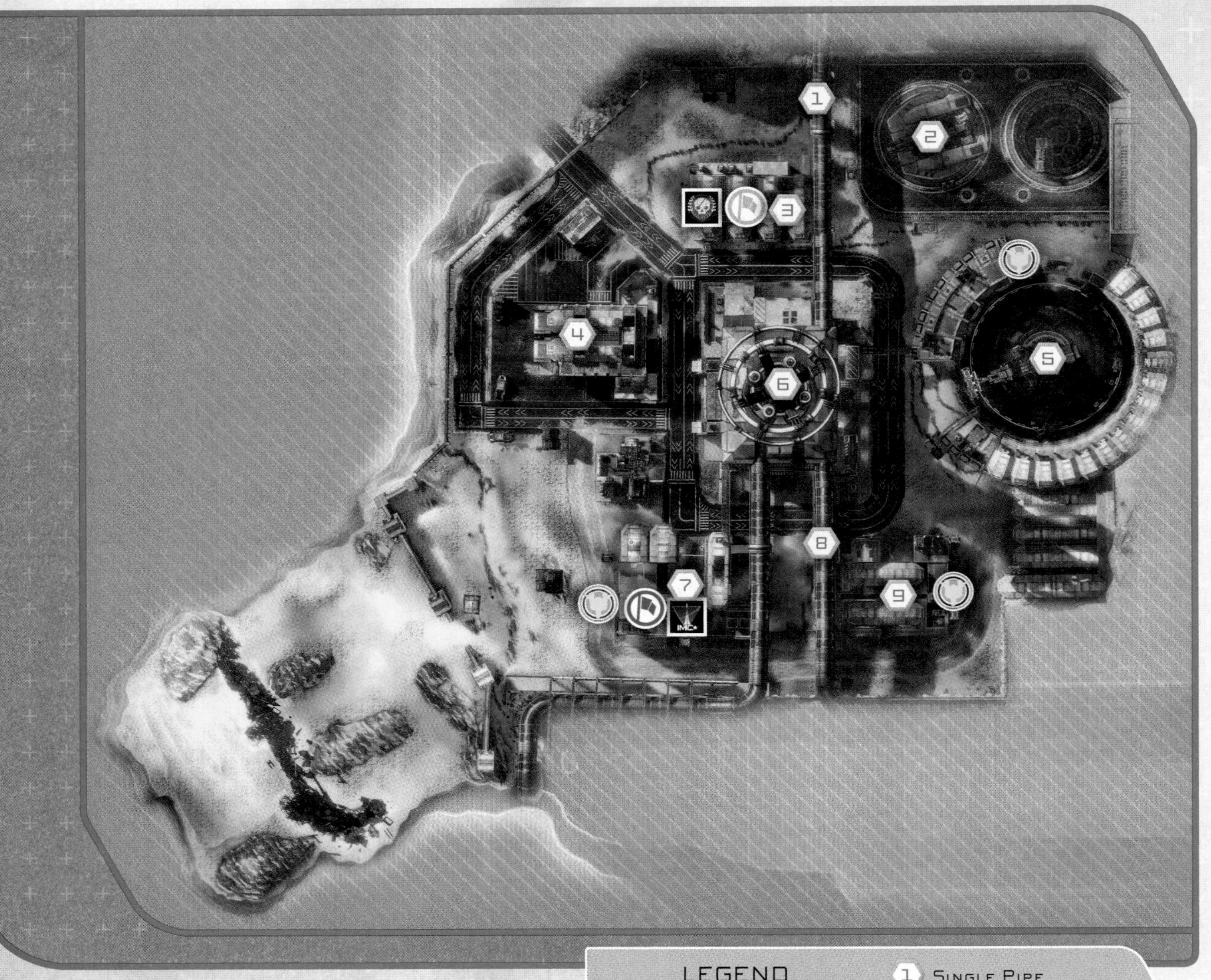

LEGEND

- IMC Deployment
- Militia Deployment
- IMC Flag
- Militia Flag
- Evac Point

1. Single Pipe
2. Stealth Bomber
3. Garage
4. Sub Station
5. Loading Bay
6. Reactor Core
7. Marvin Repair
8. Double Pipe
9. Pipe Array

NOTE

Initial flags, routes, and deployment areas shown. Factions switch sides at halftime.

TACTICS

- Escort the flag carrier around the outskirts of map with a Titan. The outskirts have a bunch of objects that can be used for cover, allowing you to safely return to your base to capture the enemy's flag.
- No matter what side you are on, you will want to hold down the top of the Reactor Core. Players up here will be able to provide suppressive fire the whole game and move in for a flag grab when the opportunity presents itself. This position will also allow you to pick off an enemy Pilot running the flag on foot.
- With each flag inside close-quarter buildings, the Garage and Marvin Repair buildings, players will want to have a class with the Tier 1 Kit Explosives Pack equipped. The extra Frag Grenade or Arc Grenade can kill players camping inside or make you aware of their location. Always toss a grenade in the building to see if someone is inside. You'll know someone is inside if you get a hit marker.
- A sniper on the Double Pipes can trap the opposing team inside of the Marvin Repair building and cover you as you charge into the enemy base. This will make it easier for friendlies to move in and kill the trapped opponents.

PRO TIP: FLAMESWORD

The Satchel Charge is a great Ordnance choice for Capture the Flag. It becomes even more effective on this map because of how small the interior of each building that holds the flag is. Place Satchel Charges around the flag and immediately detonate them when you see your flag has been stolen. Instead of pulling out the Satchel Charge detonator to detonate the charges, simply double tap your reload button to detonate the charges quicker.

HARDPOINT DOMINATION

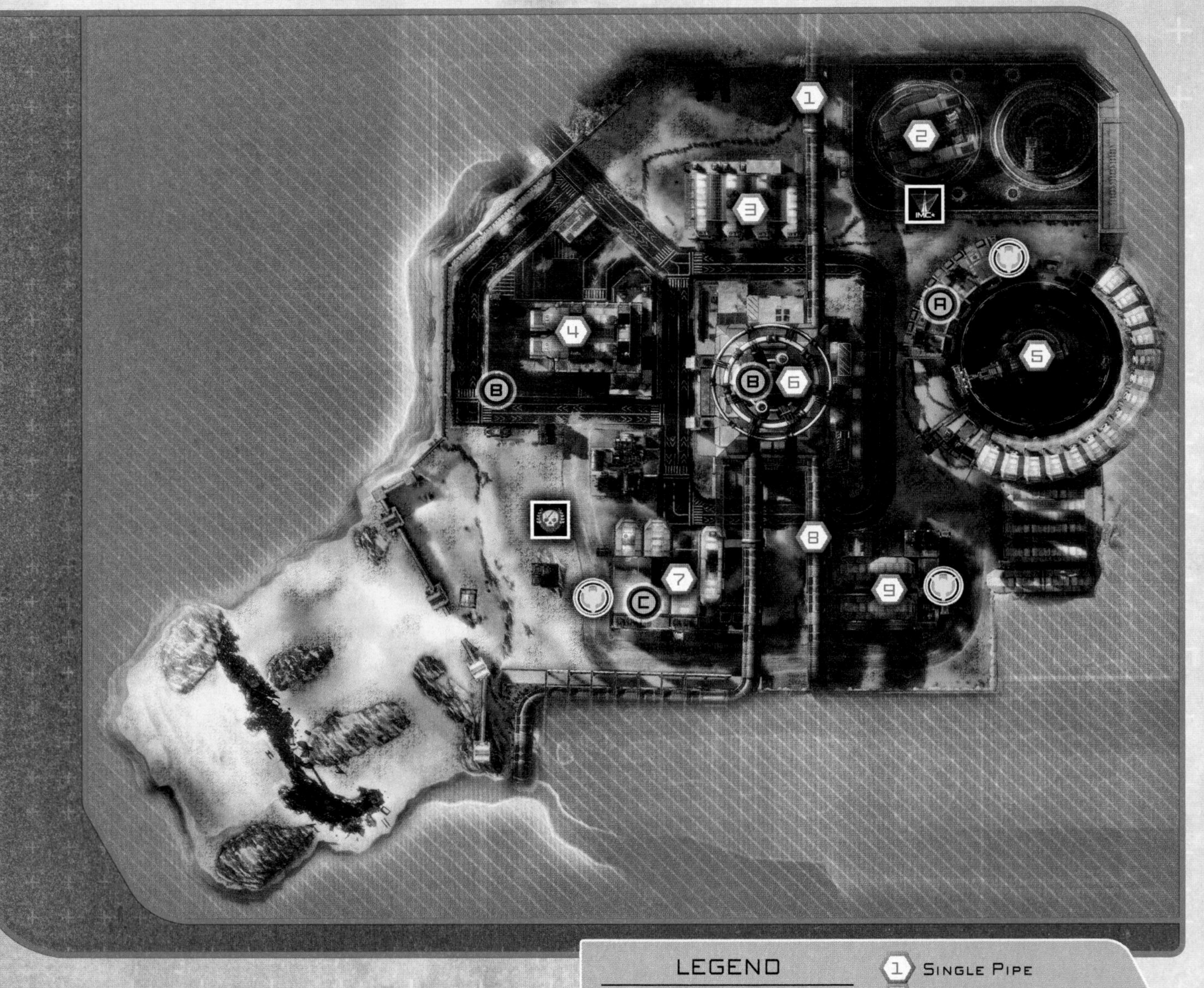

LEGEND

IMC Deployment	
Militia Deployment	
A	Hardpoint A
B	Hardpoint B
C	Hardpoint C
Evac Point	

1 Single Pipe
2 Stealth Bomber
3 Garage
4 Sub Station
5 Loading Bay
6 Reactor Core
7 Marvin Repair
8 Double Pipe
9 Pipe Array

TACTICS

PRO TIP: STRONGSIDE

An Auto-Titan placed in the Reactor Core near Hardpoint B will hold its ground and also alert you when enemies are trying to capture this objective. Placing the Auto-Titan in this building is a good bait for the enemy. As a Pilot you should play sneaky and hide around the inside of the Reactor Core building. Once you see a enemy Pilot attack your Titan, that is the golden chance to kill the enemy Pilot.

- All around Hardpoint B there are grated floors that you can shoot through. Use these to locate or kill the enemy below or above you.
- The top of the Sub Station is a perfect spot for sniping. You can catch enemies running around the outside of Hardpoint B and running out in the open from Hardpoint C.
- Running on the pipe that connects Hardpoint B to Hardpoint C is a great way to avoid enemies that are coming from Hardpoint C. Use Active Radar Pulse to see when an enemy is below you that you can easily take out.

PRO TIP: STRONGSIDE

On the second level between Hardpoints A and B is a walkway that connects both points. This position will allow you to quickly move from point to point to help your team defend both points.

- If an enemy Titan is trying to take Hardpoint B, you should easily be able to dispose of it, or at least make it run away, by using a couple Arc Grenades.

LAST TITAN STANDING

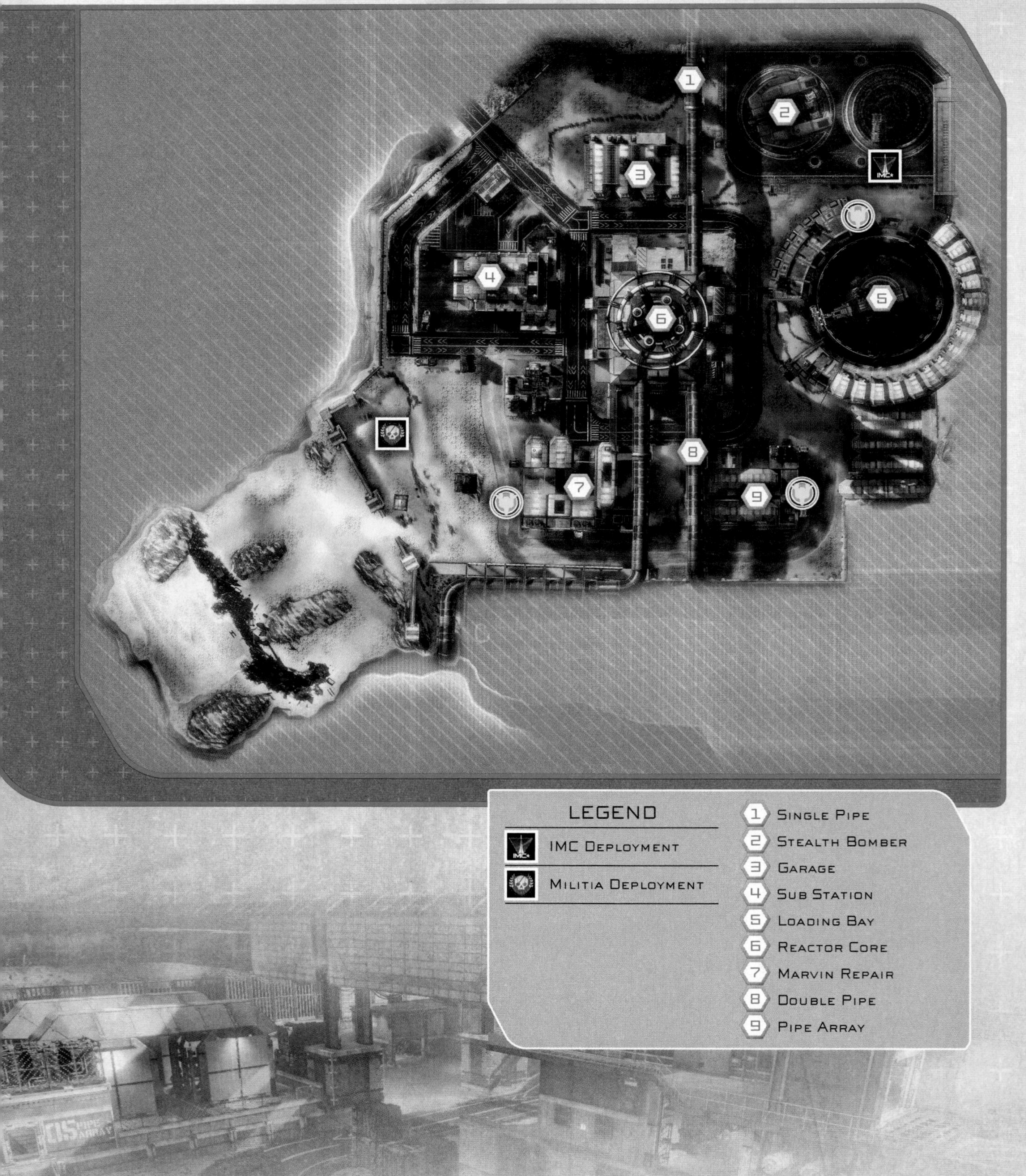

TACTICS

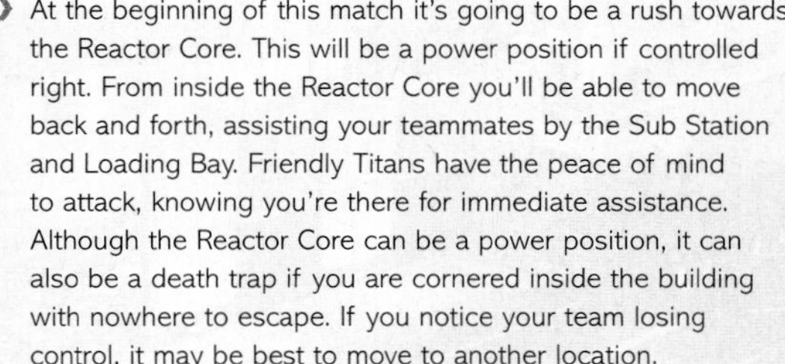

- At the beginning of this match it's going to be a rush towards the Reactor Core. This will be a power position if controlled right. From inside the Reactor Core you'll be able to move back and forth, assisting your teammates by the Sub Station and Loading Bay. Friendly Titans have the peace of mind to attack, knowing you're there for immediate assistance. Although the Reactor Core can be a power position, it can also be a death trap if you are cornered inside the building with nowhere to escape. If you notice your team losing control, it may be best to move to another location.

PRO TIP: STRONGSIDE

In this game mode, it is wise to have one Pilot on foot leaving a Titan on Auto-Titan. The Pilot can then push up with friendly Titans and use Arc Grenades to assist in battle by stunning the enemy Titans. Arc Grenades can make or break a Titan battle between the two teams.

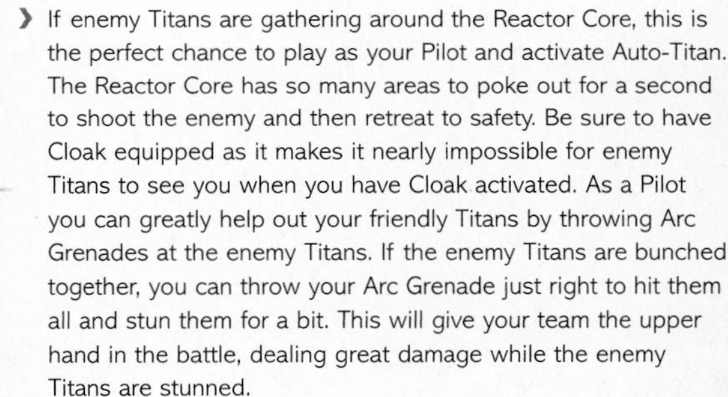

- If enemy Titans are gathering around the Reactor Core, this is the perfect chance to play as your Pilot and activate Auto-Titan. The Reactor Core has so many areas to poke out for a second to shoot the enemy and then retreat to safety. Be sure to have Cloak equipped as it makes it nearly impossible for enemy Titans to see you when you have Cloak activated. As a Pilot you can greatly help out your friendly Titans by throwing Arc Grenades at the enemy Titans. If the enemy Titans are bunched together, you can throw your Arc Grenade just right to hit them all and stun them for a bit. This will give your team the upper hand in the battle, dealing great damage while the enemy Titans are stunned.

- This map has some wide open areas to see across the map, which will allow you to take advantage of the Plasma Railgun. This weapon deals massive damage from long range, but you must be extremely accurate. This weapon works well when an enemy Titan is trying to peek shoot you from behind a building. Blast him with the Plasma Railgun as he peeks out to shoot you. With this weapon you can take down the enemy's shield completely and initiate a charge once you have weakened the enemy team. Dealing damage and dropping the enemy's shield will give your team the advantage before entering a close-range battle or initiating a charge.
- Don't get caught in the open streets on this map. Play it safe, use buildings for cover, and move around the perimeter of the map. The perimeter provides a building for cover and at least a good route to dash away to your team for help if you are in trouble.

PILOT HUNTER

LEGEND

IMC Deployment

Militia Deployment

Evac Point

1. Single Pipe
2. Stealth Bomber
3. Garage
4. Sub Station
5. Loading Bay
6. Reactor Core
7. Marvin Repair
8. Double Pipe
9. Pipe Array

TACTICS

- Controlling the inside of the Reactor Core is critical—it has plenty of walkways that lead to different wings of the reactor. Every wing of the reactor gives you a view of different parts of the map. These wings will assist you in killing minions to build your Titan and to find enemy Pilots roaming the map for you to pick off.
- Above the Garage is the Single Pipe, and near the Marvin Repair building is the Double Pipe, which connects to the Reactor Core. The height you have when on these pipes makes you a tough target and it gives you a bird's-eye view of the map, allowing you to get the jump on enemy Pilots.
- When fighting opponents from the top of the Reactor Core, always try to stick close to the reactor in the center. If the opposing team begins to pressure you, jumping up in the reactor is a great getaway. You can either wall hang in the tight space and then jump back up or fall all the way to the ground.
- Many Pilots tend to swarm towards the inside of the Reactor Core and on the roof. This gives you the opportunity to sit back and take advantage of the sniper rifle. Be patient and wait for enemy Pilots roaming the Reactor Core area. Once you kill a few enemy Pilots, prepare for them to charge you from another direction. You can also move to a different location and keep the enemy guessing your every position.
- Obtaining your Titan on this map is going to be a game changer. You'll be able to keep enemy Pilots pushed back into a building while your teammates are able to push up and surround the building to take out any enemy Pilots inside.

FRACTURE

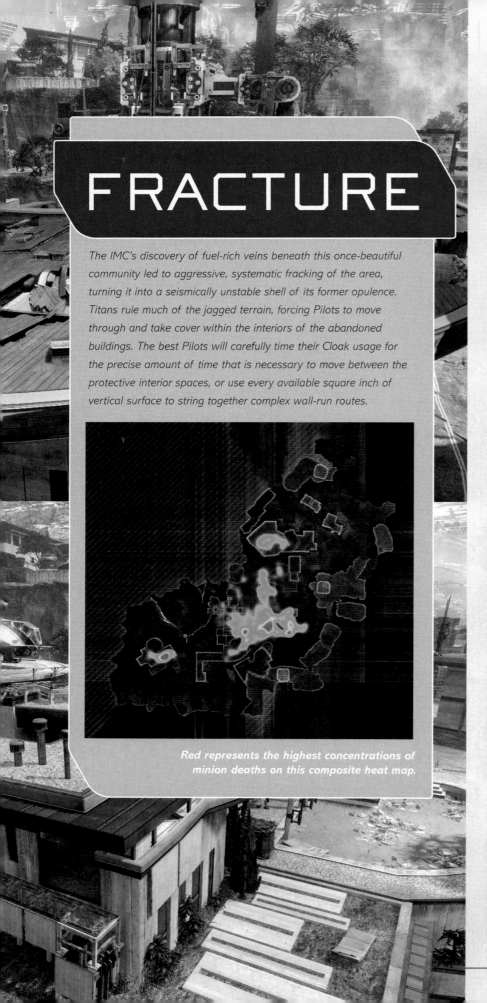

The IMC's discovery of fuel-rich veins beneath this once-beautiful community led to aggressive, systematic fracking of the area, turning it into a seismically unstable shell of its former opulence. Titans rule much of the jagged terrain, forcing Pilots to move through and take cover within the interiors of the abandoned buildings. The best Pilots will carefully time their Cloak usage for the precise amount of time that is necessary to move between the protective interior spaces, or use every available square inch of vertical surface to string together complex wall-run routes.

Red represents the highest concentrations of minion deaths on this composite heat map.

KEY LANDMARKS

ART GALLERY

TERRACE

RESIDENTIAL BUILDING

HILLTOP

LANDING PAD

SECURITY BUILDING

MAP OVERVIEW

Be prepared to face nearly every weapon in the Pilot arsenal as you fight snipers on the rooftops, shotguns in the buildings, and everything in between on this versatile map.

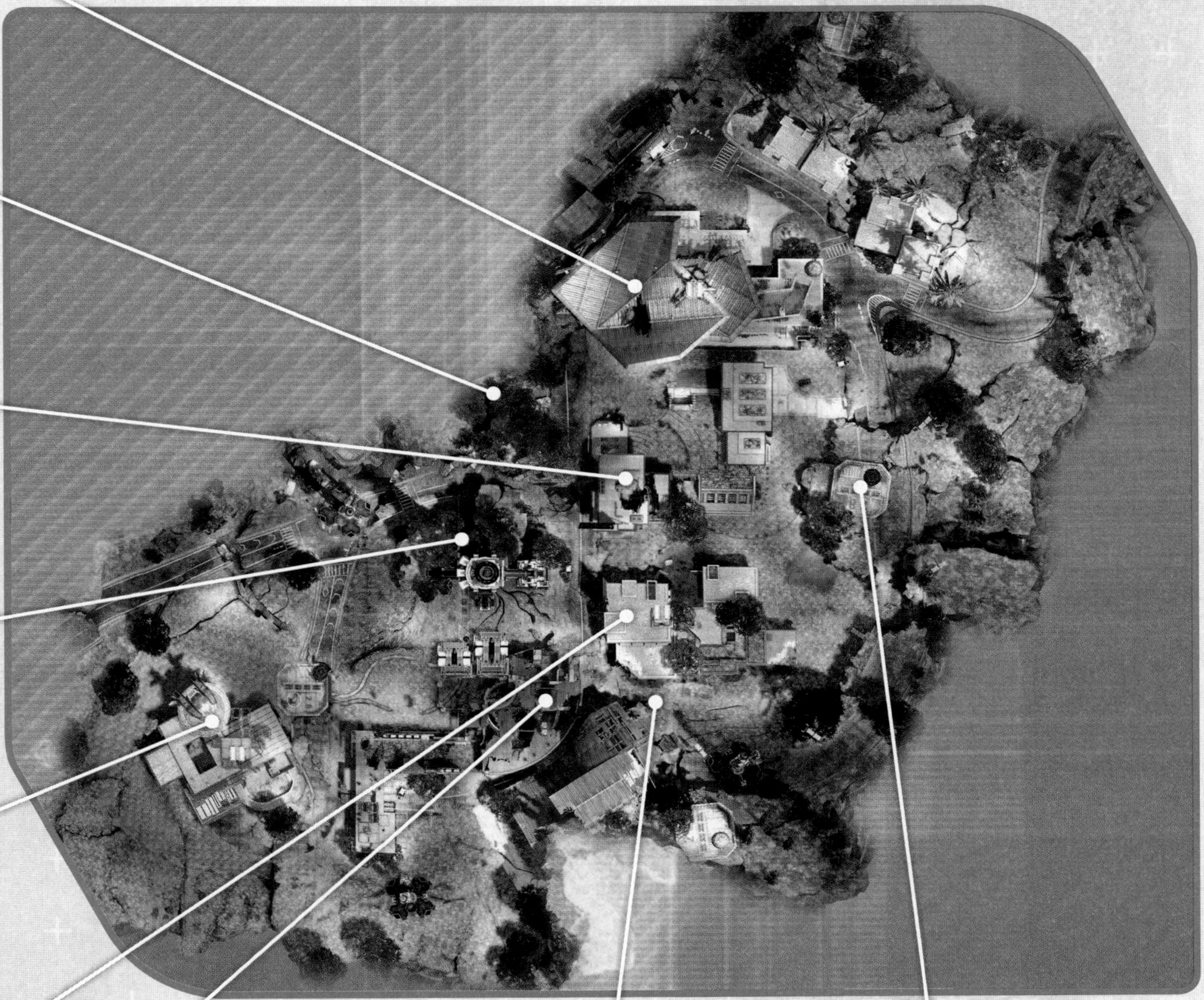

FRACTURE

BROKEN BUILDING

CLIFF

REFUELING STATION

ATTRITION

LEGEND
IMC Deployment
Militia Deployment
Evac Point
1 Art Gallery
2 Terrace
3 Residential Building
4 Hilltop
5 Landing Pad
6 Security Building
7 Broken Building
8 Cliff
9 Refuling Station

TACTICS

- Both the Security Building and Landing Pad are saturated with minions. Taking control of the Broken Building will allow you to move back and forth to pick up enemy minions. Don't stick around the eastern balcony for too long unless you have a suppressor attached—you're just asking to be killed.
- The Hilltop is a solid location to pick off enemy minions and Pilots. This area has many bushes to stay hidden behind and cover yourself if you are being shot at. This position overlooks hot spots where minions meet. Keep moving from one side of the Hilltop to another as enemy Pilots are sure to come after you.
- The top of the Security Building is a great place to hold if the enemy team is on one side of the map. If there are enemies at the Residential Building and at the Broken Building, drop down the side of the Security Building and get inside before the enemy team can easily pick you off.
- Once you call down a Titan, be sure to take the best routes by avoiding the choke point between the Broken Building and the Hilltop. Being caught in this area for too long can be the death of your Titan. Stick to roaming south of the Security Building and the back side of the Broken Building that leads to the Landing Pad.
- Avoid the open road on this map—it is a guaranteed death. It may seem obvious, but always stick to the buildings and tunnels to navigate around the map.
- Be cautious of engaging enemy Pilots while in between buildings. Many of the enemy Pilots will distract you so their teammates can try to rodeo attack you. Keep your distance from all high-traffic buildings and keep your eyes peeled for enemy Pilots using Cloak. If you lose track of a cloaked enemy Pilot, always dash away to save your Titan.
- While all the crazy minion fighting is going on around the map, there are a few spots players can take advantage of with a sniper. Posting up on the top of Broken Building, Security Building, Hilltop, or Cliff are all viable options.

CAPTURE THE FLAG

NOTE

Initial flags, routes, and deployment areas shown. Factions switch sides at halftime.

TACTICS

Reference these videos in your free mobile friendly eGuide.

- A sniper will be very effective guarding the flag in the Art Gallery. Post up on the roof, allowing you to have wide view of the map to call out enemies on the flank, especially the enemies who try to approach south of the Art Gallery. The sniper can damage or take out any enemy Pilots who run directly to your flag from the middle. Be sure to be vocal and inform your teammates of what you see.
- Winning isn't all about flashy plays and a bunch of kills. A player with an SMG or the EVA-8 Shotgun can single-handily defend the flag the entire game, making it easier for the rest of team to go on the offensive. This defensive strategy is best applied when defending the flag inside of the Broken Building because Titans can not enter inside it like they can in the Art Gallery.
- When going for the flag inside of the Art Gallery, put a Titan in Auto-Titan mode inside. This provides you with enough time to grab the flag and then run back up to jump inside of your Titan. Once you are in, kill nearby threats and quickly make it back to your base for the capture.
- If a Titan isn't an option when grabbing the flag inside the Art Gallery, use these wall runs to quickly escape the Art Gallery. Having a teammate at the Terrace will provide cover to protect the flag carrier.
- Before going inside of the Broken Building and grabbing the flag, spot out nearby enemy Pilots and take them out. If the area is clear, grab the flag and head outside to begin wall running. This wall run allows you to go from the Broken Building to the Security Building in seconds. An ally in the Residential Building needs to provide cover for the flag carrier.
- The Hilltop is your middle point between both flags. A player needs to hold down this area to spot and call out enemies. This player will be able to decide, depending on the situation, if they should either play offensively or defensively. If your team has more Pilots alive, push up. If less, play defensive until your teammates spawn.

HARDPOINT DOMINATION

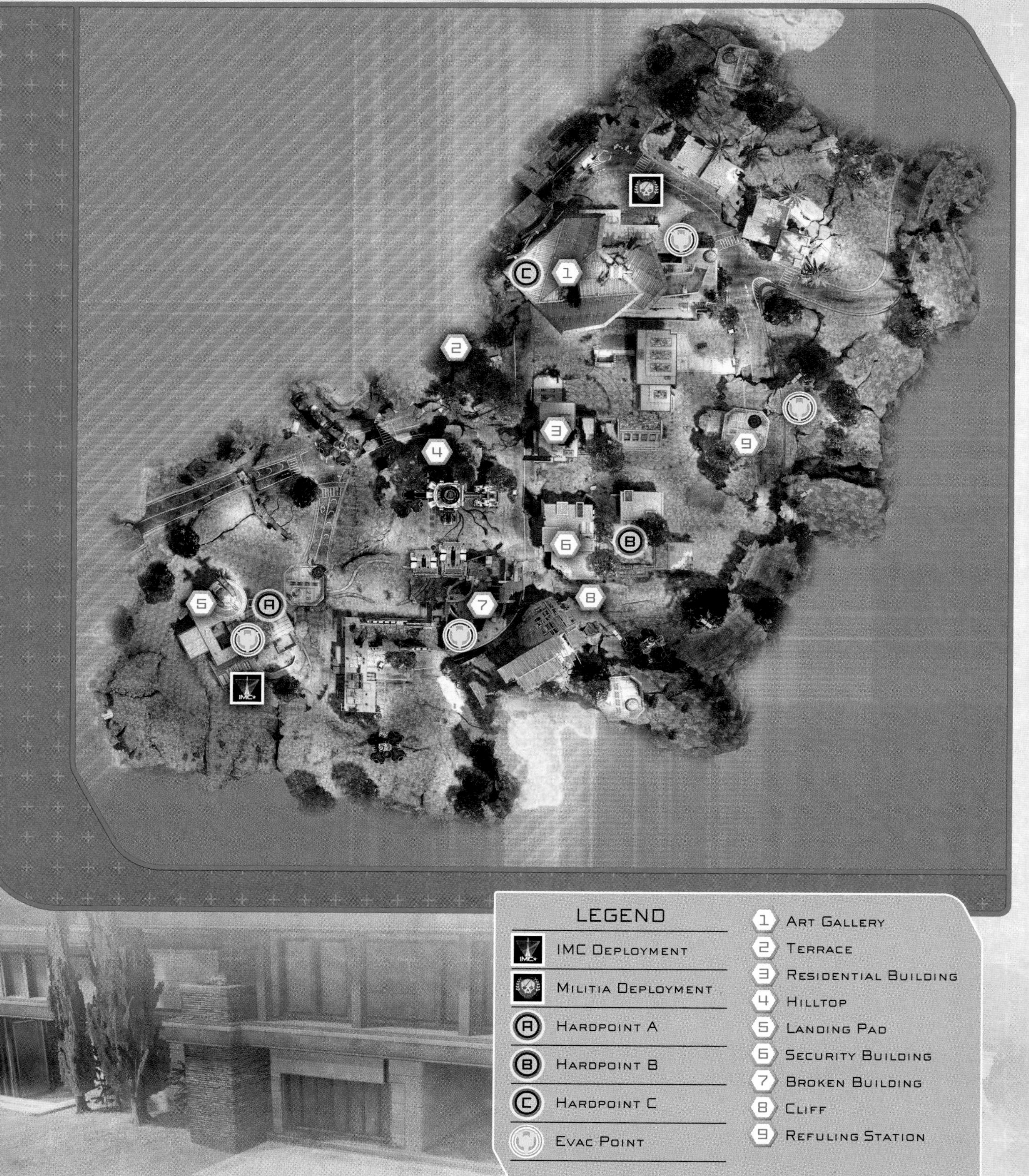
LEGEND
IMC Deployment
Militia Deployment
Hardpoint A
Hardpoint B
Hardpoint C
Evac Point
1 Art Gallery
2 Terrace
3 Residential Building
4 Hilltop
5 Landing Pad
6 Security Building
7 Broken Building
8 Cliff
9 Refuling Station

TACTICS

- Controlling Hardpoints B and C gives you the best odds to take the match since they are nearest each other. When you have a Titan keep moving back and forth from both points. Stay on defense around Hardpoint B more. Hardpoint C is easier to recapture with teammates because it is open to Titans. Don't go on your own to capture Hardpoint C if you have a Titan. Wait for teammates because enemy Pilots could be on the rooftop or inside the Art Gallery, set up to hit you with Arc Grenades and Anti-Titan weapons.

PRO TIP: FLAMESWORD

Inside of Hardpoint B is a corner that you can wall hang on that conceals your entire body, allowing you to safely capture or contest this objective while using the Enhanced Parkour Kit. You can also spot any enemies that run by as you are off the ground and looking down. Enemy Pilots almost never see you in this position.

- When defending Hardpoint A, go to the roof and scan the perimeter towards the Broken Building and Hilltop. You are able to spot and pick off enemies charging from a distance. Use the railings and turret for cover if the enemies are dealing damage to you. You can also fall down into the building and bait the enemies in.
- Hardpoint A has a small capturing radius. You want to be on the second floor when capturing this objective—a ledge provides you enough cover and enemies can only approach you from two locations. Periodically check both directions and this will be an easy capture. Placing Arc Mines around the doorway below also allows you to focus on defending the second floor.
- Hardpoints A and B cannot be accessed by Titans. Take advantage of these points by staying inside and making the enemy Pilot exit the Titan to attack you.
- Hardpoint C can be captured by a Titan, but leaves the Titan vulnerable to hit and runs. Some of the best weapons to attack a Titan with inside Hardpoint C are the Sidewinder, Mag Launcher, and Arc Grenades.

LAST TITAN STANDING

LEGEND

IMC	IMC Deployment
	Militia Deployment

1. Art Gallery
2. Terrace
3. Residential Building
4. Hilltop
5. Landing Pad
6. Security Building
7. Broken Building
8. Cliff
9. Refuling Station

TACTICS

- With such a open and mobile map, Atlas and Stryder are the safest picks. The Ogre is slow for these open fields unless you plan on playing passive.
- Nuclear Ejection is a great kit to have on for your Titan's Tier 1 Kit. Avoid battling in the open fields though. You will want to be close to buildings so enemy Titans do not have an open escape path. Played correctly you can catch multiple enemy Titans inside the explosion. If any enemy Titans are still standing, allied Titans can finish the job or you can hit them with your Anti-Titan weapon.
- With most engagements being mid-range on this map, the XO-16 Chaingun or Arc Cannon are the best choices to deal damage to Titans and pick off any Pilots that are on top of buildings as you cruise around.

PRO TIP: WALSHY

With so many large buildings on this map, you can get caught running circles chasing your opponent. When playing ring-around-the-rosie with a teammate against an enemy Titan, go the same way around the building as your teammate so the enemy can't isolate a 1v1 against your Titan. Once the enemy Titan is weak, feel free to split up to finish off the Titan so it can't regain its shields.

- Equip a long-range Anti-Titan weapon like the Heavy Archer Rocket for this map. It allows you to deal damage to Titans in the open fields. In addition, if you have to eject from your Titan, you're able to fire a rocket at the enemy Titan as you are falling from the sky.

PILOT HUNTER

1
2
3
4
5
6
7
8
9
LEGEND
IMC Deployment
Militia Deployment
Evac Point
1 Art Gallery
2 Terrace
3 Residential Building
4 Hilltop
5 Landing Pad
6 Security Building
7 Broken Building
8 Cliff
9 Refuling Station

TACTICS

- The Terrace is a great position to pick off many enemy minions and Pilots. It overlooks a big portion of the map and has a great view over the Hilltop. While at the top of the Terrace, equip a suppressor to stay unnoticed on the mini-map. Once you kill an enemy Pilot or two, be aware that they will use their death screen to find you and hunt you down.
- West of the Security Building is the Cliff—a prime location with cover from a small billboard sign and a few bushes. This is an incredible spot for a sniper to sit back and have a good view of the map. This player will be able to spot enemies and pick off Pilots that are running in the open.

PRO TIP: STRONGSIDE

The Tier 2 Kit Auto-Eject will save your life on many occasions when bailing from your Titan. The Cloak allows you to safely land and retreat to cover. In this game mode, every Pilot life counts.

- This map has so much space in between buildings that if you plan on moving from building to building use Cloak or Stim as your Tactical Ability.
- This is a great map to use the Longbow-DMR Sniper because of the open fields and not having to lead your shots on these cross-map kills. A great spot to snipe from is on the roof of the Art Gallery; on the north end of the building you can pick off enemies at the Broken Building. If you position yourself on the center of the roof of the Art Gallery, you can see Pilots on the top of the Security Building and the Residential Building.
- Once you are shot at in a location, such as the Residential Building, change your position by moving to a different floor or window. This will keep the enemy guessing. If you poke out at the same floor or window, the enemy will get the first shot on you and you will surely be dead.

LAGOON

This small fishing village on the outskirts of the Freeport system quickly became a flashpoint for IMC-Militia conflict when a distressed IMC carrier made an emergency landing nearby. Key landmarks include an abandoned temple of mysterious origin built next to the sheer cliffs behind the village, portable IMC base structures, and the ship itself. Snipers frequently clash over control of the cliffs that bisect the village, which is accessible via a small network of zip lines.

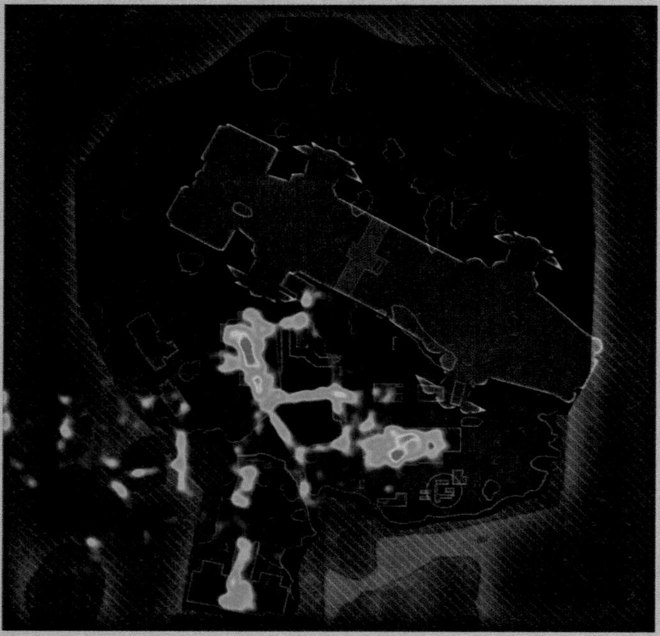

Red represents the highest concentrations of minion deaths on this composite heat map.

KEY LANDMARKS

BEACH

CLIFF HOUSE

BOATHOUSE

COMMUNICATIONS BUILDINGS

CAVES

SCIENCE LAB

MAP OVERVIEW

THE VARIOUS ZIP LINES ALLOW YOU TO QUICKLY TRAVEL AROUND THE MAP. TAKE ADVANTAGE OF THESE ZIP LINES BY USING THEM TO RUN FLAGS, GET TO AN AREA QUICKLY TO ASSIST YOUR TEAM, OR EVEN DROP IN TO RODEO ATTACK A TITAN.

TEMPLE

ARCH

LOCKWOOD BUILDING

ATTRITION

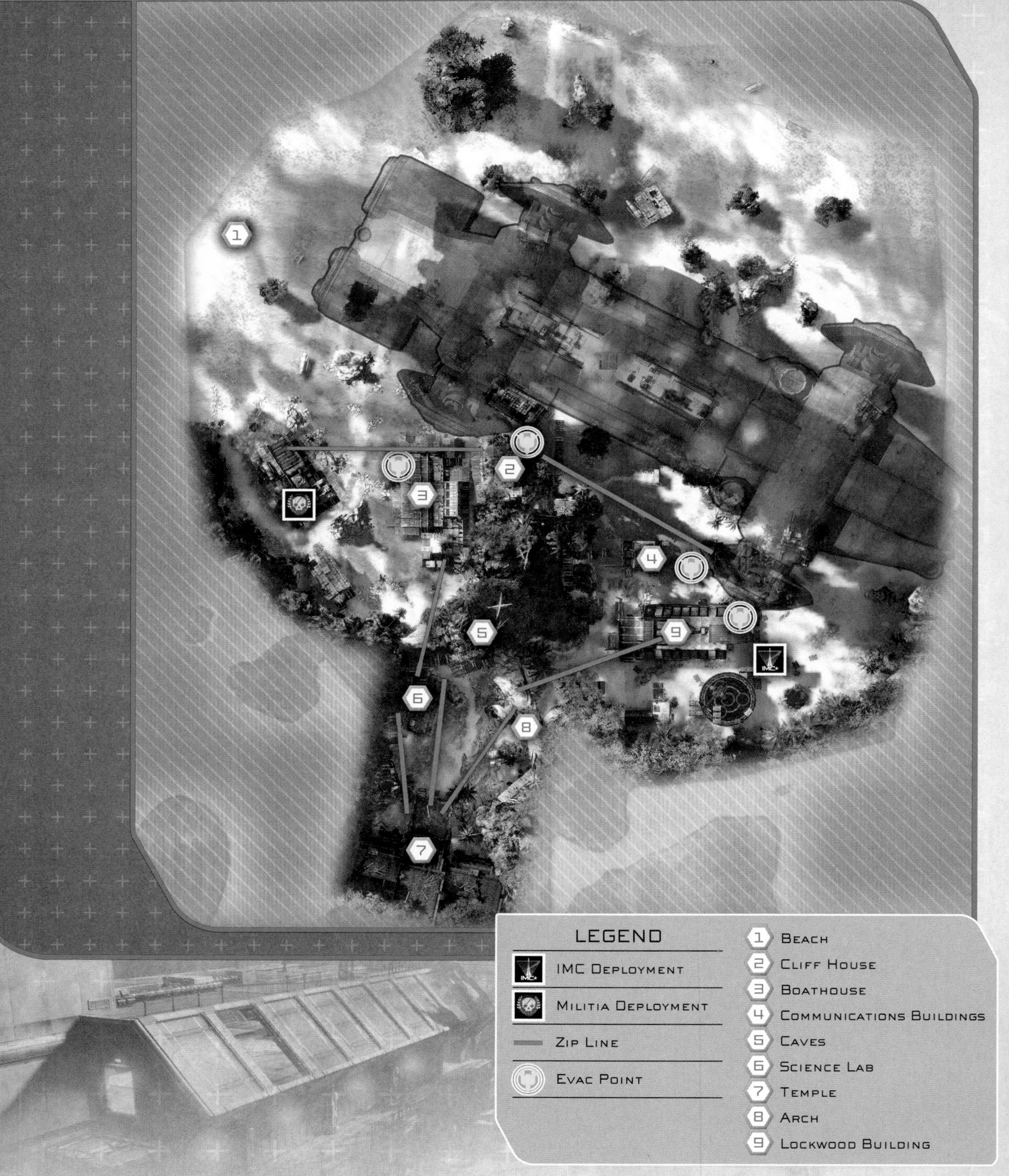
1
2
3
4
5
6
7
8
9
LEGEND
IMC Deployment
Militia Deployment
Zip Line
Evac Point
1 Beach
2 Cliff House
3 Boathouse
4 Communications Buildings
5 Caves
6 Science Lab
7 Temple
8 Arch
9 Lockwood Building

TACTICS

- You'll find that minions swarm the Lockwood Building, under the Cliff House, and under the Arch. These are locations you'll want to keep moving around to get your Titanfall quicker, but keep an eye out for enemy Pilots attempting to do the same. Sometimes using your minions as bait will get you an easy kill on an enemy Pilot.
- Holding the Arch is a great position as you have an overview of half the map and a good view of minions fighting near the Lockwood Building and underneath the Arch. The Arch also has many escape routes by taking any of the zip lines leading away from the area.

PRO TIP: FLAMESWORD

When I am controlling the Arch, I find it beneficial to have my sniper loadout. My loadout will consist of the Longbow-DMR Sniper equipped with the AOG scope attachment and Stabilizer MOD. From up here, I pick off enemies to reduce my Titanfall build time and try to spot out enemy Pilots. My Tactical Ability is Cloak, making me hard to see as I am so high up on the map. This allows me to fire upon enemy Pilots without them ever seeing me.

- The Lockwood Building is another great position to hold, with all the windows to shoot from and access to underneath the building, which has great cover and is good for patrolling the area to kill minions. You'll find many areas around this building to kill minions and bait enemy Pilots nearby. The roof of the Lockwood Building has a zip line that leads to the Arch. Use this zip line to efficiently travel back and forth.
- Once you have your Titan, patrol around the Lockwood Building and Communications Buildings to take out the many minions in these areas. These buildings will also serve for great cover if enemy Titans pursue you. This map has so much space to move around with your Titan. Take advantage of this space if you are fighting a losing battle by running away to buy time for your team to come assist you.
- Traveling through the Caves can be the safest route since it is enclosed and covered by many walls. The Caves can also lead to many minion kills, but be sure to have a suppressor attached as you'll want to stay hidden from the minimap.

CAPTURE THE FLAG

NOTE

Initial flags, routes, and deployment areas shown. Factions switch sides at halftime.

TACTICS

Reference these videos in your free mobile friendly eGuide.

PRO TIP: STRONGSIDE

Use this flag route to quickly make it back to your base when grabbing the flag from the Bungalows. Once you grab the flag, run up the stairs where you see an opening in the ceiling and wall jump out onto the roof. Then sprint to the edge of the roof and jump towards the zip line, taking that zip line to the Cliff House. Once at the Cliff House, there is another zip line leading back to your base. Take it. Lastly, when you reach the end of the zip line, jump off and wall run on the fence and then wall jump into your base through the window.

- The flag inside the Lockwood Building is completely enclosed and can be guarded with a shotgun. Watch out for enemy Titans shooting through the windows. Keep yourself hidden in a corner or behind a wall. This building has many entrances, so if you are guarding the flag, you'll want to either equip Cloak or Active Radar Pulse while inside the building. A good strategy is to hide somewhere in the Lockwood Building. Then, once you see an enemy grab the flag, come out of hiding and kill the flag runner.

PRO TIP: WALSHY

Arc Mines will be effective when defending the flag within the Lockwood Building. Plant these close by the flag, allowing you to move around the building to get better angles on incoming enemies.

- The flag inside the Bungalows can be guarded by a Pilot with a shotgun, but an enemy Titan is able to enter the building from the opening in the back and kill enemies inside. A Pilot defending this flag inside of the Bungalows will want to equip Arc Grenades to stun the enemy Titan and deal damage with an Anti-Titan weapon, forcing the enemy Titan to retreat.
- As a Titan on either team, you'll want to push up and cause a distraction when your teammates are preparing to grab the enemy's flag. This will allow your flag runner to make a flag run with fewer enemies focusing on them. If your friendly Pilot is grabbing the flag and no enemy Titans are near, tell your flag runner to hop on your Titan to assist running the flag back to your base. Once back to your base, make sure the inside of your base is clear before taking the flag in for a capture.

HARDPOINT DOMINATION

1
2
3
C
4
5
9
A
6
8
7
B
LEGEND
IMC Deployment
Militia Deployment
Hardpoint A
Hardpoint B
Hardpoint C
Zip Line
Evac Point
1 Beach
2 Cliff House
3 Boathouse
4 Communications Buildings
5 Caves
6 Science Lab
7 Temple
8 Arch
9 Lockwood Building

TACTICS

- When controlling Hardpoint B, guard the front entrance of the Temple with a Titan. Keep your view patrolling from the Arch, Science Lab, and Caves, because these are the only ways for the enemy to reach the Temple.
- Inside the Temple is a close-quarter area, so guarding it with a shotgun and Arc Mines will be extremely useful. There are only three entrances to Hardpoint B, so you can place two Arc Mines around one doorway and the third around a second doorway. This allows you to watch the third doorway as the Arc Mines will kill or alert you if an enemy Pilot is nearby.
- Inside Hardpoint B you'll see a light fixture in the corner of the room. If you stand behind this light, it is extremely hard for enemy Pilots to notice you because they are being blinded by the light that allows you to blend in with the wall. I like to use this position behind the light a few times to kill enemy Pilots and then move to another corner within Hardpoint B, since enemy Pilots are sure to catch on to this little trick.

PRO TIP: STRONGSIDE

Inside Hardpoint C you'll find a upper ceiling above a dry erase board and a generator. While wall hanging in the upper ceiling, you are still able to capture the hardpoint. If you're going to use this position, equip the Enhanced Parkour Kit, which allows you to wall hang for a much longer duration. While wall hanging, you're able to see enemies run by below—but do not get trigger happy and shoot them while you are on the ceiling. Drop down and kill them and they will be clueless to where you came from. This will allow you to keep using this position throughout the game, never letting the enemy know your position.

- Hardpoint C can be accessed by a Titan through the big opening in the back of the Bungalows, and a Titan can capture the hardpoint while in this open area. So if you are guarding at this point as a Pilot, you'll want to equip Arc Grenades to stun the enemy Titan trying to capture Hardpoint C. While the enemy Titan is stunned, use your Anti-Titan weapon to deal massive damage to the enemy Titan, which will force the enemy Titan to retreat.
- This will be a great position to capture the Hardpoint A, since there are only two entrances to this area and this area cannot be seen by a Titan. You can place Arc Mines around the doorways, so if any enemy enters, the mines will stun or kill the enemy Pilot and allow you to hold down Hardpoint A. Equipping a shotgun or SMG while defending Hardpoint A is a must due to its extremely close-quarter area.
- With a Titan on this map, you'll want to focus on Hardpoints A and C. At Hardpoint A, as a Titan you can shoot through many of the windows with the XO-16 Chaingun to kill enemy Pilots inside. At Hardpoint C, you're able to get inside the Bungalows and disrupt the enemy capture.

PRO TIP: STRONGSIDE

While playing as a Titan and attacking Hardpoint A, equip the Cluster Missile so you can shoot into the only stairway—you can't shoot enemy Pilots while they are inside. Shoot the Cluster Missile inside this stairwell and the after effects of the explosion are sure to kill anything inside.

LAST TITAN STANDING

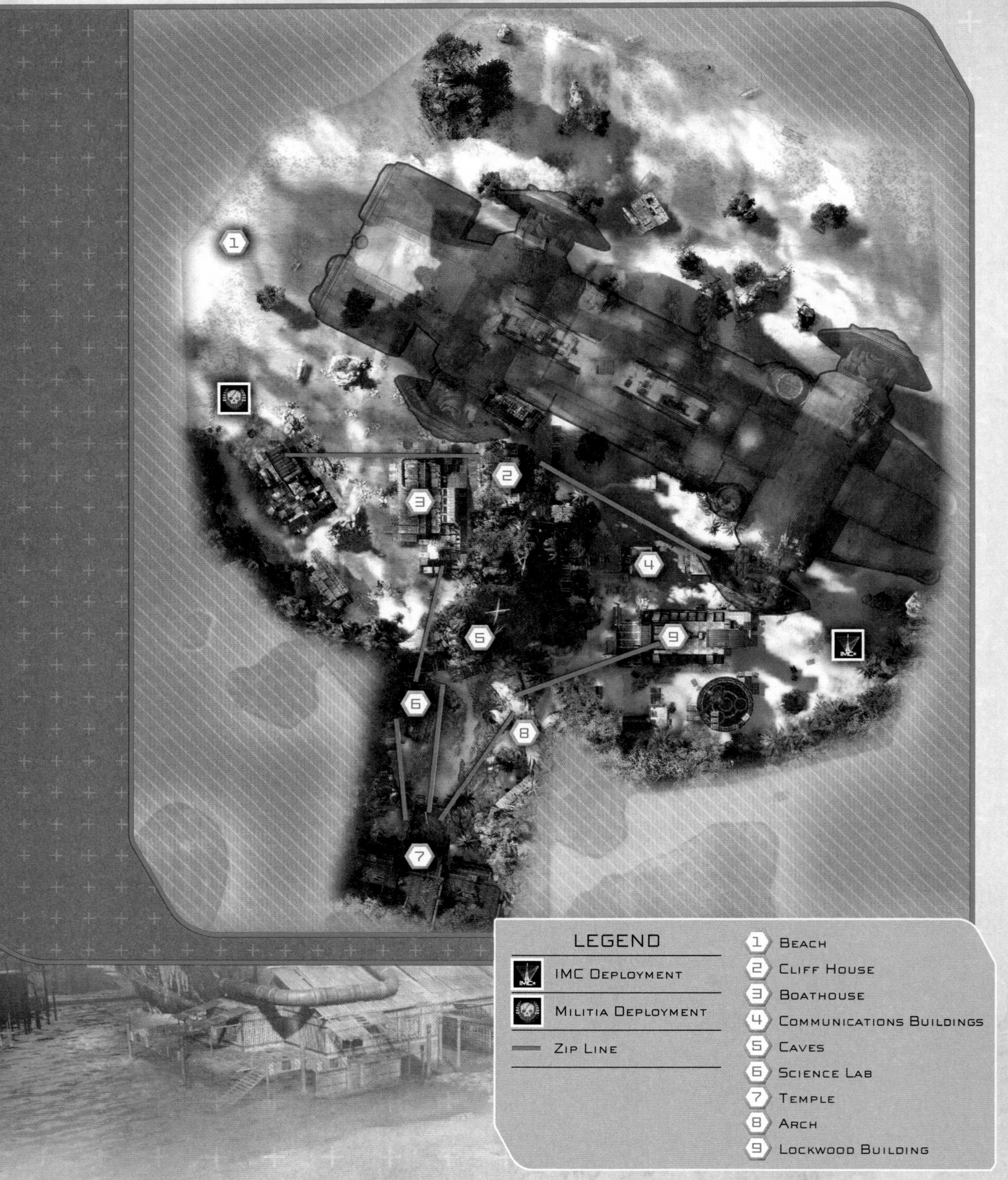

TACTICS

- A power position for Titans will be around the Lockwood Building area. This area has many buildings and structures to use for cover and to bait the enemy Titans into. From the back of the Lockwood Building you can patrol back and forth and have views towards the Arch, Beach, and Bungalows. You'll need to communicate with your team where you see enemy Titans moving too. Also, keep a lookout for enemy Titans trying to flank behind you from behind the massive battleship parked on the Beach.
- As a Pilot, you don't have too much free and covered space to roam around as a Pilot. Most buildings on the map can be seen inside by a Titan. On this map, you'll want to stay focused on keeping your Titan alive and not leaving your Titan in Auto-Titan.
- The long open areas on this map make the Plasma Railgun very useful. With this weapon you can deal massive damage on enemy Titans from long range. If you hit the enemy Titan on a weak spot with the Plasma Railgun, it will nearly destroy the enemy Titan.
- A great position to play a bit more passive on the map is on the Beach. Here you'll find many rocks protruding from the ground to use as cover so you can peek shoot enemy Titans. This works really well if your team is down Titans and trying to even out the Titan count.

PRO TIP: STRONGSIDE

This map has some extremely open areas, especially the Beach. If you know an enemy Pilot has Cloak and is coming for your Titan, stop moving for a few seconds and look for a blur on your screen. You must be completely still for this to work. Although Cloak makes it hard to see an enemy Pilot, it isn't impossible. When you stand still, the pixels on your screen stop changing. The pixels will change once a cloaked enemy Pilot passes through your view. Then you can move, but stay focused on the blur to kill the enemy Pilot.

PILOT HUNTER

1
2
3
4
5
6
7
8
9
LEGEND
IMC Deployment
Militia Deployment
Zip Line
Evac Point
1 Beach
2 Cliff House
3 Boathouse
4 Communications Buildings
5 Caves
6 Science Lab
7 Temple
8 Arch
9 Lockwood Building

TACTICS

Reference these videos in your free mobile friendly eGuide.

› This map is an extremely open map and will be great for sniper rifles. While using the sniper rifle, equip the Tactical Ability Cloak to keep yourself somewhat hidden from enemy Pilots.

PRO TIP: WALSHY

While using the Longbow-DMR Sniper, wall jump to this location above the Science Lab and you'll have an overview of the Bungalows area and the Arch area. This is a great position to cover your teammates and pick off enemy Pilots spawning near the Beach and Bungalows.

PRO TIP: STRONGSIDE

The Cliff House is a great position to hold during the match, since you're able to move quickly to either side of the map to assist your team. The Cliff House also has a complete overview of the Bungalows and the walkways around the Cliff House. If you wall jump up the side of the Cliff House, you'll find a opening where you can move around on top of the roof. Enemy Pilots don't often look up here, so you'll be able to get a few easy kills on the enemy Pilots traveling through the Cliff House area.

› As a Titan, you'll want to patrol the ramps leading up to the Cliff House and keep a eye out for enemy Pilots sneaking through the Caves. These are the two central areas of the map and the most traveled by Pilots. Watch for action happening with your teammates so you are able to assist them with your Titan in any battles they are fighting. A Titan is always a safe bet up against an enemy Pilot. Also, be sure to equip Cloak to your Pilot loadout so you can easily escape once you eject from your Titan.

PRO TIP: FLAMESWORD

A great location to patrol are the wooden ramps that lead to the Cliff House. The wooden ramps near the Lockwood Building are super useful when trying to escape enemy Pilots. Jump off the little plank and catch the cliff wall. From here, quickly jump to the panel in front of the Lockwood Building, and then to the next panel. At the end of the next panel, double jump towards the Arch. This jump provides another option to the Arch without taking the zip line from the Lockwood Building.

› If the other team has the upper hand due to having more Titans out in play, think about slowing the game down and heading inside the Lockwood Building. From within you can still pick off minions through the windows while using your Anti-Titan weapons to damage the enemy Titans. The building provides great cover, forcing the enemy Pilots to disembark their Titans and come inside to fight you. Take this to your advantage and eliminate them as they enter.

NEXUS

Long suspected by the IMC to be a hideaway for Militia personnel, this backwater outpost on the planet Harmony provides substantial contributions to the Frontier's agricultural needs. Two docking stations provide refueling to small ships in the Freeport system. The large fields provide long sight lines favoring long-range Titan weapons, while the settlement in the center gives Pilots many wall run routes and opportunities for cover.

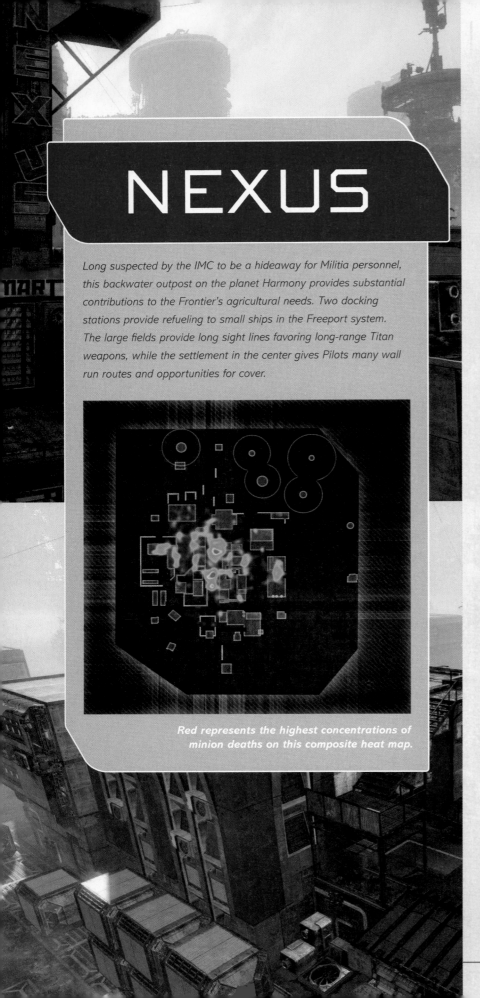

Red represents the highest concentrations of minion deaths on this composite heat map.

KEY LANDMARKS

OFFICE BUILDING

UP MART

TIFFANY'S COFFEE

FARMER'S MARKET

MARVIN'S PLACE

ZIP-LINE TOWER

MAP OVERVIEW

The zip lines across the perimeter of this map all lead to the Zip-line Tower allow you to travel to the center of the map extremely fast. The many buildings allow you to be extremely sneaky and wall jump throughout the entire match.

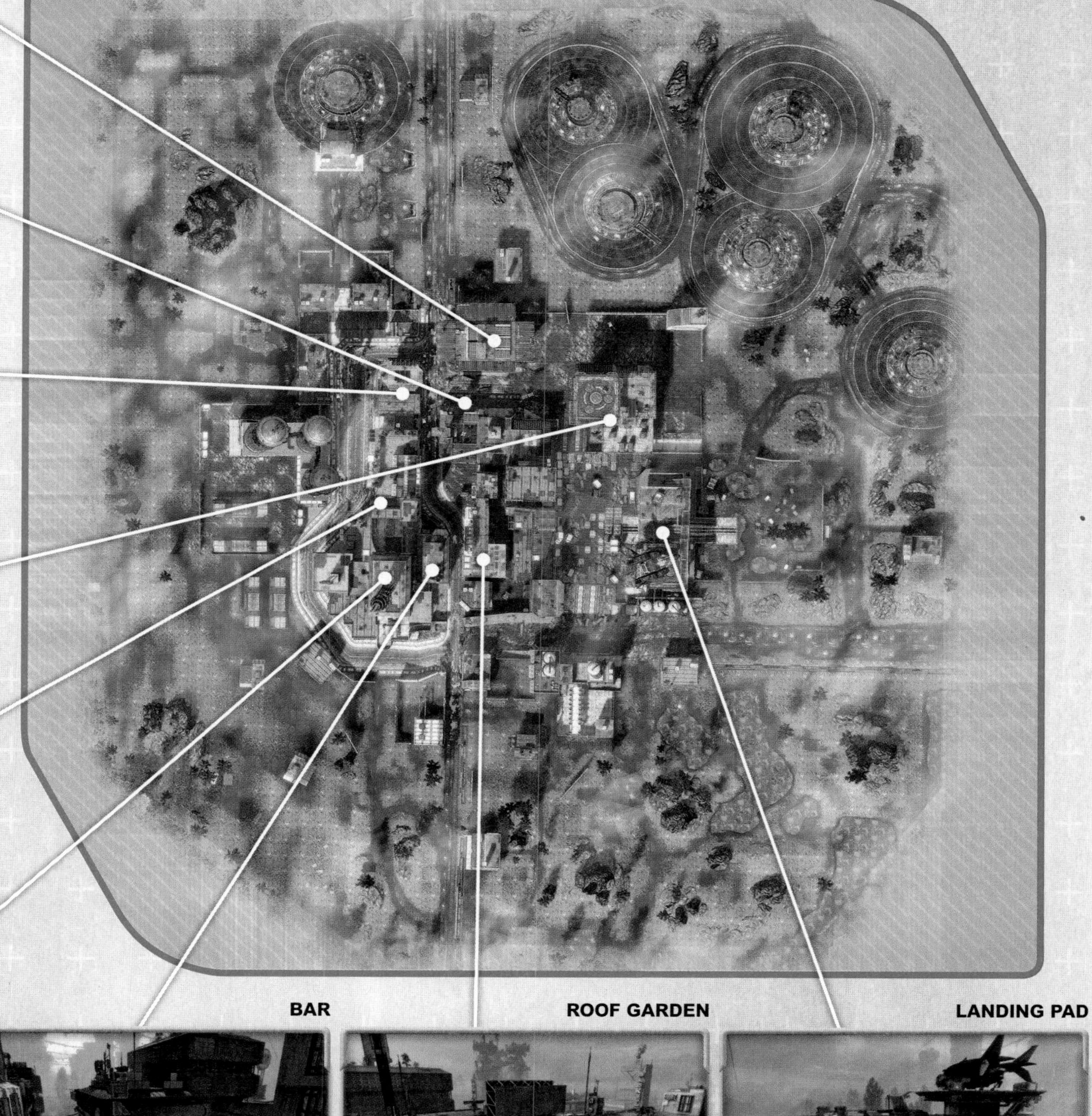

BAR

ROOF GARDEN

LANDING PAD

ATTRITION

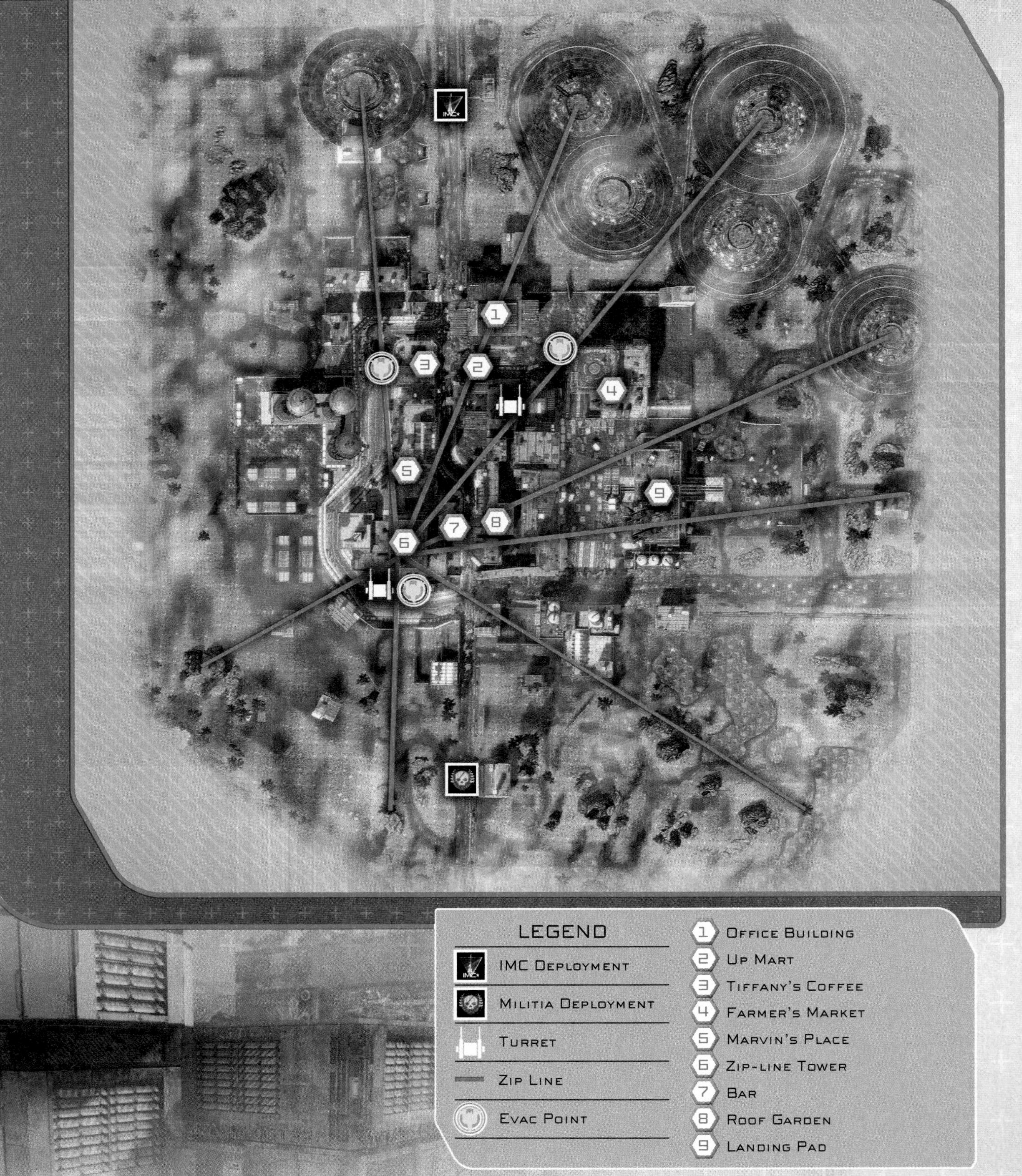
1
2
3
4
5
6
7
8
9
LEGEND
IMC Deployment
Militia Deployment
Turret
Zip Line
Evac Point
1 Office Building
2 Up Mart
3 Tiffany's Coffee
4 Farmer's Market
5 Marvin's Place
6 Zip-line Tower
7 Bar
8 Roof Garden
9 Landing Pad

TACTICS

- This game will be a battle for rooftop control surrounding the center of the map. This map provides all kinds of gameplay, from running rooftop to rooftop to playing stealthy traveling through the alleyways. The alleyways provide a great escape route and some incredible wall jumping.
- At the start of the game, the minions gravitate to the center of the map and battle one another in between the Up Mart and Roof Garden building. Head this way to get early points that will reduce your build time for Titanfall, but watch out for enemy Pilots moving towards the center of the map as well. Sometimes use the minions as bait to locate an enemy Pilot.

PRO TIP: STRONGSIDE

At the start of the match, take a zip line to the center of the map to get into the action much quicker. This will allow you to set up and prepare for enemy Pilots approaching. If you equip a sniper rifle to your loadout, once you reach the center of the map look towards the enemy's spawn to pick off a few enemy Pilots. You can also land on the Zip-line Tower and snipe enemies down below on the rooftops.

PRO TIP: FLAMESWORD

Hang around the turret near the Office Building. A Pilot will encounter a ton of minions in the middle street, between Up Mart and the Office Building. It is wise to activate the turret. The turret's kills count toward your score, allowing you to find enemy Pilots or minions that are elsewhere and watch your score quickly move up.

- Titans are capable of dominating this game. Having the Icepick equipped to your Tier 2 Kit will come in handy when activating or hacking the two turrets on the map. These turrets inflict additional damage to enemy Titans.

CAPTURE THE FLAG

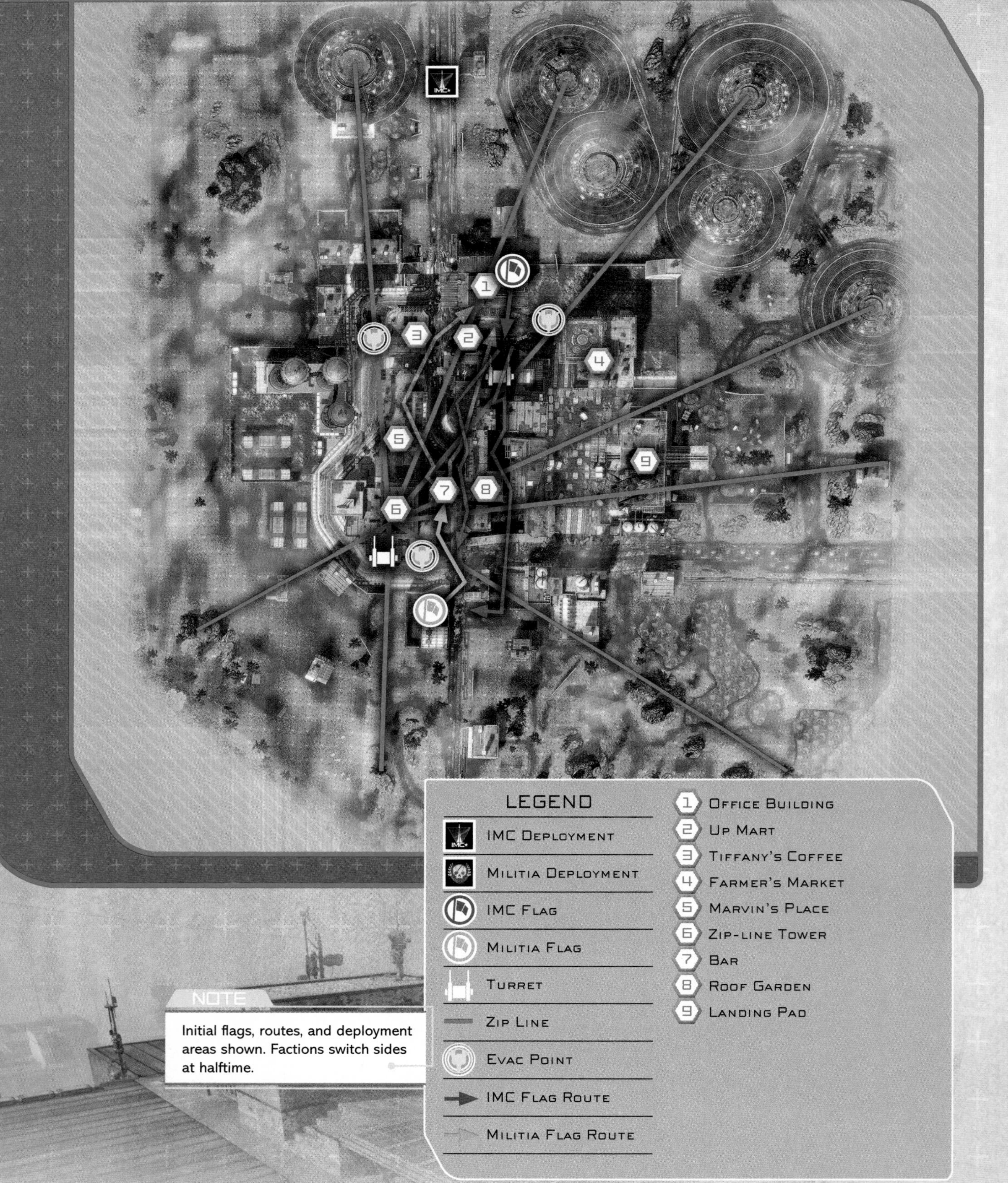

NOTE

Initial flags, routes, and deployment areas shown. Factions switch sides at halftime.

TACTICS

Reference these videos in your free mobile friendly eGuide.

- When defending the flag located in the Office Building, a player with the EVA-8 Shotgun will prove to be very effective. Take up a corner and defend the objective. Wall hanging is very useful inside. If you kill an enemy Pilot, be sure to mix up your spots from crouching in a corner to wall hanging.
- The flag on the Militia's first initial spawn side is located in an open area, so sitting near the flag is less effective. Instead, be sure to plant Arc Mines around the objective to weaken or kill enemy Pilots who try to grab your flag. Placing two Arc Mines will kill a incoming enemy Pilot. Defend this Militia flag by keeping your distance and killing incoming enemy Pilots.
- Once you grab the flag in the Office Building, get off the street as quickly as you can. Immediately use the building's doorway exit facing the Up Mart to gain momentum to make it into the Up Mart. From there, you have many paths to take to capture the flag.
- Running the flag as a Pilot down the middle isn't always the safest route, but it is definitely the quickest route when a Titan isn't available. When you grab the flag in the open area, to quickly make it to the Bar you need to exit and jump on the wall of the building to pick up speed. From here, double jump at the end to make it to the Bar. You can continue wall running or enter the Bar. Entering the Bar lets your teammates spot out the enemies so you can pick the safest path to run the flag.

PRO TIP: WALSHY

As you get closer to capturing the flag, be sure to check the corners around your base for enemy Pilots hiding with close-quarter weapons or have a teammate run into your base first to scan the area. Nothing is worse than making it right to your base and dying because an enemy was able to sneak by. This is important when capturing inside the Office Building. Enemy Pilots can be waiting inside, so throw grenades or send teammates in first to make sure it is clear.

- Overall, controlling the rooftops will be the key to success. Once you gain control, you can rain fire from above. Pilots can easily get into a rhythm and pick off opposing players as they try to jump to the top of a building. Having the height advantage allows your team to move freely around the map.

HARDPOINT DOMINATION

LEGEND
IMC Deployment
Militia Deployment
Hardpoint A
Hardpoint B
Hardpoint C
Turret
Zip Line
Evac Point
1 Office Building
2 Up Mart
3 Tiffany's Coffee
4 Farmer's Market
5 Marvin's Place
6 Zip-line Tower
7 Bar
8 Roof Garden
9 Landing Pad

TACTICS

- Hardpoint A is located within the Landing Pad and promotes close-quarter combat. Once your team has control, have a Pilot loadout that consists of either an SMG or shotgun. You will rack up on defense points as you defend the objective.
- Hardpoint A is the only point that can be captured by a Titan. If your team has fewer Titans, avoid this point until you get a Titan. Controlling this objective with Hardpoint B is the best strategy to victory.

PRO TIP: FLAMESWORD

Equip your Pilot with a sniper and scale the Farmer's Market. Up here you will be able to spot enemies coming from the Militia's main spawn and going for Hardpoint A while still being able to defend Hardpoint B. Paired with Cloak, a Pilot will be able to pick off many enemies.

- Off the initial spawn for both teams, wall run off the short walls that are along the dirt path. These will speed you up, allowing you to reach Hardpoint B faster than you would by just running.

PRO TIP: WALSHY

The grated platform above Hardpoint C is the most important area to hold to keep this capture point. Using Active Radar Pulse, you can pick off enemy Pilots, hide from enemy Titans, and even capture this point.

- Turrets provide all the extra defense you can ask for, so activate them every chance you can. This becomes very helpful once the other team starts calling down Titans. Titans can easily turn the tide of the battle, so you will want all the extra firepower you can get to deal some damage on the enemy Titans and Pilots.

Reference these videos in your free mobile friendly eGuide.

LAST TITAN STANDING

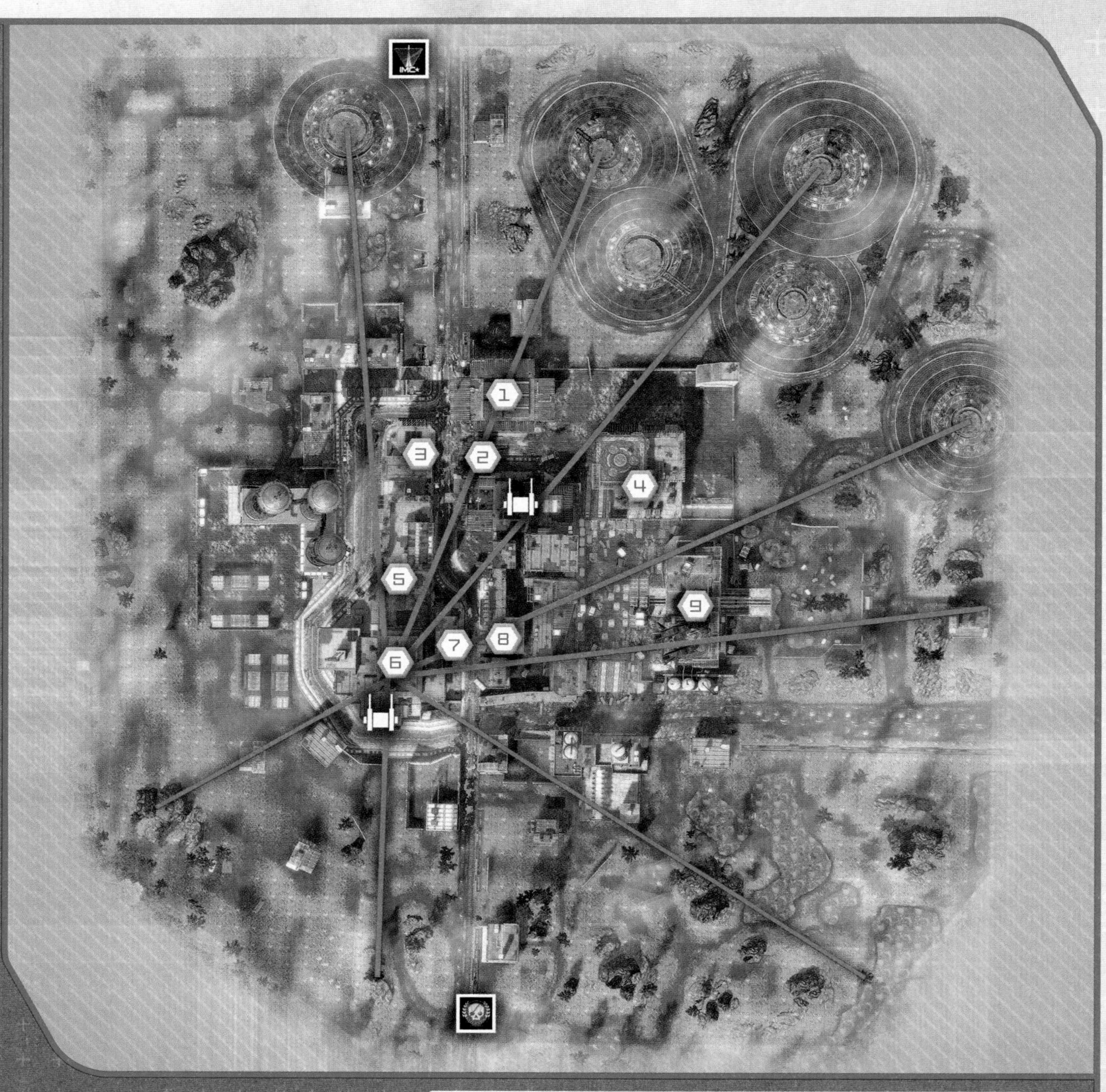

LEGEND

IMC Deployment

Militia Deployment

Turret

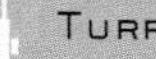

Zip Line

1. Office Building
2. Up Mart
3. Tiffany's Coffee
4. Farmer's Market
5. Marvin's Place
6. Zip-line Tower
7. Bar
8. Roof Garden
9. Landing Pad

TACTICS

PRO TIP: STRONGSIDE

When playing this game mode, equip the Spitfire LMG to your Primary Weapon Pilot loadout and equip the Slammer MOD. This can destroy an enemy Titan extremely fast when you rodeo attack the enemy. Equip the Tactical Ability Cloak as well to better your chances at getting near an enemy Titan. A good time to rodeo attack an enemy Titan is when there is a lot of action happening (so the enemy Titan's teammates won't notice as fast) or when an enemy Titan is moving around solo.

- Nexus is built for multiple Titan battles spread throughout the entire map. Teams will want to have some control of the center of the map. A Stryder can dash to the center off the start of the match to scout out the other team—have a Vortex Shield to stop incoming fire. Quickly retreat after seeing what the other team is doing and communicate the enemy's actions to your team.
- Equipping an 40mm Cannon, Plasma Railgun, or XO-16 Chaingun gives you the range to damage enemy Titans from a distance. Use the outskirts and cover around the Landing Pad to get good angles on the opposing team. Damaging enemy Titans from a distance will keep you safe and allow you to choose when you want to commit to a battle.

PRO TIP: FLAMESWORD

Group pushes are the key to success when playing Last Titan Standing. A good push off the start is sending four Titans down the street near Marvin's Place while having an Ogre Titan or two head through the middle of the map. These Ogre Titans can take a lot of damage, allowing the group of Titans to flank successfully. Once these four Titans have flanked, the two Ogre Titans should aggress forward and assist the flanking Titans.

- The Triple Threat equipped with the Mine Field MOD allows you to keep enemy Titans from pushing through the streets of the city. The Triple Threat is a great primary weapon to stop the opposing team from pushing down the middle of the city without being massively damaged.
- Off the start of the game, take your Titan near the turret close to your spawn. Disembark the Titan and quickly hack the turret. The turret can shoot enemy Titans, which will give away their position. This allows you to push up with your team and deal more damage to an enemy Titan to gain control.
- The Charge Rifle is a great Anti-Titan weapon to have equipped due to its long-range fire. Once your Titan is destroyed, escape to the many rooftops and buildings on the map. This will provide you great angles to charge up your Anti-Titan weapon and damage enemy Titans from a distance.

PILOT HUNTER

LEGEND
IMC Deployment
Militia Deployment
Turret
Zip Line
Evac Point
1 Office Building
2 Up Mart
3 Tiffany's Coffee
4 Farmer's Market
5 Marvin's Place
6 Zip-line Tower
7 Bar
8 Roof Garden
9 Landing Pad

TACTICS

- Pilots will want to control the rooftops throughout the entire game. The height advantage provides better lines of sight and cover when ground enemies shoot at you.
- A sniper positioned at the top of the Zip-line Tower can communicate the position of enemy Pilots. Even though you may be an easy target, there are many zip lines to take to escape. Once you feel it is safe, just zip back up and keep annoying the enemy.
- Early in the start of the game, enemy Pilots will go for the minions that gravitate to the center of the map. A Pilot can either flank the enemy here or sit back from a distance and pick off the minions with a sniper rifle to reduce build time.
- Fighting around turrets provides great cover. A Pilot can successfully pressure enemies and then retreat behind the turret to recover health. While you are recovering health, if you notice your turret shooting in the direction of the enemy, be prepared—that enemy might be charging you or stuck behind cover. Using Stim as your Tactical Ability also allows you to recover your health quicker once you get cover behind a structure. Then if you need to charge or run away, you have a speed boost for a short moment.
- Running around with the Tactical Ability Cloak and a shotgun as your primary weapon will help you rack up kills while moving and sneaking around the map. You usually want to take advantage of your Pilot's movement by wall jumping and running, but this map has many buildings that are connected to one another. Run into these while you wait for your Cloak to recharge. Enemies who chase after you will lose in close quarters because of your shotgun.

PRO TIP: WALSHY

Activate a turret and place Arc Mines around the turret's control panel. Enemy Pilots will make their way to the turret at some point and try to hack the turret. This will be an easy free kill.

NEXUS

OUTPOST 207

Outpost 207 is one of dozens of IMC outposts built at high altitude on a mountainous moon. The outposts' massive railguns are linked together in a defensive array to protect a nearby IMC space shipyard. Titans have three main routes: the rocky terrain in the center, the bridge at the rear of the facility, and the service route that runs through the base of the cannon. Pilots are advised to control the second floors of the Armory and Cannon Building, and to stay away from the bridge below the gondola lines, where there is little cover to protect them from Titans.

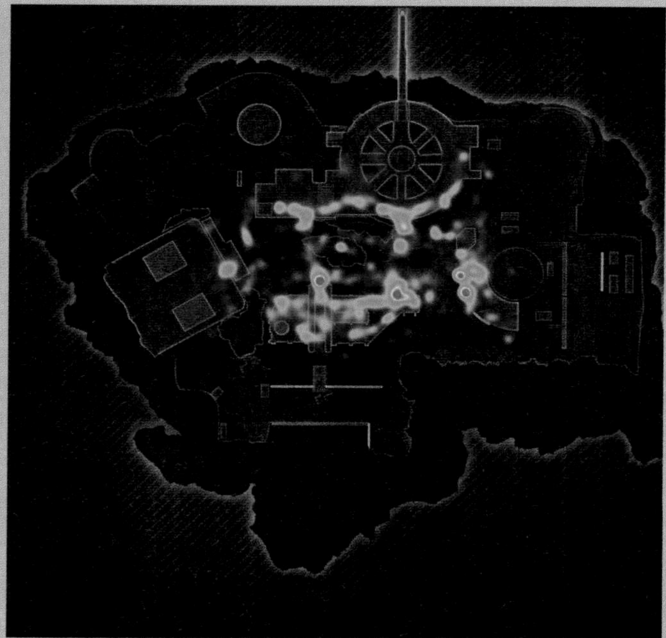

Red represents the highest concentrations of minion deaths on this composite heat map.

KEY LANDMARKS

TURRET

CANNON BUILDING

CANNON CONTROL BUILDING

GORGE

FACTORY

DELIVERY BUILDING

MAP OVERVIEW

This map may be one of the smallest of the maps, but it still both provides close-quarter combat play inside the buildings and long-range sniper play from the Observatory to the Factory.

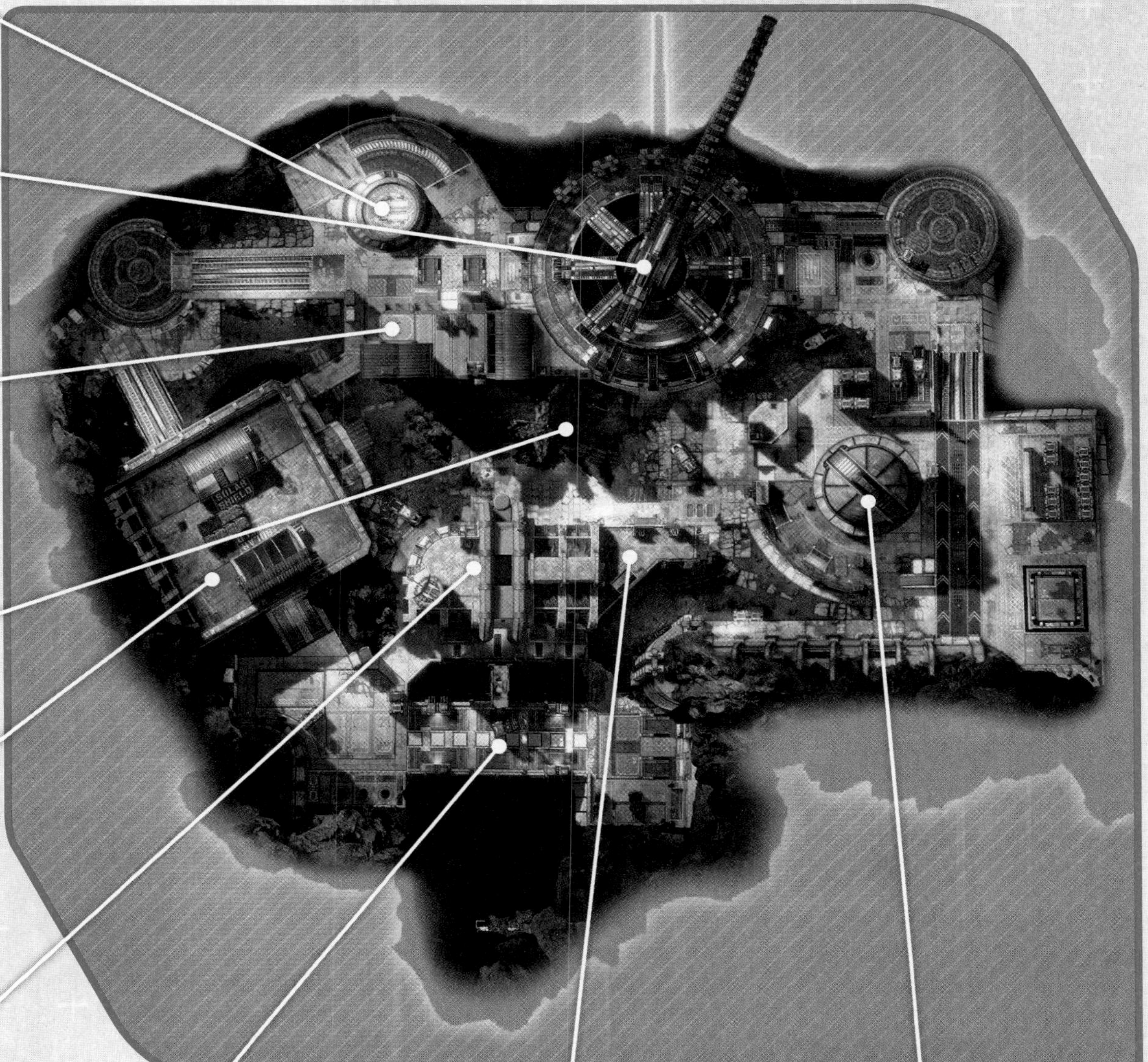

BRIDGE

ARMORY

OBSERVATORY

ATTRITION

LEGEND
IMC Deployment
Militia Deployment
Turret
Zip Line
Evac Point
1 Turret
2 Cannon Building
3 Cannon Control Building
4 Gorge
5 Factory
6 Delivery Building
7 Bridge
8 Armory
9 Observatory
IMC ARMORY 207

TACTICS

Reference these videos in your free mobile friendly eGuide.

- An initial battle between both teams' minions occurs in the Gorge and continues throughout the game. Pilots can position themselves on the Observatory to pick off a few of the minions. Equipping a long-range weapon will give you the opportunity to pick off an enemy Pilot near the Factory at the start.
- From the Cannon Building, you can pick up minion kills from the center of the map. Keep an eye on the main bubble window of the Armory to pick off enemy Pilots doing the same.
- A great jump to use off the start of the IMC spawn is to wall run off the Cannon Control Room. At the end of the wall, double jump towards the Factory, wall run once again, and then double jump towards the Delivery Building. This will aid in avoiding enemy snipers off the start of the match and is also a great jump to use throughout the match.

PRO TIP: STRONGSIDE

Patrolling both the inside and rooftops of the Armory and Delivery Building will quickly increase your Attrition score. These buildings have many windows that allow me to hunt minions while changing directions constantly. I prefer to use the R-101C Carbine when doing this so I am able to fight in both short- and long-range fights.

- The Turret is positioned away from most of the battles, but don't turn a blind eye to it. Activate the Turret, and every kill it gets will count towards your score. The kills it gets can determine who wins the match.

PRO TIP: WALSHY

The Gorge can be trouble for your Titan. Instead, use the area around the Observatory. This area will provide cover and let you kill enemy minions and Pilots gravitating to the Gorge. This area also lets you isolate enemy Titans, giving you the upper hand when fighting a Titan head on.

- Equip the Triple Threat to your Titan and bombard your enemies. This weapon's splash damage will make enemy Pilots think twice about just rushing your Titan in hopes of a rodeo attack.

CAPTURE THE FLAG

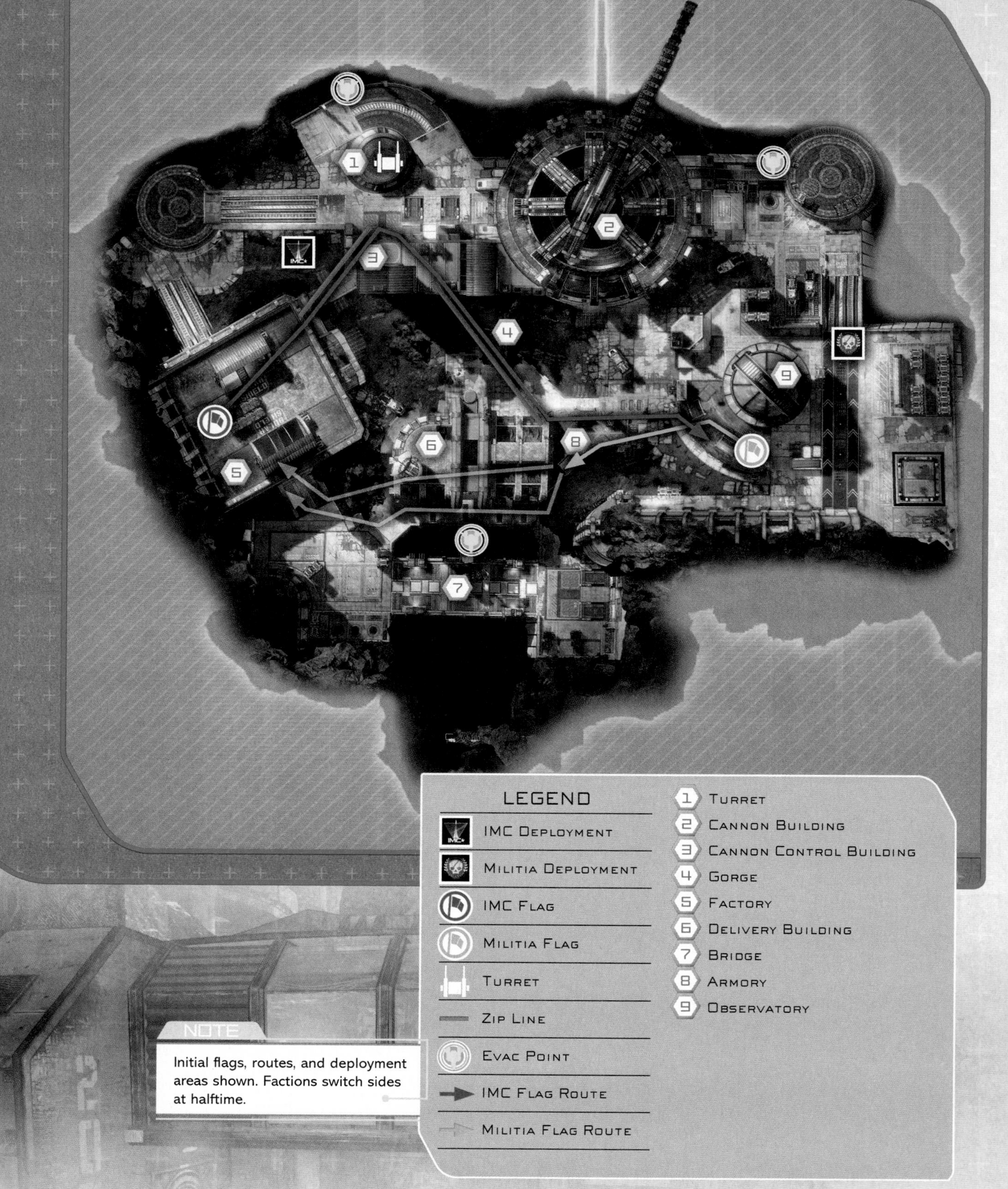

NOTE

Initial flags, routes, and deployment areas shown. Factions switch sides at halftime.

TACTICS

Reference these videos in your free mobile friendly eGuide.

- The Factory is the initial location for one of the flags. A Pilot can equip a sniper rifle of their choice and head to the rooftop of the Factory to snipe for the entire round and defend the base.
- To become the most versatile defender, the R-101C Carbine will be your best bet. Your Pilot will be able to pick off enemies at a distance and rain fire through the windows on top of the Factory to stop enemy Pilots.
- The other flag is positioned inside the Observatory and is much more exposed with the amount of entrances the building has. There are two openings from above, two windows, and a staircase from the bottom of the Observatory to the flag. Players should scatter Arc Mines around the flag to stop enemies in their tracks.

PRO TIP: WALSHY

When running the flag from the Observatory, be sure that Stim is picked for your Tactical Ability. Grab the flag and then immediately jump to the roof. Activate your Stim and jump all the way across into the Armory—Stim is essential to make this jump. You will want to make it inside so you have more cover, so either continue running through the Armory or jump through the breakable glass above it and go around the Bridge area, which provides more cover at the expense of a longer run.

- A Pilot positioned inside the Cannon Control Room can do serious damage the entire match. This Pilot can shoot through the various windows throughout the Cannon Control Room or head to the upper levels to get better angles. This Pilot can also take out enemy Pilots pursing your teammate with the flag.

Escaping with the flag inside the Factory can be tricky, but use a few wall runs and zip lines to outwit your opponent. Grab the flag and immediately head up the stairs to the upper catwalks. From here, jump onto the wall to the right and make it to the rooftop of the Factory. Across is a zip line that brings you to the Cannon Control Room. This will confuse the other team because it seems like you are going in the wrong direction to capture the flag. Quickly take the next zip line to your right that leads to the top of the Armory. The opponents will be spinning their heads because of the fast movements used. Check your corners and make your way back to your base with the flag.

PRO TIP: FLAMESWORD

Many fights occur inside the Delivery Building because that is the midpoint between both flags. Use this jump when jumping out of the bubble window to get to the roof quickly. Jump out the window and then hold back for your double jump. You will land directly above the bubble window. This can be used to evade pursuers as well.

- A Titan can't directly grab a flag from either base because of where the flag is positioned at the base, but they can be close by to escort a flag carrier back to home base by giving the friendly Pilot a ride on their Titan. The best Titan flag route when grabbing the flag from the Factory is to dash towards the Turret and go through the Cannon Building. Finally make your way to the Observatory.
- Having a Titan sit back and defend your flag base will be crucial. This map is so small that if the enemy gets your flag with a Titan, they are almost sure to get back to their base for a capture. If you have a Titan covering your base, you'll be able to deal some damage to the enemy Titan before the Titan grabs your flag. This will slow the enemy Titan down and possibly make the enemy Titan retreat.

HARDPOINT DOMINATION

LEGEND
IMC Deployment
Militia Deployment
Hardpoint A
Hardpoint B
Hardpoint C
Turret
Zip Line
Evac Point
1 Turret
2 Cannon Building
3 Cannon Control Building
4 Gorge
5 Factory
6 Delivery Building
7 Bridge
8 Armory
9 Observatory

TACTICS

- Hardpoint A is located within the Cannon Building and Titans are free to move in and out of this objective. You'll have a lot of space to move around inside the Cannon Building, so never stay in one position too long, as enemy Pilots are sure to be running around on the upper level of this building.
- Hardpoint C can also be captured and contested by a Titan. There are many catwalks within the Factory where Hardpoint C lies. Pilots need to run on them and coordinate an attack on enemy Titans. Bait and switch with teammates or rodeo attack every time an opportunity presents itself.

PRO TIP: STRONGSIDE

Titans can control the entire outcome of this game, so knowing how to take on a Titan as a Pilot is critical. You should usually avoid these fights, but they are doable. This map is small enough that you will want Cloak as your Tactical Ability. If you are above an enemy Titan, jump on top to begin a rodeo attack on it. Once the enemy Pilot disembarks, activate your Cloak so you briefly vanish and take them out. If the enemy Titan has spotted you, draw it near cover so you can Cloak and start a possible run to rodeo attack the Titan.

- At Hardpoint A, sit on top of the bottom structure that holds the cannon to hide from enemies. You can use various areas to stand on and hide. Stay close to the back side of the cannon, so if an enemy Titan engages you, you'll be able to wall jump to the upper level to take cover.
- Hardpoint B cannot be accessed or seen by Titans. This makes it an extremely valuable hardpoint to control throughout the game as there may be times you have fewer Titans than the opposing team. This is a great location to capture and contest the flag if needed. Cover is provided and you could always lock your aim on the front doors. If you see the objective is contested then you know the enemy entered through another entrance.
- If your team has the higher Titan count then controlling both Hardpoints A and C is the safest bet. With how easily Titans can move in and out of these objectives, your team will easily win the game. Once these hardpoints are captured, keep your Titans patrolling back and forth by the Turret. Once you see the objectives are being lost, dash back inside and hunt the enemies down while contesting the hardpoint.
- If you are controlling Hardpoint B, then be sure to use the zip line that leads to the Cannon Control Room. From here you can sneak to the Turret and hack it. The Turret will assist you and help delay enemy Titans so you and your team can capture one of the enemy's objectives.

LAST TITAN STANDING

LEGEND

	IMC Deployment
	Militia Deployment
	Turret
	Zip Line
	Evac Point

1. Turret
2. Cannon Building
3. Cannon Control Building
4. Gorge
5. Factory
6. Delivery Building
7. Bridge
8. Armory
9. Observatory

PRO TIP: FLAMESWORD

An Atlas can do some serious damage on this map once its Core Ability is ready for use—the Damage Core will allow you to inflict much more damage. When this is activated, you can make light work of two enemy Titans if you have the XO-16 Chaingun with the Accelerator MOD or the 40mm Cannon equipped. These paired with the Particle Wall ability allow you to evade damage and destroy the opposing team.

TACTICS

- This map is one of the smallest ones for Last Titan Standing, so you'll really want to stick together with your friendly Titans and not run off on your own. Many of the Titan battles will be within close quarters, making it feel like a Titan boxing match.
- Because of how small the map is, players can choose to use the Ogre Titan the entire match. The Stryder isn't super effective because there isn't a lot of real estate to dash around, so don't have too many of these Titans on your team.

PRO TIP: WALSHY

Most battles throughout the match consist of close-quarter combat, so be sure to equip Big Punch to your Titan's Tier 2 Kit. This will come in handy when you engage enemy titans inside the Factory or Cannon Building.

- When you spawn next to the Factory, be sure to head towards the Turret, disembark your Titan, and quickly activate the Turret. With the Turret activated, stay around this area so it can provide cover fire and aid you in taking down enemy Titans.

- The Cluster Missile is a great Ordnance for this map. Titans are constantly being forced inside the Factory and Cannon Building and get trapped in the Gorge. This allows you to shoot the Cluster Missile behind the enemy Titan near a doorway or structure that will cut off their path to retreat. This forces the enemy Titan towards you, so you can easily finish the enemy Titan off. You can also shoot the Cluster Missile in front of the enemy Titan to force it backwards so you can retreat to get your shields back or wait for a teammate to assist you.

PILOT HUNTER

TACTICS

› The Observatory is a great location to set up shop and snipe from. The dome provides you with enough cover to snipe from but avoid danger. You can pick off an enemy Pilot or two near the Factory at the start of the game before being noticed.

PRO TIP: FLAMESWORD

Control the Armory with the Observatory. If you see a teammate is sniping, start patrolling the area around the Armory. You will be able to pick off weak Pilots and call out anyone flanking your sniper. Vice versa if you are sniping: be sure to call out the locations of enemy Pilots and which ones you have weakened.

PRO TIP: STRONGSIDE

When you are in the Armory and fighting enemy Pilots at the Cannon Building, don't be predictable by always shooting from the same location. Switch windows after every engagement to throw the enemy off.

› The rooftop of the Factory is an incredible spot to be with the G2A4 Rifle or a sniper of your choice. A Pilot is provided with an incredible line of sight across the map. Pick off the minions in the middle and keep an eye to your right towards the Delivery Building for enemy Pilots.

› A player equipped with Active Radar Pulse as a Tactical Ability and a shotgun is super effective inside the Cannon Control Room and Cannon Building. This Pilot should use the ability every chance possible to spot enemies nearby. Enemy Pilots will be caught off guard as close-quarter combat dominates these two locations.

› Be aware that you can go around the top of the Cannon Building. This is an effective route because you can check the Observatory without revealing yourself too much. This allows you to spot an enemy sniper and take them out by surprise.

› The center of the map becomes congested with many enemies throughout the game. A Titan can sweep through the area to reduce its Core Ability time and pick off an enemy Pilot here and there. Don't stay focused on one enemy too long. There are rocks that make it hard to dash out. Always have an escape route ready to keep your Titan alive.

OVERLOOK

The IMC refueling and rearming facilities here date back to the early days of the Frontier conflict. Later, needing more space for prisoners of war, the IMC converted these facilities into makeshift prisons using modular container cells. Pilots are advised to learn the multiple flanking routes snaking throughout the base, while Pilots in the loading dock at the back of the level should exercise extra caution before engaging Titans, as there are precious few places to hide there. However, most of the indoor areas present good attacking opportunities for Pilots who know how to "hit and fade" against unsuspecting Titans.

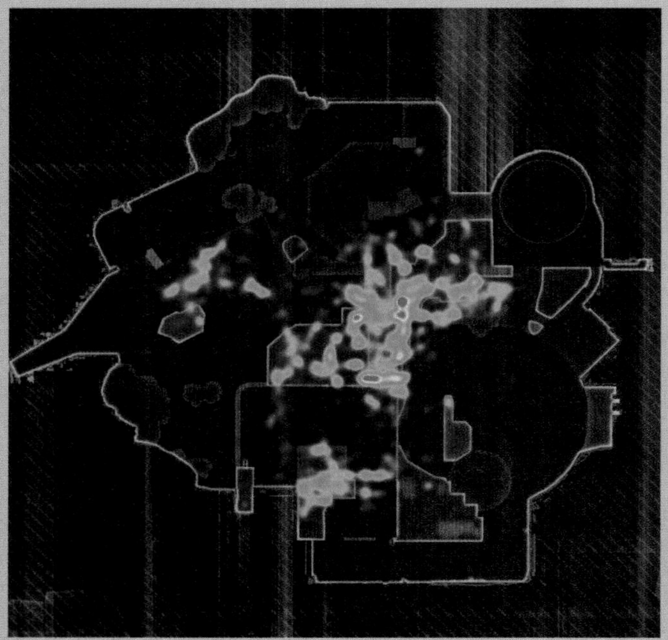

Red represents the highest concentrations of minion deaths on this composite heat map.

KEY LANDMARKS

V.O.T.L.

DRAINAGE CONTROL

GARAGE

CONTROL ROOM

WALKWAY

HANGAR

MAP OVERVIEW

THIS MAP HAS MANY CLOSE-QUARTER AREAS, BUT DON'T GET CAUGHT ON THE INSIDE OF THE MAP TOO MUCH. USE THE ZIP LINES AROUND THE PERIMETER TO GET A SURPRISE FLANK ON THE ENEMY TEAM.

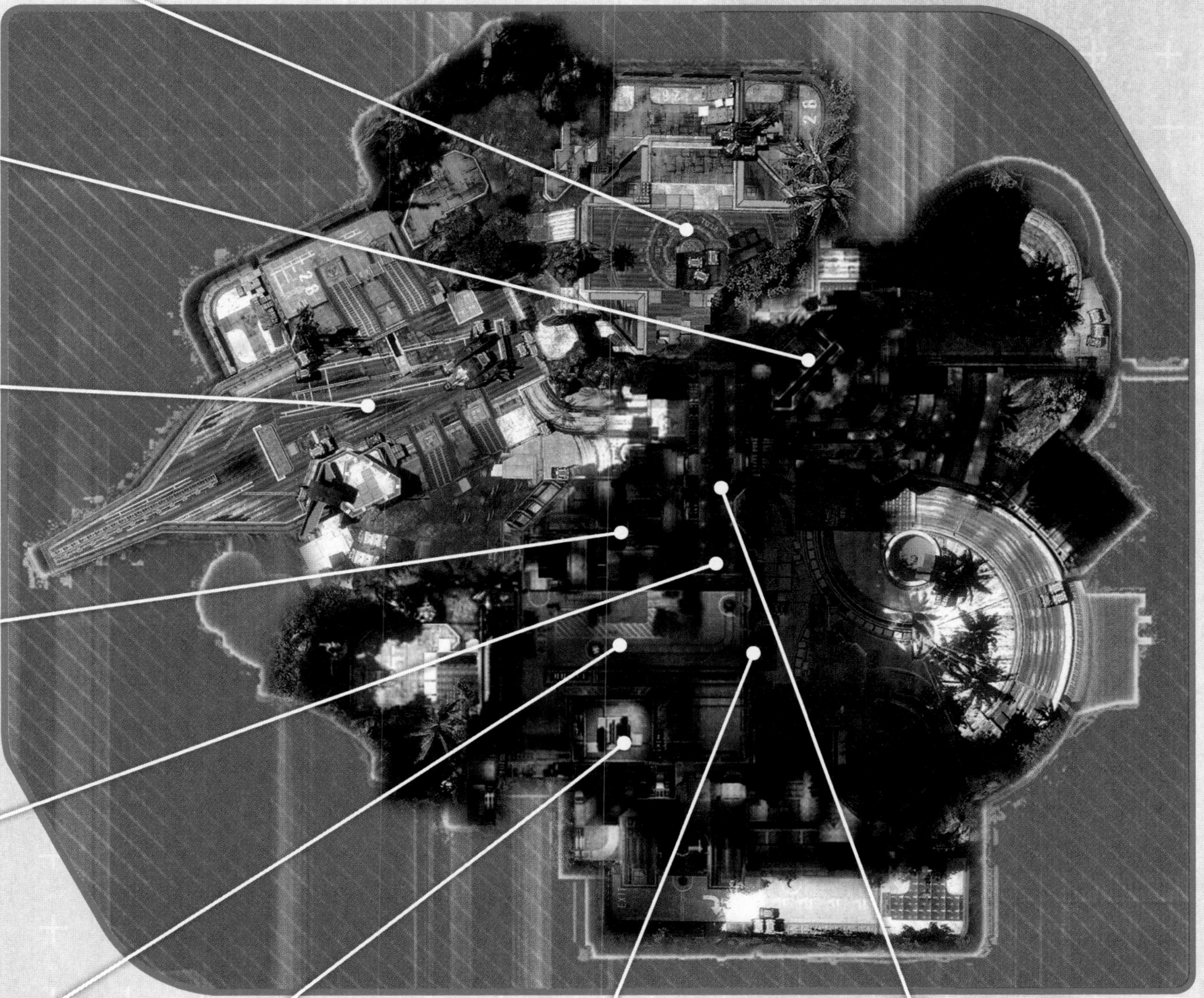

LAIR

CATWALK

STREET

ATTRITION

LEGEND

- IMC Deployment
- Militia Deployment
- Zip Line
- Evac Point

1. V.O.T.L.
2. Drainage Control
3. Garage
4. Control Room
5. Walkway
6. Hangar
7. Lair
8. Catwalk
9. Street

TACTICS

- Pilots will enjoy patrolling the Drainage Control area. The Street exit leads to minions or locations of enemy Pilots hunting your allied minions. This is a great area to rack up points on the scoreboard.
- This map is fast paced and has many close-quarter battles. There are many ways to flank, so keep moving and always check your back.
- Controlling the Walkway is a sure way to win the match. The Walkway looks out towards the V.T.O.L. where you will find a bunch of minions to score quick and easy points.
- The Hangar has a lot of jumps for you to become familiar with. These jumps help you move freely around the area and enter hot spots easily.
- Titans are safest on the outside perimeter of the map. The center of the map contains two narrow halls that are connected to one another. Apply hit and run tactics—staying in these narrow areas isn't safe as enemy Pilots can easily rodeo your Titan.
- When the enemy has Titans, lure them inside the Hangar or Street, get the high ground on the rafters, and rain down fire with your Sidewinder or Mag Launcher.
- When shooting from the Lair into the Hangar, first check the window of the Control Room so you don't get picked off by an enemy Pilot.

CAPTURE THE FLAG

LEGEND

- IMC Deployment
- Militia Deployment
- IMC Flag
- Militia Flag
- Zip Line
- Evac Point
- IMC Flag Route
- Militia Flag Route

1. V.O.T.L.
2. Drainage Control
3. Garage
4. Control Room
5. Walkway
6. Hangar
7. Lair
8. Catwalk
9. Street

NOTE

Initial flags, routes, and deployment areas shown. Factions switch sides at halftime.

TACTICS

Reference these videos in your free mobile friendly eGuide.

- Both flags are inside structures: one in the Drainage Control area and the other in the Lair. In both cases there are multiple entrances to these areas, making it difficult to wait inside and defend. Instead, hang around the many catwalks surrounding the area to cut off enemies before they enter one of the many entrances.
- Because of how narrow the center of this map is, Titans aren't the most effective way to run flags unless your team has more than the other team. Wall running and jumping are your best course of action.
- When grabbing the flag inside of the Lair, be sure to use this flag route. The flag route combines a few walls to jump off so be sure to get it down as it can lead to an easy capture.
- Gain control of the Walkway when trying to capture the flag inside of the Drainage Control. The Walkway is the perfect middle location between both flags. A player here can suppress enemies that try to come out of the V.T.O.L.
- It is smart to run the flag through the Street when grabbing the flag in Drainage Control. If you get taken out, the flag will be left in the wide open. Allied players will be able to kill enemy Pilots blindly running for the return. If you evade death, use these jumps to easily make it back to your base with the flag.
- A great route to flank and run a flag from either base is by chaining all three zip lines together. Both sides can take advantage of this, so don't miss out. The zip lines allow you to avoid the crazy action occurring between the Street and the Hangar.

HARDPOINT DOMINATION

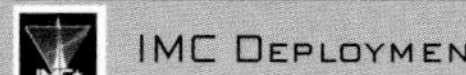

LEGEND

- IMC Deployment
- Militia Deployment
- Hardpoint A
- Hardpoint B
- Hardpoint C
- Zip Line
- Evac Point

1. V.O.T.L.
2. Drainage Control
3. Garage
4. Control Room
5. Walkway
6. Hangar
7. Lair
8. Catwalk
9. Street

TACTICS

- Hardpoint A is isolated inside the Lair and has many entrances from ground and roof level. A Titan can shoot into the Hardpoint, but cannot enter it. Equipping a Cluster Missile to your Titan makes defending this objective a lot easier.
- Capture Hardpoints without revealing your position. East of Hardpoint B is a vent that blows a little bit of smoke. This helps hide you from enemies and lets you look at the two possible areas enemies can attack you.

PRO TIP: STRONGSIDE

A manned Titan can capture a Hardpoint even when enemy Pilots are contesting the Hardpoint. The manned Titan will always trump over enemy Pilots no matter the number as long as there isn't an enemy Titan in the Hardpoint control area. Hardpoint C is completely accessible by a Titan. A Titan can freely move in and out of this area. You can really take advantage of this feature in Hardpoint C.

- All three Hardpoints are a distance away from each other. The two Hardpoints that benefit you the most will be Hardpoints A and C. Both of these objectives allow Titan support, making it difficult for the other team to capture.
- If you do have control of Hardpoints B and C, be aware of the zip lines from the top of Garage that lead towards the V.T.O.L. right outside of Drainage Control. These allow you to travel quickly between the points to better defend them.
- The Catwalk is a great median between Hardpoints A and C. A Pilot can easily patrol this area and pick up kills in both the Hangar and out in the open near Drainage Control.

LAST TITAN STANDING

TACTICS

- The Arc Cannon or XO-16 Chaingun are great primary weapons on this map because you are able to wreck enemy Titans while still being able to pick off the hard-to-hit enemy Pilots ejecting from their Titans.
- With so many corners around this map, Big Punch is an ideal Tier 2 Kit to take advantage of. You can surprise the enemy by dashing up and dealing a powerful melee attack the enemy can't avoid.
- Avoid getting bunched together around the Street area. This is a narrow passage, and if you group up with friendly Titans it becomes harder to escape as you will dash into one another.
- Most areas require you to walk up ramps or dash off ledges to reach lower areas quicker. Take this into consideration so you don't get ambushed as soon as you walk up that ramp.

PRO TIP: WALSHY

Save up your Vortex Shield when battling an enemy Titan. You always want to use your Vortex Shield after your opponent has used theirs. When the opponent thinks they are throwing all your bullets back, activate your Vortex Shield and send those bullets back again.

- Controlling the V.T.O.L. and outside around Drainage Control is a solid setup. This allows teammates to always have an area to retreat towards. Be sure to use your dashes effectively and get behind cover when fired at.

PILOT HUNTER

LEGEND
IMC Deployment
Militia Deployment
Zip Line
Evac Point
1 V.O.T.L.
2 Drainage Control
3 Garage
4 Control Room
5 Walkway
6 Hangar
7 Lair
8 Catwalk
9 Street

TACTICS

Reference these videos in your free mobile friendly eGuide.

PRO TIP: FLAMESWORD

Setting up in the Garage when your team has the lead is a great strategy to slowly take the victory. The Garage only has a few entrances, making it easy for a team to hold down and watch all of them. Be sure to communicate with each other to understand who is watching what and who needs help when the enemy team is charging.

- Players will find that a lot of Pilot fighting happens around the Walkway near the Control Room. Equip Arc Mines for your Ordnance and plant these in the small room between the Walkway and Control Room. This allows you to watch the other direction and only react when you hear the mines go off or see hit markers when the mines do damage.
- Hanging out around the V.T.O.L. area with a sniper is very effective. The sniper can pick off people who cross the Walkway and come out of the Hangar. This sniper can also check to the right to see if enemy Pilots are trying to flank from the Garage area.
- A quick jump helps you get to the Walkway. When playing Attrition, this jump would be less effective because the opposing team would be out on the Walkway killing the minions outside of Drainage Control. Since Pilot Hunter requires you to kill Pilots, enemy Pilots won't expose themselves on the Walkway, letting you sneak into the Control Room.
- When you don't have control of the Control Room, throw in Frag Grenades before assaulting the room. This will clear out anyone with a close-range weapon, and has the chance to explode any Arc Mines that might be waiting to kill you.
- When fighting in Drainage Control, be aware of this escape route. It allows you to reach the top of the Garage quickly by taking the zip lines. Check your back to see if your opponent chases you on the zip line—this will be an easy kill for you.

RELIC

The parts salvaged from this old wreck of the IMC carrier IMS Odyssey are sent into the valley below to construct and maintain the survivors' ad hoc colony. Pilots helping with the salvage operations have created clever wall running routes by hanging pieces of the wreckage between buildings, allowing them to traverse the massive work site quickly. Due to the wreck's central location, several Titans posted up inside the ship's interior can dictate combat flow quite effectively. However, the low-flanking route around the outside of the ship can be used to circumvent this strategy.

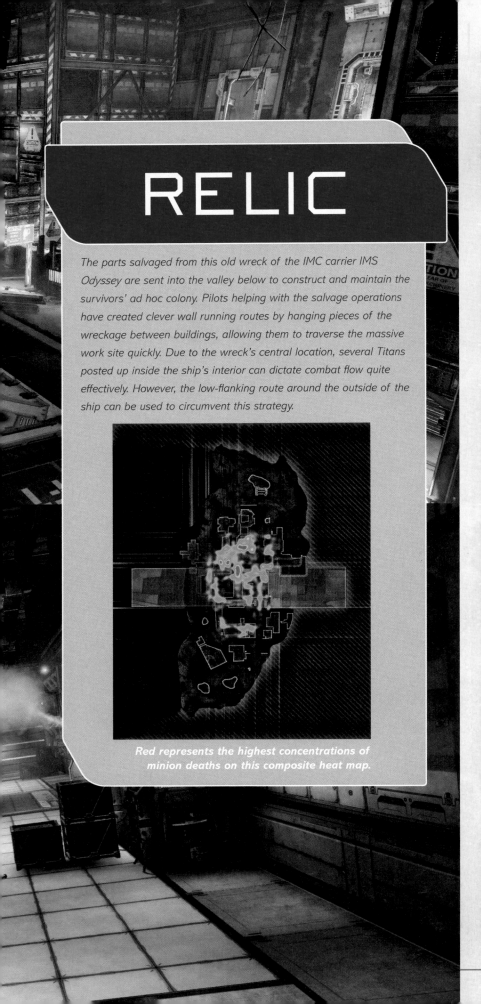

Red represents the highest concentrations of minion deaths on this composite heat map.

KEY LANDMARKS

GENERATOR BUILDING

COMMUNICATION BUILDING

ZIP-LINE BRIDGE

UNDERPASS

MED LAB

YELLOW BRIDGE

MAP OVERVIEW

You'll find out soon that all the action is near or inside the Odyssey. Pilots will find the many walkways and wall runs inside the Odyssey prove extremely useful. Do not get caught sitting in one area too long or you're sure to be killed.

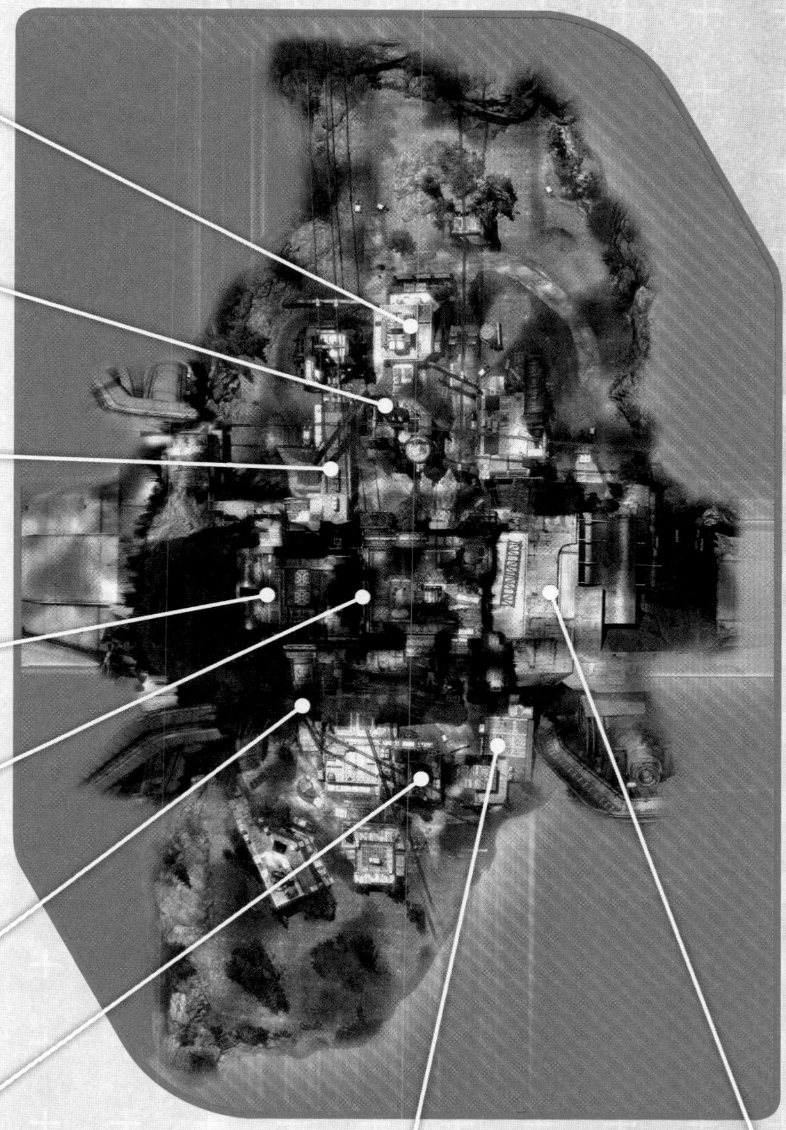

FOREMAN'S OFFICE

LAVATORY

ODYSSEY

ATTRITION

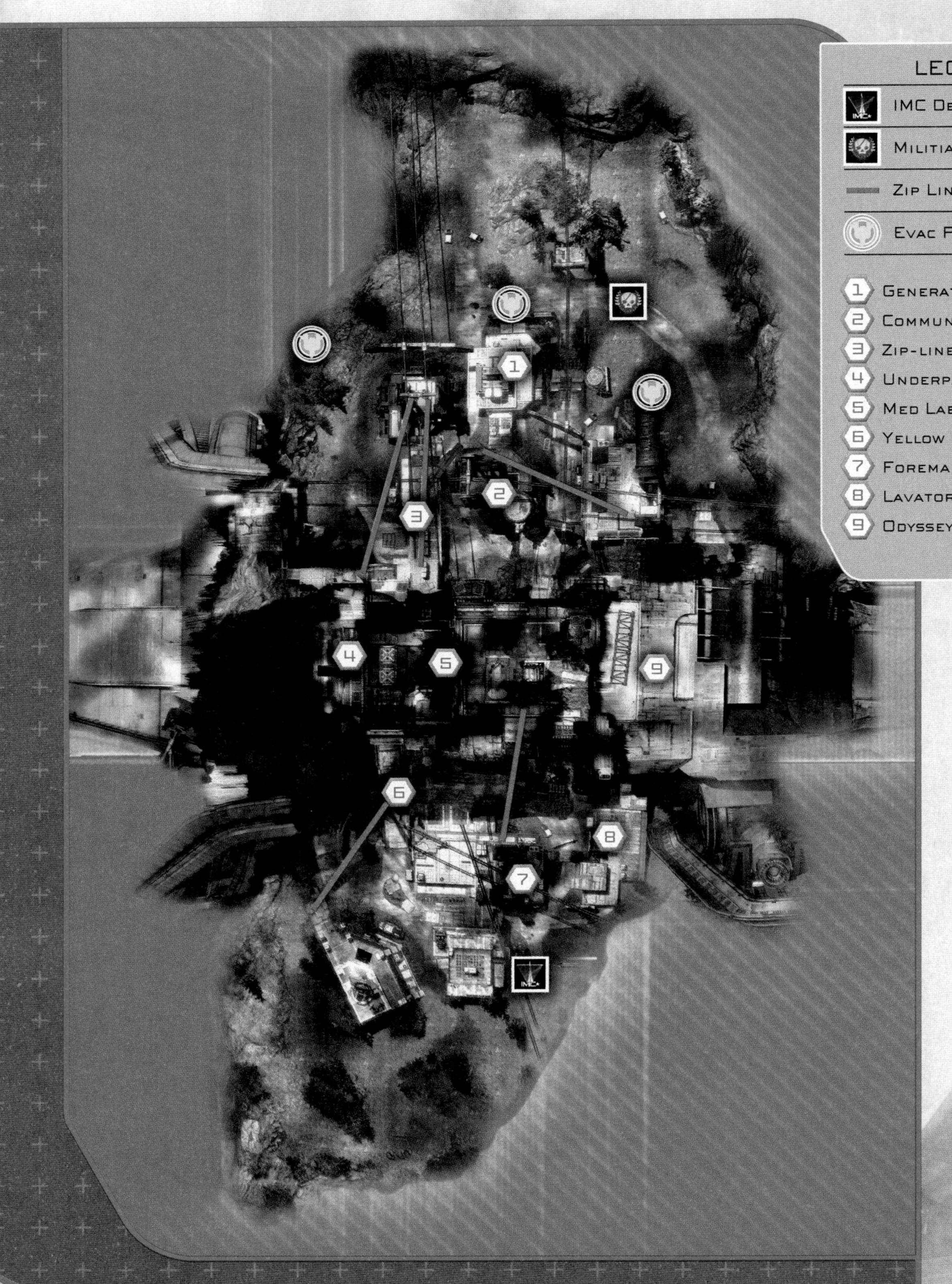
LEGEND
IMC Deployment
Militia Deployment
Zip Line
Evac Point
1 Generator Building
2 Communication Building
3 Zip-line Bridge
4 Underpass
5 Med Lab
6 Yellow Bridge
7 Foreman's Office
8 Lavatory
9 Odyssey

TACTICS

Reference these videos in your free mobile friendly eGuide.

- This map is symmetrical and most of the action will be based around the Odyssey. The Odyssey consists of a few different floors and tunnels that lead underground. Pilots will want to get familiar with this area as it will lead to many enemy Pilot and minion kills.
- Minions will make their way inside of the Odyssey the entire game, so gain height advantage to take them out as they enter. Having height advantage puts you in a better position if an enemy Pilot tries to ambush you.
- Quickly enter the Odyssey when initially spawning on the Militia side. Use the beginning wall to build momentum and then hop over to the next wall and make your way in.
- The Foreman's Office is a great building to stay on top of. Keep an eye on the path between you and the Odyssey. Pilots will find many minions heading towards the Odyssey. Take them out before they make it in to reduce your build time.
- Quickly gain access to the Med Lab inside the Odyssey when on the ground. You don't want to hang out on the ground level for too long. Use this wall to quickly run up and then jump through the door. This jump can be done on either side, making it an effective escape route.
- An interior watchtower lies within the Odyssey. This structure provides cover and a great angle to kill enemies scattered inside the Odyssey.
- The inside of the Odyssey is a cage for Titans to throw down. Pilots should be aware of the different ways to escape in case an enemy Titan has Nuclear Ejection attached. There are a few tiny tunnels and passages that lead to safety. It is a good idea to become familiar with these.
- When controlling a Titan, don't stay too long inside the Odyssey. There are many walkways inside, allowing enemy Pilots to perform rodeo attacks, and tiny entrances for enemies to take cover while still damaging your Titan. Quickly move in and out while drawing the enemies out.

CAPTURE THE FLAG

NOTE

Initial flags, routes, and deployment areas shown. Factions switch sides at halftime.

TACTICS

Reference these videos in your free mobile friendly eGuide.

- The flags are located inside the Foreman's Office and the Communication Building. Each building is designed for close-quarter combat, so be prepared for defenders to be inside with shotguns.
- The Lavatory is a great position to defend the flag within the Foreman's Office. Inside is a window that you can look through to spot enemies approaching from the Yellow Bridge or flanking underneath the bridge.
- When on the offense and trying to grab the flag inside of the Foreman's Office, quickly escape by taking the zip line on the second level. This zip line will bring you straight into the Odyssey where you then can run towards the Med Lab for cover.
- Defending the flag inside the Communication Building can be done in two different ways. One option will be to set up inside on the second level of the building and constantly look back and forth to see if enemies come out of the Odyssey. Your other choice is to control your side of the Med Lab and spot enemies before they make it on your side.

PRO TIP: FLAMESWORD

When grabbing the flag inside the Communication Building, make your way to the second level. Immediately begin wall running to clear the small window gap and jump onto the hanging wall. You will immediately have to jump off the hanging wall, but save your double jump for when you are near the next wall. This will lead you directly inside of the Odyssey.

- Players can escort flag carriers effectively through the underpass underneath the Odyssey. The bodyshield of the Titan will protect a Pilot riding on the back of a friendly Titan from enemy fire.

HARDPOINT DOMINATION

CAUTION WATCH FOR FALLING OBJECTS

REPORT ANY UNSAFE

TACTICS

- Hardpoint A is positioned on the first floor of the Communication Building, and Pilots are capable of capturing this objective anywhere once inside. A great spot to capture this point is near the door; hard aim on the door while being against the toolkit. If an enemy enters the hardpoint, you will be notified that it is being contested. Either turn around and engage the enemy or walk out and approach from a different angle.
- Hardpoint B is inside the Odyssey near the Yellow Bridge. The capture radius on this objective is fairly wide and it can be captured from high and low. The safest way to capture this hardpoint is to stay in the back room. Be warned though—after a while players will begin throwing grenades in this area. Use the drop hole to get away from the blast.

PRO TIP: STRONGSIDE

Hardpoint C is inside the Foreman's Office next to the IMC's initial spawn. In the corner of the office is a bathroom with a sun roof that can be used to escape or drop into and surprise attack the enemy. This is also a good spot to wall hang and capture the objective.

- Hardpoint B is open for Titans to roam. This makes it a lot easier to hold the objective, but a lot harder to defend it when the opposing team has a Titan. Stick to the top levels of the Odyssey and fire your Anti-Titan weapons from a distance to avoid the enemy Titan's weapons.
- When your team has a Titan or two, controlling Hardpoint B with one of the other hardpoints is the best strategy. Only one or two players need to guard the other objective while the rest of the team, including the Titan, navigate inside of the Odyssey, controlling the objective.

LAST TITAN STANDING

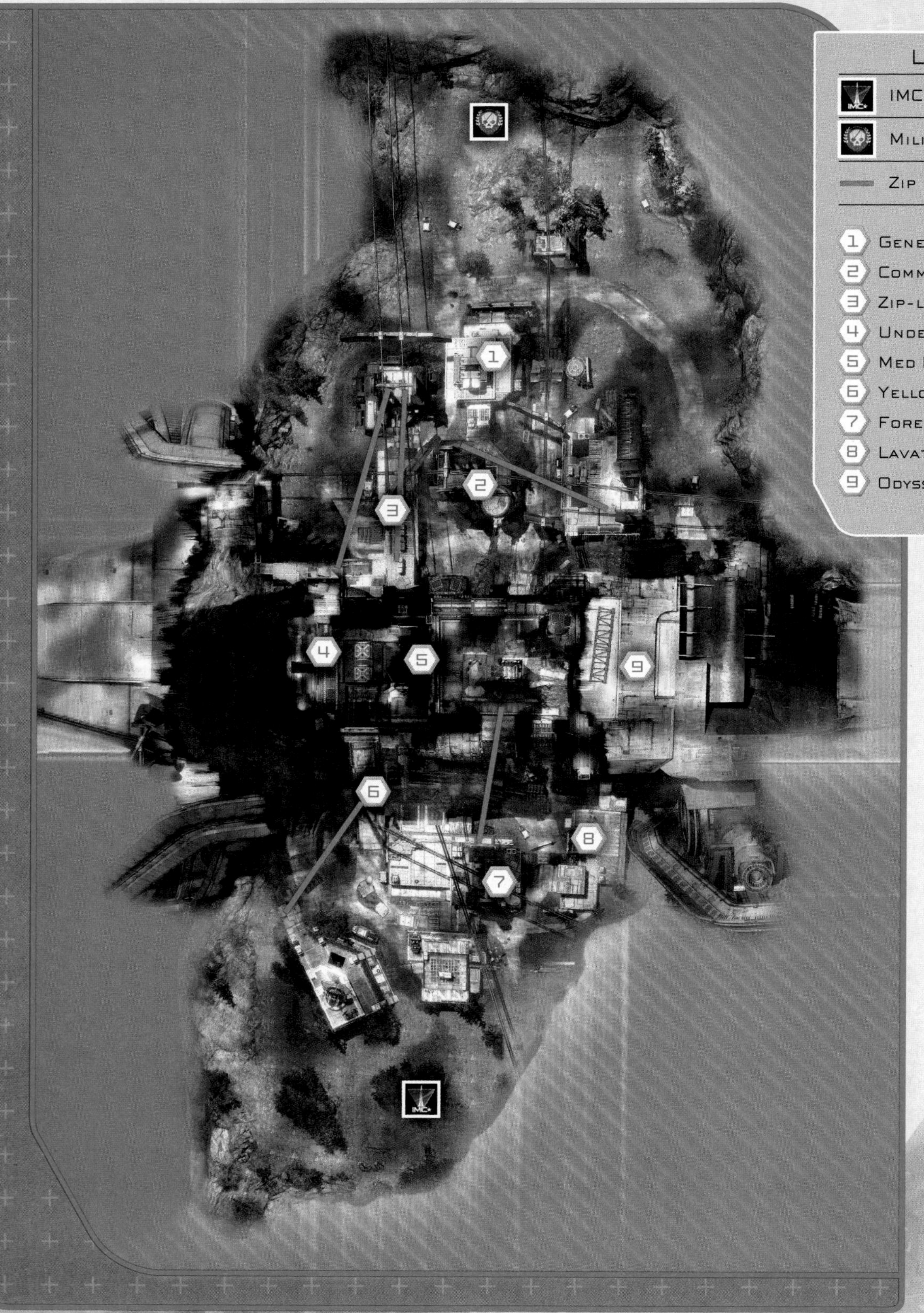
LEGEND
IMC Deployment
Militia Deployment
Zip Line
1 Generator Building
2 Communication Building
3 Zip-line Bridge
4 Underpass
5 Med Lab
6 Yellow Bridge
7 Foreman's Office
8 Lavatory
9 Odyssey
1
2
3
4
5
6
7
8
9

TACTICS

- Spawning on the Militia side gives you the advantage on this map. You are able to play passive and use the many more buildings and structures on this side for cover. If your team has the lead when on the Militia side, your entire team can sit back and watch the two choke points: Odyssey and Underpass. These two choke points are the only ways to travel from one side of the map to the other with a Titan.
- When spawning as the Militia, if your teammates are pushing into the Odyssey, use the window left of the Zip-line Bridge to see if any Titans are inside and give cover fire through the window. You can also use this window as the IMC team to shoot enemy Titans outside of the Odyssey.
- With so few paths to travel from one side of the map to the other, making an aggressive charge will be tough, unless you deal damage to the enemy Titans in small amounts. Peek shoot at the enemy by dealing damage, then backing up behind a wall or structure to reload or gain your shields back. Once you've weakened multiple enemy Titans, make a charge with three Titans through the Odyssey and three Titans through the Underpass. Focus your fire on the weak Titans.
- When traveling through the Odyssey, beware of enemy Pilots in the Med Lab and walkways where an enemy can easily hit you with an Arc Grenade. The Odyssey is a high-traffic area, but do not get caught in here as there isn't much in here to use for cover. The Particle Wall Tactical Ability will be very effective inside the Odyssey. You'll be able to throw it down at the entrance of either side of the Odyssey and fire out towards the enemy team.
- As a Pilot, moving around inside the Odyssey will work extremely well for your team because you are able to use the many walkways and Med Lab for cover. Stay alive up here and wait for your friendly Titans to get in a battle. Once your friendly Titans are in a battle, toss some Arc Grenades and deal some damage with your Anti-Titan weapon. As a Pilot, you'll never want to initiate any battles with a Titan because you are sure to be killed. Keeping your Pilot alive will allow you to still aid your team in battle with your Anti-Titan weapon and Arc Grenades against the enemy Titans.

PILOT HUNTER

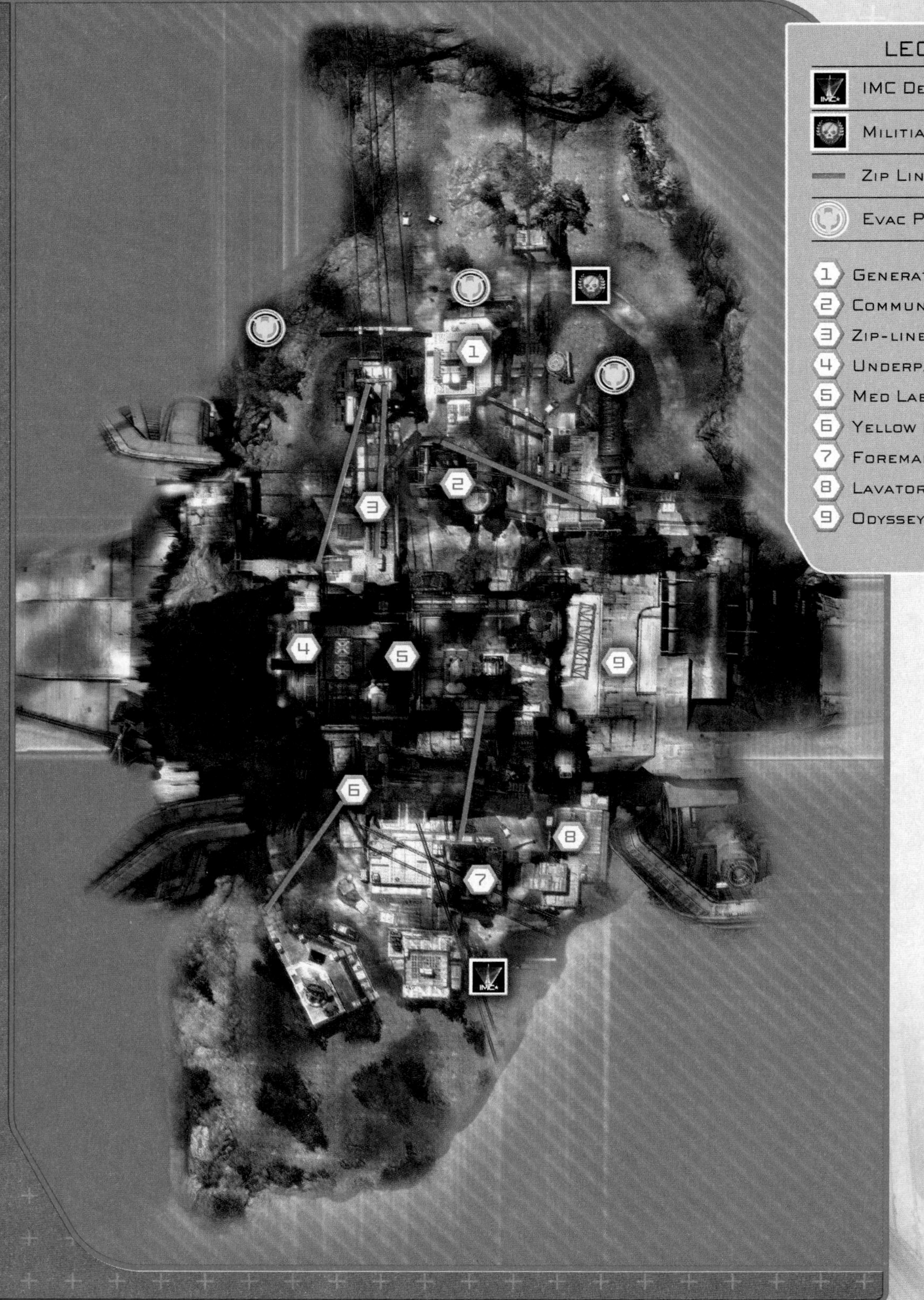

LEGEND

- IMC Deployment
- Militia Deployment
- Zip Line
- Evac Point

1. Generator Building
2. Communication Building
3. Zip-line Bridge
4. Underpass
5. Med Lab
6. Yellow Bridge
7. Foreman's Office
8. Lavatory
9. Odyssey

TACTICS

Reference these videos in your free mobile friendly eGuide.

PRO TIP: WALSHY

Pilots will want to gain control of the center of the Odyssey immediately from the beginning of the game and control the upper levels. This area is a hot spot for minions. The opposing team will constantly try to make their way in, so apply pressure from outside or wait for them to come in and then ambush them. The Active Radar Pulse Tactical Ability comes in handy when inside the Odyssey.

- From the IMC initial spawn, quickly run in the direction of the Yellow Bridge. You will see a metal plate hanging by a few cables. Jump onto this to begin wall running. At the end, jump to the top level and you will quickly enter the Odyssey.
- The Med Lab is an incredible position to hold throughout the entire game. It is interconnected with all the hallways inside the Odyssey, allowing you to freely move around while having the upper hand. Keep moving in and out of the Med Lab constantly, because enemy Pilots are sure to try and get their revenge on you. If your team is on one side of the map, the enemy Pilots are most likely coming from the other side. Focus your attention on the side your team is not on.
- Remember, minions tend to move towards the Odyssey. If the opposing team has control of the Odyssey, equip a medium- to long-range weapon and pick off minions to reduce build time. Once you are have a Titan, move into the Odyssey with friendly Pilots and regain control.

PRO TIP: FLAMESWORD

Once inside the Odyssey, stay close to every single wall. Enemy Pilots can attack you from almost anywhere, so be prepared to start jumping from wall to wall. One of my favorite areas when engaging enemies is near the Yellow Bridge. There are two walls near each other that quickly let me reach the upper level.

RISE

Militia Special Forces have set up a long-range reconnaissance outpost in this abandoned IMC reservoir, less than a hundred miles from the classified IMC proving grounds on the planet Gridiron. The reservoir's towering, sheer walls and a system of convenient zip lines provide Pilots with the perfect means to get around quickly while Titans do battle in the long corridors below. Ejecting Pilots should be very careful to avoid lingering above ground here—it only takes a few seconds to receive a lethal dose of radiation in direct sunlight.

Red represents the highest concentrations of minion deaths on this composite heat map.

KEY LANDMARKS

PIPE ROOM

STEAM ROOM

CENTRAL CONTROL

PRESSURE CONTROL

SKY BRIDGE

STORAGE

MAP OVERVIEW

Most of the action on this map takes place around the Sky Walk. If you're trying to avoid this battle area, take a zip line to the top wall of the map and wall jump your way around until you find the perfect opening for an attack or to sneak behind the enemy.

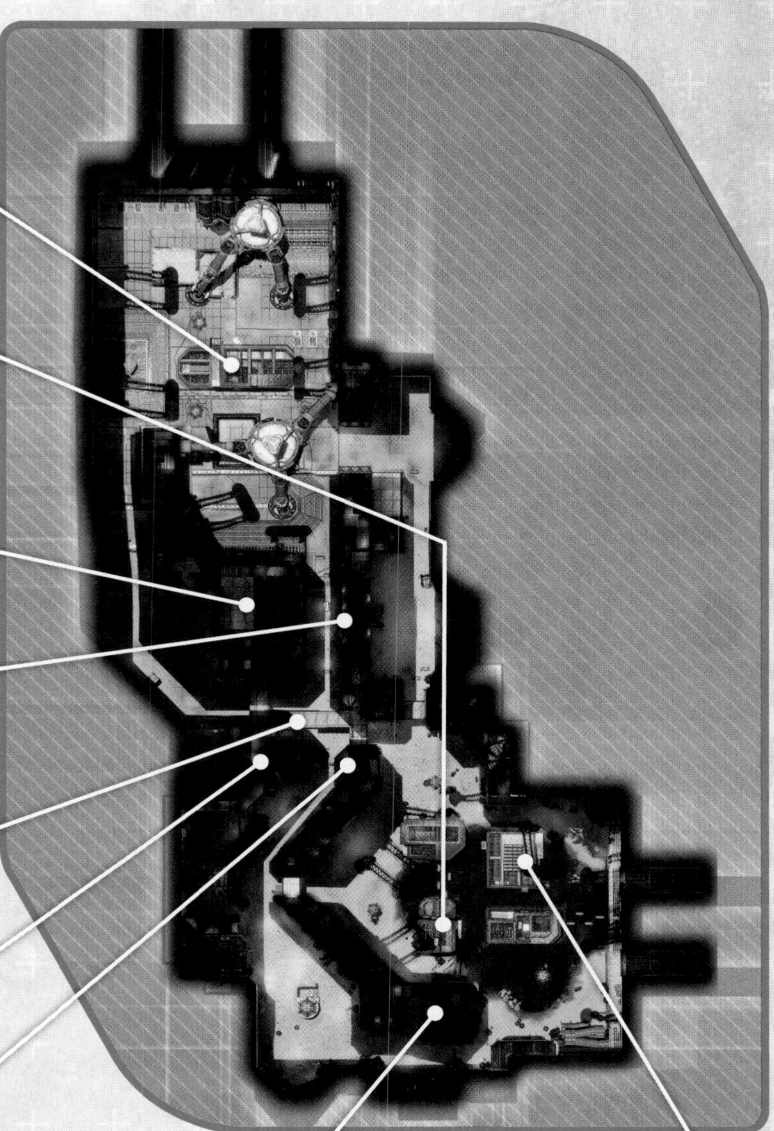

IRRIGATION CONTROL

WATER PUMP CONTROL

UTILITY BUILDING

ATTRITION

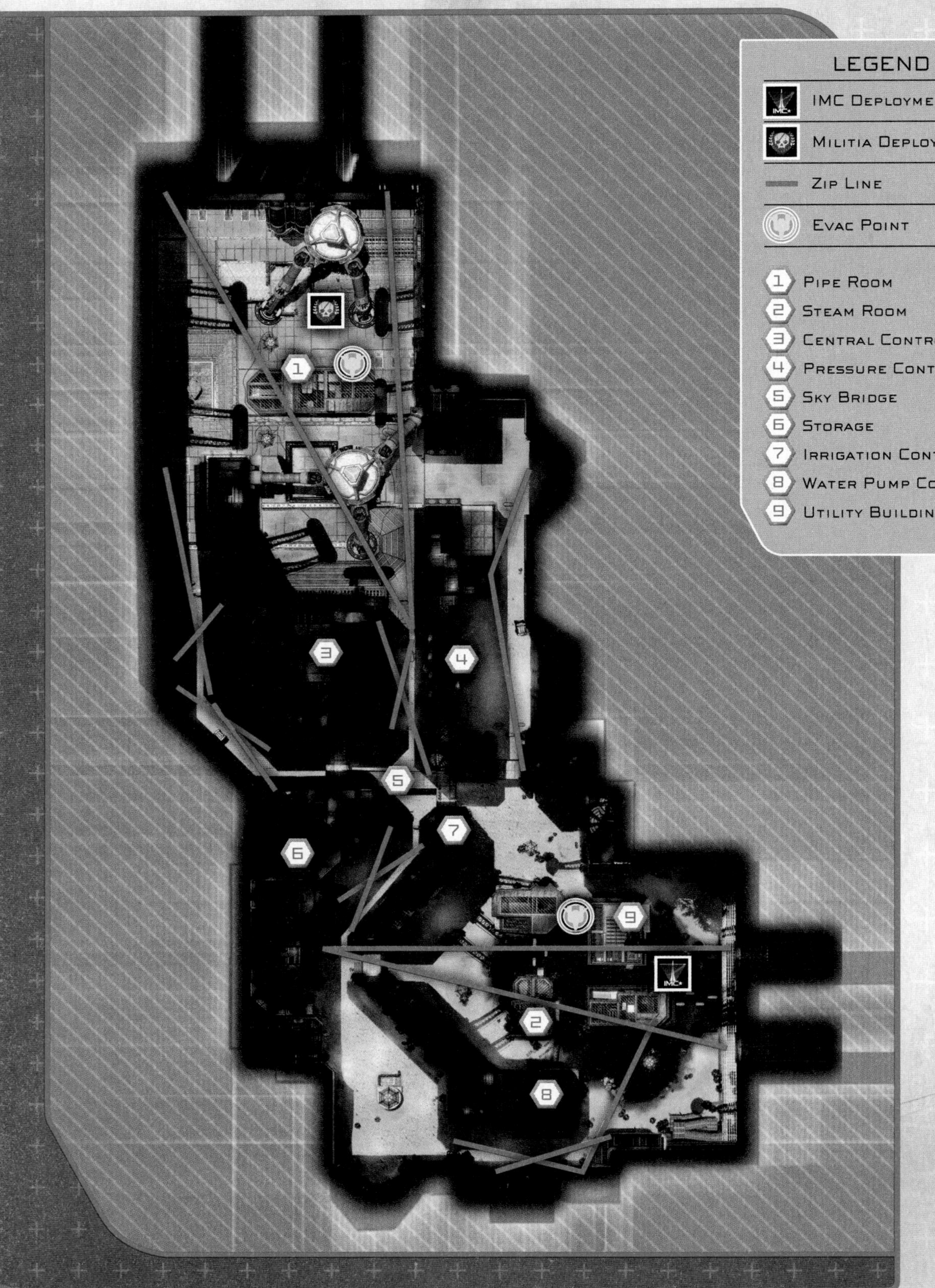
LEGEND
IMC Deployment
Militia Deployment
Zip Line
Evac Point
1 Pipe Room
2 Steam Room
3 Central Control
4 Pressure Control
5 Sky Bridge
6 Storage
7 Irrigation Control
8 Water Pump Control
9 Utility Building

TACTICS

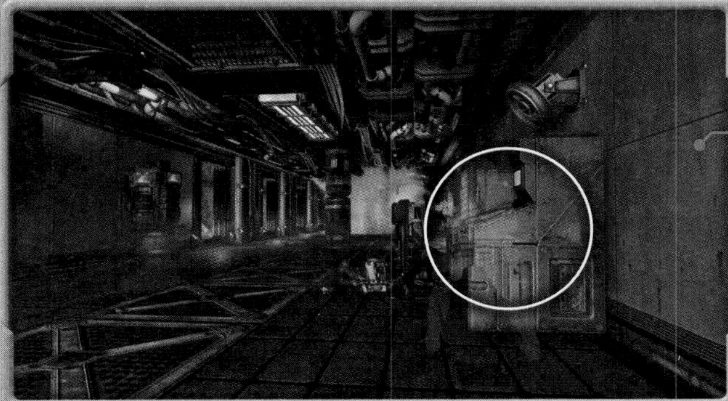

- In Rise, Attrition can be played many ways. But no matter which way you play, the most important tactic is controlling the center of the map. As the game goes on, battles tend to move towards the center around the Sky Bridge. Control this area to quickly pick off enemies.

PRO TIP: STRONGSIDE

Pilots equipped with close-quarter weapons and Cloak are very effective when patrolling the structures connected to the Sky Bridge. The insides of these structures all have cover that allow you to excel with close-quarter weapons.

- Arc Grenades are extremely useful when playing Attrition on this map. Arc Grenades help you clear out rooms, blind enemy Titans below, or throw a Hail Mary towards a group of minions to quickly score Attrition points.
- When you spawn in the far back near the Pipe Room and away from all the action, take the zip lines to quickly get back into the action. Before dropping down blindly from the wall or zip line, wall hang at the top of the map for a few seconds and scout the area out down below.
- The Ogre Titan is a great choice when you are ready for your Titanfall on this map. The Ogre is able to withstand the massive attacks in the center of the map while dishing out damage. Activating the Ogre's Core Ability before moving into battle will make your Ogre Titan an armor-packed beast. Equipping Nuclear Ejection in your Titan's Tier 1 Kit provides a brutal counterattack that can wipe out weak enemy Titans if they destroy your Titan from a close range.

RISE

CENTRAL CONTROL 1

CAPTURE THE FLAG

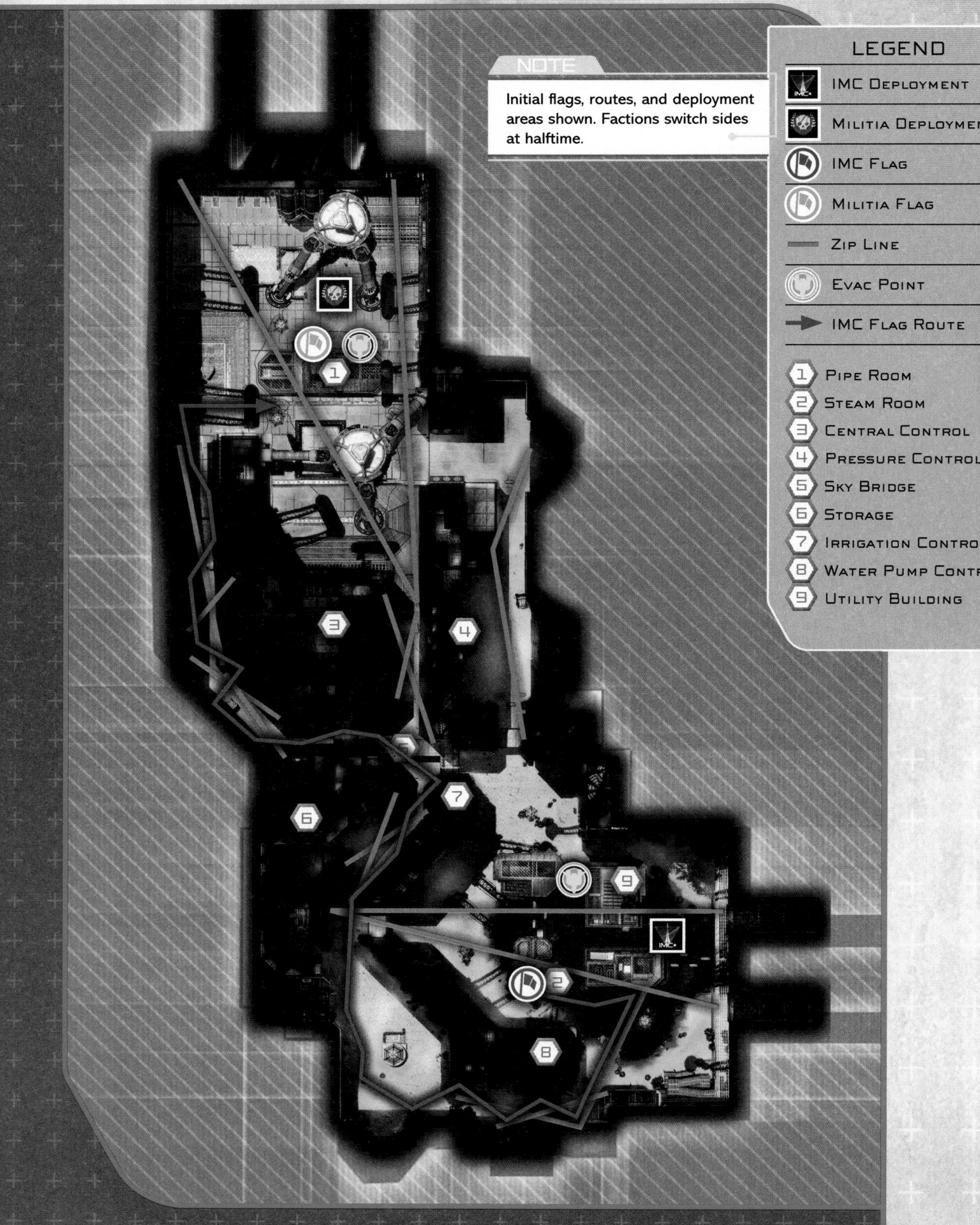
NOTE
Initial flags, routes, and deployment areas shown. Factions switch sides at halftime.
LEGEND
IMC Deployment
Militia Deployment
IMC Flag
Militia Flag
Zip Line
Evac Point
IMC Flag Route
1 Pipe Room
2 Steam Room
3 Central Control
4 Pressure Control
5 Sky Bridge
6 Storage
7 Irrigation Control
8 Water Pump Control
9 Utility Building

TACTICS

Reference these videos in your free mobile friendly eGuide.

PRO TIP: STRONGSIDE

To make this flag run a bit easier, equip the Tier 1 Kit Enhanced Parkour.

1. Once you grab the flag from the Steam Room, run to the building that has a zip line leading to the top of the map near the Water Pump Control and take the zip line to the top of the map wall.

2. Once at the top, wall run and jump all the way back to your base. Staying closer to the top of the map will make it extremely hard for enemy Pilots and Titans to kill you.

3. If you notice yourself being shot at, jump up higher than the map wall and run on the sandy floor. You will have 10 seconds up here before you are killed. This gives you more than enough time to keep moving forward and drop back in the map out of the dead zone.

4. Lastly, take either the left route or right route back to your base. It is your judgment call on which way you think is safer.

- Capture the flag on this map is extremely fast paced. Players will quickly realize that you can freely move from base to base due to all the wall runs, jumps, and zip lines. Become friendly with these as they all lead to great flag routes and escape routes.
- The Central Control and Water Pump Control are great locations to position yourself when on either team. One location will always be closer to your base, allowing you to defend your flag from a distance. The other location will be near the opponent's base, allowing you to play offensively and put pressure on the enemy team.

PRO TIP: WALSHY

When running the flag back with a Titan, once you get back to your base take your time and have a teammate clear out the area before running the flag in. Don't get careless at this last second of your flag run. The last thing you want is to have your flag run foiled by one small mistake.

- Even though it is easy to avoid enemy Titans by wall running at the top of the map, engage with the enemy Titans for a moment and deal damage to them before they grab your flag. The last thing you want to do is have to try and stop fully armored Titans running your flag.
- Enhanced Parkour Kit along with Stim are great loadout choices for this map. You can be a nuisance the entire game by getting over to the enemy base, pulling flags, and stopping enemy flag captures.

HARDPOINT DOMINATION

TACTICS

- Hardpoints A and C are both inside little buildings. Although Titans can't physically get inside of the buildings, the Titans can shoot through the small doors and openings of the buildings, so be cautious if you are inside the building for either Hardpoint A or C when an enemy Titan is nearby.
- Defending Hardpoints A and C as a Titan can be easy if you defend the points from outside the building. The objectives are inside steel cage buildings, but there are many small openings that provide an opportunity to shoot through the cage walls to kill an enemy. If an enemy Pilot sneaks by you, just shoot the enemy through the walls of the building instead of risking your life by exiting your Titan.
- Hardpoints B and A are much closer to one another, but that doesn't mean they are the two best to hold. This map involves so much jumping that you are capable of getting from one side of the map to the other in seconds. This is an excellent time to really take advantage of your Tier 1 Kit Enhanced Parkour.

PRO TIP: FLAMESWORD

The Storage area is the location of Hardpoint B. Players are able to capture and contest this hill outside near the bollards making it difficult to defend. Place a Satchel Charge inside near the objective and another outside near the bollards. Once you see the enemy is capturing, detonate the charges to have a better idea where the enemy is since you will get hit markers if you weakened them. Then move in and take them out.

RISE

LAST TITAN STANDING

LEGEND
IMC Deployment
Militia Deployment
Zip Line
1 Pipe Room
2 Steam Room
3 Central Control
4 Pressure Control
5 Sky Bridge
6 Storage
7 Irrigation Control
8 Water Pump Control
9 Utility Building

TACTICS

- Whether you're running and gunning as a Titan towards the center of the map or wall running across the top of the map as a Pilot, you'll always want to be on the lookout for a surprise attack. There are many windows and paths that you need to become familiar with so you won't be surprised by an enemy.
- If your team is going head-on towards the center of the map, be sure you and your team communicate with each other so you can focus your fire on one Titan at a time to quickly take out the enemy Titans.
- The Sky Walk is going to be a power position for Pilots on foot looking to deal damage below towards enemy Titans. Keep an eye out for enemy Pilots attempting the same maneuver. Using Arc Grenades here will be a huge step towards your team's success. If you are able to hit a group of enemy Titans with an Arc Grenade, this opens the opportunity for your team to charge in and deal massive damage to the enemy Titans.
- There isn't much cover near the center of the map, so you'll want to make sure you're traveling with other friendly Titans. If not, you could get trapped in one of the long pathways leading across the map alongside Pressure Control, Central Control, Water Pump Control, and Irrigation Control.
- If you find your team down a Titan, play passive and move back towards your initial spawn. Use the buildings in your base for cover. If you have long-range weapons attached, you'll be able to deal small amounts of damage from a distance as the enemy Titans push in to attack your team. These small amounts of damage add up when your entire team is shooting the enemy Titans and will even the playing field while your team is down a Titan.

PILOT HUNTER

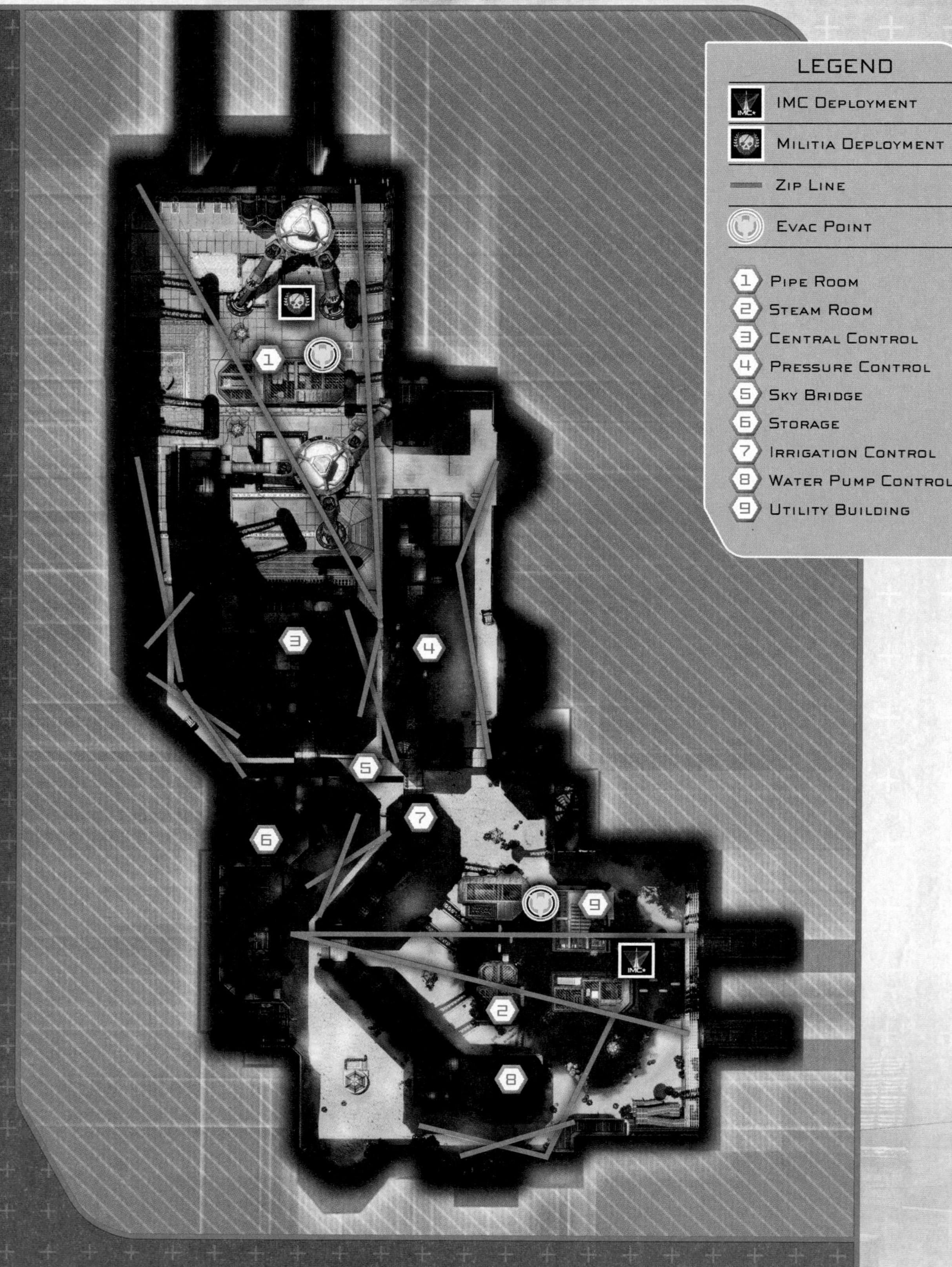
LEGEND
IMC Deployment
Militia Deployment
Zip Line
Evac Point
1 Pipe Room
2 Steam Room
3 Central Control
4 Pressure Control
5 Sky Bridge
6 Storage
7 Irrigation Control
8 Water Pump Control
9 Utility Building
1
2
3
4
5
6
7
8
9

TACTICS

› A great Ordnance choice for Rise is the Arc Mine. Throw these inside structures like Central Control, Pressure Control, Storage, Irrigation Control, and Water Pump Control. Enemy Pilots are known to run in these areas a bunch so you will be able to pick up some easy kills. If the mines don't kill them, at least you are now aware of the location of your enemy when you see a hit marker pop up on your HUD.

PRO TIP: FLAMESWORD

The Sky Bridge is very important to hold. This middle area between both sides will allow you to predict where the opponent will come from. For example, when you are controlling the Sky Bridge and if your team is spawns on one side of the map then you know the opponent must be coming from the other side of the map. When you are on the Sky Bridge, you can push towards the enemy to gain some ground to surprise attack the enemy. While you're attacking the enemy, be sure to have one of your teammates fill in your spot controlling the Sky Bridge.

› This map is meant to be played fast paced. Pilots will be constantly jumping from wall to wall. Equip the Quick Reload Kit to your Tier 1 slot. It is pretty hard to shoot enemies jumping around and ammunition gets spent quickly. Compensate for this by having a faster reload time, which will allow you to keep constant pressure on enemies jumping around.

› Scenario: Your team has the lead and all of a sudden loses control of the center area of the map. Slow the pace of the game down by taking a safe route back towards the center of the map. Take the walkways on the top level of the Water Pump Control or Central Control (depending on which side of the map you spawn on), which lead to the center of the map.

› If you turn around and look up at your initial spawn you'll see a few large open pipes at the Militia spawn or at the IMC spawn you'll see two long hall ways. These pipes and hall ways can be reached by either a zip line or wall jump. Once inside the pipes or hallways you'll have a great overview of your base and incoming enemies from the center of the map. These positions are great place to take advantage of the openness of the area to dominate Pilots with a sniper rifle and Titans with a Charge Rifle.

SMUGGLER'S COVE

Part arms bazaar and part pirate enclave, the small city of Smuggler's Cove is infamous across the Frontier for its selection of mercenaries and black market equipment. Ships arriving at the Cove must land in the shallow water outside, or risk being shot down by turrets concealed throughout the city. Visitors are searched by the pirates' "welcoming committee" and are taken by rowboat to the mainland. However, a rarely used tunnel in the corner of the harbor provides a critical flanking route into town.

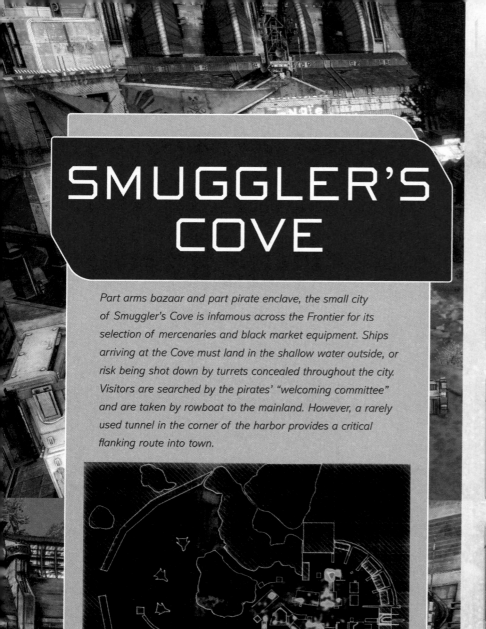

Red represents the highest concentrations of minion deaths on this composite heat map.

KEY LANDMARKS

APARTMENTS

CITY TURRET

BAY

HYDRO CONTROL BAY

HOTEX

SNACK SHOP

MAP OVERVIEW

If you like to wall run and wall jump, this map is for you. The many buildings and rooftops allow you to travel across the map quickly. If you're being attacked on the rooftops, take the alleyways as these will allow you to sneak around the map from building to building and attack the enemy from behind.

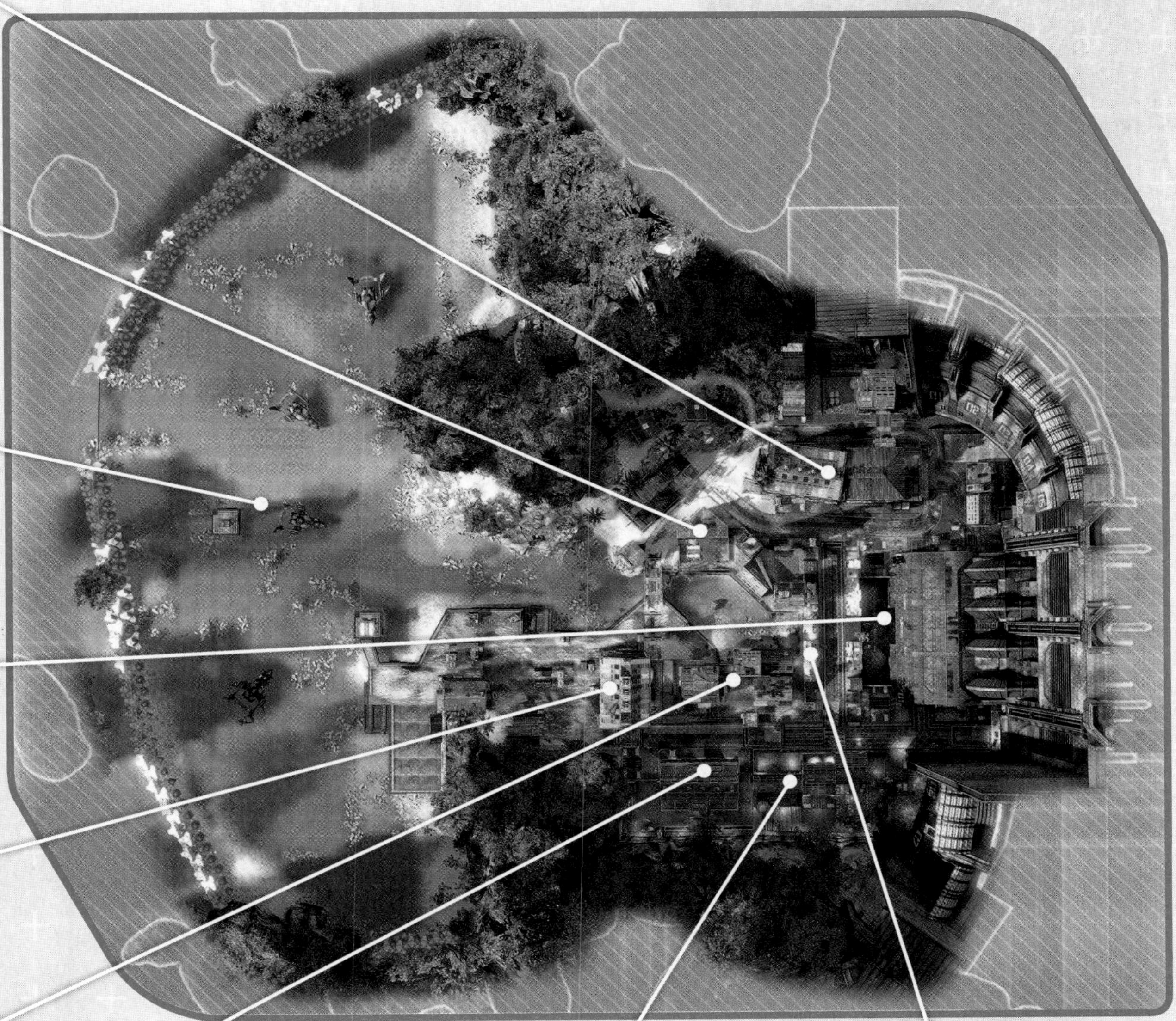

MARVIN'S PLACE

BAR

MARKET BRIDGE

ATTRITION

LEGEND
IMC Deployment
Militia Deployment
Turret
Evac Point
1 Apartments
2 City Turret
3 Bay
4 Hydro Control Bay
5 Hotex
6 Marvin's Place
7 Snack Shop
8 Bar
9 Market Bridge
IMC

TACTICS

- Around the Hotex is a great spot to pick off plenty of minions. Be sure to patrol in this area to quickly build your Attrition score and reduce your build time for a Titan. Beware though—enemy Pilots will also be heading towards this area. You can use the minions in this area as bait for the enemy Pilots. Watch the rooftops and alleyways for incoming enemy Pilots.
- Within the map there are two turrets. Activate the City Turret at all costs. This turret will be able to get a few kills that add to your Attrition score and be a nuisance to the enemy team. Check back at the turret periodically to stop any enemy Pilots from hacking it.
- Get to the higher ground on this map. This map is saturated with plenty of buildings. Be on the team to get control of the rooftops first, giving you the upper hand and better angle to take out the opposing team.
- To take down the enemy team on the rooftops, hang back with a sniper and you're sure to find some enemy Pilots jumping from building to building to take out.
- When calling down your Titan, have control of the City Turret. If you do not have control of this turret, hang out near the Hydro Control Bay and Bar. This area is out of the turret's range and allows you to go on a spree with your Titan, picking off many minions.
- Equip the Minion Detector as your Tier 2 Kit. This map has many other possible areas that minions can spawn while playing Attrition. You will want to know these locations so you can rack up some easy points.

CAPTURE THE FLAG

NOTE

Initial flags, routes, and deployment areas shown. Factions switch sides at halftime.

TACTICS

- Have your own or a friendly Titan waiting in the Hydro Control Bay. This will allow you to move in, grab the flag, and be escorted back to your base with the objective.
- When running the flag back into the Hydro Control Bay, park your Titan in the lower level of this building to ensure that you don't get picked off by a sniper as you are exiting your Titan outside the Hydro Control Bay.
- When you are a Pilot, a sneaky route to the Hydro Control Bay is to take the underpass underneath the Market Bridge. You will avoid Titans and be able to sneak into the enemy flag unseen. This is especially effective when you have a Titanfall available so you can grab the flag, drop the full-armor Titan, and run the flag back for a score.
- A sniper on top of the Hotex will prove very useful. This sniper is able to spot and call out the positions of the opposing team. The top of the Hotex has a little hidden tunnel that provides you with safe cover when you need to duck your head for a second.
- Hanging around the rooftops near the City Turret allows you to hold that side of the map. This will keep the opposing team trapped around the Hotex area. Activate the turret for more firepower.

PRO TIP: STRONGSIDE

When pulling the flag out of the Hydro Control Bay, have your teammates control the Bar and Marvin's Place. Run the flag behind these buildings as your teammates cover you back to your base. Holding the Bar and Marvin's Place should also force the opposing team to spawn around the Apartments. The teammates controlling the Bar and Marvin's Place should move back to your base and prepare for enemies attacking from the City Turret.

HARDPOINT DOMINATION

LEGEND
IMC Deployment
Militia Deployment
A Hardpoint A
B Hardpoint B
C Hardpoint C
Turret
Evac Point
1 Apartments
2 City Turret
3 Bay
4 Hydro Control Bay
5 Hotex
6 Marvin's Place
7 Snack Shop
8 Bar
9 Market Bridge

TACTICS

Reference these videos in your free mobile friendly eGuide.

- Hardpoint C is in the Hotex, which is an enclosed building. Titans are almost a non-factor once you are able to get inside the building. As long as you stay in the room with the Hardpoint in it, Titans should not be able to kill you through the windows.
- Off the start, perform this double jump to gain access to the Hotex and quickly capture Hardpoint C. During the late game, if the opposing team is holding this objective down, perform this jump once again. Many players look at the other window unaware that this jump is possible.

PRO TIP: FLAMESWORD

Take advantage of a Pilot's thruster pack. Instead of doing the norm and walking up the stairs in Hardpoint A, begin wall running up the stairs. This allows you to pick up speed, making you a harder target to hit if an enemy is defending the objective from inside.

- Titans will dominate the Market Bridge, and Hardpoint B is located in the middle of the bridge. Though there are little market shops on the bridge to use for cover, don't enter this area if the enemy team has more Titans. Plan out an attack strategy with friendlies and take advantage of the rooftops to slowly gain control of this area.
- Activating the City Turret allows you to hold down Hardpoints A and B easier. The high ground lets you rain fire on your opponents with the suppressive assistance of the turret. Players will only need to retreat back to Hardpoint A once you notice it is being neutralized by the opponent. Hold the bridge with the turret and a victory awaits you.

LAST TITAN STANDING

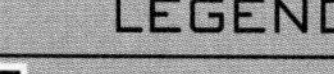

- IMC Deployment
- Militia Deployment
- Turret

1. Apartments
2. City Turret
3. Bay
4. Hydro Control Bay
5. Hotex
6. Marvin's Place
7. Snack Shop
8. Bar
9. Market Bridge

TACTICS

- Just because you are in a Titan doesn't mean you can't park it in Auto-Titan for a bit. Once you have exited your Titan, get to the City Turret as fast as possible. This turret will apply some extra damage, making the enemy Titans easier to take out. If you don't hack the turret first, have a few Titans quickly destroy the City Turret.

PRO TIP: WALSHY

A sound strategy is to play passive and hold down the Bay area. You must be really patient when using this strategy. Activate the turret near the Bay to apply secondary fire. The objective here is to use the drop ships for cover. Enemy Titans will have to step into the open to get a good point of attack in order to take you out. They will have no cover as they blindly run into the open Bay.

- If you spawned at the Hotex at the start of the game, head towards the Bay. Then move towards the side of the Bay opposite the turret on the Bay. You'll find a tunnel that is big enough for Titans to pass through. This tunnel can be used to pull off an incredible flank on the enemy team. This tunnel is an area you want to watch when playing passive and controlling the Bay.

- The Market Bridge will be a power position with a Titan. You have many options here. You have a clear view down towards the Hotex and Bay, which you can use to aid your teammates with a long-range primary weapon. You also have a path towards the Bar and Apartments to quickly rush over and help friendly Titans in the area. Don't get caught here though. If you notice enemy Titans attacking from both the Bar and Apartments, pick one side and get out of the Market Bridge because you don't want to get caught and trapped on the bridge between two enemy Titans.
- With a high presence of buildings on this map, you can use the buildings to sneak your Titan around and initiate a surprise attack or sit behind a building and wait for an enemy Titan to cross your path. Also, with all the buildings, you'll want to keep an eye out for lingering enemy Pilots looking to rodeo attack you. Stay near a friendly Titan as they are able to shoot the enemy Pilot off your back.

PILOT HUNTER

LEGEND

 IMC Deployment

 Militia Deployment

 Turret

 Evac Point

1. Apartments
2. City Turret
3. Bay
4. Hydro Control Bay
5. Hotex
6. Marvin's Place
7. Snack Shop
8. Bar
9. Market Bridge

TACTICS

- The high ground is the key to success. Control the various rooftops across the map. A good idea is to stick next to the City Turret, which will provide suppressive fire.
- Titans are usually the best way to get rid of enemy Pilots. This can prove difficult when engaging enemies near the City Turret, especially if they have control of it. If this is the case, disable the turret before engaging the enemy Pilots.
- When your initial spawn is near the Hotex, use this jump to quickly get to the Market Bridge. This jump will prove even more useful during the game when you find yourself on the lower side of the map. Use this to get back into action and better position yourself.
- A great way to bait opponents is to draw them near the Apartments. If you can get an enemy Pilot to chase you in between the Apartments, you can use this wall jump to get the upper hand.
- A great sniping location to pick off a few enemies and be a huge distraction is on the back side of the Hydro Control Bay. Both sides provide a great line of sight, but the side near the Bar is better as there is more action and minions around the Hotex.

Reference these videos in your free mobile friendly eGuide.

TRAINING GROUND

IMC Pilot training programs conducted at training facility "Whitehead" have a 98 percent fatality rate, hence the base's mantra: "Only the strong survive." Titans with ranged weapons dominate the man-made landscape, dodging behind the modular buildings that dot the training area in order to avoid enemy fire, before dashing back out to deliver precision blows to their opponents with Titan Railguns and 40mm Cannons. Pilots can avoid the outdoor carnage by moving through the basements and catwalks of the central building, while snipers can find ways to get to its rooftop for a tactically advantageous view.

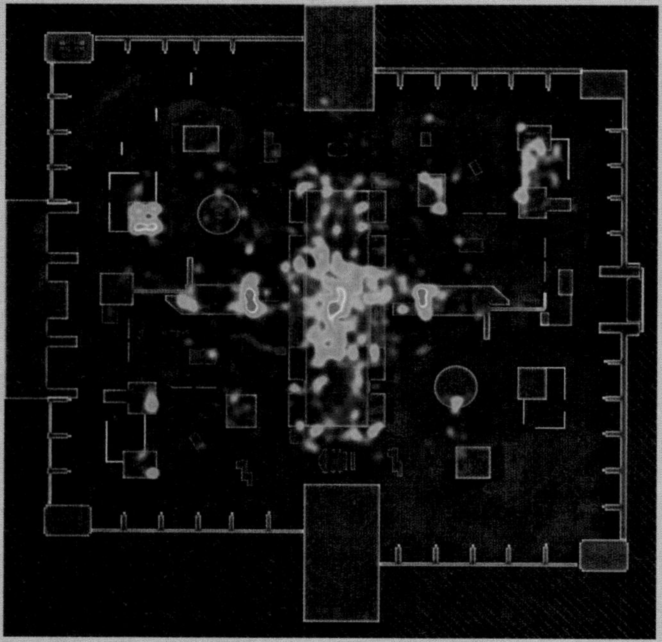

Red represents the highest concentrations of minion deaths on this composite heat map.

KEY LANDMARKS

DOZER PATH

MILITIA TOWER TURRET

IMC GROUND TURRET

TANK BAY

IMC LOCKER ROOM

IMC TOWER TURRET

MAP OVERVIEW

Being a square symmetrical map, the games on Training Ground play out a lot like a game of chess, with capturing pieces like the turrets and flying diagonally across the map like a bishop on the zip lines.

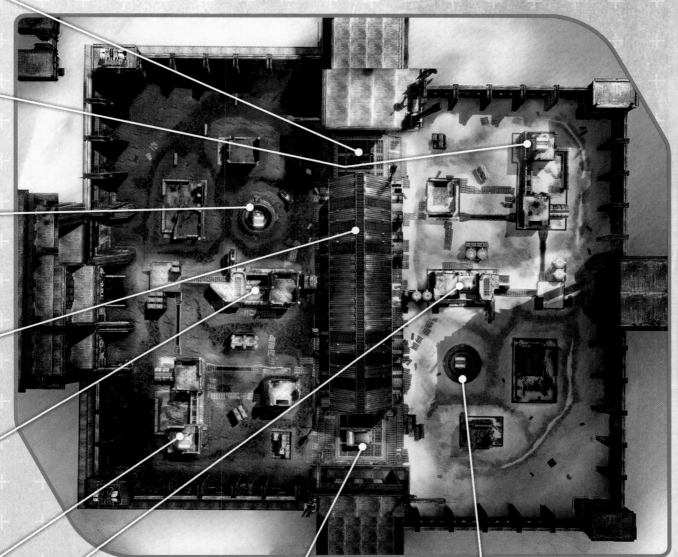

CARGO CONTAINER BUILDING

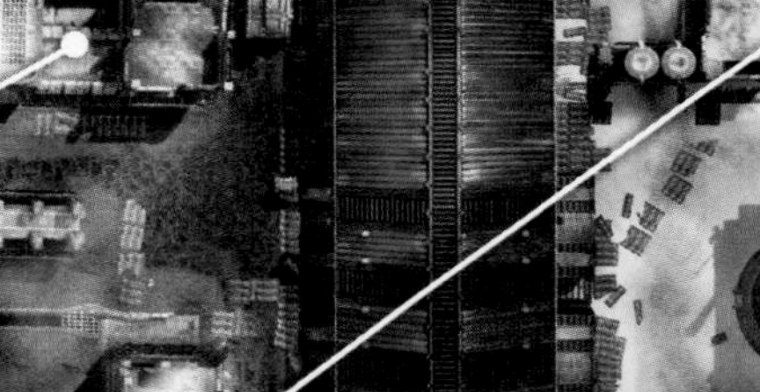

TANK PATH

MILITIA GROUND TURRET

ATTRITION

LEGEND

	IMC Deployment
	Militia Deployment
	Turret
	Zip Line
	Evac Point

1. Dozer Path
2. Militia Tower Turret
3. IMC Ground Turret
4. Tank Bay
5. IMC Locker Room
6. IMC Tower Turret
7. Cargo Container Building
8. Tank Path
9. Militia Ground Turret

TACTICS

- The roof of Tank Bay is a power position. Holding the top gives you clear lines of sight of enemies across the map, and you're able to drop down to your side of the roof for cover.
- When holding the rooftop, stay on your side of the ridge to be able to keep an eye on the enemy zip lines. Controlling these sides allows you to pick off Pilots who use the zip lines and gives you a bird's-eye view of the opposing team's side, allowing you to score points by hunting minions.

PRO TIP: STRONGSIDE

A great wall jump to get up onto the roof is by jumping up the front of the Tank Bay on either side. You're able to jump up and land on the numbered sign to easily get on the roof without being noticed by enemy Pilots watching the zip lines.

- Activate or hack turrets any chance you get because their kills go towards your score. This is a perfect time to use the Tier 2 Kit's Icepick as it reduces the time it takes to activate the turrets.
- When not on the roof, keep moving around the inside of the Tank Bay to find a bunch of easy minion kills under plenty of cover from enemy Titans that are gunning for you. Minions like to fight by the sides and entrances of the Tank Bay.
- If the opposing team controls the rooftop, pull out the Kraber-AP Sniper or the Longbow-DMR Sniper to pick off enemy Pilots on the roof. Your team's turrets and sniping will cause the other team to take cover, allowing your teammates to jump up the front of the Tank Bay or safely use the zip lines with your sniper cover.

- Players will want to use the various amount of cover with their Titans. The turrets are great areas to retreat when using a Titan. The turret provides cover for your Titan's bodyshield to recharge and provides extra firepower for pursuing enemies.
- With how open this map is, the Stryder is a great Titan choice as you can quickly dash around the map and use the cover provided.
- This is a small symmetrical map. Players will want to take control of their Titan instead of leaving it in Auto-Titan mode. Titans need to stick together on a side of a map. Close up to the Tank Bay to continue hunting minions to reduce Titan Core charge time. Titans need to work together to take down enemy turrets and push into enemy territory once the turrets are down to score points by killing enemy Pilots.

Reference these videos in your free mobile friendly eGuide.

CAPTURE THE FLAG

NOTE

Initial flags, routes, and deployment areas shown. Factions switch sides at halftime.

TACTICS

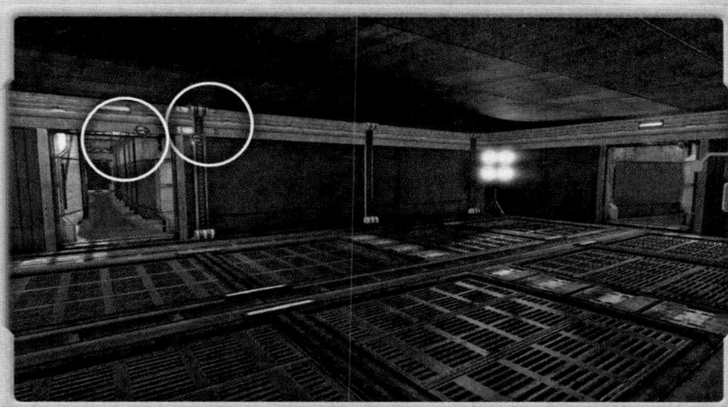

Reference these videos in your free mobile friendly eGuide.

PRO TIP: STRONGSIDE

Use the zip line route, step by step, to run the flag back to your base.

1. Once you grab the flag, wall run up to the zip line with the turret and make your way up to the roof.

2. Once on the roof, immediately run over the ridge to your team's side and then make your way over to your team's zip line that leads to your flag to score.

- On this map you're able to enter both flags' bases with your Titan and grab the flag without having to exit your Titan. With that said, the Stryder Titan will be extremely useful on this map because of its speed. To further assist your flag run, use the Stryder's Core Ability and you'll be able to use your dash to immediately get back to your base without getting caught in a battle.
- Use the trenches to sneak to the enemy's flag unnoticed. Active Radar Pulse is great here so you can spot any enemies that might be waiting around the corner for you.
- The roof is a great spot to guard your flag from being run through the zip lines—you can also zip line to their flag from here.
- Leave an Auto-Titan on guard mode with the Arc Cannon and Guardian Chip equipped at the enemy's ground turret. The Titan can pick off enemies that go on the enemy's zip line from the ground turret or pick off enemies trying to cross over to the other side of the map. This allows you to stay focused on the opposite side of the map near the enemy's tower turret.
- Use Arc Mines to boobytrap your tunnels from enemies sneaking over to your base.

HARDPOINT DOMINATION

1
2
3
4
5
6
7
8
9
A
B
C
LEGEND
IMC Deployment
Militia Deployment
Hardpoint A
Hardpoint B
Hardpoint C
Turret
Zip Line
Evac Point
1 Dozer Path
2 Militia Tower Turret
3 IMC Ground Turret
4 Tank Bay
5 IMC Locker Room
6 IMC Tower Turret
7 Cargo Container Building
8 Tank Path
9 Militia Ground Turret

TACTICS

- Hardpoint B is located in the center of the Tank Bay. This Hardpoint generally determines the winner of the game. If your team controls Hardpoint B, this center area is a perfect choke point to stop the opponents from flanking and to eventually gain control of one of the other Hardpoints. This also allows your team to apply pressure to the opponent by fighting enemies around the opponent's objective.
- Holding the IMC Locker Room building will effectively let you defend Hardpoints B and C with good cover and views over both points.
- Use the trenches to sneak up to Hardpoint A without having the enemy tower turret spot you.
- Take notice if you see your turret randomly shoot off to the side or behind itself, it is most likely shooting at an enemy Pilot.
- Don't waste too much time on the side of the map away from the Hardpoints. Even if you have a Sniper rifle, it is very difficult to get an open shot on the enemy unless you are on the roof. You'll want to stay near the Hardpoints to be in the action.
- When the opponent is converting Hardpoint B, lob grenades in the center of the crates for an easy kill.
- When defending Hardpoint B, stay hidden within the Tank Bay. Watch the side entrances for flanks, and once you see Hardpoint B being converted on your HUD then turn your attention to the center of the Tank Bay.
- Even though you are able to capture Hardpoint B with a Titan, you are extremely vulnerable to Arc Grenades and getting picked apart by Anti-Titan weapons. Keep moving and never stay stationary in this area.
- Take notice if you see your turret randomly shoot off to the side or behind itself. It is most likely shooting at an enemy Pilot.

LAST TITAN STANDING

LEGEND

IMC Deployment	1 Dozer Path
Militia Deployment	2 Militia Tower Turret
Turret	3 IMC Ground Turret
Zip Line	4 Tank Bay
Evac Point	5 IMC Locker Room
	6 IMC Tower Turret
	7 Cargo Container Building
	8 Tank Path
	9 Militia Ground Turret

TACTICS

- Because this is such a open map, it is hard to do a flank with your Titan without being noticed and overrun by multiple enemy Titans. Instead, stick with your other teammates and move around as a pack.
- Don't get caught with your team at the choke points: Dozer path or Tank path. It is easy for the enemy to damage you and hit their shots in this open area—you are just begging to get destroyed by a Cluster Missile.
- Before making a push to the enemy's side of the map, first pick off the enemy turrets.
- When making a push at the enemy team, communicate with your team to focus your fire at one enemy Titan at a time. It is better to take down a Titan rather than having two enemy Titans with half health. Eliminating one Titan at a time allows you to take less damage to your team's Titans and give you one less target to think about.
- If an enemy Pilot is on the ridge of the roof and you can't hit him, ignore the Pilot by getting closer to the Tank Bay. When the Pilot leans over to shoot you, dash away from the Tank Bay and easily pick off the Pilot who is now out in the open on the roof.
- As Training Ground is a map with standoffs and setups, using a high-powered, long-distance weapon like the Plasma Railgun is ideal.
- With this being such an open map, Particle Wall is a great Tactical Ability that allows your team to take cover in unsafe areas.

TITANFALL

PILOT HUNTER

LEGEND

	IMC Deployment
	Militia Deployment
	Turret
	Zip Line
	Evac Point

1. Dozer Path
2. Militia Tower Turret
3. IMC Ground Turret
4. Tank Bay
5. IMC Locker Room
6. IMC Tower Turret
7. Cargo Container Building
8. Tank Path
9. Militia Ground Turret

TACTICS

- Titans are the easiest and safest ways to take out enemy Pilots. Roam the perimeter of the Tank Bay to pick off minions as they try to move to the center of the map. Try to build your Titan as quickly as possible.
- The Ogre Titan is a great choice for Training Ground Pilot Hunter. You have better odds on winning the match the longer your Titan is up and running and the Ogre has the most health to get the job done.
- Getting that first strike allows your team to stay on your side of the map to defend and play passive as the opposing team tries to score points. Activating the turrets near the initial spawn will help spot enemy Pilots trying to sneak by and weaken the enemies who try to cross into your team's territory.
- Pilots need to use the cover provided on their side. The G2A4 Rifle and R-101C Carbine are great weapons to have when holding down your team's side. Each building provides enough cover for you to engage medium- to long-distance gun fights and at the same time hide behind the wall if the enemy Pilot hits you first.
- Pilots equipped with the Tier 1 Enhanced Parkour Kit will be able to wall hang on the inside of the Tank Bay for an extended amount of time. While wall hanging, you will be able to drop and kill a unsuspecting enemy Pilot.
- If the opposing team is stacked with Titans, a sure way to defeat them is to control the roof or inside the Tank Bay. The roof provides enough cover to dodge enemy Titan fire and allows you to deal damage with your Anti-Titan weapons. The inside of the Tank Bay gives you a safe area to retreat to if your team has no Titan. With a combination of Anti-Titan weapons being fired from the roof and inside of the Tank Bay, you'll catch the enemy Pilots ejecting and landing in your vicinity to finish them off.

QUICK REFERENCE

SCORING

EVENT	XP
COMBAT	
Airborne Kill	50
Beatdown	10
Comeback	100
Crushed Conscript	30
Crushed Grunt	30
Crushed Pilot	200
Crushed Spectre	40
Destroyed Crow (Militia Dropship)	100
Destroyed Goblin (IMC Dropship)	100
Destroyed Hornet (Militia Fighter)	100
Destroyed Phantom (IMC Fighter)	100
Doomed Auto-Titan	200
Doomed Titan	200
Double Kill	50
Electrocuted Grunt	20
Electrocuted Pilot	100
Electrocuted Spectre	30
First Strike	100
First Titanfall	100
Fish in a Barrel	100
Hacked Spectre	25
Hacked Spectre Killed Grunt	20
Hacked Spectre Killed Pilot	100
Hacked Spectre Killed Spectre	30
Hacked Spectre Killed Titan	200
Headshot Minion	10
Headshot Pilot	25
Killed Conscript	20
Killed Drone	50
Killed Flyer	100
Killed Grunt	20

EVENT	XP
Killed Pilot	100
Killed Search Drone	5
Killed Spectre	30
Killing Spree	25
Mayhem	50
Mega Kill	100
Nemesis	100
Pilot Assist	50
Pilot Beatdown	100
Quick Revenge	50
Rampage	50
Revenge	50
Showstopper	50
Terminated Pilot	200
Titan Assist	100
Titan Beatdown	200
Titanfall	25
Triple Kill	75
Wall Smashed Pilot	100
MELEE	
Executed Pilot	100
Executed Grunt	20
Executed Spectre	30
Jump Kicked Grunt	20
Jump Kicked Pilot	100
Jump Kicked Spectre	30
AUTO-TITAN	
Auto-Titan Killed Conscript	20
Auto-Titan Killed Grunt	20
Auto-Titan Killed Pilot	100
Auto-Titan Killed Spectre	30
Auto-Titan Killed Titan	200

EVENT	XP
RODEO	
Titan Doomed	200
Killed Rodeo Pilot	100
Rodeo Pilot Beatdown	200
Rodeoed Enemy Titan	50
TURRETS	
Hacked Turret Killed Conscript	20
Hacked Turret Killed Grunt	20
Hacked Turret Killed Pilot	100
Hacked Turret Killed Spectre	30
Hacked Turret Killed Titan	200
Killed Turret	50
Turret Activated	100
EPILOGUE	
Evac Denied	100
Get to the Chopper	200
Hot Zone Extract	200
Killed Evacuating Pilot	50
Sole Survivor	100
Solo Killed all Combatants	200
Team Bonus Full Team Evac	200
Team Bonus Killed All Combatants	100
GAME MODE	
Dominating	50
Flag Capture	500
Flag Return	250
Hardpoint Assault (Minion Kill)	25
Hardpoint Assault (Pilot Kill)	75
Hardpoint Capture Assist	75
Hardpoint Captured	150
Hardpoint Defense (Minion Kill)	25

EVENT	XP
Hardpoint Defense (Pilot Kill)	75
Hardpoint Hold	75
Hardpoint Neutralize Assist	25
Hardpoint Neutralized	50
Hardpoint Perimeter Defense (Minion Kill)	25
Hardpoint Perimeter Defense (Pilot Kill)	75
Hardpoint Ranged Support (Minion Kill)	10
Hardpoint Ranged Support (Pilot Kill)	75
Hardpoint Siege (Minion Kill)	10
Hardpoint Siege (Pilot Kill)	75
Killed Flag Carrier	150
Pilot Eliminated	150
Titan Eliminated	250
MATCH END	
Round Completion	150
Round Win	250
Victory	300
Victory Kill	100
Match Completion	200
BURN CARDS	
Burn Card Cancelled	25
Burn Card Extra Credit	1,000
Earned Burn Card	25
Earned Rare Burn Card	100
Rare Burn Card Cancelled	100
Spent Burn Card	25
Spent Rare Burn Card	100

PROGRESSION AND UNLOCKS

LEVEL	TOTAL XP	XP PER LEVEL	UNLOCK
1	—	—	—
2	1,500	1,500	CQB Pilot Loadout
3	3,300	1,800	Artillery Titan Loadout
4	5,800	2,500	Challenges
5	8,800	3,000	Custom Pilot Loadout (1-3)
6	12,500	3,700	R-97 Compact SMG
7	16,700	4,200	Arc Grenade, Burn Card Slot 1
8	21,500	4,800	Stim
9	26,900	5,400	Longbow-DMR Sniper, Burn Card Slot 2
10	32,900	6,000	Custom Titan Loadout (1-3)
11	39,400	6,500	Slaved Warheads, Burn Card Slot 3
12	46,500	7,100	Plasma Railgun
13	54,100	7,600	Electric Smoke
14	62,300	8,200	Fast Autoloader
15	71,100	8,800	Custom Pilot 4 Loadout
16	80,300	9,200	Warpfall Transmitter
17	90,100	9,800	Satchel Charge
18	100,500	10,400	G2A4 Rifle
19	111,300	10,800	Active Radar Pulse
20	122,700	11,400	Custom Titan 4 Loadout
21	134,700	12,000	Arc Cannon
22	147,100	12,400	Mag Launcher
23	160,100	13,000	Core Extender
24	173,600	13,500	Cluster Missile
25	187,600	14,000	Burn Card Pack

LEVEL	TOTAL XP	XP PER LEVEL	UNLOCK
26	202,100	14,500	Particle Wall
27	217,100	15,000	B3 Wingman
28	232,600	15,500	Triple Threat
29	248,700	16,100	Hemlok BF-R
30	265,200	16,500	Burn Card Pack, Custom Pilot 5 Loadout
31	282,300	17,100	Arc Mine
32	299,800	17,500	Multi-Target Missile System
33	317,900	18,100	Charge Rifle
34	336,500	18,600	C.A.R. SMG
35	356,000	19,500	Custom Titan 5 Loadout
36	377,000	21,000	Run N Gun Kit
37	399,000	22,000	Dead Man's Trigger
38	422,000	23,000	Dash Quickcharger
39	446,000	24,000	Spitfire LMG
40	471,000	25,000	Burn Card Pack
41	497,000	26,000	Big Punch
42	524,000	27,000	Quick Reload
43	552,000	28,000	The "Icepick"
44	581,000	29,000	Kraber-AP Sniper
45	612,000	31,000	Burn Card Pack
46	650,000	38,000	Tactical Reactor
47	695,000	45,000	Core Accelerator
48	750,000	55,000	Stealth Kit
49	818,000	68,000	Guardian Chip
50	900,000	82,000	Burn Card Pack

GEN PROGRESSION

After you Regenerate, look at the challenges you need to complete in order to regenerate again. Begin working on those as soon as possible to limit the amount of grinding needed to regenerate after reaching level 50 again.

GEN 2 PREREQUISITES

- Reach Level 50

GEN 3 PREREQUISITES

- Reach level 50
- EVA-8 Shotgun: If It Moves... Challenge
- EVA-8 Shotgun: Top Gun Challenge
- 40mm Cannon: If It Moves... Challenge
- 40mm Cannon: Titan Killer Challenge

GEN 4 PREREQUISITES

- Reach level 50
- R-97 Compact SMG: If It Moves... Challenge
- R-97 Compact SMG: Top Gun Challenge
- Plasma Railgun: If It Moves... Challenge
- Plasma Railgun: Titan Killer Challenge
- Satchel Charge: Top Gun Challenge

GEN 5 PREREQUISITES

- Reach level 50
- Longbow-DMR Sniper: If It Moves... Challenge
- Longbow-DMR Sniper: Top Gun Challenge
- Quad Rocket: If It Moves... Challenge
- Quad Rocket: Titan Killer Challenge
- Charge Rifle: Critically Conditioned Challenge
- RE-45 Autopistol: If It Moves... Challenge

GEN 6 PREREQUISITES

- Reach level 50
- R-101C Carbine: If It Moves... Challenge
- R-101C Carbine: Top Gun Challenge
- Arc Cannon: If It Moves... Challenge
- Arc Cannon: Titan Killer Challenge
- Sidewinder: Titan Killer Challenge
- Gooser Challenge

GEN 7 PREREQUISITES

- Reach level 50
- Spitfire LMG: If It Moves... Challenge
- Spitfire LMG: Top Gun Challenge
- Triple Threat: If It Moves... Challenge
- Triple Threat: Titan Killer Challenge
- Mag Launcher: Titan Killer Challenge
- Brain Surgeon Challenge

GEN 8 PREREQUISITES

- Reach level 50
- G2A4 Rifle: If It Moves... Challenge
- G2A4 Rifle: Top Gun Challenge
- XO-16 Chaingun: If It Moves... Challenge
- XO-16 Chaingun: Titan Killer Challenge
- Charge Rifle: Titan Killer Challenge
- Fresh Squeezed Challenge

GEN 9 PREREQUISITES

- Reach level 50
- C.A.R SMG: If It Moves... Challenge
- C.A.R SMG: Top Gun Challenge
- Executioner Challenge
- Archer Heavy Rocket: Titan Killer Challenge
- All I Do is Win Challenge
- Look Out Below! Challenge
- 40mm Cannon: Critically Conditioned Challenge

GEN 10 PREREQUISITES

- Reach level 50
- Smart Pistol MK5: Top Gun Challenge
- Hemlok BF-R: Top Gun Challenge
- Kraber-AP Sniper: Top Gun Challenge
- Disarmed Challenge
- MVP Challenge
- Deadly Apparition Challenge
- Death Reincarnate Challenge
- XO-16 Chaingun: Critically Conditioned Challenge
- Plasma Railgun: Critically Conditioned Challenge

CHALLENGES

NOTE

For all weapon-based challenges, see the Pilot Gear and Titans chapters.

GENERAL

GETTING REPS

TIER	CRITERIA	REWARD
1	Play 10 Rounds	500 XP
2	Play 25 Rounds	1,000 XP
3	Play 50 Rounds	2,500 XP, Fast Learner Burn Card
4	Play 100 Rounds	5,000 XP, Fast Learner Burn Card
5	Play 250 Rounds	10,000 XP, Ghost Squad, Adrenaline Transfusion, and Echo Vision Burn Cards

ALL I DO IS WIN

TIER	CRITERIA	REWARD
1	Win 10 Rounds	500 XP
2	Win 30 Rounds	1,000 XP
3	Win 50 Rounds	2,500 XP, Fast Learner Burn Card
4	Win 70 Rounds	5,000 XP, Fast Learner Burn Card
5	Win 100 Rounds	10,000 XP, Ghost Squad, Adrenaline Transfusion, and Echo Vision Burn Cards

MVP

TIER	CRITERIA	REWARD
1	Be the player with the highest score on your team 1 time	500 XP
2	Be the player with the highest score on your team 5 times	1,000 XP
3	Be the player with the highest score on your team 10 times	2,500 XP, Fast Learner, Prosthetic Legs, and Packet Sniffer Burn Cards
4	Be the player with the highest score on your team 25 times	5,000 XP, Active Camo, Smuggled Stimulant, and Aural Implant Burn Cards
5	Be the player with the highest score on your team 50 times	10,000 XP, Ghost Squad, Adrenaline Transfusion, and Echo Vision Burn Cards

RAINMAKER

TIER	CRITERIA	REWARD
1	Drop in a Titan 10 times	500 XP
2	Drop in a Titan 25 times	1,000 XP
3	Drop in a Titan 50 times	2,500 XP, Decisive Action Burn Card
4	Drop in a Titan 80 times	5,000 XP, Decisive Action, and Pull Rank Burn Cards
5	Drop in a Titan 150 times	10,000 XP, Decisive Action, Pull Rank, and Atlas Refurb Burn Cards

RODEO

TIER	CRITERIA	REWARD
1	Rodeo an enemy Titan 10 times	500 XP
2	Rodeo an enemy Titan 25 times	1,000 XP
3	Rodeo an enemy Titan 50 times	2,500 XP, Amped Sidewinder, Pull Rank, and Super Charger Burn Cards
4	Rodeo an enemy Titan 80 times	5,000 XP, Amped Charge Rifle, Satellite Uplink, and Massive Payload Burn Cards
5	Rodeo an enemy Titan 150 times	10,000 XP, Amped Mag Launcher, Pull Rank, and Super Charger Burn Cards

PUNCH OUT

TIER	CRITERIA	REWARD
1	Eject from your Titan 10 times	500 XP
2	Eject from your Titan 25 times	1,000 XP
3	Eject from your Titan 50 times	2,500 XP, Massive Payload Burn Card
4	Eject from your Titan 100 times	5,000 XP, 2 Massive Payload Burn Cards
5	Eject from your Titan 250 times	10,000 XP, 3 Massive Payload Burn Cards

MAKING FRIENDS

TIER	CRITERIA	REWARD
1	Hack 10 Spectres	500 XP
2	Hack 25 Spectres	1,000 XP
3	Hack 50 Spectres	2,500 XP, WiFi Virus, Urban Renewal, and Spectre Camo Burn Cards
4	Hack 80 Spectres	5,000 XP, WiFi Virus, Urban Renewal, and Spectre Camo Burn Cards
5	Hack 150 Spectres	10,000 XP, WiFi Virus, Urban Renewal, and Spectre Camo Burn Cards

TIME

TIME KEEPS ON SLIPPING

TIER	CRITERIA	REWARD
1	Play *Titanfall* for 1 hour	500 XP
2	Play *Titanfall* for 10 hours	1,000 XP
3	Play *Titanfall* for 20 hours	2,500 XP, Ghost Squad, Adrenaline Transfusion, and Echo Vision Burn Cards
4	Play *Titanfall* for 40 hours	5,000 XP, Ghost Squad, Adrenaline Transfusion, and Echo Vision Burn Cards
5	Play *Titanfall* for 60 hours	10,000 XP, Ghost Squad, Adrenaline Transfusion, and Echo Vision Burn Cards

PRIVATE TIME

TIER	CRITERIA	REWARD
1	Play as a Pilot for 1 hour	500 XP
2	Play as a Pilot for 5 hours	1,000 XP
3	Play as a Pilot for 10 hours	2,500 XP, Map Hack and Satellite Uplink Burn Cards
4	Play as a Pilot for 20 hours	5,000 XP, Map Hack and Satellite Uplink Burn Cards
5	Play as a Pilot for 40 hours	10,000 XP, Map Hack and Satellite Uplink Burn Cards

DOOMSDAY CLOCK

TIER	CRITERIA	REWARD
1	Play in a Titan for 1 hour	500 XP
2	Play in a Titan for 2 hours	1,000 XP
3	Play in a Titan for 5 hours	2,500 XP, Pull Rank and Super Charger Burn Cards
4	Play in a Titan for 10 hours	5,000 XP, Pull Rank and Super Charger Burn Cards
5	Play in a Titan for 20 hours	10,000 XP, Pull Rank and Super Charger Burn Cards

HANGING AROUND

TIER	CRITERIA	REWARD
1	Spend .1 hour wall hanging	500 XP
2	Spend .25 hour wall hanging	1,000 XP
3	Spend .5 hour wall hanging	2,500 XP, Spider Sense Burn Card
4	Spend 1 hour wall hanging	5,000 XP, Spider Sense Burn Card
5	Spend 1.5 hours wall hanging	10,000 XP, Spider Sense Burn Card

DISTANCE

NOMAD

TIER	CRITERIA	REWARD
1	Travel a total distance of 25 kilometers	500 XP
2	Travel a total distance of 80 kilometers	1,000 XP
3	Travel a total distance of 160 kilometers	2,500 XP, Prosthetic Legs and Decisive Action Burn Cards
4	Travel a total distance of 250 kilometers	5,000 XP, Smuggled Stimulant, Pull Rank, and Super Charger Burn Cards
5	Travel a total distance of 400 kilometers	10,000 XP, Adrenaline Transfusion, Reserve Ogre, and Super Charger Burn Cards

RUNNING MAN

TIER	CRITERIA	REWARD
1	Travel a total distance of 15 kilometers as a Pilot	500 XP
2	Travel a total distance of 40 kilometers as a Pilot	1,000 XP
3	Travel a total distance of 80 kilometers as a Pilot	2,500 XP, Prosthetic Legs Burn Card
4	Travel a total distance of 145 kilometers as a Pilot	5,000 XP, Prosthetic Legs and Smuggled Stimulant Burn Cards
5	Travel a total distance of 250 kilometers as a Pilot	10,000 XP, Prosthetic Legs, Smuggled Stimulant, and Adrenaline Transfusion Burn Cards

LONG HAUL

TIER	CRITERIA	REWARD
1	Travel a total distance of 8 kilometers in a Titan	500 XP
2	Travel a total distance of 25 kilometers in a Titan	1,000 XP
3	Travel a total distance of 50 kilometers in a Titan	2,500 XP, Decisive Action and Super Charger Burn Cards
4	Travel a total distance of 80 kilometers in a Titan	5,000 XP, Pull Rank and Super Charger Burn Cards
5	Travel a total distance of 130 kilometers in a Titan	10,000 XP, Spare Stryder and Super Charger Burn Cards

NINJA WARRIOR

TIER	CRITERIA	REWARD
1	Wall run .5 kilometer	500 XP
2	Wall run 1 kilometer	1,000 XP
3	Wall run 1.5 kilometers	2,500 XP, Prosthetic Legs Burn Card
4	Wall run 2.5 kilometers	5,000 XP, Prosthetic Legs and Smuggled Stimulant Burn Cards
5	Wall run 4 kilometers	10,000 XP, Prosthetic Legs, Smuggled Stimulant, and Adrenaline Transfusion Burn Cards

FREQUENT FLYER

TIER	CRITERIA	REWARD
1	Travel a total distance of 8 kilometers in the air	500 XP
2	Travel a total distance of 25 kilometers in the air	1,000 XP
3	Travel a total distance of 50 kilometers in the air	2,500 XP, Fast Learner Burn Card
4	Travel a total distance of 75 kilometers in the air	5,000 XP, Fast Learner Burn Card
5	Travel a total distance of 100 kilometers in the air	10,000 XP, Fast Learner Burn Card

COMMUTER FLIGHT

TIER	CRITERIA	REWARD
1	Travel .25 kilometer on zip lines	500 XP
2	Travel 1 kilometer on zip lines	1,000 XP
3	Travel 1.5 kilometers on zip lines	2,500 XP, Fast Learner Burn Card
4	Travel 3 kilometers on zip lines	5,000 XP, Fast Learner Burn Card
5	Travel 5 kilometers on zip lines	10,000 XP, Fast Learner Burn Card

SHOULDERS OF GIANTS

TIER	CRITERIA	REWARD
1	Travel .1 kilometer while hitching a ride on friendly Titans	500 XP
2	Travel .25 kilometer while hitching a ride on friendly Titans	1,000 XP
3	Travel 1 kilometer while hitching a ride on friendly Titans	2,500 XP, Titan Salvage and Amped Mag Launcher Burn Cards
4	Travel 1.5 kilometers while hitching a ride on friendly Titans	5,000 XP, Titan Salvage and Amped Mag Launcher Burn Cards
5	Travel 2.5 kilometers while hitching a ride on friendly Titans	10,000 XP, Titan Salvage and Amped Mag Launcher Burn Cards

COWBOY UP

TIER	CRITERIA	REWARD
1	Travel .1 kilometer on top of enemy Titans	500 XP
2	Travel .25 kilometer on top of enemy Titans	1,000 XP
3	Travel 1 kilometer on top of enemy Titans	2,500 XP, Titan Salvage and Amped LMG Burn Cards
4	Travel 1.5 kilometers on top of enemy Titans	5,000 XP, Titan Salvage and Amped LMG Burn Cards
5	Travel 2.5 kilometers on top of enemy Titans	10,000 XP, Titan Salvage and Amped LMG Burn Cards

KILLS

EASY PICKINGS

TIER	CRITERIA	REWARD
1	Kill 25 Grunts	500 XP
2	Kill 100 Grunts	1,000 XP
3	Kill 250 Grunts	2,500 XP, Thin the Ranks Burn Card
4	Kill 500 Grunts	5,000 XP, Thin the Ranks and Double Agent Burn Cards
5	Kill 1,000 Grunts	10,000 XP, Thin the Ranks, Double Agent, and Conscription Burn Cards

TECHNOPHOBE

TIER	CRITERIA	REWARD
1	Kill 25 Spectres	500 XP
2	Kill 100 Spectres	1,000 XP
3	Kill 200 Spectres	2,500 XP, Urban Renewal Burn Card
4	Kill 300 Spectres	5,000 XP, Urban Renewal and Spectre Camo Burn Cards
5	Kill 400 Spectres	10,000 XP, Urban Renewal, Spectre Camo, and WiFi Virus Burn Cards

INNOCENT BYSTANDER

TIER	CRITERIA	REWARD
1	Kill 10 Marvins	500 XP
2	Kill 25 Marvins	1,000 XP
3	Kill 50 Marvins	2,500 XP
4	Kill 100 Marvins	5,000 XP
5	Kill 250 Marvins	10,000 XP

ICEBREAKER

TIER	CRITERIA	REWARD
1	Get the first kill of the match 1 time	500 XP
2	Get the first kill of the match 10 times	1,000 XP
3	Get the first kill of the match 25 times	2,500 XP, Rematch Burn Card
4	Get the first kill of the match 50 times	5,000 XP, 2 Rematch Burn Cards
5	Get the first kill of the match 100 times	10,000 XP, 3 Rematch Burn Cards

GHOST HUNTER

TIER	CRITERIA	REWARD
1	Kill a cloaked Pilot 5 times	500 XP
2	Kill a cloaked Pilot 15 times	1,000 XP
3	Kill a cloaked Pilot 30 times	2,500 XP and Spider Sense Burn Card
4	Kill a cloaked Pilot 50 times	5,000 XP, Spider Sense and Satellite Uplink Burn Cards
5	Kill a cloaked Pilot 10 times	10,000 XP, Spider Sense, Satellite Uplink, and Map Hack Burn Cards

DEADLY APPARITION

TIER	CRITERIA	REWARD
1	Get 10 kills while being cloaked	500 XP
2	Get 25 kills while being cloaked	1,000 XP
3	Get 50 kills while being cloaked	2,500 XP, Double Agent Burn Card
4	Get 100 kills while being cloaked	5,000 XP, Double Agent and Active Camo Burn Cards
5	Get 200 kills while being cloaked	10,000 XP, Double Agent, Active Camo, and Ghost Squad Burn Cards

LOOK OUT BELOW!

TIER	CRITERIA	REWARD
1	Get 1 kill while dropping your Titan on the enemy	500 XP
2	Get 5 kills while dropping your Titan on the enemy	1,000 XP
3	Get 15 kills while dropping your Titan on the enemy	2,500 XP, Atlas Refurb Burn Card
4	Get 30 kills while dropping your Titan on the enemy	5,000 XP, Atlas Refurb and Spare Stryder Burn Cards
5	Get 50 kills while dropping your Titan on the enemy	10,000 XP, Atlas Refurb, Spare Stryder, and Reserve Ogre Burn Cards

SIC 'EM!

TIER	CRITERIA	REWARD
1	Have your Auto-Titan get 10 kills while in Follow mode	500 XP
2	Have your Auto-Titan get 25 kills while in Follow mode	1,000 XP
3	Have your Auto-Titan get 50 kills while in Follow mode	2,500 XP, Titan Salvage Burn Card
4	Have your Auto-Titan get 100 kills while in Follow mode	5,000 XP, Titan Salvage and Decisive Action Burn Cards
5	Have your Auto-Titan get 200 kills while in Follow mode	10,000 XP, Titan Salvage and Pull Rank Burn Cards

GUARD DOG		
TIER	CRITERIA	REWARD
1	Have your Auto-Titan get 10 kills while in Guard mode	500 XP
2	Have your Auto-Titan get 25 kills while in Guard mode	1,000 XP
3	Have your Auto-Titan get 50 kills while in Guard mode	2,500 XP, Titan Salvage Burn Card
4	Have your Auto-Titan get 100 kills while in Guard mode	5,000 XP, Titan Salvage and Decisive Action Burn Cards
5	Have your Auto-Titan get 200 kills while in Guard mode	10,000 XP, Titan Salvage and Pull Rank Burn Cards

MOBILITY KILLS

DEATH REINCARNATE		
TIER	CRITERIA	REWARD
1	Get a kill while ejecting 5 times	500 XP
2	Get a kill while ejecting 15 times	1,000 XP
3	Get a kill while ejecting 30 times	2,500 XP, Massive Payload Burn Card
4	Get a kill while ejecting 50 times	5,000 XP, Massive Payload Burn Card
5	Get a kill while ejecting 75 times	10,000 XP, Massive Payload Burn Card

GOOSER		
TIER	CRITERIA	REWARD
1	Kill 5 Pilots while they are ejecting	500 XP
2	Kill 15 Pilots while they are ejecting	1,000 XP
3	Kill 30 Pilots while they are ejecting	2,500 XP and Massive Payload Burn Card
4	Kill 50 Pilots while they are ejecting	5,000 XP and Massive Payload Burn Card
5	Kill 75 Pilots while they are ejecting	10,000 XP and Massive Payload Burn Card

PEST CONTROL		
TIER	CRITERIA	REWARD
1	Kill 1 Pilot while they are wall running	500 XP
2	Kill 5 Pilots while they are wall running	1,000 XP
3	Kill 15 Pilots while they are wall running	2,500 XP, Most Wanted List Burn Card
4	Kill 30 Pilots while they are wall running	5,000 XP, Most Wanted List Burn Card
5	Kill 50 Pilots while they are wall running	10,000 XP, Most Wanted List Burn Card

FLYSWATTER		
TIER	CRITERIA	REWARD
1	Kill 1 Pilot while they are wall hanging	500 XP
2	Kill 5 Pilots while they are wall hanging	1,000 XP
3	Kill 15 Pilots while they are wall hanging	2,500 XP, Most Wanted List Burn Card
4	Kill 30 Pilots while they are wall hanging	5,000 XP, Most Wanted List Burn Card
5	Kill 50 Pilots while they are wall hanging	10,000 XP, Most Wanted List Burn Card

DRIVE-BY		
TIER	CRITERIA	REWARD
1	Get 5 kills while wall running	500 XP
2	Get 15 kills while wall running	1,000 XP
3	Get 30 kills while wall running	2,500 XP, Satellite Uplink Burn Card
4	Get 50 kills while wall running	5,000 XP, 2 Satellite Uplink Burn Cards
5	Get 75 kills while wall running	10,000 XP, 2 Satellite Uplink and 1 Map Hack Burn Cards

WALLFLOWER		
TIER	CRITERIA	REWARD
1	Get 5 kills while wall hanging	500 XP
2	Get 15 kills while wall hanging	1,000 XP
3	Get 30 kills while wall hanging	2,500 XP, Double Agent Burn Card
4	Get 50 kills while wall hanging	5,000 XP, Double Agent and Active Camo Burn Cards
5	Get 75 kills while wall hanging	10,000 XP, Double Agent, Active Camo, and Ghost Squad Burn Cards

ROADKILL		
TIER	CRITERIA	REWARD
1	Run over 25 enemies with your Titan	500 XP
2	Run over 50 enemies with your Titan	1,000 XP
3	Run over 100 enemies with your Titan	2,500 XP, Fast Learner Burn Card
4	Run over 200 enemies with your Titan	5,000 XP, Fast Learner Burn Card
5	Run over 500 enemies with your Titan	10,000 XP, Fast Learner Burn Card

WHAT PILOT?		
TIER	CRITERIA	REWARD
1	Run over 5 Pilots with your Titan	500 XP
2	Run over 15 Pilots with your Titan	1,000 XP
3	Run over 30 Pilots with your Titan	2,500 XP, Fast Learner Burn Card
4	Run over 50 Pilots with your Titan	5,000 XP, Fast Learner Burn Card
5	Run over 100 Pilots with your Titan	10,000 XP, Fast Learner Burn Card

BRAIN SURGEON		
TIER	CRITERIA	REWARD
1	Kill 1 Titan by rodeo	500 XP
2	Kill 5 Titans by rodeo	1,000 XP
3	Kill 15 Titans by rodeo	2,500 XP, Titan Salvage Burn Card
4	Kill 30 Titans by rodeo	5,000 XP, Titan Salvage Burn Card
5	Kill 50 Titans by rodeo	10,000 XP, Titan Salvage Burn Card

MELEE KILLS

HEAD TURNER		
TIER	CRITERIA	REWARD
1	Execute 5 Pilots as a Pilot	500 XP
2	Execute 15 Pilots as a Pilot	1,000 XP
3	Execute 30 Pilots as a Pilot	2,500 XP, Most Wanted List Burn Card
4	Execute 50 Pilots as a Pilot	5,000 XP, Most Wanted List Burn Card
5	Execute 100 Pilots as a Pilot	10,000 XP, Most Wanted List Burn Card

JACKBOOT		
TIER	CRITERIA	REWARD
1	Get 10 kills using a melee kick	500 XP
2	Get 25 kills using a melee kick	1,000 XP
3	Get 50 kills using a melee kick	2,500 XP, Most Wanted List Burn Card
4	Get 100 kills using a melee kick	5,000 XP, Most Wanted List Burn Card
5	Get 200 kills using a melee kick	10,000 XP, Most Wanted List Burn Card

SWEEP THE LEG		
TIER	CRITERIA	REWARD
1	Kill 10 Pilots using melee kick	500 XP
2	Kill 25 Pilots using melee kick	1,000 XP
3	Kill 50 Pilots using melee kick	2,500 XP, Most Wanted List Burn Card
4	Kill 100 Pilots using melee kick	5,000 XP, Most Wanted List Burn Card
5	Kill 200 Pilots using melee kick	10,000 XP, Most Wanted List Burn Card

MISMATCH		
TIER	CRITERIA	REWARD
1	Kill 5 enemies with melee as a Titan	500 XP
2	Kill 20 enemies with melee as a Titan	1,000 XP
3	Kill 50 enemies with melee as a Titan	2,500 XP, Titan Salvage Burn Card
4	Kill 100 enemies with melee as a Titan	5,000 XP, Titan Salvage Burn Card
5	Kill 200 enemies with melee as a Titan	10,000 XP, Titan Salvage Burn Card

BRASS KNUCKLES		
TIER	CRITERIA	REWARD
1	Kill 5 Pilots with melee as a Titan	500 XP
2	Kill 15 Pilots with melee as a Titan	1,000 XP
3	Kill 30 Pilots with melee as a Titan	2,500 XP, Titan Salvage Burn Card
4	Kill 50 Pilots with melee as a Titan	5,000 XP, Titan Salvage Burn Card
5	Kill 100 Pilots with melee as a Titan	10,000 XP, Titan Salvage Burn Card

FRESH SQUEEZED		
TIER	CRITERIA	REWARD
1	Get 1 execution kill as a Stryder Titan	500 XP
2	Get 5 execution kills as a Stryder Titan	1,000 XP
3	Get 10 execution kills as a Stryder Titan	2,500 XP, Titan Salvage Burn Card
4	Get 15 execution kills as a Stryder Titan	5,000 XP, Titan Salvage Burn Card
5	Get 25 execution kills as a Stryder Titan	10,000 XP, Titan Salvage Burn Card

EXECUTIONER		
TIER	CRITERIA	REWARD
1	Get 1 execution kill as an Atlas Titan	500 XP
2	Get 5 execution kills as an Atlas Titan	1,000 XP
3	Get 10 execution kills as an Atlas Titan	2,500 XP, Titan Salvage Burn Card
4	Get 15 execution kills as an Atlas Titan	5,000 XP, Titan Salvage Burn Card
5	Get 25 execution kills as an Atlas Titan	10,000 XP, Titan Salvage Burn Card

DISARMED		
TIER	CRITERIA	REWARD
1	Get 1 execution kill as an Ogre Titan	500 XP
2	Get 5 execution kills as an Ogre Titan	1,000 XP
3	Get 10 execution kills as an Ogre Titan	2,500 XP, Titan Salvage Burn Card
4	Get 15 execution kills as an Ogre Titan	5,000 XP, Titan Salvage Burn Card
5	Get 25 execution kills as an Ogre Titan	10,000 XP, Titan Salvage Burn Card

NOTE

For all weapon-based challenges, see the Pilot Gear and Titans chapters.

BURN CARDS

WEAPON BURN CARDS

These cards increase the damage of the specified weapon, usually increasing damage output or through the addition of a special attribute. The weapon's attachments and mods are determined by the card, not the Pilot's preferred loadout.

Amped Archer

Description: Replace Anti-Titan weapon with an Archer firing powerful Titanhammer Missiles.

Rarity: Common

Amped Archer
Replace Anti-Titan Weapon with an Archer firing powerful Titanhammer Missiles
We traced the modification. Hammond Robotics has a weapons division? -Bish

Tactics

- Best used in Last Titan Standing
- This already powerful Anti-Titan weapon gets a damage boost, making the Archer Heavy Rocket a great Anti-Titan weapon for dropping an enemy Titan's shield...or taking it out. However, the projectile travels at a slower speed, so make sure you have a clear shot.

Amped C.A.R.

Description: Replace Primary Weapon with a more lethal C.A.R. SMG.

Rarity: Common

Amped C.A.R.
Replace Primary Weapon with a more lethal C.A.R. SMG
It's not all trash on the black market. -Blisk

Tactics

- Dominate close-quarter combat with this super-charged C.A.R. SMG; it makes defending objectives much easier.

Amped Charge Rifle

Description: Replace Anti-Titan Weapon with a faster charging Charge Rifle.

Rarity: Common

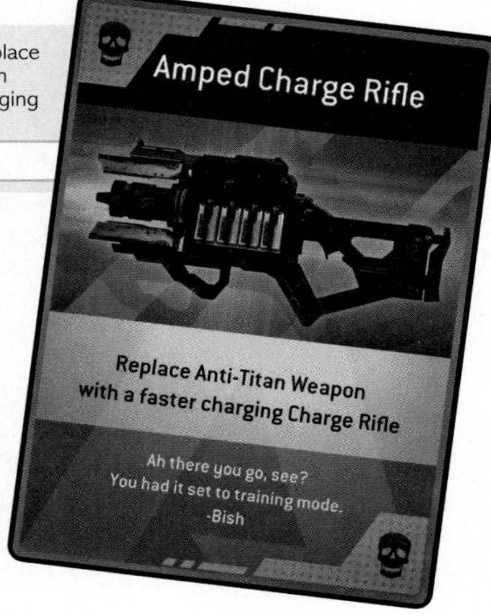

Amped Charge Rifle
Replace Anti-Titan Weapon with a faster charging Charge Rifle
Ah there you go, see?
You had it set to training mode.
-Bish

Tactics

- Best used in Last Titan Standing
- The Charge Rifle is the most powerful Anti-Titan weapon. This Burn Card increases the charge speed, allowing it to fire more energy beams at a faster rate, significantly increasing the weapon's overall damage output.

Amped DMR

Description: Replace Primary Weapon with a sonar scope Longbow-DMR Sniper.

Rarity: Common

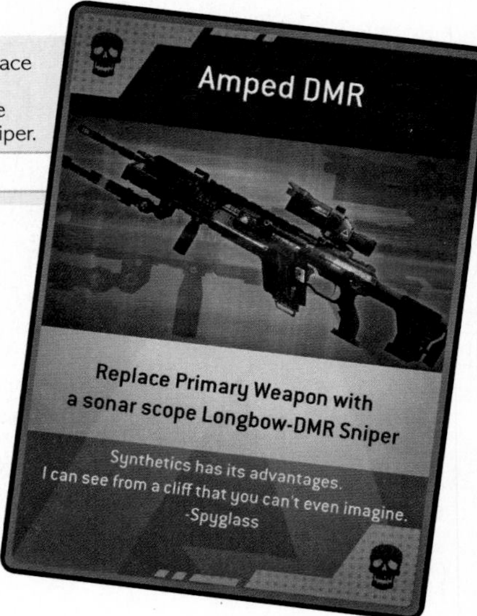

Amped DMR
Replace Primary Weapon with a sonar scope Longbow-DMR Sniper
Synthetics has its advantages.
I can see from a cliff that you can't even imagine.
-Spyglass

Tactics

- This Burn Card adds Active Radar Pulse when zoomed in with the Longbow-DMR Sniper. An excellent card to use to communicate the location of enemies to your teammates.

Amped EVA-8

Description: Replace Primary Weapon with an automatic EVA-8 Shotgun.

Rarity: Common

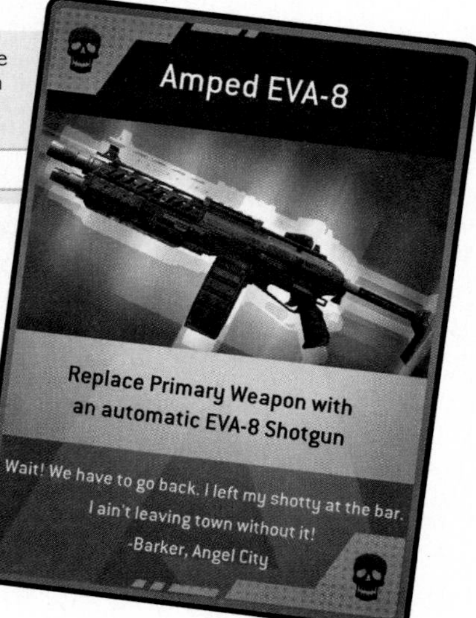

Tactics

- Catch enemies by surprise when roaming the interiors of buildings with this powerful auto-shotgun; reload often.

Amped G2A4

Description: Replace Primary Weapon with a more lethal G2A4 Rifle.

Rarity: Common

Amped G2A4
Replace Primary Weapon with a more lethal G2A4 Rifle
Grab the rifle, boy.
There's something moving in the fields,
and it ain't natural.
-Albert Woodman, Colony hydro farmer

Tactics

- This enhanced G2A4 Rifle allows you to take precision shots across the map and take down enemies.

Amped Hemlok

Description: Replace Primary Weapon with a more lethal Hemlok BF-R.

Rarity: Common

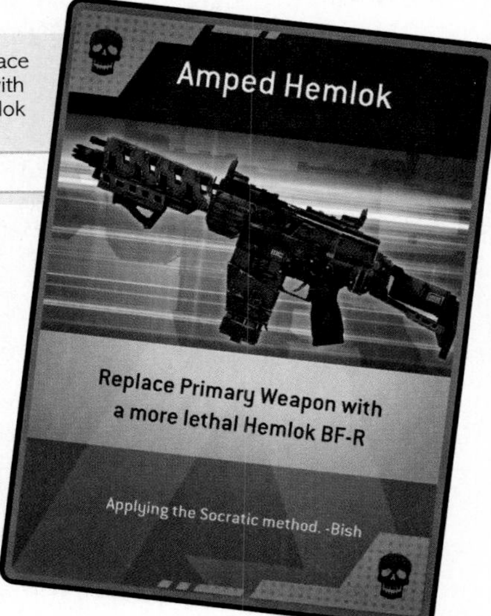

Amped Hemlok
Replace Primary Weapon with a more lethal Hemlok BF-R
Applying the Socratic method. -Bish

Tactics

- This Hemlok BF-R allows you to dominate Pilots, delivering more damage per burst.

Amped Kraber

Description: Replace Primary Weapon with a Kraber-AP Sniper that fires explosive rounds.

Rarity: Common

Tactics

- Explosive rounds have small splash damage radius, ideal for damaging/killing tight groups of minions. Rounds also inflict light damage against Titans.

Amped LMG

Description: Replace Primary Weapon with a rapid-fire Spitfire LMG.

Rarity: Common

Amped LMG
Replace Primary Weapon with a rapid-fire Spitfire LMG
I approve these changes. -Charles Griffith, Pilot

Tactics

- If there are multiple Titans on the map, combine this Burn Card with Cloak and rodeo attack as many enemy Titans as you can. The higher rate of fire allows the Spitfire LMG to tear through a Titan's internal systems in no time.

Amped Mag Launcher

Description: Replace Anti-Titan Weapon with a high-capacity, automatic Mag Launcher.

Rarity: Common

Amped Mag Launcher
Replace Anti-Titan Weapon with a high-capacity, automatic Mag Launcher
Just because they call it the Titan Wars doesn't mean we always had Titans. Sometimes you had to improvise. -Graves

Tactics

- Best used in Last Titan Standing
- With a larger magazine capacity and a higher rate of fire, the Mag Launcher is more devastating against enemy Titans; engage at close range, preferably while the Titan's bodyshield is down.

Amped P2011

Description: Replace Sidearm Weapon with a burst fire Hammond P2011.

Rarity: Common

Amped P2011
Replace Sidearm Weapon with a burst fire Hammond P2011
There was a fella from the backwaters that could shoot three times before yer pinky touched the holster. I'm that fella. -Blisk

Tactics

› An excellent Burn Card for a rifleman or sniper, the Hammond P2011 is now set to burst fire instead of single fire, allowing for a faster rate of fire.

Amped R-101C

Description: Replace Primary Weapon with a more lethal R-101C Carbine.

Rarity: Common

Amped R-101C
Replace Primary Weapon with a more lethal R-101C Carbine
They'll call us terrorists or worse, but we can't win playing by their rules. -MacAllan

Tactics

› The carbine is already the most versatile Pilot weapon; take advantage of the extra firepower and dominate the enemy in all distances.

Amped R-97

Description: Replace Primary Weapon with a more lethal R-97 Compact SMG.

Rarity: Common

Amped R-97
Replace Primary Weapon with a more lethal R-97 Compact SMG
Merc gear. Better keep moving, nobody hires just one bounty hunter. -Sarah, outside Cobalt Station

Tactics

› Dominate close-quarter combat with this super-charged R-97; it makes defending objectives much easier.

Amped RE-45

Description: Replace Sidearm Weapon with a more lethal RE-45 Autopistol.

Rarity: Common

Amped RE-45
Replace Sidearm Weapon with a more lethal RE-45 Auto-Pistol
Presuming you don't want to become a critter's lunch, take this time to locate and secure your hollow point rounds. -Graves, approaching Boneyard

Tactics

› This Burn Card benefits the Pilot that likes to snipe, giving them a more powerful RE-45 Autopistol as a close-quarter backup.

Amped Sidewinder

Description: Replace Anti-Titan Weapon with a double ammo capacity Sidewinder.

Rarity: Common

Tactics

- Best used in Last Titan Standing
- With double the ammo, this Burn Card makes the Sidewinder a great Anti-Titan weapon; target the red glowing sections on a Titan's hull to score one critical hit after another.

Amped Smart Pistol
So it'll do calculus now? -Sarah

Description: Replace Primary Weapon with a more lethal Smart Pistol MK5.

Rarity: Common

Tactics

- Best used in Attrition
- Quickly blast through squads of minions with this enhanced Smart Pistol MK5.

Amped Wingman

Description: Replace Sidearm Weapon with a match trigger B3 Wingman.

Rarity: Common

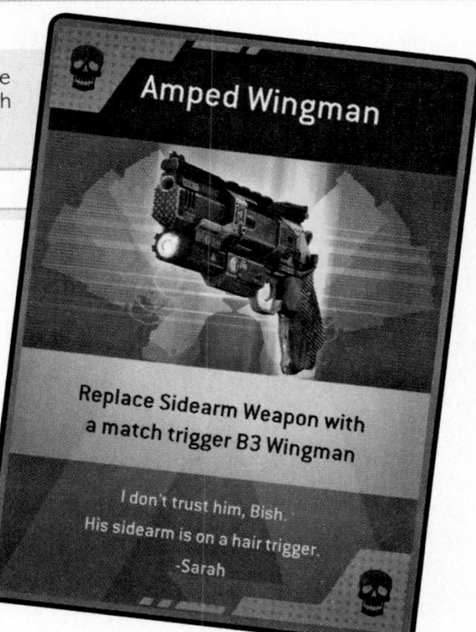

Amped Wingman
Replace Sidearm Weapon with a match trigger B3 Wingman
I don't trust him, Bish. His sidearm is on a hair trigger. -Sarah

Tactics

- The B3 Wingman is a powerful revolver, but its only down side is its slow fire rate. Equip this card to have a match trigger equipped, allowing a Pilot to fire the Wingman as quick as they can pull the trigger.

Bottomless Frags

Description: Replace Ordnance Weapon with infinite, more lethal Frag Grenades.

Rarity: Common

Tactics

- This is an excellent card to use while playing Pilot Hunter; a direct Frag Grenade will kill an enemy Pilot and having the addition of infinite grenades makes it even more worthwhile.
- Great Burn Card to clear out rooms of enemies that are guarding objectives.
- Grenades replenish with time.

Shock Rocks

Description: Replace Ordnance Weapon with infinite magnetic Arc Grenades.

Rarity: Common

Shock Rocks
Replace Ordnance Weapon with infinite, magnetic Arc Grenades
Give it a rub on the trim here before ya toss. Gives it a wicked curve.
-Blisk, above Angel City

Tactics

- A great Burn Card to use when the enemy team has multiple Titans out. These new and improved Arc Grenades will have an magnetic attribute. Throw these near enemy Titans and watch these grenades stick to the enemy Titan. The Arc Grenade will damage and blur the vision of the Titan.
- Grenades replenish with time.

Personal Alarm System

Description: Replace Ordnance Weapon with infinite Arc Mines with a larger blast radius.

Rarity: Common

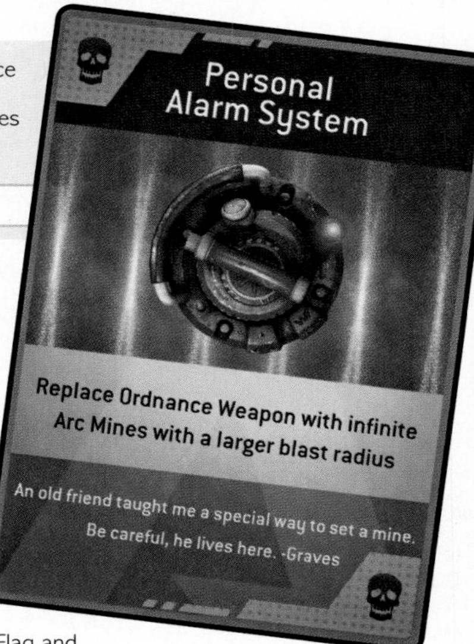

Personal Alarm System
Replace Ordnance Weapon with infinite Arc Mines with a larger blast radius
An old friend taught me a special way to set a mine. Be careful, he lives here. -Graves

Tactics

- This Burn Card can be optimized within Capture the Flag and Hardpoint Domination. Place these Arc Mines around the objective and become the ultimate defender.
- If a Pilot sets any more mines after initially setting three down, the previous ones will disappear, since you are only allowed to have three out at once.
- Mines replenish with time.

Surplus Satchels

Description: Replace Ordnance Weapon with infinite, more lethal Satchels,

Rarity: Common

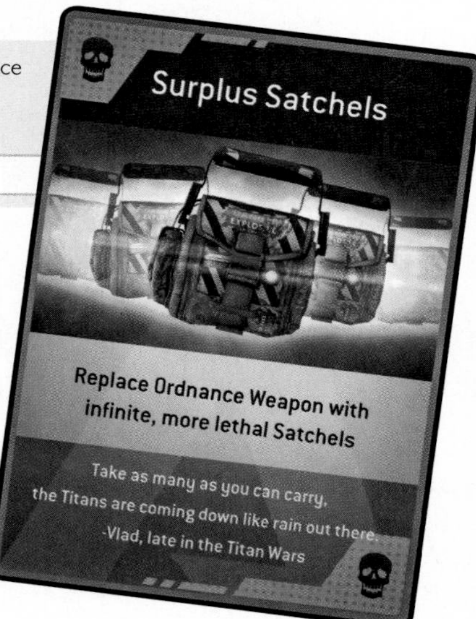

Surplus Satchels
Replace Ordnance Weapon with infinite, more lethal Satchels
Take as many as you can carry, the Titans are coming down like rain out there.
-Vlad, late in the Titan Wars

Tactics

- Best used in Capture the Flag and Hardpoint Domination
- Pilots should use Satchels to defend objectives and place on enemy Titans. The Satchel Charges now have a more lethal blast, doing more damage to enemy Titans; ideal for rodeo attacks.
- Charges replenish with time.

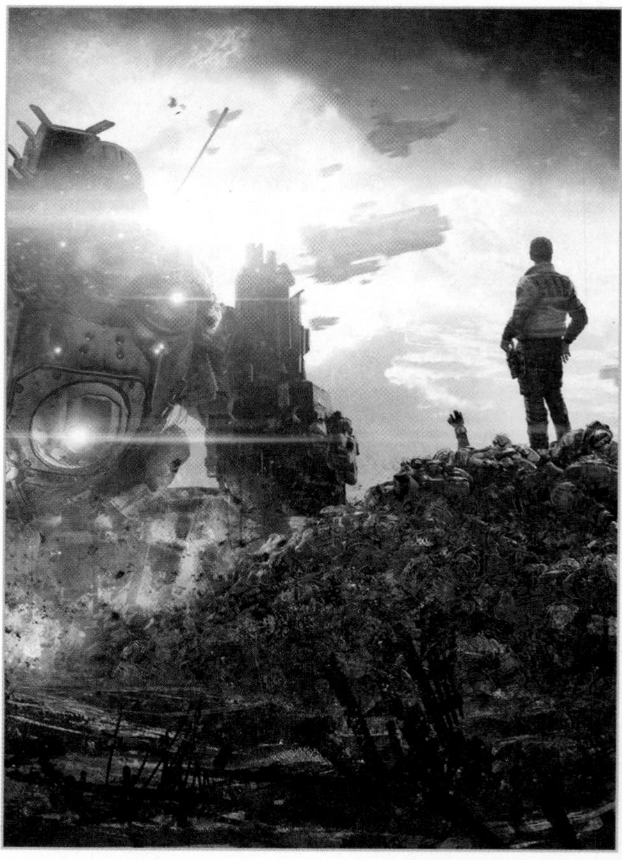

STEALTH BURN CARDS

These Burn Cards allow you to traverse the map in a stealthier fashion, allowing a Pilot to take out enemies without being seen.

Active Camo
The suit worked, Bish. They never saw me coming. Prepare to move in 3, 2... -Sarah

Description: Replace Pilot Tactical Ability with longer-lasting Cloak.

Rarity: Common

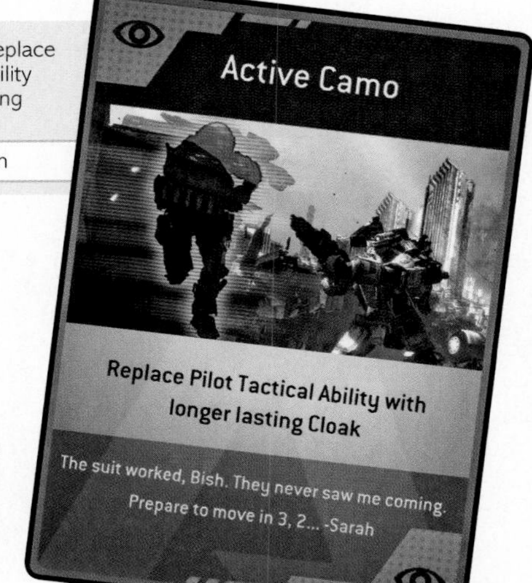

Tactics

- Using this Burn Card during Hardpoint Domination is super effective. The longer-lasting Cloak allows a Pilot to change locations and hide from enemies when neutralizing or defending the objective.
- A great Burn Card for escaping or rodeo attacking enemy Titans.

Ghost Squad
A crack team of invisible special forces? Sounds like a story meant to frighten over-privileged children. -Sarah

Description: Permanently cloaked as a Pilot, in addition to having your Pilot Tactical Ability.

Rarity: Rare

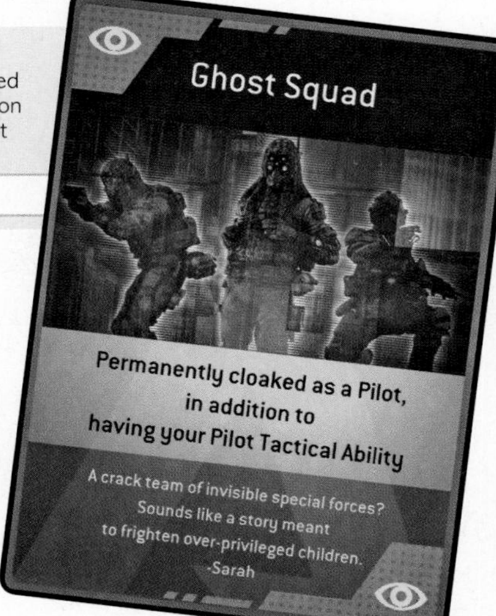

Tactics

- This rare Burn Card excels in many game modes and is super effective to use with a sniper. Easily move around the map while cloaked, but be sure to have Stim or Active Radar Pulse equipped as the card does not take up your Tactical Ability slot.
- This card is effective when performing rodeo attacks on enemy Titans.

SPEED BURN CARDS

If racing around the map is your thing, then these Burn Cards are what you're looking for. Quickly change positions on the map while using these cards.

Adrenaline Infusion

Description: Permanently stimmed as a Pilot, in addition to having your Pilot Tactical Ability.

Rarity: Rare

Adrenaline Transfusion
Permanently stimmed as a Pilot, in addition to having your Pilot Tactical Ability
We clone your own adrenaline; trust me, it is undetectable. -Dr. Yisv, Regenerative Specialist

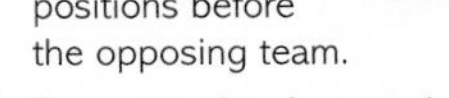

Tactics

- This rare Burn Card keeps Stim active permanently. Use it at the beginning of the game to quickly cut off the opposing team. Permanent Stim means a Pilot's health will be regenerated constantly as long as they are not being shot at.
- Make jumps that a normal Pilot isn't capable of, allowing for new wall runs and escape routes.

Prosthetic Legs

Description: Faster Pilot movement speed.

Rarity: Common

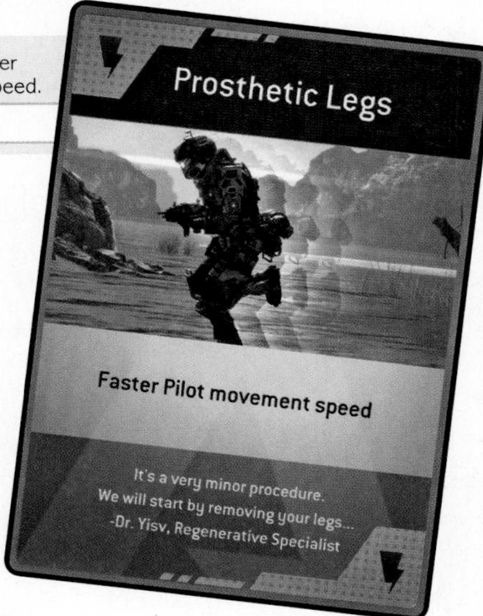

Tactics

- The Prosthetic Legs Burn Card is best used at the start of matches; use the increased Pilot speed to reach power positions before the opposing team.
- Extra speed makes you harder to hit, particularly while wall running.
- Using Prosthetic Legs with Stim does not make you go faster than normal Stim. So you may want to select a different Tactical Ability when playing this card.

QUICK REFERENCE

Smuggled Stimulant

Description: Replace Pilot Tactical Ability with longer-lasting Stim.

Rarity: Common

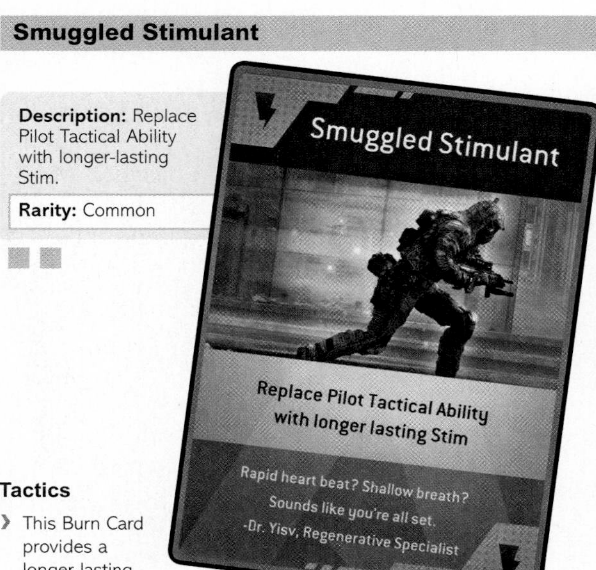

Smuggled Stimulant
Replace Pilot Tactical Ability with longer lasting Stim
Rapid heart beat? Shallow breath? Sounds like you're all set.
-Dr. Yisv, Regenerative Specialist

Tactics

- This Burn Card provides a longer-lasting Stim, allowing a Pilot to escape losing firefights a lot easier.
- Longer-lasting Stim also allows a Pilot to regenerate health faster, making them more durable during firefights. But you must still take cover to regenerate health.

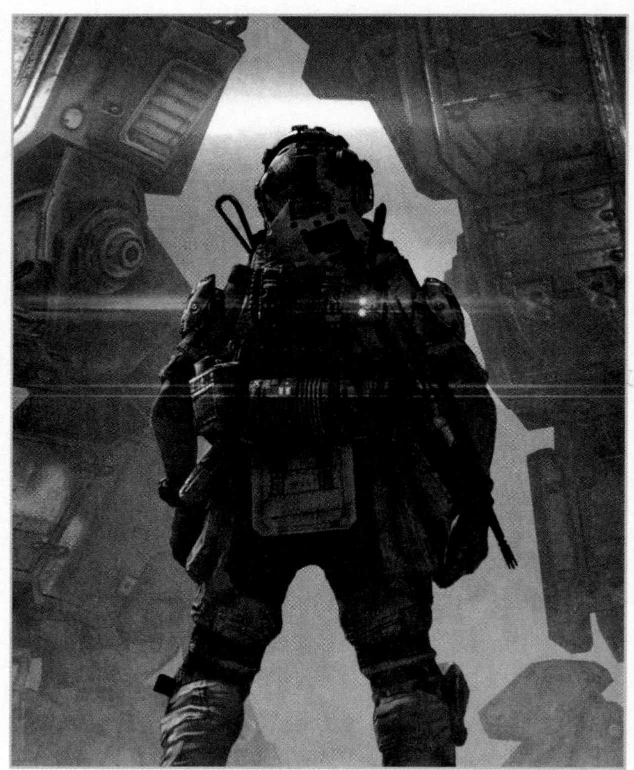

INTEL BURN CARDS

A Pilot's situational awareness is increased when using these Burn Cards; quickly locate the positions of the enemies and relay them to your team.

Aural Implant
It's not a hearing aid! -MacAllan

Description: Replace Pilot Tactical Ability with longer-lasting Active Radar Pulse.

Rarity: Common

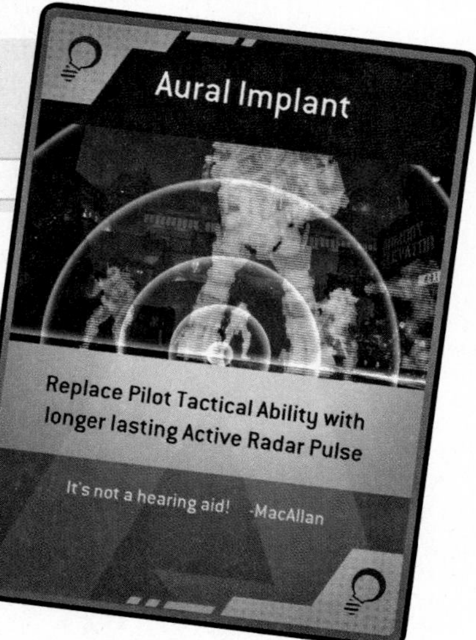

Tactics

- A longer-lasting Active Radar Pulse allows a Pilot to scan the inside of a building before going inside to kill enemies, grab a flag, or neutralize a hardpoint.

Echo Vision
Keep it. I have 20/20 hearing. -Bish

Description: Active Radar Pulse is permanently active, in addition to having your Pilot Tactical Ability.

Rarity: Rare

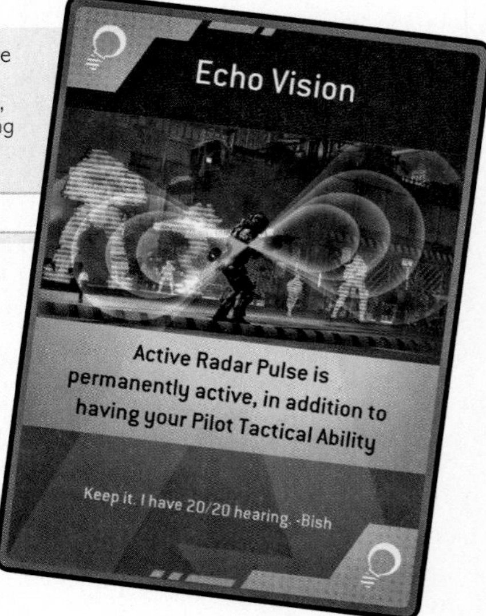

Tactics

- Equip when defending a hardpoint or flag. Equip your Pilot with a shotgun and kill enemies as they walk through an entrance.

Map Hack

Description: Full minimap vision.

Rarity: Rare

Map Hack
Full minimap vision
OSET? I've heard their security is unbreakable.
That's good, I needed something to do after lunch.
-Bish

Tactics

- A top five Burn Card. Pilots will want to play safe when using this card, as it grants a Pilot full minimap vision...as long as they stay alive.
- This card is great to use during Pilot Hunter; enemy Pilot locations are shown on the minimap at all times, allowing you to quickly rack up points.

Packet Sniffer

Description: You automatically generate Active Radar Pulses periodically.

Rarity: Common

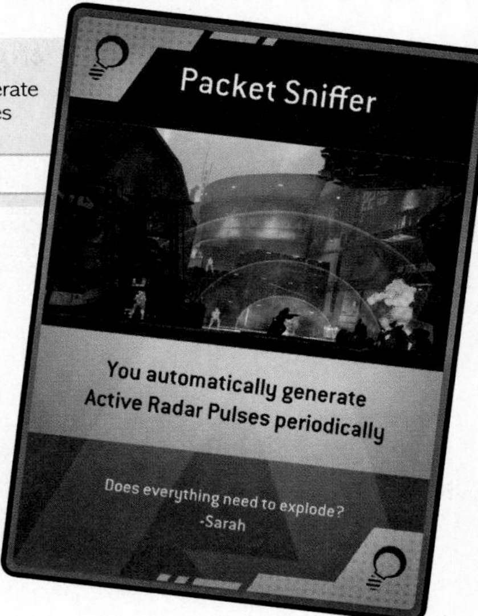

Packet Sniffer
You automatically generate
Active Radar Pulses periodically
Does everything need to explode?
-Sarah

Tactics

- A pulse is sent out from a Pilot every few seconds, revealing the position of enemies. Equip this card when playing as a sniper and watch your kills increase.

Satellite Uplink

Description: Reveal all enemies on the minimap every ten seconds.

Rarity: Common

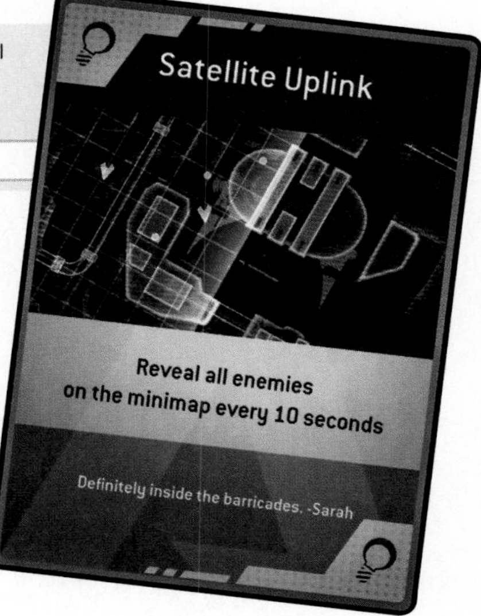

Satellite Uplink
Reveal all enemies
on the minimap every 10 seconds
Definitely inside the barricades. -Sarah

Tactics

- This Burn Card is an excellent choice in all game modes. The enemies are constantly shown on the minimap every ten seconds. This allows a Pilot to take their time, flanking unsuspecting enemy minions and Pilots.

Spider Sense

Description: There is an audible warning when enemy players are nearby.

Rarity: Common

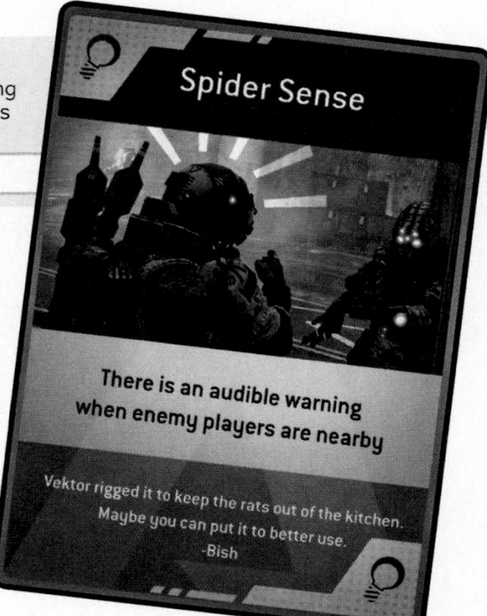

Spider Sense
There is an audible warning
when enemy players are nearby
Vektor rigged it to keep the rats out of the kitchen.
Maybe you can put it to better use.
-Bish

Tactics

- This is an excellent Burn Card to use when defending an objective or hanging on walls as you wait to ambush nearby enemies. This card triggers a sound that alerts a Pilot when enemies are near.

NPC BURN CARDS

These Burn Cards allow Pilots to make use of the multiple minions on the map, great for scoring big points in Attrition.

Conscription
Under whose authority? Oh, his.

Description: Nearby friendly Grunts fight for you—their kills count toward your score.

Rarity: Common

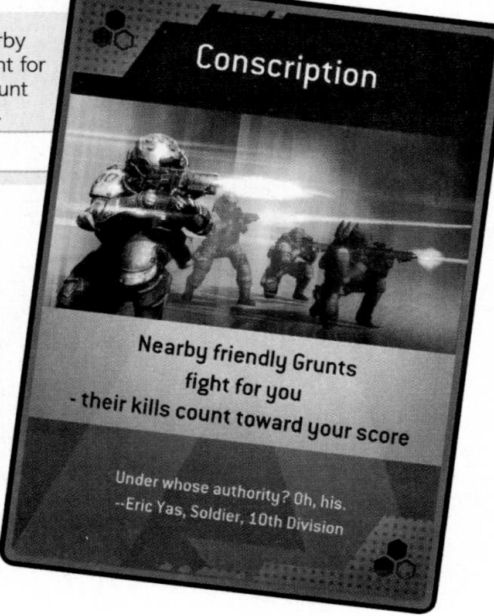

Tactics

- This is an excellent Burn Card to use when playing Attrition. Engage enemy Pilots while friendly Grunts assist, either shooting other minions or damaging the opposing Pilot.

Double Agent

Description: Grunts, Spectres, Auto-Titans, and turrets ignore you.

Rarity: Common

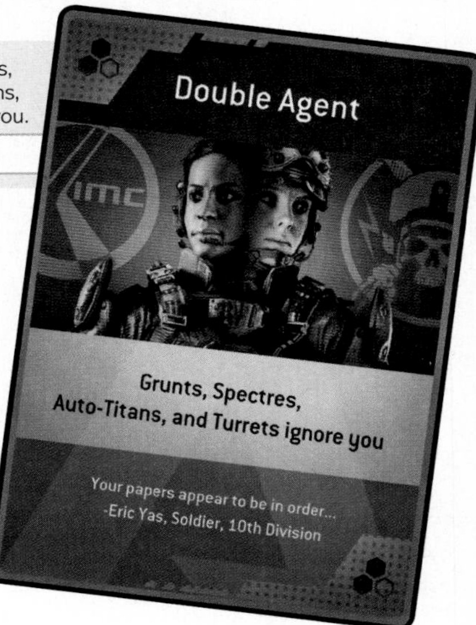

Double Agent
IMC
Grunts, Spectres, Auto-Titans, and Turrets ignore you
Your papers appear to be in order...
-Eric Yas, Soldier, 10th Division

Tactics

- Use this Burn Card to kill enemy Pilots, evade taking damage from minions and Auto-Titans, and battle an enemy Pilot on an even playing field.

WiFi Virus

Description: Automatically capture nearby enemy Spectres.

Rarity: Common

WiFi Virus
Automatically capture nearby enemy Spectres
You saw how those machines fight.
We need an answer and we need it fast.
-Sarah

Tactics

- Best used in The Colony in the campaign when playing as the Militia. The card is also effective in Made Men when playing as either faction.
- This card is of great use when playing on maps heavily saturated with Spectres. Simply walk past enemy Spectres to automatically hack them. Hacked Spectres then follow you around the map, engaging enemies and giving you all the credit for their kills.

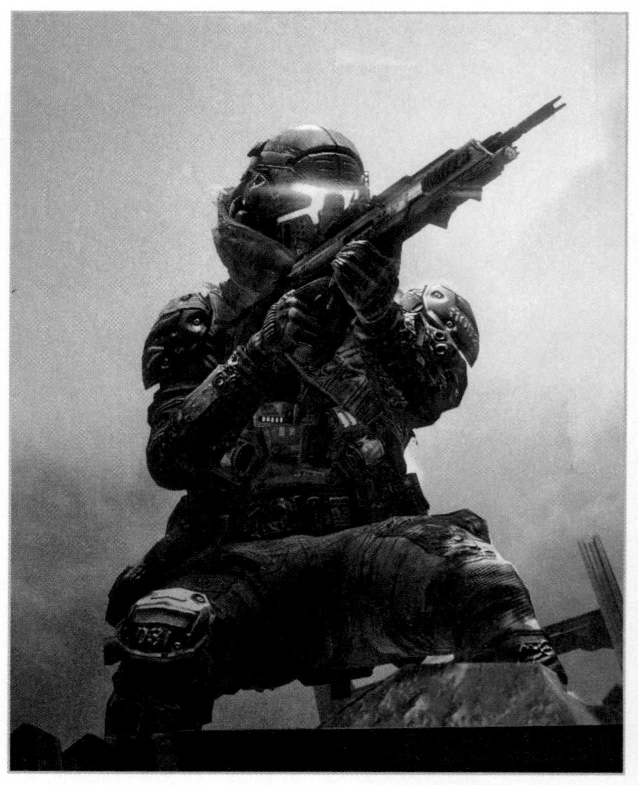

MISCELLANEOUS BURN CARDS

These cards don't fit into any specific category. Instead, they provide a wide range of benefits, often helping trick or catch your opponents off-guard.

Massive Payload

Description: Your Titan Eject causes an extended nuclear explosion.

Rarity: Common

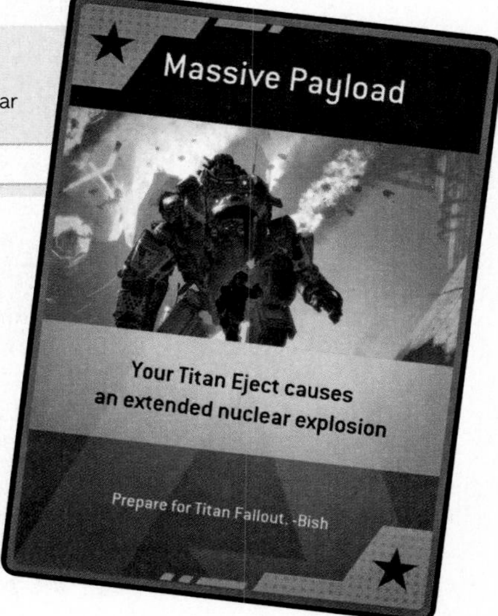

Tactics

- Best used in Last Titan Standing
- This Burn Card allows a Titan to have two Tier 1 Kits, one of them being Nuclear Ejection because of the Burn Card. This gives your Titan a significant advantage when battling enemy Titans.
- The closer the Titan is to enemies, the more damage the nuclear explosion will cause. So always dash near enemies to catch them in the blast radius before you eject from your doomed Titan.

Rematch

Description: Respawn where you died.

Rarity: Common

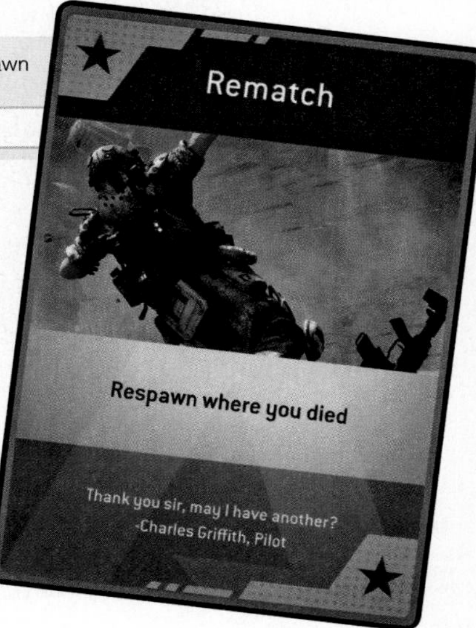

Tactics

- Wait a few seconds before using this Burn Card. Watch the death cam to make sure the area is clear and then use this card to respawn where your Pilot just died.
- In Pilot Hunter, if you die in an elevated position and see the enemy jump down, use this card to catch the enemy off-guard.

Spectre Camo

Description: You are a Spectre.

Rarity: Rare

Tactics

- Wait to play this card until Spectres have entered the battle, shortly after Titans arrive.
- Advance alongside friendly Grunts and Spectres, attempting to blend in. Many times enemy Pilots will ignore minions and only focus on finding Pilots. Now that your Pilot looks like a Spectre, you will be able to kill the enemy Pilot once they turn their back.

Super Charger

Description: Your Titan has a pre-charged Titan Core ability.

Rarity: Common

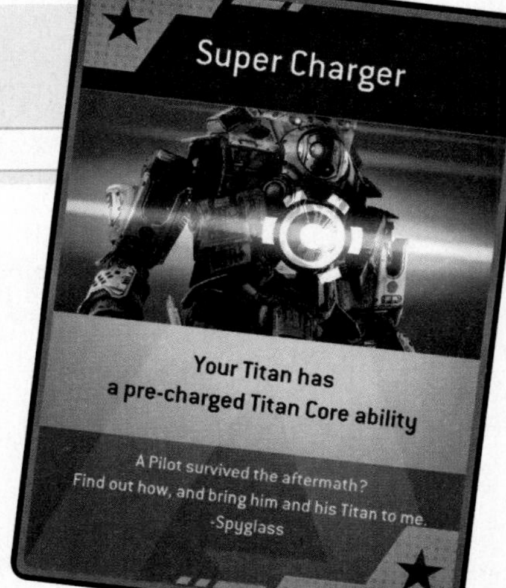

Tactics

- Best used in Last Titan Standing
- This card allows an Atlas Titan to have its Core Ability, Damage Core, at the beginning of each deployment. Equipped with the 40mm Cannon, the Atlas can make quick work of enemies with Damage Core activated.

BONUS BURN CARDS

These cards are great to use in all situations, rewarding you with bonus XP while reducing your build times.

Atlas Refurb

Description: Call in an Atlas Titan.

Rarity: Rare

Atlas Refurb
Call in an Atlas Titan
If your Auto-Titan exhibits signs of stress or anxiety, check for enemy riders and then relocate to a calmer environment.
-Owner's Manual

Tactics

- This Burn Card is perfect to use at the start of any of the game modes listed above. Having a Titan at the beginning will allow you to get off to an early lead.
- During the beginning of a Capture the Flag map, flank all the way around to grab the enemy's flag. Call an Atlas down and ride it back to your base to capture the flag.

Decisive Action

Description: Forty seconds off build time or Titan Core charge.

Rarity: Common

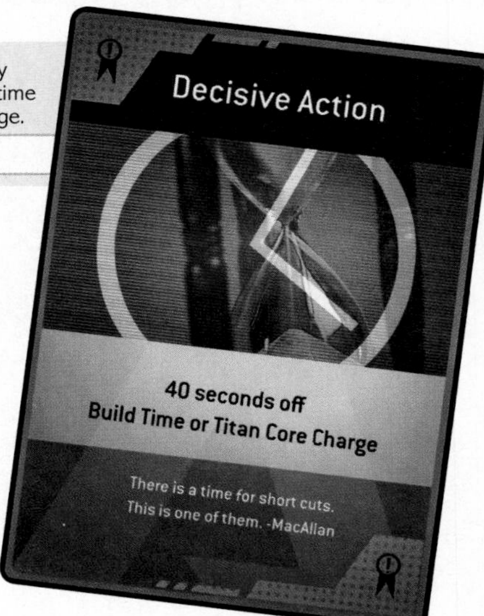

Decisive Action
40 seconds off
Build Time or Titan Core Charge
There is a time for short cuts.
This is one of them. -MacAllan

Tactics

- Best used at the start of the game to quickly reduce Titanfall build time; getting a Titan early in the game gives your team a huge advantage.
- This Burn Card is great to use off the start of Last Titan Standing. The quicker you get your Titan's Core Ability, the better.

DEVELOPER TIP (Respawn Entertainment)

You can pick a Burn Card from the menu at the beginning of the match, and it will activate when you get out of the dropship.

DEVELOPER TIP (Respawn Entertainment)

If you die, you may be able to find your Amped weapon on the ground where you left it.

DEVELOPER TIP (Respawn Entertainment)

Keep an eye out for "Cancelled Burn Card", the enemy may have dropped an Amped weapon on the ground.

Fast Learner

Description: You earn double XP.

Rarity: Common

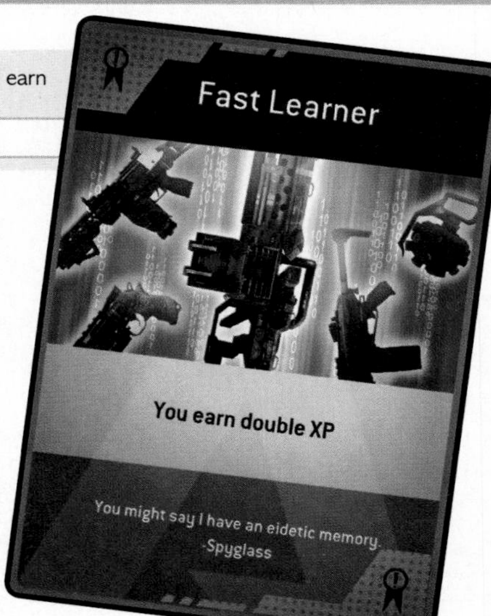

Fast Learner
You earn double XP
You might say I have an eidetic memory.
-Spyglass

Tactics

- Best used in Attrition
- This Burn Card grants you double XP. Attrition is a great game mode for accumulating XP. Pilots can go around the map with Minion Detector as their Tier 1 Kit and hunt minions to level up faster.

Most Wanted List

Description: Scoring hits on Pilots earns extra XP and reduces build time.

Rarity: Common

Tactics

- This Burn Card works with all the game modes listed above, but excels most in Pilot Hunter, since you must kill enemy Pilots in order to win the game mode.

Outsource

Description: Earn extra build time and Titan Core charge reductions during combat.

Rarity: Common

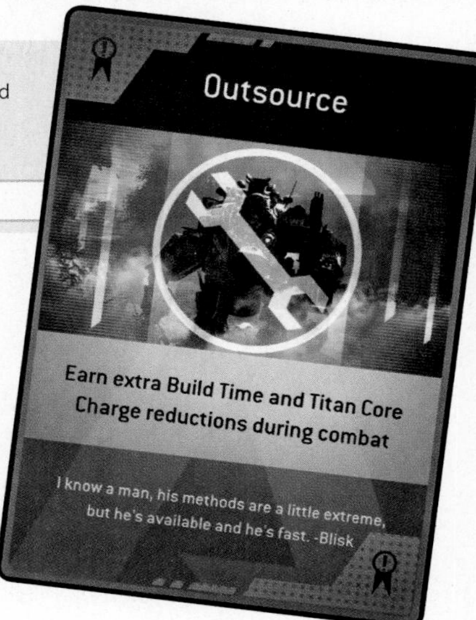

Tactics

- Want to be rewarded for engaging enemies? This Burn Card is for you! Either fight as a Pilot or Titan and watch your build time or Titan Core charge be reduced significantly as you damage enemies.

Pull Rank

Description: Eighty seconds off build time or Titan Core charge.

Rarity: Common

Tactics

- Best used at the start of the game to quickly reduce Titanfall build time.
- This Burn Card is great to use off the start of Last Titan Standing; the quicker you get your Titan's Core Ability, the better.

Reserve Ogre

Description: Call in an Ogre Titan.

Rarity: Rare

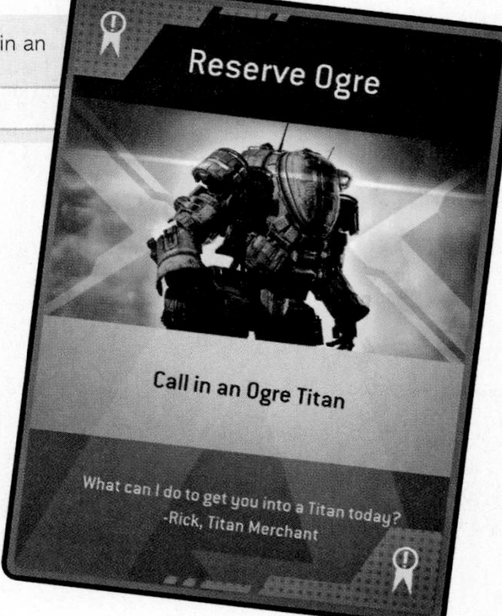

Tactics

- This Burn Card is perfect to use at the start of any of the game modes listed above. Having a Titan at the beginning will allow you to get off to an early lead.
- During the beginning of a Capture the Flag map, flank all the way around to grab the enemy's flag. Then call an Ogre down and ride it back to your base to capture the flag.

Spare Stryder

Description: Call in a Stryder Titan.

Rarity: Rare

Spare Stryder

Call in a Stryder Titan

I like having plan A, plan B, plan C...
-Graves

Tactics

- This Burn Card is perfect to use at the start of any of the game modes listed above. Having a Titan at the beginning will allow you to get off to an early lead.
- During the beginning of a Capture the Flag map, flank all the way around to grab the enemy's flag. Then call a Stryder down and ride it back to your base to capture the flag.

Thin the Ranks

Description: Scoring hits on Grunts earns extra XP and reduces build time.

Rarity: Common

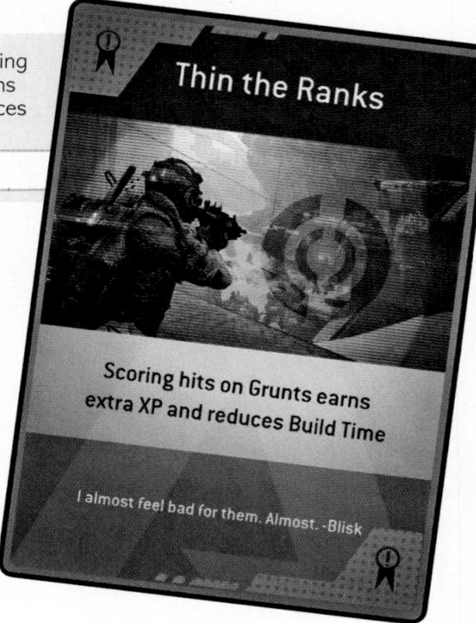

Tactics

- Equip the Minion Detector Tier 1 Kit and quickly hunt minions. This Burn Card reduces your build time, allowing you to get your Titan faster. The sooner you get your Titan, the more damage you can dish out, earning your Titan's Core Ability faster.

Titan Salvage

Description: Scoring hits on Titans earns extra XP and reduces build time.

Rarity: Common

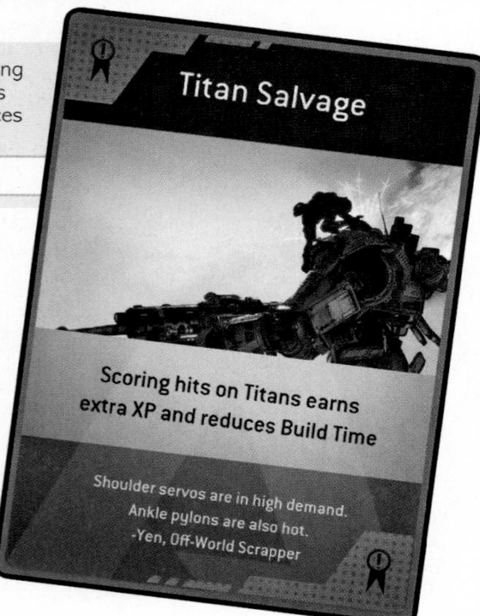

Titan Salvage
Scoring hits on Titans earns extra XP and reduces Build Time
Shoulder servos are in high demand.
Ankle pylons are also hot.
-Yen, Off-World Scrapper

Tactics

- This Burn Card works with all the game modes listed above, but is most effective in Last Titan Standing. Since everyone is in a Titan already, you will gain a lot of bonus XP as you damage the enemy Titans.

Urban Renewal

Description: Scoring hits on Spectres earns extra XP and reduces build time.

Rarity: Common

Urban Renewal
Scoring hits on Spectres earns extra XP and reduces Build Time
Place the terminated artificial life form
in the appropriate receptacle.
-Spyglass

Tactics

- Equip the Minion Detector Tier 1 Kit and quickly hunt minions. This Burn Card reduces your build time, allowing you to get your Titan faster. Getting your Pilot allows you to kill Pilots and defend objectives with relative ease.

ACHIEVEMENTS

XBOX ONE	XBOX 360	NAME	DESCRIPTION	GAMERSCORE
		IMC Pilot	Complete the IMC Campaign	50
		Militia Pilot	Complete the Militia Campaign	50
		My Generation	Become a second-generation Pilot	50
		IMC Elite Pilot	Win every Campaign level as an IMC Pilot	25
		Militia Elite Pilot	Win every Campaign level as a Militia Pilot	25
		Death From Above	Kill 5 enemies by dropping a Titan on them	25
		Build Yourself	Create a custom Pilot loadout	15
		Customize Your Ride	Create a custom Titan loadout	15
		Halfway There	Reach Level 25	25
		Maxed Out	Reach Level 50	50
		Flag Runner	Win 50 Capture the Flag matches	25
		I Wore 'Em Down	Win 50 Attrition matches	25
		Pilot Hunter	Win 50 Pilot Hunter matches	25
		Captured Everything	Win 50 Hardpoint Domination matches	25
		I Stand Alone	Win 50 Last Titan Standing matches	25
		I've Seen It All	Play every gameplay mode on every map	25
		Ride 'Em Cowboy	Rodeo kill a Titan	25
		Best In Class	Finish as the top player on your team once	25

XBOX ONE	XBOX 360	NAME	DESCRIPTION	GAMERSCORE
		All Charged Up	Kill 5 enemies with one Arc Cannon shot	25
		Like A Vacation	Complete training	25
		Look Around	Snap the necks of 10 Pilots	10
		Pull!	Kill 10 ejecting Pilots	25
		Pull Harder!	Kill an ejecting Pilot with the Plasma Railgun	25
		All The Cards	Earn 500 burn cards	25
		All The Hardware	Unlock everything	50
		My Robot Army	Hack 20 Spectres using the Data Knife	20
		Refuge	Survive an evacuation	50
		I Like A Challenge	Complete all challenges for a single weapon	50
		Vortex Volley	Catch a projectile shot from a Vortex Shield with your own Vortex Shield	15
		Frequent Flyer	Play 50 Campaign matches	50
		I Killed Them All	Kill all Pilots during the evacuation single-handedly	25
		Freerunner	Wall run for 5 kilometers	25
		Gen 10	Reach the highest Pilot generation	0
		Superior In Every Way	Kill 1,000 AI soldiers	25
		Titanfall	Call in your Titan 25 times	25

DEVELOPER TIPS

PILOT COMBAT/MOBILITY

- *Careful! Your jump jets are still visible when they fire, even while you are cloaked.*
- *The Pilot's cloaking device was built to fool Titan optics, and is less effective against the naked eye.*
- *Hang from the walls! You can come to a stop and hang onto a wall by holding the zoom button while wall running.*
- *Each time you inflict damage on an enemy, you reduce the time it takes to get your next Titan.*
- *Get there faster. You get a big speed boost while you are wall running.*
- *Check your minimap for enemies and friendlies on foot—large dots are Pilots, small dots are Grunts. Titans appear as large triangles on the minimap.*
- *Get the drop. You can detach from walls at any time by pressing the crouch button.*
- *Stand on the shoulders of giants—you can get to higher locations by double jumping off of other Titans.*
- *Leverage your momentum. When landing while in motion, jump as you touch the ground to go even faster.*
- *Create a personal army. Get close to a Spectre to hack it. This will also automatically hack other nearby Spectres.*
- *As a Pilot, you can ride on zip lines in both directions, thanks to your Jump Kit.*
- *Using Cloak before using a zip line can help you avoid enemy fire.*
- *Keep 'em guessing. Press the crouch button to suddenly drop from zip lines without carrying speed.*
- *Swoop into the action! Jump to detach from zip lines without losing speed.*

WEAPONS

- *Get refreshed. Every time you enter your Titan, your Pilot ammo is automatically refilled.*
- *Be quick on the draw. Switching to your sidearm is faster than reloading.*
- *The Smart Pistol will lock onto live grenades. Be careful not to blow yourself up!*
- *Be patient. The basic Smart Pistol takes three lock-ons to kill a Pilot with one trigger pull.*
- *Be prepared to do it yourself. The Smart Pistol's auto-targeting shuts off when you aim manually.*
- *If you are equipped with the Cloak ability, it will slow down enemy lock-ons when active, while you are a Pilot.*
- *Give it some time. Fired continuously, the Spitfire LMG kicks heavily on the first few shots, but stabilizes soon afterward.*
- *Arc Grenades disorient and reveal cloaked Pilots.*
- *The Arc Grenade is highly effective against a Titan's shields, and temporarily distorts a Titan's vision.*
- *Remotely detonate satchels by double tapping the fire button.*
- *Zap it. The Arc Cannon can destroy rockets in flight.*
- *The Arc Cannon drains energy from an enemy's Vortex Shield.*
- *Pilots can jump above explosions created from Triple Threat grenades.*
- *Scratch your back! As a Titan, you can use the explosions from your Cluster Missile to hurt a Pilot on your back.*

TITAN COMBAT

- *Watch for weak points. Taking down a Titan's bodyshield will expose bright red weak points to certain weapons.*
- *Don't hesitate! You can board your Titan from any direction—even from mid-air!*
- *Heads up! Titans falling into the battle will kill any enemy combatants they land on.*
- *Go for the rodeo! You can kill a Titan by jumping on its back and firing into its internal systems.*
- *Get under their skin. When you rodeo an enemy Titan and shoot its internal systems, your attack bypasses the shields.*
- *Don't rest on your laurels—a doomed Titan is still a threat.*
- *Finish them! You can rip an enemy out of a doomed Titan with a well-timed melee attack.*
- *Switch to your Anti-Titan weapon to do the most damage to Titans when you're on foot as a Pilot.*
- *Getting outnumbered in a Titan fight is very dangerous—your Titan will tell you if you are in danger.*
- *Always check your teammates' Titans—there may be enemy Pilots on their backs.*
- *Your Titan is programmed to follow you around unless you manually switch it to Guard Mode.*
- *When you switch your Titan to Guard Mode, it will face in the direction you were looking at the time.*
- *When you hitch a ride on a friendly player's Titan, its shields will protect you too.*
- *When a Titan is doomed, its health bar will change to a striped pattern*
- *If your Titan is not doomed, your shields will begin recharging if you avoid getting hit for a short time.*
- *A Titan's built-in shields are not impenetrable—the armor underneath just takes a lot less damage.*
- *Live to fight another day! When your Titan's bodyshield is low or depleted, take cover from enemy fire to recharge it.*
- *Get punchy. Prevent enemy Pilots from jumping on your Titan by punching them at close range.*
- *A doomed Titan gets a striped health bar and will soon self-destruct. The Pilot who dooms an enemy Titan scores the kill.*

BURN CARDS

- *Respawn with a vengeance! Remember to select and activate a Burn Card after you die—it will take effect when you respawn.*
- *Get a head start. Select and activate a Burn Card before the start of every match—it will take effect when you spawn.*
- *Burn Cards give you special abilities that last until you die or the match ends. Try them out!*
- *Out of Burn Cards? Challenge yourself—many Challenges have Burn Card rewards.*
- *Burn Card effects carry over during round-based game modes, such as Last Titan Standing, if you manage to stay alive.*
- *Make some space. If your Burn Card collection is full, discard or use your existing Burn Cards so that you may earn more.*

MEET THE PROS

For Titanfall we have assembled a team of gamers with an eclectic mix of skills, backgrounds, and professional gaming experience. Together they have put hundreds of hours into Titanfall with the end goal of creating the most complete and comprehensive guide available.

STRONGSIDE

Name: Michael Cavanaugh

Michael has extensive knowledge in competitive FPS gaming and has been competing for the past nine years. Known to pick up any game and become a master at it, Michael's dedication and drive are key factors behind his gaming success, winning several major professional tournaments in the last five years. Most recently, Michael took first place in a worldwide tournament held by 343 Industries and Virgin Gaming's Infinity Challenge (Halo 4), winning a 2013 Halo Edition Ford F-150 Raptor. Outside of FPS gaming, Cavanaugh enjoys rock climbing, wake boarding, skydiving and many other action sports. He is also an avid old-school gamer.

Author Acknowledgements

I'd like to give a BIG thanks to everyone at Respawn Entertainment for letting us work on this remarkable game. It has been an honor and so much fun playing Titanfall. I can't wait to spend many more hours on this game! Thank you Abbie Heppe for teaching me to run on walls and wall jump. Joel Emslie for intriguing me with the many ideas that inspired Titanfall. Ryan "Brockhaurd" Lastimosa for the great games during the Alpha and Beta. Dominic McCarthy for all the insight on the game at the Titanfall event. Game Testers for spending a day gaming with us and teaching us a few new tricks. Thanks to everyone at Prima for an incredible visit. The best welcome ever. #Incredible

Thank you to my family and my beautiful girlfriend Ellen for supporting me. Thank you to all my fans and friends—I wouldn't be here without any of you.

WALSHY

Name: David Walsh

A true veteran, David enjoyed a successful professional gaming career for ten years, winning more than 30 major tournaments over five different game titles. One of his biggest victories was winning GameStop's Battlefield 2: Modern Combat tournament in 2005 where he won a Dodge Charger SRT8. In addition to his numerous wins and sponsorships, David popularized the "Claw" grip as a way of holding the Xbox controller. Although he retired from competing in 2012, David is still active in the competitive scene, serving as a tournament commentator. He's also a member of the board of directors for Gamers Outreach, a charity which donates games and gaming equipment to children's hospitals and troops overseas. Outside of gaming David enjoys reading and traveling the world.

Author Acknowledgements

I want to thank Prima Games, Electronic Arts, and Respawn Entertainment for the opportunity to work on this guide. I want to thank my family for always supporting me while I follow my dreams. I want to say thank you to Michael Cavanaugh, Steve Herbert, Chris Posthumus, and Zach Wigal; a few close friends of mine who have been there for me during some tough times in my life. Last I want to say thank you to my fans out there—I'm optimistic about the future of gaming and plan to be involved in this field for the rest of my life!

FLAMESWORD

Name: Michael Chaves

Sponsored by Red Bull, Michael "Flamesword" Chaves has been a professional gamer since 2009. A natural leader, Mike found success in 2008 when he created the prestigious Halo team "Status Quo"; where he won several tournaments. Waiting for the next big competitive shooter, Flamesword has joined the OpTic Gaming organization and coached two events for the Greenwall. Now known as the infamous OpTicBeard, Mike enjoys bouldering, Crossfit, biking, and other action sports which keeps his reflexes and hand-eye coordination above the competition. Mike believes in hard work and pursues excellence in everything he does, always striving to better himself and the ones around him.

Author Acknowledgements

I would like to thank Respawn, EA, and Prima Games for allowing me and the team to work on this project. Abbie Heppe for her incredible cooperation and guidance throughout the entire experience. Dom McCarthy I know you must have been incredibly busy, but you my friend are a hero! Thank you for taking the time out of your busy day to send over the assets we needed, they were a game changer. Mathew Everett, thank you for the invite to the private Titanfall event where we got to meet and game with members of Respawn. Vince Zampella, one word for you, GENIUS!

I want to thank my family and dog "Lucky" for all their love and support, Joe (my mentor) and Gina Pennacchio, Sam and Audrey (it all started with you two), my extended family, my fans from the beginning and new, the Buffalo Brotherhood, and Red Bull for giving me wings to better myself each and everyday.

MABOOZA

Name: David Knight

David is a veteran Prima Games author, writing more than 50 guides over the past decade. Specializing in first-person shooters, David jumped at the chance to be part of the Titanfall team. Over the last 12 years, David has written guides for dozens of games including Battlefield 1942, Battlefield 2, Tom Clancy's Rainbow Six Vegas, Shadowrun, Far Cry 2, Left 4 Dead, Medal of Honor (2010), Bulletstorm, Rage, Battlefield 3, Tom Clancy's Ghost Recon: Future Soldier, Medal of Honor: Warfighter, and Battlefield 4. When he's not rodeo attacking enemy Titans, David enjoys biking, target shooting, and playing basketball.

Author Acknowledgements

Creating this guide was a true team effort, so there's many people I'd like to acknowledge. First I'd like to thank our dedicated team of pro gamers, Michael "StrongSide" Cavanaugh, David "Walshy" Walsh, and Michael "Flamesword" Chaves; the long hours paid off! Thanks to Loren "Evil Drew" Gilliland for not only creating our maps, but for providing critical technical assistance. Another special thanks to our team at Prima Games including Paul Giacomotto, Jesse Anderson, Don Tica, and JJ Zingale. Working with Respawn Entertainment was a great experience; a huge thanks to Abbie Heppe for being such an awesome and responsive contact...and for introducing us to Bottle Caps at Blue Dog Beer Tavern.

TITANFALL™
Building Sets From K'NEX
K'NEX®
Building Worlds Kids Love®
Available in stores and online starting July 2014
Respawn ENTERTAINMENT
©2014 Respawn
facebook.com/buildknex
KNEX·COM

The Prima Games logo is a registered trademark of Random House LLC, registered in the United States and other countries. Primagames.com is a registered trademark of Random House LLC, registered in the United States. Prima Games is an imprint of Random House LLC, New York, a Penguin Random House Company.

IMPORTANT:
Prima Games has made every effort to determine that the information contained in this book is accurate. However, the publisher makes no warranty, either expressed or implied, as to the accuracy, effectiveness, or completeness of the material in this book; nor does the publisher assume liability for damages, either incidental or consequential, that may result from using the information in this book. The publisher cannot provide any additional information or support regarding gameplay, hints and strategies, or problems with hardware or software. Such questions should be directed to the support numbers provided by the game and/or device manufacturers as set forth in their documentation. Some game tricks require precise timing and may require repeated attempts before the desired result is achieved.

AUSTRALIAN WARRANTY STATEMENT:
This product comes with guarantees that cannot be excluded under the Australian Consumer Law. You are entitled to a replacement or refund for a major failure and for compensation for any other reasonably foreseeable loss or damage. You are also entitled to have the goods repaired or replaced if the goods fail to be of acceptable quality and the failure does not amount to a major failure.

This product comes with a 1 year warranty from date of purchase. Defects in the product must have appeared within 1-year, from date of purchase in order to claim the warranty.

All warranty claims must be facilitated back through the retailer of purchase, in accordance with the retailer's returns policies and procedures. Any cost incurred, as a result of returning the product to the retailer of purchase - are the full responsibility of the consumer.

AU wholesale distributor: Bluemouth Interactive Pty Ltd, Suite 1502, 9 Yarra Street, South Yarra, Victoria, 3141. (+613 9646 4011)

EMAIL: support@bluemouth.com.au

ISBN:
978-0-804-16290-6 / 978-0-804-16293-7

Printed in the United States of America

Prima Games
An Imprint of Random House LLC,
a Penguin Random House Company

3000 Lava Ridge Court, St. 100
Roseville, CA 95661

WWW.PRIMAGAMES.COM

TITANFALL™

PRIMA OFFICIAL GAME GUIDE

Authors – David Knight, Michael Cavanaugh, Michael Chaves, David Walsh

Product Manager – Paul Giacomotto
Design and Layout – In Color Design
Maps – Loren Gilliland
Copy Editor – Julia Mascardo

PRIMA GAMES WOULD LIKE TO THANK –
Respawn Entertainment and Electronic Arts for the opportunity to work on a brand new, highly anticipated, and incredibly fun game. The following people at Respawn provided tremendous support in the making of this guide- Vince Zampella, Abbie Heppe, Drew McCoy, Dom McCarthy, Chad Grenier, Joel Emslie, Justin Hendry, Paul Messerly, Steve Fukuda, Jon "Slothy" Shiring, Erik Kraber, Ryan Lastimosa, and so many more behind the scenes. Thank you, your team is impressive and loaded with talent. We'd also like to thank our partners at Electronic Arts- Patrick O'Brien, Alexander Lee, Ryan Gagerman, and Mathew Everett for always wanting the best for us. Extra kudos goes to Abbie Heppe, Dom McCarthy, Mathew Everett, Donato Tica, Jesse Anderson, Julie Asbury, Andrea Hill, and Shaida Boroumand for your incredible efforts.